CHINA'S "AUTONOMOUS" CITIES

This book explores the constitutional evolution of Hong Kong and Macau as Beijing asserts "comprehensive jurisdiction" over both Special Administrative Regions, compelling them to align with the national agenda of security, patriotic education, and Mainland integration.

The book delivers a comparative study of Hong Kong alongside its "younger sibling" Macau – just 3% of its land size and 38 miles away – where, unlike their Hong Kong counterparts, Macau's residents have been politically quiescent and street protests remain rare. It examines Hong Kong's notable judicial autonomy, particularly in advancing gay rights, and the dramatic expansion of national security laws in both cities, with enforcement concentrated in Hong Kong. Readers gain critical insights into the differing levels of political quiescence and judicial independence between the two territories, as Beijing reshapes them under a unified framework of central control.

China's "Autonomous" Cities is essential reading for students and scholars of Chinese politics, comparative constitutional law, and East Asian studies, as well as policymakers and analysts focused on Hong Kong, Macau, and China's governance strategies.

Po Jen Yap is Professor of Law at The University of Hong Kong.

Han Zhu is Research Assistant Professor at The University of Hong Kong.

Shiling Xiao is Lecturer in Public Law at the University of Manchester.

Routledge Contemporary China Series

270 **The Chinese Censorship Discourse on Television Dramas**
Worrying about the Audience in Postsocialist China
How Wee Ng

271 **A History of Chinese Orchestras in Greater China**
Ming-yen Lee

272 ***Tianxia* and Its Discontents**
Confucian Political Theology, Coloniality, and the Global Order
Joyce C.H. Liu

273 **Negative Incentives and Disciplinary Action in China's Food Safety Regulation**
Jia Liu

274 **China's "Autonomous" Cities**
The Constitution and Reconstruction of Hong Kong and Macau
Po Jen Yap, Han Zhu, and Shiling Xiao

For more information about this series, please visit: www.routledge.com/Routledge-Contemporary-China-Series/book-series/SE0768

CHINA'S "AUTONOMOUS" CITIES

The Constitution and Reconstruction of Hong Kong and Macau

Po Jen Yap, Han Zhu, and Shiling Xiao

Routledge
Taylor & Francis Group
LONDON AND NEW YORK

Designed cover image: Getty Images

First published 2027
by Routledge
4 Park Square, Milton Park, Abingdon, Oxon OX14 4RN

and by Routledge
605 Third Avenue, New York, NY 10158

Routledge is an imprint of the Taylor & Francis Group, an informa business

British Library Cataloguing-in-Publication Data
A catalogue record for this book is available from the British Library

Library of Congress Cataloging-in-Publication Data
Names: Yap, Po Jen author | Zhu, Han author | Xiao, Shiling (Law teacher) author
Title: China's "autonomous" cities : the constitution and reconstruction of Hong Kong and Macau / Po Jen Yap, Han Zhu, and Shiling Xiao.
Description: First. | London : Routledge, 2027. |
Series: Routledge contemporary china series |
Includes bibliographical references and index.
Identifiers: LCCN 2026027139 (print) | LCCN 2026027140 (ebook) |
ISBN 9781041163152 hardback | ISBN 9781041163145 paperback |
ISBN 9781003683872 ebook
Subjects: LCSH: Constitutional law–China–Hong Kong |
Constitutional law–China–Macau | National security–Law and legislation–China–Hong Kong | National security–Law and legislation–China–Macau | Hong Kong (China)–Politics and government |
Macau (China)–Politics and government
Classification: LCC KNQ2080 .Y375 2026 (print) | LCC KNQ2080 (ebook)
LC record available at https://lccn.loc.gov/2026027139
LC ebook record available at https://lccn.loc.gov/2026027140

ISBN: 9781041163152 (hbk)
ISBN: 9781041163145 (pbk)
ISBN: 9781003683872 (ebk)

DOI: 10.4324/9781003683872

Typeset in Times New Roman
by Newgen Publishing UK

CONTENTS

1
INTRODUCTION

Hong Kong has long been hailed as a gateway between communist China and the capitalist West, but in this tumultuous decade, it has only drawn international attention for all the wrong reasons. In 2019, this so-called autonomous[1] Special Administrative Region (SAR) was roiled by relentless months-long street protests as the people rose up against a rendition bill that would have authorised extradition to Mainland China.[2] In 2020, as the COVID-19 pandemic engulfed the globe, China foisted a customised National Security Law on the hunkered-down unsuspecting city[3] and cleansed the local legislature of political opposition in 2021,[4] so that similar uprisings could never occur again. With the decimation of civil society and the imposition of a punishing "zero-COVID" policy that quarantined Hong Kong from the rest of the world for close to three years, residents and expatriates fled the city by the tens of thousands.[5] Today, this international financial hub stands at the

1 Both Hong Kong and Macau are constitutionally guaranteed a "high degree of autonomy". See Article 2 of Hong Kong Basic Law and Article 2 of Macau Basic Law.

2 Jeff Li, 'Hong Kong-China extradition plans explained' *BBC* (13 December 2019). <www.bbc.com/news/world-asia-china-47810723> last accessed 3 January 2026.

3 Law of the People's Republic of China on Safeguarding National Security in the Hong Kong Special Administrative Region (Adopted at the 20th Session of the Standing Committee of the 13th National People's Congress on 30 June 2020).

4 Annex II to the Basic Law of the Hong Kong Special Administrative Region of the People's Republic of China: Method for the Formation of the Legislative Council of the Hong Kong Special Administrative Region and Its Voting Procedures (Amended at the 27th Meeting of the Standing Committee of the 13th National People's Congress on 30 March 2021).

5 Yiran Yu, 'Brain Drain and Brain Gain in Hong Kong's Population Shuffle' *Migration Policy Institute* (3 April 2024). <www.migrationpolicy.org/article/hong-kong-migration-shuffle> last accessed 19 March 2026.

DOI: 10.4324/9781003683872-1

crossroads, seeking to restore its global reputation tarnished by years of pandemic self-isolation and perceived repression.

For all of Hong Kong's fame and infamy, far fewer international observers know that it has a younger sibling situated 38 miles away and only 3% of its land area: the Macau Special Administrative Region (MASAR).[6] Macau is one of China's only *two* SARs, and it too is governed under a formal "One Country, Two Systems" (OCTS) constitutional model that has allowed that city to thrive as the world's top casino hub.[7]

The MASAR operates under a Basic Law that was carved from Hong Kong's constitutional template. But from birth (1999 for Macau and 1997 for Hong Kong), the two siblings were as different as they could get, despite their near-identical genetic make-up. In Macau, its residents were and are politically obedient; street protests were and are rare and have never reached the scale we witnessed in boisterous Hong Kong,[8] where political mass mobilisation and huge protests were regular and distinct features of the city.[9] Operating within this rambunctious milieu, the Hong Kong Court of Final Appeal (HKCFA) decisively exercised the powers of constitutional review and nullified legislation in its very first constitutional decision in 1999.[10] And to date, the HKCFA has declared laws unconstitutional on 27 occasions.[11] In contrast, the Macau Court of Final Appeal (MACFA) has only declared laws unconstitutional in three cases,[12] and in all three cases, the unconstitutional laws are only inapplicable vis-à-vis the successful claimants but remain operative otherwise.

To date, Eric Ip is the only other author who has examined the operation of the two SARs closely and offered a compelling explanation for the divergence in the two cities, despite their sharing of near-identical genetic traits. In an important monograph published in April 2019,[13] Eric Ip argued that "regime

6 '澳門地理位置 Macau's Location'. <www.dscc.gov.mo/zh-hans/geographical_location.html> last accessed 3 January 2026; 'Hong Kong Geographic Data 2026'. <www.landsd.gov.hk/en/resources/mapping-information/hk-geographic-data.html> last accessed 19 March 2026.

7 Elaine Yu, 'Macau Reclaims Crown from Vegas as World's Top Gambling Hub' *The Wall Street Journal* (19 August 2023) <www.wsj.com/business/hospitality/macau-reclaims-crown-from-vegas-as-worlds-top-gambling-hub-edf318cd> last accessed 3 January 2026.

8 The largest protest in Macau occurred in 2014 when 20,000 demonstrators rallied against the Macau government's attempt to pass an exorbitant retirement package for its Chief Executive and principal officials. See Meng U Ieong, 'Macao and Hong Kong, Convergence or Divergence?: The 2014 Retirement Package Bill Protest and Macao's Governance Crisis' (2017) 57(3) *Asian Survey* 504, 509.

9 Nearly two million people took to the streets on 16 June 2019 to oppose the HKSAR government's extradition bill. 'Hong Kong protest: "Nearly two million" join demonstration' *BBC* (17 June 2019) <www.bbc.com/news/world-asia-china-48656471> last accessed 3 January 2026.

10 *Ng Ka Ling v Director of Immigration* (1999) 2 HKCFAR 4.

11 See Appendix 1 of Chapter 3.

12 See Appendix 2 of Chapter 3.

13 Eric Ip, *Hybrid Constitutionalism: The Politics of Constitutional Review in the Chinese Special Administrative Regions* (CUP 2019).

fragmentation"[14] within the legislature stacked with pro-Beijing allies and the "external resistance"[15] to this governing coalition – a vibrant civil society and a sizable elected pro-democracy camp in opposition – imposed a prohibitively "high political transaction cost"[16] on the Hong Kong government, which hampered its ability to effectively rein in the courts or its people. Echoing Ip, Wanli Wang has also attributed the "asymmetric evolution"[17] of the two SARs to the low social mobilisation and the lack of democratisation in Macau. But from 2020 onwards, with the passage of the National Security Law in Hong Kong and the institution of a "patriots-only" legislature, civil society in the city has been decimated and the Hong Kong legislature is now derided as an echo chamber[18] or a rubber-stamp.[19] While Hong Kong is no longer as free-wheeling as before, by many measures, it is still significantly freer than Macau. Since 2011, the MACFA has ceased declaring any local legislation unconstitutional. On the other hand, the HKCFA unanimously ruled in 2023 that it was unconstitutional for the government to require transgender persons to undergo full sex reassignment surgery before they can alter their gender markers on the government-issued identity cards.[20] At the heart of this constitutional controversy was the transgender persons' desire to legally access public bathrooms that aligned with their gender identity. Later that same year, the HKCFA declared that the local government's *failure* to provide an alternative legal framework for protecting the core rights of same-sex partnerships was unconstitutional, and the Court gave the government two years to enact remedial legislation.[21]

What explains this post-2021 semi-resilience of the HKCFA? Put another way, if intense political fragmentation and opposition within the legislature, and a strong mobilised civil society were determinative of Hong Kong's pre-2021 divergence from Macau, why hasn't Hong Kong simply caved and converged with Macau in all aspects after the former was politically tamed by Beijing? In this book, we seek to address this puzzle.

14 Eric Ip, *Hybrid Constitutionalism: The Politics of Constitutional Review in the Chinese Special Administrative Regions* (CUP 2019) 24–25.

15 Eric Ip, 'The Evolution of Constitutional Adjudication in the Chinese Special Administrative Regions: Theory and Evidence' (2013) 61(4) *American Journal of Comparative Law* 799, 817–821; Eric Ip, *Hybrid Constitutionalism: The Politics of Constitutional Review in the Chinese Special Administrative Regions* (CUP 2019) 185–192.

16 Eric Ip, *Hybrid Constitutionalism: The Politics of Constitutional Review in the Chinese Special Administrative Regions* (CUP 2019) 200.

17 Wanli Wang, 'The Asymmetric Evolution of the Basic Laws of Hong Kong and Macao' (2024) 54(1) *Hong Kong Law Journal* 15, 49.

18 Michael Shum, 'Legco "Becoming More Like NPC" ' *The Standard* (9 May 2024) <www.thestandard.com.hk/hong-kong-news/article/62629/> last accessed 3 January 2026.

19 Frank Ching, 'Is Hong Kong Headed for a Rubber-Stamp Legislature?' *The Japan Times* (25 March 2024) <www.japantimes.co.jp/commentary/2024/03/25/world/hong-kong-rubber-stamp-legislature/> last accessed 3 January 2026.

20 *Q and Tse Henry Edward v Commissioner of Registration* (2023) 26 HKCFAR 25.

21 *Sham Tsz Kit v Secretary for Justice* (2023) 26 HKCFAR 385.

In essence, we argue that two *additional* variables existed and remain extant in Hong Kong, which explain the continuing divergence. First, the Hong Kong judiciary, particularly its Court of Final Appeal, is different from Macau because of their dramatically distinct judicial appointment systems. Both Basic Laws promise that their judges would be selected by independent judicial commissions,[22] but in practice Macau's "Independent" Judicial Officers Nomination Commission has always been chaired by a local high-ranking pro-Beijing lawmaker[23] and the entire Commission is stacked with members with explicit pro-Beijing political affiliations, with very few members possessing legal training.[24] Notably, Chief Justice Sam Hou Fai – the MASAR's first Chief Justice – received Beijing's blessing to resign in August 2024 and ran *unopposed* in October 2024 to become the current Chief Executive of Macau.[25] To be endorsed by the Central Government to take on the city's top job, Chief Justice Sam's political reliability must be unassailable. Conversely, Hong Kong's Judicial Officers Recommendation Commission is chaired by its non-partisan Chief Justice and the Commission is dominated by serving appellate judges and leading lawyers. This crucial difference in judicial appointment directly impacts the composition of the bench and results in Macau and Hong Kong appointing different kinds of judges to their cities' top courts.

Second, Hong Kong is an international financial hub, while Macau is not. As of 2025, Hong Kong is the world's third leading global financial centre.[26] With capital controls firmly in place within Mainland China, the Hong Kong Stock Exchange – with its advanced financial infrastructure and access to foreign capital – is the gateway through which Chinese state-owned enterprises, state-supported transnational corporations, and private conglomerates raise capital to enter global markets.[27] China's connection to the global economy hinges on Hong

22 Article 88 of the Hong Kong Basic Law (HKBL); Article 87 of the Macau Basic Law (MABL).

23 Since the handover in 1999, Macau's Commission has been chaired by Lau Cheok Va, who concurrently served as Vice President (1999–2009) and President (2009–2013) of the Macau Legislative Assembly, and he was a Macau delegate to the 10th and 11th National People's Congress (2003–2013).

24 Unlike Hong Kong, there have been only five legally trained persons serving on Macau's Commission since the handover on 20 December 1999. Mr. Sam Hou Fai (岑浩輝), the first Chief Justice of the MACFA, was a member from December 1999 to August 2024. Philip Xavier (許輝年), a lawyer, served as a member of the Commission from 1999 to 2025 and he was a Macau delegate to the 10th National People's Congress (2003–2008). Mr. Wang Yu (王禹), a professor of public law at the University of Macau, was appointed as a member of the Commission in 2021. Chief Justice Song Man Lei (宋敏莉) was appointed to the Commission in 2025 in place of Mr. Sam Hou Fai. Mr. António José Dias Azedo, a lawyer of Portuguese descent, was appointed in 2025 in place of Philip Xavier.

25 'Sam Hou Fai Elected as Next Macau Leader; Beijing Lauds Him as Unifier and Reformer' *SCMP* (13 October 2024) <www.scmp.com/news/hong-kong/politics/article/3282151/voting-starts-macau-leadership-election-ex-judge-sam-hou-fai-runs-uncontested> last accessed 3 January 2026.

26 'The Global Financial Centres Index 38' (September 2025) <www.longfinance.net/media/documents/GFCI_38_Report_2025.09.25_v1.0.pdf> last accessed 3 January 2026.

27 Yan-leung Cheung, Yuk-shing Cheng, and Chi-keung Woo, *Hong Kong's Global Financial Centre and China's Development: Changing Roles and Future Prospects* (Routledge 2017) 4–7.

Kong, which maintains a "semi-porous and heavily regulated economic border"[28] with Mainland China but a free financial border with the rest of the world. In this way, China gets the best of both worlds: capping capital flight *from* the Mainland, while attracting *foreign* capital through Hong Kong. It is noteworthy that 68.1% of Mainland China's inward Foreign Direct Investment (FDI) originated from Hong Kong in 2024.[29] Furthermore, by expanding the controlled circulation of "offshore" Renminbi (RMB) in Hong Kong, China succeeded in getting the International Monetary Fund to include the RMB in its Special Drawing Rights currency basket in 2016 – thereby expanding China's global economic clout – while still keeping its currency capital account largely closed to the world.[30] "Free market constitutionalism"[31] was codified in Hong Kong's Basic Law to serve China's economic interests. With Beijing's tightened grip over Hong Kong, the HKCFA is obviously no longer as confrontational as it used to be, especially on national security issues. But so long as the Hong Kong and Central Governments still want the city to remain a top international financial centre attractive to *overseas* financial and human capital, the politicians understand that the rule of law undergirded by an independent judiciary must remain a cornerstone of the city's governance, and they therefore cannot neuter the courts or overrule the HKCFA at every turn. Macau, on the other hand, is not an international financial centre, and its economy is founded on a one-way dependence on Mainland China. This fundamental difference in Hong Kong's political economy therefore provides the HKCFA with some capacity to chart a path less taken from the rest of communist China, especially on LGBT rights.

In addition, this book will also analyse the key constitutional developments in Hong Kong and Macau that post-dated Ip's book. In 2021, Beijing overhauled Hong Kong's electoral system such that only "patriots" can now run for political office, leaving only *one* "non-establishment" politician in the legislative chamber in 2021, and none in 2025. The Macau government – on its own initiative – upped the ante and simply barred *all* pro-democracy candidates from contesting its 2021 legislative election and even the centrist candidates in the 2025 election.

28 Ho-fung Hung, *City on the Edge: Hong Kong under Chinese Rule* (CUP 2022) 51.

29 National Bureau of Statistics of China 中国国家统计局, *2025中国统计年鉴 2025 China Statistical Yearbook*, section 11–14 (Foreign Direct Investment by Country (Region)) <www.stats.gov.cn/sj/ndsj/2025/indexch.htm> last accessed 3 January 2026. See also 'Hong Kong is China's Financial Gateway to the World' *Forbes* (13 September 2022 updated) <www.forbes.com/sites/hongkong/2021/11/01/hong-kong-is-chinas-financial-gateway-to-the-world/> last accessed 3 January 2026.

30 Ho-fung Hung, *City on the Edge: Hong Kong under Chinese Rule* (CUP 2022) 65–67; Yan-leung Cheung, Yuk-shing Cheng, and Chi-keung Woo, *Hong Kong's Global Financial Centre and China's Development: Changing Roles and Future Prospects* (Routledge 2017) 39–50. 'IMF Adds Chinese Renminbi to Special Drawing Rights Basket' *IMF News* (30 September 2016) <www.imf.org/en/news/articles/2016/09/29/am16-na093016imf-adds-chinese-renminbi-to-special-drawing-rights-basket> last accessed 3 January 2026.

31 Gonzalo Villalta Puig and Eric Ip, *The Freest Market in the World: The Constitutional Logic of Economic Liberty in China's Hong Kong* (Routledge 2023).

The neutering of democracy in both cities is now complete. On national security, Beijing annexed a customised National Security Law to Hong Kong's Basic Law in 2020, and the "patriots-only" legislature *unanimously* passed local national security legislation in 2024[32] to complement the Beijing-imposed one. From the start of the public consultation to the passage of the local law, the entire process took less than 50 days – the fastest Bill passed in the history of the HKSAR.[33] Not to be outdone by Hong Kong, the Macau legislature also enacted a "toughened" National Security Law in 2023,[34] even though it already had one in place since 2009.

To understand how Hong Kong reached this inflection point in its history, it would be timely for us to review how the two SARs were conceived and how the epochal political movements that occurred in Hong Kong changed the destinies of both cities forever.

Conception and Construction of the SARs

The "OCTS" constitutional model was originally designed for Taiwan by China's Paramount Leader Deng Xiaoping in 1979.[35] But as the "renegade province" showed no interest in subservience, Deng retrofitted this framework for Hong Kong and Macau as China sought to reclaim both cities from the United Kingdom[36] and Portugal,[37] respectively, in the early 1980s.[38]

Beijing commenced negotiations with the British first, and the Sino-British Declaration on the Question of Hong Kong was signed in 1984. Negotiations with Portugal followed soon after, and the Sino-Portuguese Declaration on the Question of Macau was inked in 1987. Unlike the British, Portugal did not have the same

32 Safeguarding National Security Ordinance (維護國家安全條例). The full text of the law is available at www.elegislation.gov.hk/hk/a305, last accessed 3 January 2026.

33 See Chapter 4 for a full discussion of this law.

34 2023 Law on Safeguarding National Security (維護國家安全法). A bilingual (Chinese and Portuguese) version of the law is available at https://images.io.gov.mo/bo/i/2023/24/despce-79-2023.pdf, last accessed 3 January 2026.

35 Christopher Hughes, 'Regional Perspectives and Domestic Imperatives: Living with "One Country, Two Systems"?: The Future of Beijing's Taiwan Policy' (2001) 14(2) *Cambridge Review of International Affairs* 124, 125; '邓小平提出"一国两制" Deng Xiaoping Proposed "One Country Two Systems"' *CNR* (17 August 2014) <http://news.cnr.cn/special/dengxiaoping/latest/201408/t20140817_516235884.shtml> last accessed 3 January 2026.

36 The acquisition of Hong Kong by the British government was achieved via the conclusion of three unequal treaties with China – the Treaty of Nanking of 1842, the Convention of Peking of 1860, and the Convention Respecting an Extension of Hong Kong Territory of 1898 – over the span of approximately 60 years. See Yash Ghai, *Hong Kong's New Constitutional Order: The Resumption of Chinese Sovereignty and the Basic Law* (2nd edn, HKU Press 1999) 1–80.

37 In 1887, China agreed unwillingly to Portugal's 'perpetual occupation and government of Macau'. See Article II of the 1887 Sino-Portuguese Treaty of Friendship and Commerce.

38 See Xiaobo Zhai, 'Macao's Constitutional Founding' in Kevin Tan and Michael Ng (eds), *Constitutional Foundings in Northeast Asia* (Hart 2022) 79.

political leverage to negotiate from a position of strength with China.[39] This "asymmetrical bargaining"[40] meant that Portugal strategically never pushed for democratisation – a fundamental concern of the British[41] – and focused its efforts on preserving its "cultural heritage"[42] in Macau and the interests of its Portuguese descendants.[43]

Based on the respective Declarations, Beijing proceeded to draft the Basic Laws for both cities – the mini-constitutions that would govern the two cities after China resumed sovereignty over the territories. China drafted both Basic Laws[44] without the *formal* participation of either Britain or Portugal, but behind-the-scenes both colonial governments were consulted on the drafts of the respective charters.[45] The drafting of the Hong Kong Basic Law (HKBL) commenced in 1985 and it was finally promulgated in 1990.[46] As the HKBL was drafted first, the Chinese drafters were able to use that as a template for the Macau version when they commenced drafting the Macau Basic Law (MABL) in 1988, and the MABL was finally promulgated in 1993.[47] Given that both Basic Laws were drafted around the same time with the Hong Kong version serving as a template for Macau, it is unsurprising that both Basic Laws were strikingly similar – at least on paper. Each SAR is authorised "a high degree of autonomy";[48] the "previous capitalist system and way of life"[49] shall remain unchanged for 50 years; private ownership of property shall be protected by law;[50] laws in each SAR shall be enacted by its local legislature;[51] National Laws shall not be applied in the SAR except for those listed in the respective Annex of the Basic Law;[52] each SAR shall enact a national security law "on its own";[53] their courts will enjoy "independent judicial power,

39 Carmen Amado Mendes, *Portugal, China and the Macau Negotiations, 1986–1999* (HKU Press 2013) 110.
40 Carmen Amado Mendes, *Portugal, China and the Macau Negotiations, 1986–1999* (HKU Press 2013) 113.
41 While the Sino-British Declaration required the Hong Kong legislature to be constituted by elections (Annex 1, art I), the Sino-Portuguese one only mandated "a majority" of Macau's legislature to be elected. (Annex 1, art III).
42 See Sino-Portuguese Declaration, Annex 1, art VII.
43 See Sino-Portuguese Declaration, art 2(6).
44 In 1985, China appointed 59 members to Hong Kong's Basic Law Drafting Committee, of which 23 members were from Hong Kong. In 1988, China appointed 48 members to Macau's Basic Law Drafting Committee, of which 19 were from Macau.
45 See Yash Ghai, 'The Basic Law of the Special Administrative Region of Macau: Some Reflections' (2000) 49(1) *International and Comparative Law Quarterly* 183.
46 See Albert Chen and Po Jen Yap, *The Constitutional System of the Hong Kong SAR* (Hart 2023) 6–12.
47 See Jason Buhi, *Global Constitutional Narratives of Autonomous Regions: The Constitutional History of Macau* (Routledge 2021) 176–177.
48 HKBL, art 2; MABL, art 2.
49 HKBL, art 5; MABL, art 5.
50 HKBL, art 6; MABL, art 6.
51 HKBL, art 17; MABL, art 17.
52 HKBL, art 18; MABL, art 18.
53 HKBL, art 23; MABL, art 23.

including that of final adjudication";[54] residents are guaranteed the freedom of speech, press, expression, assembly,[55] and freedom of religion;[56] residents shall not be subjected to arbitrary or unlawful arrest, detention or imprisonment, and torture is prohibited;[57] the Central Government shall not levy taxes on the SARs;[58] both SARs shall continue to use their local currency which shall be freely convertible;[59] no foreign exchange control policies shall be applied in the SARs and the free flow of capital shall be safeguarded;[60] each SAR shall be a separate customs territory and each may participate in international organisations and international trade agreements using its SAR designation, etc.[61] On paper, the Basic Laws purport to create two liberal, autonomous enclaves within China, distinct from the communist way of life up-north.

But of course there are textual differences between the two Basic Laws. Some distinctions were simply attributable to the divergent historical socio-economic characteristics of the two cities. Hong Kong was – and is – a global financial and aviation hub, so its Basic Law spelt out specific injunctions on preserving these attributes.[62] For Macau, the casino industry was – and is – a bedrock of its economy and the MABL authorises the local government to make policies on "tourism and recreation"[63] – the drafters' chosen euphemism for "casino gambling".[64] In the same vein, the common law[65] and jury trials[66] are preserved in Hong Kong, but both are inapplicable to Macau's civil law system. Interestingly, the MABL codifies far more constitutional rights than its Hong Kong counterpart.[67] The legitimate rights and interests of women,[68] minors, the aged, and the disabled[69]

54 HKBL, art 19; MABL, art 19.
55 HKBL, art 27; MABL, art 27.
56 HKBL, art 32; MABL, art 34.
57 HKBL, art 28; MABL, art 28.
58 HKBL, art 106; MABL, art 104.
59 HKBL, arts 111–112; MABL, arts 108–109.
60 HKBL, art 112; MABL, art 109.
61 HKBL, art 116; MABL, art 112.
62 HKBL, art 109 and Ch 5, s 4.
63 MABL, art 118.
64 Paul Fifoot, 'One Country, Two Systems – Mark II: From Hong Kong to Macao' (1994) 12(1) *International Relations* 25, 54.
65 HKBL, art 8.
66 HKBL, art 86.
67 One notable exception relates to the constitutional right of abode. Macau's Basic Law [Article 24(2)] explicitly states that Mainland Chinese children born outside of Macau would only obtain the right of permanent residency through their parents if the child was born *after* a parent obtains Macau permanent residency. For Hong Kong, its Basic Law did not impose an explicit time-of-birth stipulation on the child, but the local legislature by ordinary legislation imposed a similar stipulation in 1997 and the issue was subject to a major constitutional litigation in Hong Kong. See discussion of *Chan Kam Nga v Director of Immigration* (1999) 2 HKCFAR 82 in Chapter 3 of this book.
68 MABL, art 38.
69 MABL, art 38.

are all codified in the MABL, with no equivalent found in the HKBL.[70] The right to habeas corpus[71] and prohibitions against inhuman treatment[72] and retrospective criminal punishment[73] are also expressly enshrined in the MABL; for Hong Kong, the right to habeas corpus is only protected under the common law and the two prohibitions are codified under the Hong Kong Bill of Rights Ordinance – an ordinary law passed by the British colonial government in 1991. Macau even has an inviolable constitutional right to "human dignity",[74] which again is absent from the HKBL or any local Hong Kong law. The constitutional potential of the more extensive rights regime enshrined in the MABL was, however, nipped in the bud by two significant differences between the constitutional set-up of the MASAR judiciary and the Hong Kong one. First, the HKBL allows all pre-existing colonial judges to "remain in employment and retain their seniority"[75] after the handover, but no such provision was included for Macau, thereby allowing the Macau government to sinicise the bench swiftly. Second, the HKBL allows "judges from other common law jurisdictions"[76] – to be designated as overseas Non-Permanent Judges (NPJs) – to sit on the HKCFA, the territory's highest court after the handover. Again, for Macau, no such provisions were provided. Continued Western confidence in the rule of law in Hong Kong after the handover was pivotal to preserving the city as an international financial hub,[77] and these concessions for Hong Kong served that purpose; China had no reason to be as accommodating with the Portuguese on Macau. Therefore, it is unsurprising that only the HKBL contains a constitutional promise that the ultimate aim is for the election of its Chief Executive – the head of the HKSAR government – and all members of its Legislative Council by "universal suffrage".[78] But it is noteworthy that no timeline for universal suffrage was codified. As for Macau, China simply kept to its promise of preserving Portugal's cultural legacy in Macau[79] and protecting the interests of its Portuguese descendants.[80]

70 But notably in 1995, the colonial British government passed both the Sex Discrimination Ordinance and Disability Discrimination Ordinance to respectively prohibit sex-based and disability-related discrimination.
71 MABL, art 28.
72 MABL, art 28.
73 MABL, art 29.
74 MABL, art 30.
75 HKBL, art 93.
76 HKBL, art 82.
77 See Yash Ghai, *Hong Kong's New Constitutional Order: The Resumption of Chinese Sovereignty and the Basic Law* (2nd edn, HKU Press 1999) 301–304, 332–33.
78 HKBL, arts 45 and 68.
79 MABL, art 125.
80 MABL, arts 42, 24(3) and 24(4).

Epochal Political Movements in the Hong Kong SAR

From birth, the MASAR was China's obedient child: the political orientation of Macau residents was and remains homogeneously conservative;[81] civil society groups in Macau were and remain weak;[82] and its people have always preferred to focus on livelihood issues.[83] Macau never saw protests of the magnitude we have witnessed in Hong Kong – not even close.[84]

On the other hand, from its early years, the Hong Kong SAR began tugging at its political leash. In 2003, when the local government – upon Beijing's prompting – sought to enact a local national security law in the city, half a million people took to the streets to oppose its passage; and this one-day "uprising" successfully pressured the government to abort the bill.[85] Success begets success and civil society in Hong Kong further flourished.

In 2013, law professor Benny Tai floated the idea of "Occupy Central" in a local newspaper.[86] His plan was to mobilise pro-democracy activists to occupy the central financial district in Hong Kong – à la Occupy Wall Street Movement of 2011 – to pressure the local and central governments to take substantive genuine steps towards universal suffrage for both the city's Chief Executive and the local legislature. This idea gained traction, and local pro-democracy political parties and student groups chimed in, but each group possessed its own vision of what political reforms were needed. Beijing was unsurprisingly infuriated by this social movement, viewing the public mobilisation as a political plot orchestrated by the West to launch a "Colour Revolution" in the city.[87] While the Central Government

81 Eilo Yu Wing-yat and Natalie Chin Ka-man, 'The Political Opposition and Democracy in Macao: Revolutionaries or Loyalists?' (2012) 47(1) *Government and Opposition* 97, 102.

82 Sonny Shiu-hing Lo, 'Consultative Governance, Legitimacy Problem and Democracy Deficit in Macau' (2011) 7 *"一國兩制"研究 Journal of "One Country Two Systems" Studies* 90, 94.

83 C. S. Bryan Ho, 'Political Culture, Social Movements, and Governability in Macao' (2011) 38(2) *Asian Affairs: An American Review* 59, 62.

84 The largest protest in Macau occurred in 2014 when 20,000 demonstrators rallied against the Macau government's attempt to pass an exorbitant retirement package for its Chief Executive and principal officials. See Meng U Ieong, 'Macao and Hong Kong, Convergence or Divergence?: The 2014 Retirement Package Bill Protest and Macao's Governance Crisis' (2017) 57(3) *Asian Survey* 504, 509.

85 See Fu Hualing, Carole J. Petersen, and Simon N. M. Young (eds), *National Security and Fundamental Freedoms: Hong Kong's Article 23 Under Scrutiny* (HKU Press 2005).

86 Benny Tai, '公民抗命的最大殺傷力武器, The Most Lethal Weapon Of Civil Disobedience' *信報 Hong Kong Economic Journal* (16 January 2013) <https://sparkpost.wordpress.com/2013/01/19/戴耀廷：公民抗命的最大殺傷力武器/> last accessed 3 January 2026; Karita Kan, 'Occupy Central and Constitutional Reform in Hong Kong' (2013) 3 *China Perspectives* 73, 75.

87 Zuoer Chen 陈佐洱, '"占中"是街头政治和颜色革命 "Occupy Central" is street politics and colour revolution' *BBC* (14 October 2014) <www.bbc.com/zhongwen/simp/china/2014/10/141014_hk_chenzuoer_umbrella_revolution> last accessed 3 January 2026. Chen was then the president of the Chinese Association of Hong Kong and Macau Studies and the former Executive Deputy Director of the Hong Kong and Macau Affairs Office of the PRC State Council.

blustered about its full prerogative to exercise "comprehensive jurisdiction"[88] in Hong Kong, it did make one significant concession in August 2014: The Chief Executive could be elected by the people in a "universal suffrage" election going forward, but the candidates had to be pre-screened by a nominating committee heavily stacked with pro-Beijing delegates,[89] thereby ensuring that the people could only choose from a slate of pro-Beijing candidates. Hitherto, the Chief Executive was "elected" by this 1200-member committee alone, with the general public totally excluded from this franchise. But to the pro-democracy groups, this was "fake" universal suffrage, and they retaliated by commencing their occupation of Hong Kong's financial district in the early morning of 28 September 2014. With the benefit of hindsight, the local government soon after made one tactical error: they dispatched the riot police to deploy tear gas to disperse the crowd. This proved to be counterproductive: television images of Hong Kongers being teargassed by the police (hitherto unseen since the 1960s) – and using *umbrellas* to shield themselves – shocked the city and drew thousands more people into the streets in solidarity with the protesters. The Umbrella Movement was born. Reportedly, the Central Government responded by formulating a policy of "No compromise, and no blood":[90] Beijing would not relent on its Decision of August 2014, but neither would it repeat the bloodshed of Tiananmen Square in its dear global financial hub. The riot police were withdrawn; the protesters were allowed to blockade the major arteries of the financial district; the local government would wait out the crisis and allow for public fatigue to set in and shore up legitimacy for future site clearance. Camping tents of all colours and sizes sprang up on the austere asphalt of the financial district and they would remain there for 79 days until they were all cleared by the police with minimal opposition and fanfare on 15 December 2014. By that time, some 1.4 million Hong Kong residents – approximately 20% of the city's population – had participated in this unprecedented occupation for democracy.[91] Among all the abandoned banners and posters cleared from the Occupy Central site were slogans carrying this same prophetic promise: "We Will Be Back".

And the street protesters indeed returned five years later, and with unexpected vengeance. But the triggering event was stranger than fiction. In February 2018, a

88 The State Council, 'White Paper on the Practice of "One Country, Two Systems" Policy in the Hong Kong Special Administrative Region' <https://english.www.gov.cn/archive/white_paper/2014/08/23/content_281474982986578.htm> last accessed 3 January 2026.

89 Decision of the Standing Committee of the National People's Congress on Issues Relating to the Selection of the Chief Executive of the Hong Kong Special Administrative Region by Universal Suffrage and on the Method for Forming the Legislative Council of the Hong Kong Special Administrative Region in the Year 2016 (Adopted at the 10th Session of the Standing Committee of the 12th National People's Congress on 31 August 2014).

90 Yongshun Cai, *The Occupy Movement in Hong Kong: Sustaining Decentralized Protest* (Routledge 2016) 55.

91 Shibani Mahtani and Timothy McLaughlin, *Among the Braves: Hope, Struggle, and Exile in the Battle for Hong Kong and the Future of Global Democracy* (Hachette Books 2023) 94.

young Hong Kong man murdered his girlfriend in Taiwan and fled back to Hong Kong after the crime. As there was no extradition treaty between Hong Kong and Taiwan, he could not be returned to face trial for his offence. To address this legal lacuna, Carrie Lam – the Chief Executive of Hong Kong – decided in February 2019 to push for local legislation that would authorise the rendition of Hong Kong residents to jurisdictions, with which Hong Kong did not have any pre-existing extradition agreement, to face trial for offences allegedly committed there. For reasons unclear, Lam decided to include Mainland China in the designated list.[92] Unsurprisingly, public opposition to the bill grew, gained steam, and mass street protests returned to the streets of Hong Kong. To fend off the street protesters, the police frequently deployed tear gas and rubber bullets, with violent altercations between law enforcement and the protesters becoming a regular feature of the Hong Kong streetscape. On 15 June 2019, the bill was "suspended"; but on that fateful night, a street protester fell to his death after slipping on scaffolding and his misadventure became a rallying cry that brought nearly two million people – the largest demonstration in the history of Hong Kong – into the streets the very next day.[93] The unrest persisted as protesters demanded that the government grant arrested protesters amnesty and conduct an independent inquiry into alleged police misuse of force,[94] concessions which the Hong Kong government refused to make. And the street protests became increasingly violent. Public facilities were vandalised and set on fire;[95] the Legislative Council was stormed and ransacked;[96] and university campuses became war zones despite the formal "withdrawal" of the bill in October 2019.[97]

92 David Lague, James Pomfret, and Greg Torode, 'How Murder, Kidnappings and Miscalculation Set off Hong Kong's Revolt' *Reuters* (20 December 2019) <www.reuters.com/investigates/special-report/hongkong-protests-extradition-narrative/> last accessed 3 January 2026.

93 'Hong Kong protest: "Nearly two million" join demonstration' *BBC* (17 June 2019) < www.bbc.com/news/world-asia-china-48656471> last accessed 3 January 2026.

94 The protesters wanted the government to fulfil five demands: (1) withdrawal of the extradition bill, (2) an independent inquiry into the use of force by police, (3) amnesty for arrested protesters, (4) a halt to categorising the protests as riots, and (5) the implementation of universal suffrage: see Jeffie Lam, '"Five Key Demands, Not One Less": Hong Kong Protesters Make Clear that Chief Executive Carrie Lam's Bill Withdrawal Is Not Enough' *SCMP* (4 September 2019) <www.scmp.com/news/hong-kong/politics/article/3025750/five-key-demands-not-one-less-hong-kong-protesters-make> last accessed 3 January 2026.

95 'Fire and Fear: Hong Kong Lit by Protests after Dark – in Pictures' *The Guardian* (2 September 2019) <www.theguardian.com/world/gallery/2019/sep/02/fire-and-fear-hong-kong-lit-by-protests-after-dark-in-pictures> last accessed 3 January 2026.

96 Naomi Ng, Alvin Lum, and Su Xinqi, 'Hong Kong Protesters' Damage to Legislative Council Building Could Exceed HK $10 Million and Take Weeks to Repair' *SCMP* (2 July 2019) <www.scmp.com/news/hong-kong/politics/article/3016996/hong-kong-protesters-damage-legislative-council-building> last accessed 3 January 2026.

97 Lily Kuo and others, 'Hong Kong University Siege: A Visual Guide' *The Guardian* (18 November 2019) <www.theguardian.com/world/2019/nov/18/hong-kong-university-siege-a-visual-guide> last accessed 3 January 2026; 'Hong Kong's Universities Now Citadels Under Siege' *Bangkok*

As relentless protests roiled the city,[98] prominent Hong Kong pro-democracy activists were in Washington, lobbying the Trump administration and US Congress to penalise Hong Kong economically.[99] The Hong Kong Human Rights and Democracy Act (HKHRDA) was passed in November 2019, which authorised sanctions against Mainland China and Hong Kong officials for human rights abuses in Hong Kong and required the US government to annually review whether Hong Kong was sufficiently autonomous to justify "special treatment" apart from the rest of China – Hong Kong lost its special trade privileges with the USA in 2020 and every year since then.[100] Once again, Beijing saw a "colour revolution" instigated by Western hostile forces that threatened to engulf Hong Kong and infect the rest of China.

Days before President Trump signed the HKHRDA into law, another seismic political event shook Hong Kong. On 24 November 2019, pro-democracy politicians scored a landslide victory in the city's District Council (DC) election, sweeping 392 out of 452 seats.[101] The DC election was a mere municipal election, but it had been framed as a *de facto* referendum on the protest movement, and the crushing defeat for the pro-Beijing camp was a harbinger of the consequential Legislative Council election hitherto scheduled 10 months away. Equally important was the fact that elected District Councillors were at that time eligible to vote in the Chief Executive election. While a pro-democracy politician would never win this race, the pro-democracy faction on that Chief Executive Election Committee, whose coalition had now expanded with the newly elected District Councillors, could play kingmaker in a contest between two pro-Beijing candidates.[102] The Central Government was stunned. Its loyalists had privately given assurances that the silent majority in Hong Kong was exasperated by the street violence and would

Post (14 November 2019) <www.bangkokpost.com/world/1794044/hong-kongs-universities-now-citadels-under-siege> last accessed 3 January 2026.

98 For a detailed account, see Zuraidah Ibrahim and Jeffie Lam (eds), *Rebel City: Hong Kong's Year of Water and Fire* (World Scientific Publishing Co. Pte. Ltd. and South China Morning Post Publishers Limited 2020).

99 Chris Fuchs, 'Activist Joshua Wong Brings Hong Kong Fight to U.S. with Upcoming Congressional Testimony' *NBC News* (16 September 2019) <www.nbcnews.com/news/asian-america/activist-joshua-wong-brings-hong-kong-fight-u-s-upcoming-n1054971> last accessed 3 January 2026.

100 Hillary Leung, 'US has "Persecutory Delusion," Beijing Says after Joe Biden Renews "Emergency Status" for Hong Kong' *HKFP* (11 July 2024) <https://hongkongfp.com/2024/07/11/us-has-persecutory-delusion-beijing-says-after-joe-biden-renews-emergency-status-for-hong-kong/> last accessed 3 January 2026; 'Trump ends preferential economic treatment for Hong Kong' *BBC* (15 July 2020) <www.bbc.co.uk/news/world-us-canada-53412598> last accessed 20 March 2026.

101 Kinling Lo, 'Hong Kong Election Success for Pro-Democracy Camp Gives Beijing a Headache When Dealing with "Kingmaker" Tycoons' *SCMP* (28 November 2019) <www.scmp.com/news/china/politics/article/3039832/hong-kong-election-success-pro-democracy-camp-gives-beijing> last accessed 3 January 2026.

102 Prior to China's overhaul of Hong Kong's electoral system in 2021, the District Council lawmakers could choose 117 of their members to vote in the 1200-member Chief Executive Election Committee.

come out in full force to vote for the pro-Beijing politicians.[103] But the thumping they received instead displayed the complete disconnect between the government and the governed.

The social unrest eventually receded but not because of any new measures passed or concessions made by the hapless local administration. Instead, the street protesters retreated because of a new contagion: COVID-19. As the pandemic swept over China and across the globe, Hong Kong hunkered down and there was a silent truce. Beijing used this time-out most shrewdly. Behind the scenes, it quietly crafted a bespoke National Security Law for Hong Kong and foisted it on the city in June 2020, bypassing the local legislature in the process and taking the entire city by surprise. Next, China's National People's Congress overhauled Hong Kong's electoral system such that going forward only "patriots" – as certified by a government-appointed committee – can run for public office. The Central Government was determined to eradicate all the anti-China forces once and for all.

Macau was an innocent witness to Hong Kong's unravelling. But as Hong Kong was taken to task by the central authorities in Beijing, Macau – through no fault of its own – felt it had to do more and genuflect to the national zeitgeist. The MASAR government of its own accord disqualified all pro-democracy candidates from even contesting its 2021 Legislative Assembly election and even the centrist candidates in the subsequent 2025 election, and it swiftly strengthened its national security law in 2023, even though it already had a comprehensive one since 2009.

Conclusion

China's two SARs have been perceived as a "constitutional experiment".[104] For Hong Kong especially, it was intended to be a liberal enclave constructed within a dual state:[105] a normative state that rules in accordance with law co-existing with a prerogative state exercising unlimited arbitrary power.

103 Shibani Mahtani and Timothy McLaughlin, *Among the Braves: Hope, Struggle, and Exile in the Battle for Hong Kong and the Future of Global Democracy* (Hachette Books 2023) 213; James Palmer, 'Hong Kongers Break Beijing's Delusion of Victory' *Foreign Policy* (25 November 2019) https://foreignpolicy.com/2019/11/25/hong-kong-election-beijing-media-delusions-victory/ last accessed 3 January 2026; Feng Lin 林枫, '香港区议会选举建制派惨败北京或误判形势 Pro-Establishment Camp Suffers a Crushing Defeat in Hong Kong District Council Elections; Beijing May Have Misjudged The Situation' *VOA* (25 November 2019) <www.voachinese.com/a/Beijing-Shocked-By-Stunning-Defeat-Of-Pro-Beijing-Candidated-In-HK-Election-20191125/5179974.html> last accessed 3 January 2026.

104 Cora Chan and Albert Chen, 'Yash Ghai and the Constitutional Experiment of "One Country, Two Systems" in Hong Kong' in Humphrey Sipalla and J. Osogo Ambani (eds), *Furthering Constitutions, Birthing Peace: Liber Amicorum Yash Pal Ghai* (Strathmore University Press 2021) 303–335.

105 Cora Chan, 'From Legal Pluralism to Dual State: Evolution of the Relationship between the Chinese and Hong Kong Legal Orders' (2022) 16(1) *Law & Ethics of Human Rights* 99–135.

But with China's authoritarian turn, questions are now regularly raised about whether Hong Kong can still preserve its common law values within a communist statist state.[106] At the heart of this concern lie unallayed anxieties about the future of Hong Kong's vaunted judiciary and its ability to remain independent amid the city's political changes. Global confidence in Hong Kong's rule of law had been bolstered by the city's erstwhile ability to attract a stream of prestigious overseas jurists to sit on its highest court. At its peak in 2019, Hong Kong had 15 overseas NPJs rostered to hear cases before the top court with luminaries who included Baroness Hale of Richmond (President of the UK Supreme Court), Anthony Murray Gleeson (Chief Justice of Australia), and Beverley McLachlin (Chief Justice of Canada). But since 2020, at least five overseas judges have resigned from the HKCFA, explicitly citing their concerns about the political situation in Hong Kong or its national security laws.[107] While Beverley McLachlin only cited family reasons for retiring from the HKCFA, it is noteworthy that she renewed her position as an international judge in Singapore for another three years a few months before leaving her post in Hong Kong.[108] The HKCFA is now left with six overseas judges, with fewer joining the ranks as incumbents retire.

Comparative studies are replete with outstanding scholarship on how courts judge under authoritarianism.[109] This book will add to this chorus of important voices by examining how the Hong Kong judiciary navigates this shrinking space of autonomy in the post-2020 era of "coercive assimilation".[110]

Our book is organised as follows: Chapter 2 of this book will analyse the political systems of the two SARs, with a particular focus on how Hong Kong was electorally overhauled in 2021. We will also illustrate how the pre-2021 electoral configurations fostered gridlock in the Hong Kong legislature, which Beijing ended with its unceremonious exclusion of all perceived "troublemakers" from the legislature. Chapter 3 proceeds by contrasting Hong Kong's and Macau's Courts of Final Appeal and explains the *continued* post-2021 divergence between the two top courts. Chapter 4 compares the national security laws enacted in both cities, including their post-enactment implementation by their governments and judicial

106 Cora Chan, 'Thirty Years from Tiananmen: China, Hong Kong, and the Ongoing Experiment to Preserve Liberal Values in an Authoritarian State' (2019) 17(2) *International Journal of Constitutional Law* 439–452.

107 These five overseas NPJs were James Spigelman, Lord Reed, Lord Hodge, Lord Sumption and Lord Collins. See Chapter 4 for a discussion of their resignations.

108 'McLachlin Renewed with Singapore Court Months before Leaving Hong Kong Court To Be with Family' *National Post* (17 June 2024) <https://nationalpost.com/news/canada/beverley-mclachlin-singapore-court-hong-kong-court> last accessed 3 January 2026.

109 See Julius Yam, 'Judging under Authoritarianism' (2024) 87(4) *Modern Law Review* 894–925; Tom Ginsburg and Tamir Moustafa, *Rule by Law: The Politics of Courts in Authoritarian Regimes* (CUP 2008); Tamir Moustafa, 'Law and Courts in Authoritarian Regimes' (2014) 10 *Annual Review of Law and Social Science* 281; Po Jen Yap, *Courts and Democracies in Asia* (CUP 2017).

110 Ho-fung Hung, *City on the Edge: Hong Kong under Chinese Rule* (CUP 2022) 122.

interpretation by the courts. Finally, in Chapter 5, we explore the constitutional interface between the respective SARs and Mainland China and examine how the relationship has evolved through the years, from "a high degree of autonomy"[111] granted at conception to their current consigned role of integrating into the country's developmental plans.[112]

"OCTS" may seem like a constitutional contradiction in terms or even a perennial paradox. But its inherent nebulousness has allowed this phrase to be rhetorically deployed by persons across the ideological spectrum. Pro-democracy politicians in Hong Kong used to view OCTS as a promise of a "political system" in Hong Kong distinct from the Mainland, while Beijing saw OCTS as codifying primarily two *economic* systems and no more.[113] The Basic Laws of both Hong Kong and Macau guarantee that the OCTS arrangement will endure for 50 years.[114] Whether this constitutional promise can be kept – in both form and substance – will be the real question.

References

Buhi, Jason, *Global Constitutional Narratives of Autonomous Regions: The Constitutional History of Macau* (Oxford, Routledge 2021).

Cai, Yongshun, *The Occupy Movement in Hong Kong: Sustaining Decentralized Protest* (Oxford, Routledge 2016).

Chan, Cora, 'Thirty Years from Tiananmen: China, Hong Kong, and the Ongoing Experiment to Preserve Liberal Values in an Authoritarian State' (2019) 17(2) *International Journal of Constitutional Law* 439.

Chan, Cora, 'From Legal Pluralism to Dual State: Evolution of the Relationship between the Chinese and Hong Kong Legal Orders' (2022) 16(1) *Law & Ethics of Human Rights* 99.

Chan, Cora and Albert Chen, 'Yash Ghai and the Constitutional Experiment of "One Country, Two Systems" in Hong Kong', in Humphrey Sipalla and J. Osogo Ambani (eds), *Furthering Constitutions, Birthing Peace: Liber Amicorum Yash Pal Ghai* (Nairobi, Strathmore University Press 2021) 303.

111 HKBL, art 2; MABL, art 2.

112 Natalie Wong and Lilian Cheng, 'China's "Two Sessions" 2023: Xi Jinping Ties Hong Kong's Future to Country's, Vows to "Firmly" Push Forward "One Country, Two Systems"' *SCMP* (14 March 2023) <www.scmp.com/news/hong-kong/hong-kong-economy/article/3213297/xi-jinping-stresses-hong-kongs-role-chinas-development-he-kicks-third-term-president> last accessed 3 January 2026; Yu Hong, 'China's Grand Plans to Further Integrate Hong Kong and Macau. Will They Work?' *Think China* (17 January 2022) <www.thinkchina.sg/economy/chinas-grand-plans-further-integrate-hong-kong-and-macau-will-they-work> last accessed 3 January 2026.

113 Zheng Ge 鄭戈, '"一國兩制"與國家整合 "One Country Two Systems" and National Integration' (2017) 161 *二十一世紀 Twenty-First Century* 17, 20; also see Shuwen Wang 王叔文, *香港基本法导论 Introduction to the Basic Law of the Hong Kong Special Administrative Region* (中共中央党校出版社 CCP Central Party School Press 1997) 327; Albert Chen, 'Foreword' in Gonzalo Villalta Puig and Eric Ip (eds), *The Freest Market in the World: The Constitutional Logic of Economic Liberty in China's Hong Kong* (Routledge 2023) xix.

114 HKBL, art 5; MABL, art 5.

Chen, Albert, 'Foreword' in Gonzalo Villalta Puig and Eric Ip (eds), *The Freest Market in the World: The Constitutional Logic of Economic Liberty in China's Hong Kong* (Oxford, Routledge 2023) xix.

Chen, Albert and Po Jen Yap, *The Constitutional System of the Hong Kong SAR* (Oxford, Hart 2023).

Cheung, Yan-leung, Yuk-shing Cheng, and Chi-keung Woo, *Hong Kong's Global Financial Centre and China's Development: Changing Roles and Future Prospects* (Oxford, Routledge 2017).

Fifoot, Paul, 'One Country, Two Systems – Mark II: From Hong Kong to Macao' (1994) 12(1) *International Relations* 25.

Fu, Hualing, Carole J Petersen, and Simon N M Young (eds), *National Security and Fundamental Freedoms: Hong Kong's Article 23 Under Scrutiny* (Hong Kong, Hong Kong University Press 2005).

Ghai, Yash, *Hong Kong's New Constitutional Order: The Resumption of Chinese Sovereignty and the Basic Law* (2nd edn, Hong Kong, Hong Kong University Press 1999).

Ghai, Yash, 'The Basic Law of the Special Administrative Region of Macau: Some Reflections' (2000) 49(1) *International and Comparative Law Quarterly* 183.

Ginsburg, Tom and Tamir Moustafa, *Rule by Law: The Politics of Courts in Authoritarian Regimes* (Cambridge, Cambridge University Press 2008).

Ho, Chiew Siang Bryan, 'Political Culture, Social Movements, and Governability in Macao' (2011) 38(2) *Asian Affairs: An American Review* 59.

Hughes, Christopher, 'Regional Perspectives and Domestic Imperatives: Living with "One Country, Two Systems"?: The Future of Beijing's Taiwan Policy' (2001) 14(2) *Cambridge Review of International Affairs* 124.

Hung, Ho-fung, *City on the Edge: Hong Kong under Chinese Rule* (Cambridge, Cambridge University Press 2022).

Ibrahim, Zuraidah and Jeffie Lam (eds), *Rebel City: Hong Kong's Year of Water and Fire* (Singapore, World Scientific Publishing Co. Pte. Ltd.; South China Morning Post Publishers Limited 2020).

Ieong, Meng U, 'Macao and Hong Kong, Convergence or Divergence?: The 2014 Retirement Package Bill Protest and Macao's Governance Crisis' (2017) 57(3) *Asian Survey* 504.

Ip, Eric, 'The Evolution of Constitutional Adjudication in the Chinese Special Administrative Regions: Theory and Evidence' (2013) 61(4) *American Journal of Comparative Law* 799.

Ip, Eric, *Hybrid Constitutionalism: The Politics of Constitutional Review in the Chinese Special Administrative Regions* (Cambridge, Cambridge University Press 2019).

Kan, Karita, 'Occupy Central and Constitutional Reform in Hong Kong' (2013) 3 *China Perspectives* 73.

Lo, Sonny Shiu-hing, 'Consultative Governance, Legitimacy Problem and Democracy Deficit in Macau' (2011) 7 *"一國兩制"研究 Journal of "One Country Two Systems" Studies* 90.

Mahtani, Shibani and Timothy McLaughlin, *Among the Braves: Hope, Struggle, and Exile in the Battle for Hong Kong and the Future of Global Democracy* (New York, Hachette Books 2023).

Mendes, Carmen Amado, *Portugal, China and the Macau Negotiations, 1986–1999* (Hong Kong, Hong Kong University Press 2013).

Moustafa, Tamir, 'Law and Courts in Authoritarian Regimes' (2014) 10 *Annual Review of Law and Social Science* 281.

Puig, Gonzalo Villalta and Eric Ip, *The Freest Market in the World: The Constitutional Logic of Economic Liberty in China's Hong Kong* (Oxford, Routledge 2023).

Wang, Shuwen 王叔文, *香港基本法导论 Introduction to the Basic Law of the Hong Kong Special Administrative Region* (Beijing, 中共中央党校出版社 CCP Central Party School Press 1997).

Wang, Wanli, 'The Asymmetric Evolution of the Basic Laws of Hong Kong and Macao' (2024) 54(1) *Hong Kong Law Journal* 15.

Yam, Julius, 'Judging under Authoritarianism' (2024) 87(4) *Modern Law Review* 894.

Yap, Po Jen, *Courts and Democracies in Asia* (Cambridge, Cambridge University Press 2017).

Yu, Eilo Wing-yat and Natalie Chin Ka-man, 'The Political Opposition and Democracy in Macao: Revolutionaries or Loyalists?' (2012) 47(1) *Government and Opposition* 97.

Zhai, Xiaobo, 'Macao's Constitutional Founding' in Kevin Tan and Michael Ng (eds), *Constitutional Foundings in Northeast Asia* (Oxford, Hart 2022) 73.

Zheng, Ge 鄭戈, '"一國兩制"與國家整合 "One Country Two Systems" and National Integration' (2017) 161 *二十一世紀 Twenty-First Century* 17.

2

POLITICAL SYSTEMS OF HONG KONG AND MACAU

Introduction

Both the Hong Kong Special Administrative Region (HKSAR) and Macau Special Administrative Region (MASAR) were similarly structured at conception. Each SAR is headed by its Chief Executive (CE). Both CEs cannot be members of any political party and are elected by a small circle of pro-Beijing loyalists in each city, with the general public excluded from the franchise. The public can directly vote for a segment of the seats in the legislature, but such "universal suffrage" seats co-exist with legislative seats that are reserved for business and professional sectors that are overwhelmingly pro-Beijing. In both cities, there has never been a dominant political party in power as the pro-Beijing coalition is splintered into different factions. This was part of Beijing's original design as it never wanted a strong CE or political party resisting its control,[1] and the fragmentation of political power allowed the Central Authorities in Beijing – through the Liaison Offices of the Central People's Government in Hong Kong and Macau – to coordinate among its allies and determine core personnel and policy decisions.

But as this chapter will explain, the deliberate fragmentation of political power among all the pro-China allies led to legislative gridlock and fomented social unrest in Hong Kong. Unlike Macau, pro-democracy lawmakers in Hong Kong used to be electorally successful before Beijing overhauled Hong Kong's electoral system in 2021, and the Hong Kong pro-democracy camp (also known as pan-democrats) used to occupy between 33%–40% of the seats in the city's legislature, giving them significant leverage to decry and delay governmental policies. In

1 Ngok Ma, 'Party Underdevelopment in Hong Kong: Hybrid Constraints and Value Changes' (2018) 58(3) *Asian Survey* 416, 419.

DOI: 10.4324/9781003683872-2

contrast, no more than three pro-democracy legislators have ever been elected to the Macau legislature, and the legislative agenda of the Macau CEs has typically passed unimpeded.[2]

As elaborated upon in Chapter 1, 2019 was an epochal year in Hong Kong as the city witnessed months of public protests arising from the HKSAR government's attempt to pass a law that would allow residents to be extradited to Mainland China to face criminal proceedings.[3] To prevent such uprisings from ever occurring again, Beijing foisted a National Security Law on Hong Kong in 2020, which we will discuss in Chapter 4, and also overhauled Hong Kong's political system in 2021 to create a "patriots-only" legislature that can swiftly pass local laws the Central Government needs. Only one "non-establishment" lawmaker was elected in 2021 after this electoral revamp in Hong Kong. In 2025, the pro-establishment camp swept the Legislative Council and won all seats. Moreover, 30% of all elected members are now deputies of the National People's Congress, the Standing Committee of the National People's Congress, and the Chinese People's Political Consultative Conference.[4] The Macau government – on its own initiative – barred all pro-democracy candidates from contesting its 2021 legislative election and even disqualified all candidates from the centrist camp in the 2025 legislative election. The neutering of democracy in both cities is now complete.

This chapter begins by examining colonial rule in Portuguese Macau and British Hong Kong. Next, the chapter proceeds by analysing the political systems of the SARs, in particular the constitutional powers of their respective CEs and legislatures, and the methods by which they are elected, and how Hong Kong was overhauled in 2021 such that only "patriots" can govern the city going forward.

Political Systems of the Colonies

Portuguese Macau

According to Portugal's official narrative, Portuguese rule in Macau began in 1557 after the Chinese Emperor authorised the settlement of Portuguese in Macau as a reward for defeating pirate fleets on China's southern coast.[5] The subsequent

2 The only significant exception was when public backlash forced the Macau SAR government to withdraw a legislative bill that would have conferred an exorbitant retirement package on its CE and principal officials. Meng U Ieong, 'Macao and Hong Kong, Convergence or Divergence?: The 2014 Retirement Package Bill Protest and Macao's Governance Crisis' (2017) 57(3) *Asian Survey* 504, 509.

3 Heike Holbig, 'Be Water, My Friend: Hong Kong's 2019 Anti-Extradition Protests' (2020) 50(4) *International Journal of Sociology* 325–337.

4 Carlos Araujo, Joe Lo and Matthew Cheng, '2025 LegCo election: who are the winners?' *SCMP* (8 December 2025) <https://multimedia.scmp.com/infographics/news/hong-kong/article/3334034/legco-election-2025/> last accessed 3 January 2026.

5 Paulo Cardinal, 'Macau: Transformation of an Historic Autonomy' in Yash Ghai and Sophia Woodman (eds), *Practising Self-Government: A Comparative Study of Autonomous Regions* (CUP 2013) 384–385.

four centuries of Portuguese rule in Macau can be divided into three periods: the period of mixed jurisdiction and administration (1557–1849), the colonial period (1849–1976), and the transitional period prior to China's resumption of sovereignty (1976–1999).[6]

During the period of mixed jurisdiction and administration (1557–1849), both the Chinese and Portuguese monarchies exercised jurisdictional powers over Macau.[7] Macau was included in the jurisdiction of Xiangshan County in China and the Chinese had the powers *inter alia* to maintain military camps, collect tariffs, levy rent from the Portuguese, and resolve disputes between the Chinese and the Portuguese and between the Chinese themselves.[8] The national laws of China were applied in Macau. Additionally, China made specific regulations that governed the Portuguese living in Macau. For example, five prohibitive rules were promulgated in 1614, which banned the Portuguese from owning Japanese slaves, trafficking Chinese citizens, evading taxes, purchasing smuggled goods, and constructing buildings without permission.[9] The Senate was the most critical and influential governing institution for the Portuguese community during this period.[10] It exercised administrative and judicial powers[11] and was in charge of safeguarding security, levying taxes, and hearing civil and criminal cases in the Portuguese community.[12] The first governor of Macau was only appointed in 1616, and 128 Portuguese Governors were appointed in total until Macau was returned to China in 1999.[13] Throughout the 17th and most of the 18th Century, the Governor possessed military powers but could not question the Senate's ruling authority.[14]

6 Shenghua Lou 婁勝華 and Chan U Chan 陳震宇, *澳門行政 Administration of Macau* (三聯書店和澳門基金會 Joint Publishing HK and Macau Foundation 2013) 9; Zhihui He 何志辉, *澳门法制史新编 A New Study on the Legal History of Macau* (社会科学文献出版社 Social Sciences Academic Press 2019) 3–4.

7 Richard Louis Edmonds and Herbert S. Yee, 'Macau: From Portuguese Autonomous Territory to Chinese Special Administrative Region' (1999) 160 *The China Quarterly* 801, 803.

8 Zhihui He 何志辉, *澳门法制史新编 A New Study on the Legal History of Macau* (社会科学文献出版社 Social Sciences Academic Press 2019) 7–8.

9 Shenghua Lou 婁勝華 and Chan U Chan 陳震宇, *澳門行政 Administration of Macau* (三聯書店和澳門基金會 Joint Publishing HK and Macau Foundation 2013) 14.

10 Kaijian Tang 湯開建, '澳門議事會的起源、發展與衰落 The Origin, Development and Decline of Macau Senate' (2016) 2 *澳門研究 Journal of Macau Studies* 81, 98.

11 Jason Buhi, *Global Constitutional Narratives of Autonomous Regions: The Constitutional History of Macau* (Routledge 2021) 10.

12 Zhihui He 何志辉, *澳门法制史新编 A New Study on the Legal History of Macau* (社会科学文献出版社 Social Sciences Academic Press 2019) 69.

13 Zhihui He 何志辉, *澳门法制史新编 A New Study on the Legal History of Macau* (社会科学文献出版社 Social Sciences Academic Press 2019) 80; Juxin Wang 王巨新 and Xin Wang 王欣, *明清澳门涉外法律研究 A Research on Foreign-Related Laws in Macao of the Ming and Early Qing Dynasties* (社会科学文献出版社 Social Sciences Academic Press 2010) 241.

14 Paulo Cardinal, 'Macau: Transformation of an Historic Autonomy' in Yash Ghai and Sophia Woodman (eds), *Practising Self-Government: A Comparative Study of Autonomous Regions* (CUP 2013) 385.

Eventually, in 1783, Queen Maria I of Portugal issued the *Royal Provisions* and granted the Governor more critical powers, including the power to veto decisions of the Senate.[15] Over time, the Governor's powers were expanded and the Senate in turn became an insignificant advisory body.[16] Eventually, Governor Bernardo José de Sousa Soares disbanded the Senate and replaced it with a municipal council within the government structure in 1835.[17]

Macau's era of mixed jurisdiction ended in 1849 after Governor João Maria Ferreira do Amaral began to bring Macau and all its residents (Chinese, Portuguese, and other foreign nationals) under Portugal's control.[18] Governor João Maria Ferreira do Amaral ruled with an iron fist, requiring Chinese citizens to pay taxes to Portugal, expelling Chinese officials from Macau, destroying Chinese customs facilities, and ceasing lease payments to China.[19] In essence, Macau became a *de facto* Portuguese colony.[20] The Treaty of Friendship and Commerce between Portugal and China was signed in 1887, whereby the Qing Government officially recognised Portuguese governance over Macau.[21] Between 1849 and 1976, Portuguese rule in Macau was codified under the colonial acts[22] and Macau organic laws enacted by Portugal.[23] The Governor of Macau appointed by Portugal was the

15 Jason Buhi, *Global Constitutional Narratives of Autonomous Regions: The Constitutional History of Macau* (Routledge 2021) 54.

16 Kaijian Tang 湯開建, '澳門議事會的起源、發展與衰落 The Origin, Development and Decline of Macau Senate' (2016) 2 *澳門研究 Journal of Macau Studies* 81, 98–102. Zhihui He 何志辉, *澳门法制史新编 A New Study on the Legal History of Macau* (社会科学文献出版社 Social Sciences Academic Press 2019) 89.

17 Zhihui He 何志辉, *澳门法制史新编 A New Study on the Legal History of Macau* (社会科学文献出版社 Social Sciences Academic Press 2019) 105; Avelino Rosa, '澳門市政廳的前途 The Future of Macau Municipal Council' (1997) 3 *澳門公共行政雜誌 Macau Public Administration Journal* 967–983.

18 Paulo Cardinal and Luís Pessanha, 'Macau' in David S. Law and others (eds), *Oxford Handbook of Constitutional Law in Asia* (OUP forthcoming); Macau comprises three parts: Macau Peninsula, Taipa, and Coloane. Portugal took over control of Taipa and Coloane in 1851 and 1864, respectively. Zhihui He 何志辉, *澳门法制史新编 A New Study on the Legal History of Macau* (社会科学文献出版社 Social Sciences Academic Press 2019) 123.

19 Zhihui He 何志辉, *澳门法制史新编 A New Study on the Legal History of Macau* (社会科学文献出版社 Social Sciences Academic Press 2019) 112–114.

20 Shenghua Lou 婁勝華 and Chan U Chan 陳震宇, *澳門行政 Administration of Macau* (三聯書店和澳門基金會 Joint Publishing HK and Macau Foundation 2013) 21.

21 Zhihui He 何志辉, *澳门法制史新编 A New Study on the Legal History of Macau* (社会科学文献出版社 Social Sciences Academic Press 2019) 124–125.

22 For example, see the Decree on Overseas Colonial Constitutional Organisation of 1869 (海外殖民憲制組織大綱), the Colonial Act of 1930 (殖民地條例), the Organic Charter of the Portuguese Colonial Empire of 1933 (葡萄牙殖民地帝國組織章程), the Organic Law of the Portuguese Overseas of 1953 (葡萄牙海外組織法), and the New Organic Law of Overseas of 1972 (新海外組織法).

23 For example, the Organic Statute of Macau Province of 1917 (澳門省組織章程), the Organic Statute of Macau Colony of 1926 (澳門殖民地組織章程), the Statute of Macau Province of 1955 (澳門省章程), the Political and Administrative Statute of Macau Province of 1963 (澳門省政治行

highest-ranking person in colonial Macau and he was vested with administrative and legislative powers. The Governing Council was an executive agency led by the Governor and was an advisory body of the Governor.[24]

The Political and Administrative Statute of Macau Province of 1963 made significant changes to Macau's political structure by establishing the Legislative Assembly, which shared legislative powers with the Governor.[25] The Legislative Assembly consisted only of 12 members.[26] The Governor was the Chair of the Legislative Assembly and he could veto laws passed by the Legislative Assembly unless the veto was overridden by a two-thirds legislative supermajority vote.[27]

Following the Carnation Revolution in 1974, the new Portuguese Government started decolonising its overseas colonies.[28] In 1976, the new Organic Statute of Macau (澳門組織章程) came into force and served as Macau's governing framework during the transitional period leading up to the resumption of Chinese sovereignty over Macau.[29] The Governor and the Legislative Assembly remained Macau's governing institutions.[30] While the Governor was appointed by the Portuguese President,[31] consultations with Macau residents were required before his appointment, but such consultations were confined to members of the Legislative Assembly and prominent local interest organisations.[32] The Governor was vested with wide administrative powers[33] and he was assisted by the Consultative

政章程), and the Political and Administrative Statute of Macau Province of 1972 (澳門省政治行政章程).

24 Zhihui He 何志辉, *澳门法制史新编 A New Study on the Legal History of Macau* (社会科学文献出版社 Social Sciences Academic Press 2019) 136.

25 Political and Administrative Statute of Macau Province of 1963 (澳門省政治行政章程), arts 10 and 18 <https://diariodarepublica.pt/dr/detalhe/decreto/45377-611511> last accessed 3 January 2026.

26 Political and Administrative Statute of Macau Province of 1963 (澳門省政治行政章程), art 20 <https://diariodarepublica.pt/dr/detalhe/decreto/45377-611511> last accessed 3 January 2026. The Legislative Assembly included three *ex officio* members (the Secretary General of the Government, the Public Prosecutor, and the Head of the Department of Finance and Accounting); one representative of the Chinese community appointed by the Governor; three members directly elected by citizens registered as voters; one member elected by the taxpayers; three members elected by administrative organisations and public interest associations (e.g., Kiang Wu Hospital Charitable Association and Macau Tung Sin Tong Charitable Society); and one member elected by associations or institutes of private nature (e.g., Macau Chamber of Commerce).

27 Political and Administrative Statute of Macau Province of 1963 (澳門省政治行政章程), arts 13(2), 19(1), and 32(2) <https://diariodarepublica.pt/dr/detalhe/decreto/45377-611511> last accessed 3 January 2026.

28 Paulo Cardinal and Luís Pessanha, 'Macau' in David S. Law and others (eds), *Oxford Handbook of Constitutional Law in Asia* (OUP forthcoming).

29 Shiu-Hing Lo, *Political Development in Macau* (The Chinese University of Hong Kong Press 1995) 26.

30 Organic Statute of Macau (澳門組織章程) (Law No. 1/76), art 4.

31 Organic Statute of Macau (澳門組織章程) (Law No. 1/76), art 7(1).

32 Organic Statute of Macau (澳門組織章程) (Law No. 1/76), art 7(2).

33 Organic Statute of Macau (澳門組織章程) (Law No. 1/76), arts 11–12, 15.

Council – the Governor's top policy-making advisory body.[34] The Governor also possessed legislative powers,[35] which he shared with the Legislative Assembly.[36]

Under the 1976 Organic Statute of Macau, the Legislative Assembly comprised 17 members.[37] Five members were appointed by the Governor, six were directly elected by universal suffrage, and six were indirectly elected by groups from four functional sectors.[38] This colonial model served as a prototype for Macau's political system after China resumed sovereignty over the city.[39] The four sectors were as follows: economic (經濟), morality (道德), welfare (救濟), and culture (文化) sectors. Directors and supervisors (理監事會的成員) of any association legally formed with the aim of promoting economic, moral, cultural, and welfare interests were eligible to vote in these indirect elections.[40] In the 1976 and 1980 direct elections, franchise favoured Portuguese nationals. Chinese citizens and foreigners were only eligible to vote if they could claim 5 years (Chinese) or 7 years (foreigners) of residency in Macau, while there was no such residential requirement imposed on Portuguese citizens.[41] These discriminatory restrictions were removed by the Governor in 1984.[42] From 1984 to 1990, residents of Macau, whether Portuguese, Chinese, or foreigners, who held identification documents issued by Portuguese authorities were eligible to vote in the direct elections.[43]

After the Sino-Portuguese Joint Declaration was signed on 13 April 1987, Macau's colonial Legislative Assembly enacted various key legislative instruments that remain operative today: the Penal Code, the Criminal Procedure Code, the Civil Code, the Commercial Code, and the Civil Procedure Code. In the 1990s – the final decade leading up to Macau's return to China – there was limited political reform towards greater democratisation in the city as Portugal sought to maintain cordial

34 Organic Statute of Macau (澳門組織章程) (Law No. 1/76), art 4.

35 Organic Statute of Macau (澳門組織章程) (Law No. 1/76), art 13.

36 Organic Statute of Macau (澳門組織章程) (Law No. 1/76), art 5.

37 Organic Statute of Macau (澳門組織章程) (Law No. 1/76), art 21.

38 Rules on Voters Registration and the Election of Members of the Legislative Assembly and the Consultative Council of Macau of 1976 (訂定有關辦理選民登記及澳門立法會暨咨詢會成員之選舉應遵規則), art 42(3), (Decree No. 4/76/M); Organic Statute of Macau of 1976 (澳門組織章程) (Law No. 1/76), art 21.

39 Xiaobo Zhai, 'Macao's Constitutional Founding' in Kevin Y. L. Tan and Michael Ng (eds), *Constitutional Founding in Northeast Asia* (Hart 2022) 77.

40 Rules on Voters Registration and the Election of Members of the Legislative Assembly and the Consultative Council of Macau (訂定有關辦理選民登記及澳門立法會暨咨詢會成員之選舉應遵規則), (Decree No. 4/76/M), art 6(1).

41 Rules on Voters Registration and the Election of Members of the Legislative Assembly and the Consultative Council of Macau (訂定有關辦理選民登記及澳門立法會暨咨詢會成員之選舉應遵規則), (Decree No. 4/76/M), art 2.

42 Decree on the Voter Registration in the Consultative Council and the Legislative Assembly Election (關於訂定咨詢會及立法會選舉之選民登記事宜), (Decree No. 9/84/M), art 4(1).

43 Decree on the Voter Registration in the Consultative Council and the Legislative Assembly Election (關於訂定咨詢會及立法會選舉之選民登記事宜), (Decree No. 9/84/M), art 4(1)(A).

relations with China,[44] and Macau only saw a meagre expansion of its Legislative Assembly seats in 1990. That year, the Organic Statute of Macau was amended and the Legislative Assembly was enlarged to 23 members, comprising 7 appointed members, 8 directly elected members, and 8 indirectly elected members from four new functional sectors.[45] The new sectors were as follows: (1) employers (雇主利益); (2) labour (勞工利益); (3) professional (專業利益); and (4) charity, culture, education, and sports (慈善、文化、教育及體育利益).[46] Four seats were allocated to the employers sector; two to the labour sector; one to the professional sector; and one to the charity, culture, education, and sports sector.[47] Associations belonging to these four sectors were eligible to register as electors in indirect elections,[48] with each association entitled to 11 votes, exercisable by the organisation's leadership team or managers (領導機構成員或經理).[49] In direct elections held after 1990, all adult Macau residents who had lived in Macau for at least 7 years were eligible to vote.[50] After 1990, seats returned from direct and indirect elections were allocated using the *modified* d'Hondt Method, and this method is still used in Macau. We will explain how this *modified* d'Hondt Method works in the next section of this chapter. Suffice to say here, this electoral method prevents any singular political party from gaining a majority of seats in the Legislative Assembly.[51] The 1996 election of the Legislative Assembly was also conducted on the same basis and the last colonial legislature proceeded to operate as the 1st Legislative Assembly of the MASAR after the 1999 handover, until the 2nd Legislative Assembly of the MASAR was duly elected in 2001.

China's resumption of sovereignty over Macau was scheduled for 20 December 1999, following extensive negotiations and compromises between China and Portugal. China initially proposed the handover in 1998, while Portugal favoured

44 Richard Louis Edmonds and Herbert S. Yee, 'Macau: From Portuguese Autonomous Territory to Chinese Special Administrative Region' (1999) 160 *The China Quarterly* 801, 802, 806.

45 Organic Statute of Macau (澳門組織章程) (Law No. 1/76, amended by Law No. 13-A/90), art 21; Electoral Regime of the Legislative Assembly of Macau (澳門立法會選舉法) (Law No. 4/91/M), arts 8, 15.

46 Organic Statute of Macau (澳門組織章程) (Law No. 1/76, amended by Law No. 13-A/90), art 21; Electoral Regime of the Legislative Assembly of Macau (澳門立法會選舉法) (Law No. 4/91/M), art 15.

47 Electoral Regime of the Legislative Assembly of Macau (澳門立法會選舉法) (Law No. 4/91/M), art 15(1).

48 Electoral Regime of the Legislative Assembly of Macau (澳門立法會選舉法) (Law No. 4/91/M), art 6.

49 Electoral Regime of the Legislative Assembly of Macau (澳門立法會選舉法) (Law No. 4/91/M), art 15(3).

50 Electoral Regime of the Legislative Assembly of Macau (澳門立法會選舉法) (Law No. 4/91/M), art 2.

51 Chan U Chan 陳震宇, '比例代表制與澳門立法機關的直接選舉 Proportional Representation and the Direct Election of the Legislature of Macau' (2021) 4 *澳門研究 Journal of Macau Studies* 23, 26.

a handover after 2000.[52] But China's Paramount Leader Deng Xiaoping insisted that Macau must return to China before the end of the 20th Century. Finally, on 6 January 1987, Portugal's Council of State agreed to return Macau to China in 1999. Subsequently, during a visit to China on 20 January 1987, Portugal's Secretary for Foreign Affairs and Cooperation and Zhou Nan, the head of the Chinese delegation, agreed to a handover date of 20 December 1999.[53]

British Hong Kong

The acquisition of Hong Kong by the British government was achieved via the conclusion of three treaties with China over the span of approximately 60 years.[54] Following the confiscation and destruction of opium stocks belonging to the British in 1839, war broke out between the British government and the imperial Chinese government, and this culminated in the Treaty of Nanking in 1842 that formally ceded in perpetuity Hong Kong Island to Britain. Following another altercation between the two governments in 1856, the Anglo–French forces went on to occupy Beijing in 1860 and compelled China to conclude a second treaty, the Convention of Peking, which ceded the Kowloon peninsula in perpetuity to Britain. Subsequently, as Britain observed how Japan, Russia, France, and Germany had successfully obtained leases over different ports in China, it decided to follow suit, and this culminated in the third treaty, the Convention respecting an Extension of Hong Kong Territory of 1898, which provided for a 99-year lease of the immediate hinterland of Kowloon, including land still known today as the New Territories. The lease would expire on 30 June 1997, an event too remote and far into the future for the British government then to consider the consequences following its expiration. As a Crown Colony, Hong Kong was governed pursuant to the Letters Patent of 1843, which, as amended through the years, formed the Constitution of Hong Kong until 30 June 1997.

The Letters Patent authorised the establishment of the Governor, the Executive Council, and the Legislative Council in Hong Kong. In 1843, Queen Victoria appointed Henry Pottinger as the first Governor of Hong Kong. From that point until Hong Kong's return in 1997, there were a total of 28 Governors appointed in Hong Kong.[55] The Governor held the highest colonial office in Hong Kong,

52 Xiaobo Zhai, 'Macao's Constitutional Founding' in Kevin Y. L. Tan and Michael Ng (eds), *Constitutional Founding in Northeast Asia* (Hart 2022) 87.

53 Jie Chen 陈杰, '中葡两国关于澳门回归时间问题的外交博弈及其历史经验 The Diplomatic Bargain between China and Portugal over the Time of Macau's Handover and Its Historical Experience' (2022) 1 *统一战线学研究 Journal of United Frontier Science* 28, 33.

54 Yash Ghai, *Hong Kong's New Constitutional Order: The Resumption of Chinese Sovereignty and the Basic Law* (2nd edn, HKU Press 1999) 1–80.

55 Lianxing Zhang 張連興, *香港二十八總督 Hong Kong's 28 Governors* (2nd edn, 三聯書店 Joint Publishing HK 2022).

wielding extensive powers.[56] Following an amendment to the Letters Patent which took effect from 19 January 1888, the Governor was required to seek the consent of the Legislative Council when enacting laws.[57] In addition, the Governor could also appoint judges, members of the Executive and Legislative Councils and other public officers.[58]

When exercising his gubernatorial powers, the Governor was expected to consult his Executive Council.[59] The Executive Council was a formal body of advisers to the Governor, serving as a core policy-making organ assisting the Governor. Generally, the Governor would follow the advice given by the Executive Council. But if he went against the Council's advice, he had to report to the UK government with reasons.[60]

The Legislative Council (LegCo) was established in 1843. Initially, there were three official members and the Governor served as the President of LegCo. (Governor Chris Patten ceased to be the President of LegCo in 1993). In 1850, two unofficial members were appointed to LegCo with the aim of broadening community representation. By 1964, the membership of LegCo had increased to 26, with an equal number of official and unofficial members.

As the critical date of 1 July 1997 approached, the Functional Constituencies (FC) electoral system was introduced in 1984 by the British, as part of an overall plan to develop a representative government in Hong Kong.[61] The aims of such FC elections were to allow the economic and professional sectors to be well-represented in the legislature and to maintain Hong Kong's stability and prosperity after the handover. Critically, under the FC system, only individuals working in certain professions were eligible to vote. Furthermore, in many FCs, it was only the recognised corporate bodies operating in these professions that were eligible to vote, and they would select their authorised representatives to vote as their proxies.[62] Such "indirect" elections were held for the first time in 1985 and the FC electoral system remains operative in Hong Kong today.

For the legislative term commencing in 1985, the size of LegCo was increased from 47 to 57 seats, of which there were 24 elected members, 29 appointed members, and 4 *ex officio* members. 12 of the 24 elected legislators were returned from 11 FCs. In the 1985 LegCo election, the 11 FCs were Commercial (First); Commercial (Second); Industrial (First); Industrial (Second); Finance; Labour; Medical;

56 Letters Patent 1843 <www.legco.gov.hk/general/chinese/procedur/companion/chapter_1/mcp-part1-ch1-n13-ce-a.pdf> last accessed 3 January 2026.

57 Letters Patent 1888, s 9 <https://oelawhk.lib.hku.hk/items/show/1021> last accessed 3 January 2026.

58 Letters Patent 1843 <www.legco.gov.hk/general/chinese/procedur/companion/chapter_1/mcp-part1-ch1-n13-ce-a.pdf> last accessed 3 January 2026.

59 Royal Instructions, s 10. (Adopted on 14 February 1917, amended on 28 February 1969).

60 Royal Instructions, s 12. (Adopted on 14 February 1917).

61 Green Paper on the Further Development of Representative Government in Hong Kong (July 1984).

62 Green Paper on the Further Development of Representative Government in Hong Kong (July 1984), para. 37.

Teaching; Legal; Social Services; and Engineering, Architectural and Surveying. One seat was allocated to each FC except Labour, which had two seats.[63] For the five professional constituencies (Medical; Teaching; Legal; Social Services; and Engineering, Architectural and Surveying), individuals working in those sectors possessing the requisite professional qualifications were eligible to vote; for the remaining six constituencies, only corporate bodies were eligible to vote.[64] Another 12 elected members were drawn from 12 electoral college constituencies.[65] Members serving on the Boards and Councils in these 12 constituencies, alongside the Chairman and two Vice-Chairmen of the Heung Yee Kuk (who voted in the Regional Council Constituency),[66] could vote in the electoral college elections.[67] Two additional FCs – Health Services and Accountancy – were added for the 1988 election, replacing two of the appointed legislators.[68]

In 1991, the size of LegCo was increased from 57 to 60 seats. The number of members appointed by the Governor was reduced from 27 to 18 and the number of *ex officio* members was reduced from 4 to 3.[69] The number of legislators

63 '1985年9月26日，首次立法局間接選舉 On 26 September 1985, the first indirect election of the Legislative Council' <https://oldhkphoto.com/legcoindirectelection/> last accessed 3 January 2026; Norman Miners, 'The Transformation of the Hong Kong Legislative Council 1970–1994: From Consensus to Confrontation' (1994) 16(2) *Asian Journal of Public Administration* 224, 229.

64 Norman Miners, 'The Transformation of the Hong Kong Legislative Council 1970–1994: From Consensus to Confrontation' (1994) 16(2) *Asian Journal of Public Administration* 224, 229.

65 In the 1985 election, the 12 electoral college constituencies were Urban Council (市政局), Provisional Regional Council (臨時區域市政局), and 10 electoral college constituencies consisting of 19 district boards (區議會): Hong Kong Island (East); Hong Kong Island (West); Kwun Tong; Wong Tai Sin; Kowloon City; Sham Shui Po; South Kowloon; New Territories (East); New Territories (West); and New Territories (South). The Urban Council was a financially autonomous statutory body funded from the rates and licence fees, with responsibility for environmental health, markets, abattoirs, recreational facilities, the City Hall, libraries, museums, the issue of liquor and entertainment and the control, and the licensing of street traders. The Provisional Regional Council (it was called Regional Council after 1986) was responsible for providing municipal services to people in the New Territories and island areas. The council played a key role in safeguarding environmental hygiene and public health as well as providing cultural services and venues and recreational facilities and programmes. Brian Hook, 'The Government of Hong Kong: Change within Tradition' (1983) 95 *The China Quarterly* 491, 494–495.

66 Heung Yee Kuk is a pro-Beijing statutory body established in 1926 that represents the indigenous inhabitants of the New Territories in advising the government on socio-economic matters pertaining to their welfare. See <www.hyknt.org/about> last accessed 3 January 2026.

67 Legislative Council (Electoral Provisions) Ordinance (6 April 1985), s 13 and First Schedule.

68 *A Companion to the history, rules and practices of the Legislative Council of the Hong Kong Special Administrative Region, Appendix 3 – A Composition of the Legislative Council of Hong Kong (from October 1985 to June 1997) and the Legislative Council of HKSAR (from July 1997 onwards)*, page 2, <www.legco.gov.hk/general/english/procedur/companion/chapter3_toc.html> last accessed 3 January 2026.

69 Norman Miners, 'The Transformation of the Hong Kong Legislative Council 1970–1994: From Consensus to Confrontation' (1994) 16(2) *Asian Journal of Public Administration* 224, 233. Between 1985 and 1991, the tenure of office of the LegCo members was 3 years. Elections were held in 1985, 1988, and 1991. Since 1991, the tenure of office has been extended to 4 years.

returned from both direct and FC elections increased to 39 and the electoral college constituencies were abandoned.[70] 21 legislators were thereafter elected from 16 FCs: Regional Council (1 member); Urban Council (1 member); Heung Yee Kuk (1 member); Accountancy (1 member); Commercial (2 members); Engineering, Architectural, Surveying and Planning (2 members); Finance and Financial Services (2 members); Health Services (1 member); Industrial (2 members); Labour (2 members); Legal (1 member); Medical (1 member); Real Estate and Construction (1 member); Social Services (1 member); Teaching (1 member); and Tourism (1 member).[71] Most importantly, and for the first time, 18 legislative members were directly elected by the Hong Kong people living in nine geographical constituencies (GCs). This election adopted the first-two-past-the-post system. Each GC returned two legislators, and each elector could cast votes for up to two candidates in their constituencies.[72] The two candidates who received the highest votes were elected. In this landmark 1991 GC election, a total of 18 candidates from pro-democracy parties[73] and pro-democracy non-party independents[74] were duly elected. No one from the pro-Beijing camp was elected in the direct elections.[75] For the FC elections, the pro-democracy camp won five seats and the pro-Beijing camp won 16 seats.[76]

70 See *A Companion to the history, rules and practices of the Legislative Council of the Hong Kong Special Administrative Region, Appendix 3 – A Composition of the Legislative Council of Hong Kong (from October 1985 to June 1997) and the Legislative Council of HKSAR (from July 1997 onwards)*, page 3, <www.legco.gov.hk/general/english/procedur/companion/chapter3_toc.html> last accessed 3 January 2026.

71 See *A Companion to the history, rules and practices of the Legislative Council of the Hong Kong Special Administrative Region, Appendix 3 – A Composition of the Legislative Council of Hong Kong (from October 1985 to June 1997) and the Legislative Council of HKSAR (from July 1997 onwards)*, page 3, <www.legco.gov.hk/general/english/procedur/companion/chapter3_toc.html> last accessed 3 January 2026.

72 Chung Fun Steven Hung, 'Reviewing and Evaluating the Direct Elections to the Legislative Council and the Transformation of Political Parties in Hong Kong, 1991–2016' (2016) 13(8) *Journal of US-China Public Administration* 499, 503–504.

73 Initially, the United Democrats won 12 seats, the Meeting Point won two, and the Association for Democracy and People's Livelihood won one. In a subsequent by-election held in December 1991, Meeting Point won its third seat. See Norman Miners, 'The Transformation of the Hong Kong Legislative Council 1970–1994: From Consensus to Confrontation' (1994) 16(2) *Asian Journal of Public Administration* 224, 233–234.

74 Two pro-democracy independents, Emily Lau Wai-hing and Andrew Wong Wang-fat, were elected in the 1991 direct elections. See Jingxuan Lei 雷競璇 and Guoxiang Shen 沈國祥, *香港選舉資料匯編： 1982年–1994年 Compendium of Hong Kong Election Materials: From 1982 to 1994* (香港中文大學香港亞太研究所 Hong Kong Institute of Asia-Pacific Studies, CUHK 1995) 177–181.

75 Wing K. Fung, 'The Last Legislative Election of Hong Kong under British Rule, 1995' (1996) 15(1) *Electoral Studies* 119, 120.

76 See Jingxuan Lei 雷競璇 and Guoxiang Shen 沈國祥, *香港選舉資料匯編： 1982年–1994年 Compendium of Hong Kong Election Materials: From 1982 to 1994* (香港中文大學香港亞太研究所 Hong Kong Institute of Asia-Pacific Studies, CUHK 1995) 174–176.

In 1992, Christopher Patten – Hong Kong's last British governor – assumed office. Notably, Patten attempted to expand the electoral base for the FCs in the mid-1990s by replacing corporate voting with votes cast by individuals/ employees in all the FCs; and he further created nine new FCs that included all of Hong Kong's working population.[77] The Legislative Council elections of 1995 took place on this basis. The last LegCo under British rule comprised 60 seats, the same as the previous legislative term. However, all legislators were elected, and the remaining three *ex officio* legislators were removed. There were three avenues of entry into LegCo in the 1995 election. First, 30 legislators were elected by 29 FCs (Labour FC had two seats and the rest with one seat each).[78] Second, 20 legislators were elected from 20 GCs[79] and the first-past-the-post system was adopted for the first time instead of the prior first-two-past-the-post system.[80] In the 1995 GC elections, the pro-democracy parties and non-party independents obtained 17 seats.[81] By contrast, the pro-Beijing parties only obtained three seats (the Democratic Alliance for the Betterment of Hong Kong with two seats and the Liberal Party with one). For the FC elections, the pro-democracy camp won ten seats and the pro-Beijing camp won 20 seats.[82] Third, ten members were elected from the newly established Election Committee (EC) that comprised 283 District Board[83] members who were previously elected in the District Board elections held in 1994. For the EC legislative constituency,

77 *Research Paper: Political Development in Hong Kong since the 1980s published by the Research and Library Division of the Legislative Council Secretariat* (September 1996) <www.legco.gov.hk/general/english/procedur/companion/chapter_3/mcp-part1-ch3-n1-e.pdf> last accessed 3 January 2026.

78 Wing K. Fung, 'The Last Legislative Election of Hong Kong under British Rule, 1995' (1996) 15(1) *Electoral Studies* 119, 122–123; Richard Baum, 'Democracy Deformed: Hong Kong's 1998 Legislative Elections – and Beyond' (2000) 162 *The China Quarterly* 439, 444.

79 Paul S. F. Yip and Christopher J. Lloyd, 'Statistical Analysis of the 1995 Hong Kong Legislative Council Election Results' (1996) 18(1) *Asian Journal of Public Administration* 119, 119–120.

80 Lo Shiu-Hing and Yu Wing-Yat, 'The Politics of Electoral Reform in Hong Kong' (2001) 39(2) *Commonwealth & Comparative Politics* 98, 101–103.

81 The Democratic Party – founded in 1994 following the merger of United Democrats of Hong Kong and Meeting Point – won 12 seats. The Association for Democracy and People's Livelihood won two seats. Three pro-democracy non-party affiliated independents (Emily Lau Wai-hing, Andrew Wong Wang-fat, and Christine Loh Kung-wai) won one seat each. See Jingxuan Lei 雷競璇 and Guoxiang Shen 沈國祥, *香港選舉資料匯編: 1995 Compendium of Hong Kong Election Materials: 1995* (香港中文大學香港亞太研究所 Hong Kong Institute of Asia-Pacific Studies, CUHK 1996) 95–97.

82 See Jingxuan Lei 雷競璇 and Guoxiang Shen 沈國祥, *香港選舉資料匯編: 1995 Compendium of Hong Kong Election Materials: 1995* (香港中文大學香港亞太研究所 Hong Kong Institute of Asia-Pacific Studies, CUHK 1996) 90–94.

83 The Hong Kong District Boards were founded in 1982 and they served as local councils that advised the government on municipal matters relating to the public. On 10 March 1999, they were renamed DCs. See *A Companion to the history, rules and practices of the Legislative Council of the Hong Kong Special Administrative Region, Appendix 3 – A Composition of the Legislative Council of Hong Kong (from October 1985 to June 1997) and the Legislative Council of HKSAR (from July 1997 onwards)*, page 5 <www.legco.gov.hk/general/english/procedur/companion/chapter3_toc.html> last accessed 3 January 2026.

each voter had to rank any ten candidates in order of preference, and the single transferable voting system was adopted.[84] Only members of the District Boards were eligible to vote in the EC elections.[85] For the EC elections, the pro-democracy camp won four seats and the pro-Beijing camp won six seats.[86] Basically, these reforms left the pro-Beijing lawmakers with 29 out of 60 seats in total for the last legislature of colonial Hong Kong.

China vehemently objected to these Patten reforms as it perceived them to be inconsistent with the Basic Law promulgated in 1990.[87] In China's view, both governments had reached a tacit understanding – when the Basic Law was enacted – that the last legislature of colonial Hong Kong would form the first legislature of the HKSAR, and the massive expansion of the electoral franchise for the FC elections undercut the prior consensus. China therefore decided that after it resumed control over Hong Kong on 1 July 1997, these Patten reforms would be reversed and repealed. Furthermore, instead of allowing the last colonial legislature to become the first Legislative Council of the HKSAR, China established an unelected Provisional Legislative Council for Hong Kong in December 1996[88] – with a term-limit of about one year – to take charge of Hong Kong's legislative affairs until the first HKSAR Legislative Council could be constituted under its revised electoral rules in 1998.

Chief Executive Elections in the SARs

In both Hong Kong and Macau, their CEs are heads of their respective SARs.[89] Their terms of office are five years, and they are limited to two consecutive terms.[90] Both CEs are elected by their respective EC and appointed by the Central People's Government in Beijing.[91] Notably, for Hong Kong, its EC votes for the CE and also elects lawmakers to the Legislative Council. In Macau, the EC votes only for the CE. As members of the ECs in both Hong Kong and Macau are stacked with

84 Wing K. Fung, 'The Last Legislative Election of Hong Kong under British Rule, 1995' (1996) 15(1) *Electoral Studies* 119, 122.

85 Legislative Council (Electoral Provisions) (Amendment) Ordinance (Ordinance No. 57 of 1994) (7 July 1994), ss 11 and 21.

86 See Jingxuan Lei 雷競璇 and Guoxiang Shen 沈國祥, *香港選舉資料匯編: 1995 Compendium of Hong Kong Election Materials: 1995* (香港中文大學香港亞太研究所 Hong Kong Institute of Asia-Pacific Studies, CUHK 1996) 90.

87 Lo Shiu-Hing and Yu Wing-Yat, 'The Politics of Electoral Reform in Hong Kong' (2001) 39(2) *Commonwealth & Comparative Politics* 98, 105.

88 Decision of the National People's Congress Preparatory Committee for the HKSAR on the Establishment of the Provisional Legislative Council of the HKSAR (全国人民代表大会香港特别行政区筹备委员会关于设立香港特别行政区临时立法会的决定) (Adopted at the Second Plenary Session of the Preparatory Committee for the HKSAR on 24 March 1996).

89 Macau Basic Law (MABL), art 45; Hong Kong Basic Law (HKBL), art 43.

90 MABL, art 48; HKBL, art 46.

91 MABL, art 47; HKBL, art 45.

pro-Beijing loyalists, only the CE candidate pre-endorsed by Beijing would be elected.

Another significant difference between Hong Kong and Macau is that the Hong Kong Basic Law explicitly states that the "ultimate aim" is for the selection of the CE "by universal suffrage upon nomination by a broadly representative nominating committee"[92], but this constitutional promise of universal suffrage is absent in Macau. In August 2014, the National People's Congress Standing Committee (NPCSC) agreed to a political reform which would allow the existing Hong Kong EC to serve as a nominating committee that would select two or three CE candidates who would be voted upon by the Hong Kong population in a universal suffrage CE election.[93] The NPCSC's Decision was derided by the "pro-democracy" forces in Hong Kong as "fake universal suffrage" as only pro-Beijing political figures would be shortlisted by this nominating committee to be CE candidates whom the people could vote for. The pan-democrats in the Hong Kong Legislative Council therefore voted against the constitutional proposal in June 2015, such that the constitutional bill failed to secure the requisite two-thirds majority for a constitutional amendment of the Hong Kong Basic Law to pass. In view of the current political climate, which we will elaborate upon below, it is unlikely that universal suffrage for the Hong Kong CE election would be entertained again in the foreseeable future.

In Macau, its EC was initially composed of 300 members, but it was expanded to 400 members in 2012 for the 2014 Macau CE election and beyond,[94] ostensibly to enhance the representativeness of the EC.[95] The Macau EC is elected every five years.[96] The members are drawn from various sectors of society and are divided into four sectors (see Table 2.1).[97] In theory, the vast majority of the current Macau EC members (344 out of 400 members) are supposed to be elected by corporate bodies

92 HKBL, art 45.

93 Decision of the Standing Committee of the National People's Congress on Issues Relating to the Selection of the CE of the HKSAR by Universal Suffrage and on the Method for Forming the Legislative Council of the HKSAR in the Year 2016 (Adopted at the 10th Session of the Standing Committee of the 12th National People's Congress on 31 August 2014).

94 Amendment to Annex I to the Basic Law of the Macau Special Administrative Region of the People's Republic of China concerning the Method for the Selection of the CE of the Macau Special Administrative Region, art 1(1) (Adopted at the 27th Session of the Standing Committee of the 11th National People's Congress on 30 June 2012).

95 Shenghua Lou 婁勝華, '競爭性與認受性辨析：以第四任行政長官選舉為中心 Debate about Competitiveness and Recognition – Focus on the Election of the Fourth Chief Executive' (2014) 22 *"一國兩制"研究 Journal of "One Country Two Systems" Studies* 21, 24.

96 Amendment to Annex I to the Basic Law of the Macau Special Administrative Region of the People's Republic of China concerning the Method for the Selection of the CE of the Macau Special Administrative Region, art 1(2) (Adopted at the 27th Session of the Standing Committee of the 11th National People's Congress on 30 June 2012).

97 Amendment to Annex I to the Basic Law of the Macau Special Administrative Region of the People's Republic of China concerning the Method for the Selection of the CE of the Macau Special Administrative Region, art 1(1) (Adopted at the 27th Session of the Standing Committee of the 11th National People's Congress on 30 June 2012).

in their respective constituencies.[98] This includes the EC members representing the first and second sectors, as well as the members representing the labour and social services subsectors in the third sector.[99] Each registered corporate body is supposed to choose – from its respective organisation's leadership and management team (領導機關或管理機關) – no more than 22 people as voters (投票人).[100] But in reality, the membership of the EC is negotiated behind closed doors between the leaders of the dominant and pro-Beijing social organisations and corporate bodies, rather than according to the "one-voter, one-vote" rule.[101] Aside from the 344 EC members "elected" by these social and corporate groups, 22 representatives of the Legislative Assembly are elected by all Macau Legislative Assembly members, two representatives from municipal organisations are elected from among all members of municipal organisations, and 14 representatives are elected from among the Macau members of the Chinese People's Political Consultative Conference (CPPCC) National Committee.[102] Six members from the religious subsector within the third sector are nominated by religious groups[103] and 12 Macau deputies to the National People's Congress (NPC) are *ex officio* EC members.[104] In view of the composition of the EC, it is obvious that most members of the EC are pro-Beijing elites[105] and the EC members are hardly representative of the Macau public[106] (see Table 2.1).

Each member of the Macau EC can only nominate one candidate for the office of CE.[107] To run for Macau CE, a candidate must be nominated by at least 66 Macau EC members (16.5% of all EC members).[108] The members of the Macau EC will cast their votes amongst the nominees in a secret ballot, and the candidate who garners a majority of the votes will be elected as Macau CE.[109]

98 Law on Chief Executive Election (行政長官選舉法) (Law No. 3/2004), art 12 and Annex 1.
99 Law on Chief Executive Election (行政長官選舉法) (Law No. 3/2004), art 12 and Annex 1.
100 Law on Chief Executive Election (行政長官選舉法) (Law No. 3/2004, amended by Law No. 11/2012), art 19.
101 Bill K. P. Chou, 'Politics and Social Organisations in Macao: A Historical Institutionalist Analysis' (2015) 12(1) *China: An International Journal* 22, 33.
102 Law on Chief Executive Election (行政長官選舉法) (Law No. 3/2004, amended by Law No. 11/2012 and Law No. 13/2018), art 14 and Annex 1.
103 Law on Chief Executive Election (行政長官選舉法) (Law No. 3/2004), art 13 and Annex 1.
104 Law on Chief Executive Election (行政長官選舉法) (Law No. 3/2004), art 10 and Annex 1.
105 Shiu-Hing Lo, *Political Change in Macao* (Routledge 2009) 47.
106 Bill K. P. Chou, 'Interest Group Politics in Macau after Handover' (2005) 14(43) *Journal of Contemporary China* 191, 197.
107 Amendment to Annex I to the Basic Law of the Macau Special Administrative Region of the People's Republic of China: Method for the Selection of the CE of the Macau Special Administrative Region, art 2, (Adopted at the 27th Session of the Standing Committee of the 11th National People's Congress on 30 June 2012).
108 Amendment to Annex I to the Basic Law of the Macau Special Administrative Region of the People's Republic of China concerning the Method for the Selection of the CE of the Macau Special Administrative Region, art 2 (Adopted at the 27th Session of the Standing Committee of the 11th National People's Congress on 30 June 2012).
109 Law on Chief Executive Election (行政長官選舉法) (Law No. 3/2004), arts 59 and 60.

TABLE 2.1 Composition of the Election Committee for the Macau Chief Executive

Sectors	*Seats in the 2004 and 2009 CE Elections*	*Seats in the 2014 CE Election and beyond*
First Sector: industrial, commercial and financial sectors	100	120
Second Sector: culture, education, and other professions	80	115
Third Sector: labour, social services, religious sectors	80	115
Fourth Sector: representatives of members of the Legislative Assembly, representatives of members of municipal organs, MASAR deputies to the NPC, and MASAR members of the CPPCC National Committee	40	50
Total:	300	400

In contrast, the Hong Kong CE was originally elected by an EC composed of 800 members, with 200 members fielded from four sectors that were very similar to Macau's.[110] In 2010, the size of the Hong Kong EC was expanded to 1200 members, with 300 members drawn from the same four sectors.[111]

Like the Macau EC, the Hong Kong EC members are elected every five years,[112] and the methods for constituting the ECs are very similar. Between 2002 and 2021, all Hong Kong EC members were drawn from four sectors of society, which were further divided into 38 subsectors. The vast majority of Hong Kong EC members (664 out of 800 from 2002-2012, 1034 out of 1200 from 2012–2021) were elected by registered corporate bodies and/or individuals within each subsector.[113] Members

110 Annex I to the Basic Law of the HKSAR of the People's Republic of China: Method for the Selection of the CE of the HKSAR, art 2 (Adopted at the Third Session of the Seventh National People's Congress on 4 April 1990).

111 Amendment to Annex I to the Basic Law of the HKSAR of the People's Republic of China Concerning the Method for the Selection of the CE of the HKSAR, art 1(1) (Adopted at the 16th Session of the Standing Committee of the 11th National People's Congress on 28 August 2010).

112 Amendment to Annex I to the Basic Law of the HKSAR of the People's Republic of China Concerning the Method for the Selection of the CE of the HKSAR, art 1(2) (Adopted at the 16th Session of the Standing Committee of the 11th National People's Congress on 28 August 2010).

113 Chief Executive Election Ordinance, Schedule: EC, s 2. For some subsectors, there were only individual voters, including Accountancy, Chinese Medicine, Education, Engineering, Health Services, Higher Education, Legal, etc. For other subsectors, there were only corporate bodies registered as voters, such as Commercial (First), Employers' Federation of Hong Kong, Finance, Finance Services, and Industrial (Second). In some subsectors, there were both corporate bodies and individuals registered as voters, for instance, Catering, Commercial (Second), Import and Export, Real Estate and Construction, and Information Technology. See Report on the 2012 Chief Executive Election Appendix II: 2011 Election Committee Subsector Elections Breakdown of Voters for Election Committee Subsectors,

from the religious subsector (40 from 2002–2012, 60 from 2012–2021) were nominated by religious groups in this subsector.[114] Lastly, Hong Kong deputies to the NPC (36 members) and LegCo members (60 from 2002–2012, 70 from 2012–2021) were *ex officio* members of the Hong Kong EC.[115]

Like the Macau CE Election, each Hong Kong EC member can only nominate one person for CE. A candidate for the office of Hong Kong CE had to be nominated by no less than 100 EC members from 1997–2012 and 150 EC members from 2012–2021 (12.5% of all EC members).[116] This threshold was slightly lower than Macau's 16.5%. After nomination, the members of the Hong Kong EC will cast their votes from the slate of eligible nominees in a secret ballot,[117] and the candidate who obtains a majority of the votes will be elected as Hong Kong CE.[118]

In 2021, Beijing overhauled the electoral system to entrench its control over the selection of the Hong Kong CE.[119] The Hong Kong EC now comprises 1500 members, an increase of 300 members. A new fifth sector has now been added, comprising 300 members that consist of HKSAR deputies to the NPC, HKSAR members of the CPPCC National Committee, and representatives of Hong Kong members in China's designated national organisations[120] (see Table 2.2).

Alongside the expansion of the EC, important changes were made to each sector. A small and medium enterprises subsector of 15 seats was added to the first sector. In the second sector, higher education was no longer a subsector on its own but was merged with the original education subsector. The medical subsector and the health services subsector were also merged to form a new medical and health

<www.eac.hk/en/elections/chief/2012ce_election/report/detailreport.html> last accessed 3 January 2026; Report on the 2017 Chief Executive Election Appendix II: 2016 Election Committee Subsector Elections Breakdown of Voters for Election Committee Subsectors, <www.eac.hk/en/elections/chief/2017ce_election/report/detailreport.html> last accessed 3 January 2026.

114 Chief Executive Election Ordinance, Schedule: Election Committee, ss 2 and 6.

115 Chief Executive Election Ordinance, Schedule: Election Committee, s 2.

116 Annex I to the Basic Law of the HKSAR of the People's Republic of China: Method for the Selection of the CE of the HKSAR, art 4 (Adopted at the Third Session of the Seventh National People's Congress on 4 April 1990); Amendment to Annex I to the Basic Law of the HKSAR of the People's Republic of China Concerning the Method for the Selection of the CE of the HKSAR, art 2 (Adopted at the 16th Session of the Standing Committee of the 11th National People's Congress on 28 August 2010).

117 Chief Executive Election Ordinance, s 25(2).

118 Chief Executive Election Ordinance, ss 26–27.

119 Decision of the National People's Congress on Improving the Electoral System of the HKSAR (Adopted at the Fourth Session of the 13th National People's Congress on 11 March 2021).

120 Annex I to the Basic Law of the HKSAR of the People's Republic of China: Method for the Selection of the CE of the HKSAR, art 2 (Amended at the 27th Meeting of the Standing Committee of the 13th National People's Congress on 30 March 2021). These designated national organisations include the All-China Women's Federation (中華全國婦女聯合會), the All-China Federation of Industry and Commerce (中華全國工商業聯合), the All-China Federation of Returned Overseas Chinese (中華全國歸國華僑聯合會), the All-China Youth Federation (中華全國青年聯合會), and the China Overseas Friendship Association (中華海外聯誼會). See Chief Executive Election Ordinance, Schedule: Election Committee, s 39ZJ.

TABLE 2.2 Composition of the Election Committee for the Hong Kong Chief Executive

Sectors	*2002 and 2007 CE Elections*[a]		*2012 and 2017 CE Elections*[b]		*2022 CE Election and beyond*[c]	
First Sector	Industrial, commercial and financial sectors	200 seats	Industrial, commercial and financial sectors	300 seats	Industrial, commercial and financial sectors	300 seats
Second Sector	The professions	200 seats	The professions	300 seats	The professions	300 seats
Third Sector	Labour, social services, religious and other sectors	200 seats	Labour, social services, religious and other sectors	300 seats	Grassroots, Labour, religious and other sectors	300 seats
Fourth Sector	Members of the Legislative Council, representatives of district-based organisations, HKSAR deputies to the NPC, HKSAR members of the CPPCC National Committee	200 seats	Members of the Legislative Council, representatives of the District Councils, representatives of the Heung Yee Kuk, HKSAR deputies to the NPC, HKSAR members of the CPPCC National Committee	300 seats	Members of the Legislative Council, representatives of district organisations and other organisations	300 seats
Fifth Sector	NA		NA		HKSAR deputies to the NPC, HKSAR members of the CPPCC National Committee, and representatives of Hong Kong members of relevant national organisations	300 seats
Total Seats		800 seats		1200 seats		1500 seats

a Annex I to the Basic Law of the HKSAR of the People's Republic of China: Method for the Selection of the CE of the HKSAR, art 2 (Adopted at the Third Session of the Seventh National People's Congress on 4 April 1990).

b Amendment to Annex I to the Basic Law of the HKSAR of the People's Republic of China Concerning the Method for the Selection of the CE of the HKSAR, art 1 (Adopted at the 16th Session of the Standing Committee of the 11th National People's Congress on 28 August 2010).

c Annex I to the Basic Law of the HKSAR of the People's Republic of China: Method for the Selection of the CE of the HKSAR, art 2 (Amended at the 27th Meeting of the Standing Committee of the 13th National People's Congress on 30 March 2021).

services subsector. These mergers have the effect of reducing representation from the education and healthcare subsectors by 30 seats for each. Similarly, the social welfare subsector also had its seats reduced from 60 to 30. The subsector of sports, performing arts, culture, and publication which originally belonged to the third sector, was moved to the second sector, and its seats were also reduced to 30 seats from 60 seats. It is also important to note that, prior to the overhaul, members from these EC seats tended to be pro-democracy figures, and these electoral changes were intended to reduce the influence of this camp on the EC.

In the third sector, the grassroots associations and the associations of Chinese fellow townsmen were added as new subsectors, each with 60 seats. The recognised grassroots associations[121] are all pro-Beijing and pro-establishment organisations.[122] Similarly, the associations of Chinese fellow townsmen are associations that comprise Hong Kong people who were originally from various provinces and major cities in Mainland China.[123] These associations are vocal about upholding patriotism and promoting exchanges and cooperation between Hong Kong and the Mainland.[124]

In the fourth sector, the most conspicuous change was the removal of District Councillors (117 seats) from the EC. Notably, in 2019, pro-democracy candidates swept 392 out of 452 seats in the local District Council (DC)[125] election. Retaining District Councillors in the EC would mean that these pro-democracy politicians would have played an outsized role in the then-upcoming 2022 CE election. Three new subsectors were also added to the fourth sector. They are (1) Representatives of members of Area Committees, District Fight Crime Committees, and District Fire Safety Committees of Hong Kong Island and Kowloon (76 seats);

121 Chief Executive Election Ordinance, Schedule: Election Committee, s 39ZE.

122 For example, the New Territories Association of Societies states its purpose on its website, as follows: (1) To love the country and Hong Kong, uphold the Basic Law, and maintain the long-term prosperity and stability of Hong Kong; (2) To promote liaison among New Territories associations; (3) To care for the livelihood of the New Territories residents, safeguard their reasonable rights and interests, and promote and develop social welfare services; (4) To advocate healthy cultural, recreational, and entertainment activities, and to promote friendship. (In Chinese, (1) 愛國愛港，擁護《基本法》，維護香港的長期繁榮穩定；(2) 促進新界社團間之聯繫；(3) 關心新界居民的生活，維護新界居民的合理權益，推動和發展社會福利事業；(4) 提倡健康的文娛康樂活動，增進友誼。) <http://ntas.org.hk/mixmedia/a/202301/06/WS63b8020912344756cbb1fcb0.html> last accessed 3 January 2026.

123 Chief Executive Election Ordinance, Schedule: Election Committee, s 39ZD.

124 For an overview of the Federation of Hong Kong Guangdong Community Organisations Limited (香港廣東社團總會有限公司) <www.guangdong.com.hk/a-list/13985-cht> last accessed 3 January 2026.

125 Kinling Lo, 'Hong Kong Election Success for Pro-Democracy Camp Gives Beijing a Headache When Dealing with "Kingmaker" Tycoons' *South China Morning Post* (28 November 2019) <www.scmp.com/news/china/politics/article/3039832/hong-kong-election-success-pro-democracy-camp-gives-beijing> last accessed 3 January 2026. DCs are local municipalities that advise the Hong Kong government on the well-being of the people and the provision of public services in 18 localities across the city.

(2) Representatives of members of Area Committees, District Fight Crime Committees, and District Fire Safety Committees of the New Territories (80 seats); and (3) Representatives of associations of Hong Kong residents in the Mainland (27 seats). These representatives are unsurprisingly pro-establishment and pro-Beijing.[126] 20 additional seats were allocated to the Legislative Council subsector and one more seat was given to the pre-existing Heung Yee Kuk subsector. Heung Yee Kuk is a statutory body that represents the indigenous inhabitants of the New Territories in advising the government on socio-economic matters pertaining to their welfare, and this organisation is also fervently pro-Beijing.

In the newly created fifth sector, a new subsector was created: representatives of Hong Kong members of relevant national organisations (110 seats). As their name indicates, these national organisations are registered and operate in Mainland China.[127] Furthermore, the HKSAR deputies to the NPC and the HKSAR members of the CPPCC National Committee were also transferred from the fourth sector to the fifth sector. While the number of seats of the HKSAR deputies to the NPC was retained at 36 members, the number of seats of the HKSAR members of the CPPCC National Committee was increased to 154 from 51 (see Table 2.3).

As Table 2.3 clearly indicates, subsectors that were traditionally more liberal or pro-democracy were shrunk or removed altogether. Concurrently, more pro-Beijing seats were created. Beijing claimed that these changes were merely intended to uphold the principle of "patriots administering Hong Kong",[128] but they clearly stymie the fair participation of the pro-democracy camp in Hong Kong.[129]

In 2021, on top of the changes to the sectors and subsectors of the EC, the way the members were constituted was also revised. In 2021, 982 EC members were elected[130]– a significant decrease from 1034 in 2017. Conversely, the number of

126 Shiu-Hing Lo 盧兆興 '中國式選舉在香江 Chinese Style Election in Hong Kong' *灼見名家 Master-Insight Com* (16 August 2021) <www.master-insight.com/%E4%B8%AD%E5%9C%8B%E5%BC%8F%E9%81%B8%E8%88%89%E5%9C%A8%E9%A6%99%E6%B1%9F/> last accessed 3 January 2026.

127 Chief Executive Election Ordinance, Schedule: Election Committee, s 39ZJ. These national organisations include:
a HKSAR delegates of the All-China Women's Federation;
b HKSAR executive members of the All-China Federation of Industry and Commerce;
c HKSAR committee members of the All-China Federation of Returned Overseas Chinese;
d HKSAR committee members of the All-China Youth Federation; and
e HKSAR directors of the China Overseas Friendship Association.
All of them are pro-Beijing organisations.

128 'Explanation on the Draft Decision of the National People's Congress on Improving the Electoral System of the HKSAR' (关于《全国人民代表大会关于完善香港特别行政区选举制度的决定（草案）》的说明) <www.basiclaw.gov.hk/filemanager/content/tc/files/basiclawtext/basiclawtext_doc30.pdf> last accessed 3 January 2026.

129 Chao Wang, 'Hong Kong in the Age of the PRC's Alienation from the International System: In Search of Normative Consensus' (2024) 13(1) *Global Constitutionalism* 53, 68.

130 Annex I to the Basic Law of the HKSAR of the People's Republic of China: Method for the Selection of the CE of the HKSAR, art 4(3) (Amended at the 27th Meeting of the Standing Committee of the 13th National People's Congress on 30 March 2021); See Report on the 2022

TABLE 2.3 Major Changes Made to the Election Committee of the Hong Kong CE in 2021

Sector	*Subsectors*	*Reduce*	*Increase*
1	Small and medium enterprises (New)		15 ↑
2	Social welfare	30 ↓	
2	Sports, performing arts, culture, and publication	30 ↓	
2	Education (Removal of Higher Education Subsector)	30 ↓	
2	Medical and Health Services (Medical and Health Services are Combined)	30 ↓	
3	Grassroots associations (New)		60 ↑
3	Associations of Chinese fellow townsmen (New)		60 ↑
4	Removed: All District Council Seats	117↓	
4	Area Committees, District Fight Crime Committees, and District Fire Safety Committees of Hong Kong, Kowloon, and New Territories (New)		156 ↑
4	Representatives of associations of Hong Kong residents in the Mainland (New)		27 ↑
4	Legislative Council		20 ↑
5 (New)	Hong Kong members of relevant national organisations		110 ↑
5 (New)	Hong Kong members of the CPPCC National Committee		154 ↑

nominated persons on the EC was significantly increased from 60 in 2017 to 156 in 2021.[131] 60 nominated members from the religious subsector were retained, but 96 new members from six groups were added. The added nominated members are (1) 15 members of the technology and innovation subsector (2nd Sector) nominated from among Hong Kong academicians of the Chinese Academy of Sciences and the Chinese Academy of Engineering; (2) 15 members of the accountancy subsector (2nd Sector) nominated from among Hong Kong Accounting Advisors appointed by the Ministry of Finance of the PRC; (3) 9 members of the legal subsector (2nd Sector) nominated from among Hong Kong members of the Council of the China Law Society; (4) 15 members of the sports, performing arts, culture and publication subsector (2nd Sector) nominated respectively by the Sports Federation and Olympic Committee of Hong Kong, the China Federation of Literary and Art Circles Hong Kong Member Association, and the Hong Kong Publishing Federation; (5) 15 members of the Chinese medicine subsector (2nd Sector) nominated from among Hong Kong members of the Council of the World Federation of Chinese

Chief Executive Election Appendix I: Number of Members for the Election Committee, its Sectors and Subsectors <www.eac.hk/en/elections/chief/2022ce_election/report/detailreport.html> last accessed 3 January 2026.

131 For a comparison see Schedule: Election Committee, s 2(7)(a) of the pre-2021 Chief Executive Election Ordinance and Annex I to the Basic Law of the HKSAR of the People's Republic of China: Method for the Selection of the CE of the HKSAR, art 4(2) (Amended at the 27th Meeting of the Standing Committee of the 13th National People's Congress on 30 March 2021).

Medicine Societies; and (6) 27 members of the new subsector of representatives of associations of Hong Kong residents in the Mainland nominated by such associations (4th Sector).[132] As their titles indicate, all the added nominated groups have close connections with associations and groups in the Mainland.

The number of new *ex officio* members serving on the EC also increased in 2021. In 2021, the number of *ex officio* members was increased to 362 from 106 in 2017.[133] These added *ex officio* members are (1) Hong Kong members of the CPPCC National Committee (154 members in the 5th Sector); (2) Hong Kong members of the Committee for the Basic Law of the HKSAR under the NPCSC (6 members in the 2nd Sector); (3) Legislative Council members (20 members in the 4th Sector); (4) university presidents or chairpersons of the board of governors or the council of universities (11 members in the 2nd Sector); (5) responsible persons of statutory bodies, advisory bodies and relevant associations of the subsectors of engineering (15 members in the 2nd Sector), architectural, surveying, planning and landscape (15 members in the 2nd Sector), education (5 members in the 2nd Sector), medical and health services (15 members in the 2nd Sector), and social welfare (15 members in the 2nd Sector).[134]

After the 2021 electoral overhaul, a candidate for the office of the Hong Kong CE must be nominated by no less than 188 members[135] (12.5% of all Hong Kong EC members, which was also the operative percentage threshold pre-2021). But an extra requirement was added in 2021: every Hong Kong CE candidate must now be nominated by at least 15 members from each of the five EC sectors.[136] This new requirement basically means that Beijing through its proxies in any of the

132 Annex I to the Basic Law of the HKSAR of the People's Republic of China: Method for the Selection of the CE of the HKSAR, art 4(2) (Amended at the 27th Meeting of the Standing Committee of the 13th National People's Congress on 30 March 2021). The representatives of associations of Hong Kong residents in the Mainland are a new subsector, and all members of this subsector are nominated.

133 For a comparison, see Schedule: Election Committee, s 2(7)(c) of the pre-2021 Chief Executive Election Ordinance (Amended in 2012) and Annex I to the Basic Law of the HKSAR of the People's Republic of China: Method for the Selection of the CE of the HKSAR, art 4(1) (Amended at the 27th Meeting of the Standing Committee of the 13th National People's Congress on 30 March 2021).

134 Annex I to the Basic Law of the HKSAR of the People's Republic of China: Method for the Selection of the CE of the HKSAR, art 4(1) (Amended at the 27th Meeting of the Standing Committee of the 13th National People's Congress on 30 March 2021). Before the 2021 electoral overhaul, the number of seats of the HK members of the CPPCC was 51, and they were elected by the HK members of the CPPCC. In 2021, the number of seats for this subsector increased to 154, and the 154 members all serve as *ex officio* members.

135 Annex I to the Basic Law of the HKSAR of the People's Republic of China: Method for the Selection of the CE of the HKSAR, art 6 (Amended at the 27th Meeting of the Standing Committee of the 13th National People's Congress on 30 March 2021).

136 Annex I to the Basic Law of the HKSAR of the People's Republic of China: Method for the Selection of the CE of the HKSAR, art 6 (Amended at the 27th Meeting of the Standing Committee of the 13th National People's Congress on 30 March 2021).

sectors, especially those in the new fifth sector, can veto a pro-democracy politician from being even nominated. In the past, Hong Kong pro-democracy politicians had been successfully nominated when they managed to get the support of at least 150 members in the EC.

In Macau, only the first CE election in 1999 was contested. For all subsequent Macau CE elections, only one pro-Beijing candidate was put forward each time. In contrast, for Hong Kong – at least before the electoral overhaul of 2021 – there were regular contests for the top job,[137] and hustings and campaigns were boisterous and often acrimonious affairs. But in 2022, the 5th Hong Kong CE John Lee was elected unopposed, foreshadowing the placid state-of-affairs to come.

Neither CE elections in Macau nor those in Hong Kong are democratic. Except for the expansion of the EC to 400 members from 300 members in 2012, there has been no progress in Macau.[138] The situation in Hong Kong is arguably even more dire as we have witnessed a democratic regression. Pre-2021, while it was always a foregone conclusion that a pro-Beijing candidate would be elected, pro-democracy candidates used to be able to get onto the ballot. After the electoral overhaul of 2021, CE elections in Hong Kong would likely be uncontested or uneventful affairs going forward, as is the case in Macau.

Legislative Elections in the SARs

The Legislative Assembly of Macau is the unicameral legislature of the MASAR. Elected lawmakers serve a term of four years (except for the first term which lasted two years) and there are no term limits.[139] The members of the Legislative Assembly are elected in three ways: direct election (直接選舉), indirect election (間接選舉), and appointed by the CE (行政長官委任).[140]

While the total number of Macau Legislative Assembly members has increased from 23 to 33, the number of legislators returned by direct election has always been less than half of the total number of seats in the Legislative Assembly (see Table 2.4).

All adult Macau permanent residents can be electors (選民) in direct elections.[141] Unlike Hong Kong, the whole of Macau is one singular GC without

137 Prior to the electoral overhaul of 2021, only the 2002 and 2005 Hong Kong CE elections were uncontested. The 2005 CE election was a special election held after the CE Tung Chee-hwa resigned mid-term.

138 Eilo Yu Wing-yat and Natalie Chin Ka-man, 'The Political Opposition and Democracy in Macao: Revolutionaries or Loyalists' (2012) 46 *Government and Opposition* 97.

139 MABL, art 69.

140 Amendment to Annex II to the Basic Law of the Macau Special Administrative Region of the People's Republic of China Concerning the Method for the Formation of the Legislative Assembly of the Macau Special Administrative Region, art 1 (Recorded at the 27th Session of the Standing Committee of the 11th National People's Congress on 30 June 2012).

141 Law on the Election of the Legislative Assembly of the Macau Special Administrative Region (澳門特別行政區立法會選舉法) (Law No. 3/2001), arts 2 and 3.

TABLE 2.4 Composition of the Legislative Assembly of the MASAR (1996–2029)

Year	*Directly elected*	*Indirectly elected*	*Appointed*	*Total*
1996–2001	8	8	7	23
2001–2005	10	10	7	27
2005–2009	12	10	7	29
2009–2013	12	10	7	29
2013–2017	14	12	7	33
2017–2021	14	12	7	33
2021–2025	14	12	7	33
2025–2029	14	12	7	33

electoral divisions. Electors can also form a nomination committee of 300–500 members to nominate their preferred candidates for direct elections.[142] All adult permanent residents can be nominated as candidates for the direct elections.[143] Each nomination committee can submit only one list of candidates (no less than four candidates and no more than the total number of legislators that are returnable by direct election).[144] Political parties can also nominate candidates in the parties' names,[145] but in all the past MASAR elections, no political party has ever done so.[146] Instead, the party members prefer to use nominating committees as a proxy so that each political party can form more than one nomination committee to contest direct elections.

Each Macau voter would cast their vote in favour of one list of candidates put forward by the nominating committees. Voters vote for their preferred slate of candidates and not individual candidates on the list.[147] The legislative seats are distributed using the "list system of proportional representation (比例代表制)".[148] Specifically, after all votes in the direct elections are counted, the seats will be allocated using the *modified* d'Hondt Method. Under this method, the number of

142 Law on the Election of the Legislative Assembly of the Macau Special Administrative Region (澳門特別行政區立法會選舉法) (Law No. 3/2001), art 28.

143 Law on the Election of the Legislative Assembly of the Macau Special Administrative Region (澳門特別行政區立法會選舉法) (Law No. 3/2001), art 5.

144 Law on the Election of the Legislative Assembly of the Macau Special Administrative Region (澳門特別行政區立法會選舉法) (Law No. 3/2001), arts 16 and 27(2).

145 Law on the Election of the Legislative Assembly of the Macau Special Administrative Region (澳門特別行政區立法會選舉法) (Law No. 3/2001), art 27(1).

146 Yu Wang 王禹 and Ran Shen 沈然, *澳门特别行政区立法会产生办法研究 A Study on the Method for the Formation of the Legislative Assembly of the Macau Special Administrative Region* (社会科学文献出版社和澳门基金会 Social Sciences Academic Press and Macau Foundation 2017) 99.

147 Law on the Election of the Legislative Assembly of the Macau Special Administrative Region (澳門特別行政區立法會選舉法) (Law No. 3/2001), art 15.

148 Law on the Election of the Legislative Assembly of the Macau Special Administrative Region (澳門特別行政區立法會選舉法) (Law No. 3/2001), art 15.

TABLE 2.5 Hypothetical Example of How Legislative Seats Are Allocated under the Modified d'Hondt Method for Direct Elections

Candidates' list	*Votes Received*	*1 (Divisor)*	*2 (Divisor)*	*4 (Divisor)*	*8 (Divisor)*	*16 (Divisor)*
A	100,000	**Quotient: 100,000 Priority 1**	**Quotient: 50,000 Priority 3**	**Quotient: 25,000 Priority 6**	Quotient: 12,500	Quotient: 6,250
B	80,000	**Quotient: 80,000 Priority 2**	**Quotient: 40,000 Priority 4**	**Quotient: 20,000 Priority 7**	Quotient: 10,000	Quotient: 5,000
C	30,000	**Quotient: 30,000 Priority 5**	Quotient: 15,000	Quotient: 7,500	Quotient: 3,750	Quotient: 1,875
D	20,000	**Quotient: 20,000 Priority 7**	Quotient: 10,000	Quotient: 5,000	Quotient: 2,500	Quotient: 1,250

valid votes received by each list of candidates is repeatedly divided by the divisor 1, 2, 4, 8 and successive multipliers of 2. Each quotient (total votes attained ÷ divisor) will be ranked in priority based on the numerical size.[149] The number of "winning" quotients will be the number of legislative seats available.[150] The legislative seats will be awarded to the "winning" list in order of the quotient's numerical size.[151] The "winning" list will allocate the seats to candidates in order of the candidates' rankings on the respective list.[152]

Take the hypothetical below as an example, where there are 8 legislative seats up for contest, with 4 lists of candidates in competition, and a total of 230,000 votes cast in the election (see Table 2.5).

With eight legislative seats up for contest, the seats will be awarded to the highest eight "winning" quotients. After all the "winning" quotients are ranked, List A wins three seats, List B wins three seats, List C one seat, and List D one seat.

For indirect elections, the legislative seats are reserved for social and economic sectoral constituencies recognised by the Macau government. Since the 2013 Legislative Election, there have been five such sectoral constituencies: (1) industry, commerce, and finance (four seats); (2) labour (two seats); (3) the professions

149 Law on the Election of the Legislative Assembly of the Macau Special Administrative Region (澳門特別行政區立法會選舉法) (Law No. 3/2001), art 17(2).

150 Law on the Election of the Legislative Assembly of the Macau Special Administrative Region (澳門特別行政區立法會選舉法) (Law No. 3/2001), art 17(2).

151 Law on the Election of the Legislative Assembly of the Macau Special Administrative Region (澳門特別行政區立法會選舉法) (Law No. 3/2001), art 17(3).

152 Law on the Election of the Legislative Assembly of the Macau Special Administrative Region (澳門特別行政區立法會選舉法) (Law No. 3/2001), art 18.

TABLE 2.6 Macau Legislative Assembly Indirect Election in 2021 and 2025[a]

Sectors	*Total number of Seats*	*Total number of Registered corporate bodies*		*Total number of valid votes*	
		2021	*2025*	*2021*	*2025*
Industry, commerce and finance	4	109	108	969	1021
Labour	2	73	68	1074	1062
Professions	3	62	63	624	720
Social service and education	1	159	162	1776	1969
Culture and sports	2	410	382	2317	1648

a '按選舉組別劃分的結果 Results by Electoral Sector' <www.eal.gov.mo/pdf/2021/final/FinalRptID01.pdf> last accessed 3 January 2026; '按選舉組別劃分的結果 Results by Electoral Sector' <www.eal.gov.mo/pdf/2025/final/FinalRptID01.pdf> last accessed 3 January 2026.

(three seats); (4) social service and education (one seat); and (5) culture and sports (two seats) (see Table 2.6).[153] Before 2013, the current fourth and fifth sectoral constituencies existed as one sector, from which two seats were returned.[154] Notably for the indirect elections, it is not individuals but corporate bodies that can register as electors (選民) in indirect elections.[155] The registered corporate bodies can also form nomination committees to nominate election candidates. For indirect elections, each nomination committee must comprise no less than 20% of the registered corporate bodies within the respective sectoral constituency (before 2013, the minimum threshold was 25%).[156] Each nomination committee can submit one list of candidates from their constituencies to contest the indirect election and the number of nominated candidates has to equal the number of seats allocated to the sectoral constituency they belong to.[157] Like direct elections, all adult permanent residents can be nominated as candidates for the indirect elections.[158] The law does not specify that the candidates must work in the registered corporate bodies that nominated them, but in practice the candidates are usually eminent and reputable persons from those respective sectors.[159]

153 Law on the Election of the Legislative Assembly of the Macau Special Administrative Region (澳門特別行政區立法會選舉法) (Law No. 3/2001, amended by Law No. 12/2012), art 22(2).
154 Law on the Election of the Legislative Assembly of the Macau Special Administrative Region (澳門特別行政區立法會選舉法) (Law No. 3/2001), art 22(1).
155 Law on the Election of the Legislative Assembly of the Macau Special Administrative Region (澳門特別行政區立法會選舉法) (Law No. 3/2001), art 7(1).
156 Law on the Election of the Legislative Assembly of the Macau Special Administrative Region (澳門特別行政區立法會選舉法) (Law No. 3/2001, amended by Law No. 12/2012), art 43.
157 Law on the Election of the Legislative Assembly of the Macau Special Administrative Region (澳門特別行政區立法會選舉法) (Law No. 3/2001), art 23.
158 Law on the Election of the Legislative Assembly of the Macau Special Administrative Region (澳門特別行政區立法會選舉法) (Law No. 3/2001), art 8.
159 Yu Wang 王禹 and Ran Shen 沈然, *澳门特别行政区立法会产生办法研究 A Study on the Method for the Formation of the Legislative Assembly of the Macau Special Administrative Region* (社会科学文献出版社和澳门基金会 Social Sciences Academic Press and Macau Foundation 2017) 118.

Aside from nominating candidates, each registered corporate body can also choose – from its respective organisation's leadership and management team (領導機關或管理機關) – no more than 22 people as voters (投票人) in the indirect elections.[160] The law does not specify how each registered corporate body should pick its corporate electors and the corporate "selected" voters will vote in their *personal* capacity for the preferred list of candidates in the relevant sector. After all the votes are counted, the seats will be allocated by the same *modified* d'Hondt Method used in direct elections.[161]

Under Portuguese rule, the Governor could appoint seven persons to the Legislative Assembly. This practice of appointed lawmakers was retained after the handover and the Macau CE continues to appoint seven legislative members.[162]

Since the handover, Macau has held seven Legislative Assembly elections. But unlike Hong Kong, the pro-Beijing camp in Macau always won handily. In fact, the pro-democracy Macau politicians have never won more than three seats in the direct elections.[163] The two pro-democracy political parties that found some electoral success were the New Macau Association (新澳門學社) and its splinter party – New Democratic Macau Association (澳門社區發展新動力). Both parties worked closely with local labour organisations to pressure the MASAR to better protect civil and political rights.[164]

As for indirect elections, pro-democracy groups have never taken part in them. Without sufficient financial resources and deep business ties, it is practically impossible for these pro-democracy groups to get nominated by the relevant functional sectors.[165] In turn, indirect elections were and still are dominated by pro-Beijing commercial and neighbourhood associations.[166] Notwithstanding the

160 Law on the Election of the Legislative Assembly of the Macau Special Administrative Region (澳門特別行政區立法會選舉法) (Law No. 3/2001, amended by Law No. 12/2012), art 22(4).

161 Law on the Election of the Legislative Assembly of the Macau Special Administrative Region (澳門特別行政區立法會選舉法) (Law No. 3/2001), art 24.

162 MABL, Annex II, art 1.

163 For our purposes, we do not count New Hope (新希望) as one of these pro-democracy political parties. New Hope is a political party founded by the Association of Civil Servants of Macau to focus on defending the rights and interests of all civil servants in Macau. In 2005, New Hope ran for the Legislative Assembly direct election for the first time and won one seat. It won one seat in the 2009 Legislative Assembly direct elections, two seats in the 2013 direct elections, and only one seat in the 2017 direct elections. In 2021, while all candidates from pro-democracy groups were disqualified from running for office, candidates from New Hope were unaffected and they gained two seats in the 2021 direct elections. See Shiu-Hing Lo and Eric King-Man Chong, 'Casino Interests, Fujian Tongxianghui and Electoral Politics in Macao' (2016) 46 *Journal of Contemporary Asia* 286, 299.

164 Eilo Yu Wing-yat and Natalie Chin Ka-man, 'The Political Opposition and Democracy in Macao: Revolutionaries or Loyalists' (2012) 46 *Government and Opposition* 97, 102.

165 Yufan Hao, Li Sheng, and Guanjin Pan, *Political Economy of Macao since 1999: The Dilemma of Success* (Palgrave Macmillan 2017) 165.

166 Yu Wang 王禹 and Ran Shen 沈然, *澳门特别行政区立法会产生办法研究 A Study on the Method for the Formation of the Legislative Assembly of the Macau Special Administrative Region* (社会科学文献出版社和澳门基金会 Social Sciences Academic Press and Macau Foundation 2017) 115–116, 123.

limited influence of the pro-democracy camp in the Legislative Assembly, all aspiring candidates from the pro-democracy political parties were disqualified from running in the 2021 Legislative Assembly election. Specifically, prior to the 2021 legislative election, the Macau Legislative Assembly Electoral Affairs Commission (立法會選舉管理委員會, MALAEAC) disqualified 21 people from contesting the 2021 Legislative Assembly election, 15 of whom were from the pro-democracy political parties.[167] The MALAEAC asserted that these pro-democracy candidates had been disloyal to Macau and China, and therefore had failed to comply with the Basic Law and the Law on the Election of the Legislative Assembly of the MASAR (澳門特別行政區立法會選舉法).[168] The disqualification was based on the fact that many of these candidates had organised and participated in the candlelight vigils hitherto held annually in Macau on June 4th – the anniversary of the Tiananmen Square military crackdown[169] – or took part in past public assemblies in Macau to commemorate Chinese dissident Liu Xiaobo and the pro-democracy manifesto Charter 08.[170] All these disqualifications were also upheld by the Macau Court of Final Appeal (MACFA)[171] and the pro-Beijing politicians now have a clean sweep in the Macau legislature.

In the 2025 elections, no pro-democracy candidates contested. But this time, the MALAEAC even disqualified 12 candidates from the centrist camp, including one incumbent legislator Ron Lam U Tou (林宇滔).[172] These 12 candidates belonged to two centrist political groups – Synergy of Macau (傳新澳門協會)

167 The disqualified pro-democracy candidates were from three pro-democracy groups: the Macau Democratic Prosperity Association (民主昌澳門), the New Macau Progressives (學社前進), and the New Macau Progressive Association (新澳門進步協會). Besides the 15 candidates from pro-democracy parties, 6 were from labour and other groups. '澳門立法會候選人遭集體 DQ,「愛國愛澳」面臨重新定義 Macau Legislative Assembly Candidates Face Mass Disqualification, 'Love the Motherland, Love Macau' Faces Redefinition' *BBC* (14 July 2021) <www.bbc.com/zhongwen/trad/chinese-news-57811700> last accessed 3 January 2026.

168 Art 6(8) of the Law on the Election of the Legislative Assembly of the MASAR written in Chinese: '拒絕聲明擁護《中華人民共和國澳門特別行政區基本法》和效忠中華人民共和國澳門特別行政區者；或事實證明不擁護《中華人民共和國澳門特別行政區基本法》或不效忠中華人民共和國澳門特別行政區者。'

169 Case 113/2021, at 191 (31 July 2021).

170 Case 113/2021, at 204–209 (31 July 2021). Liu Xiaobo was one of China's most prominent dissidents and well-known human rights activists. He was arrested in December 2008 and was imprisoned for inciting subversion of state power in December 2009. His alleged crime was the public criticism of the Chinese government and being one of the main drafters of Charter 08, a manifesto calling for democracy, respect for human rights and the rule of law in China. Liu Xiaobo was awarded the Nobel Peace Prize on 8 October 2010, but he was absent from the ceremony and was represented by an empty chair. On 13 July 2017, Liu Xiaobo died of liver cancer in a hospital in Shenyang. Jean-Philippe Beja, Fu Hualing, and Eva Pils (eds), *Liu Xiaobo, Charter 08 and the Challenges of Political Reform in China* (HKU Press 2012).

171 Case 113/2021 (31 July 2021). See Chapter 3 for a fuller discussion of this case.

172 'Disqualified Candidate Group Demands Clarification from CAEAL on Eligibility Decision' *Macau Daily Times* (17 July 2025) <https://macaudailytimes.com.mo/disqualified-candidate-group-demands-clarification-from-caeal-on-eligibility-decision.html> last accessed 3 January 2026.

and Macau Create People's Livelihood Force (澳門創建民生力量). Both groups differentiated themselves from the pro-democracy camp insofar as they focused on livelihood issues instead of democratic reform.[173] Still, they were not welcomed by the government as the candidates were deemed not to have upheld the Basic Law and borne allegiance to the MASAR. Notably, prior to this election, Macau amended the Law on the Election of the Legislative Assembly in April 2024, which introduced two significant changes. Reviews on the eligibility of legislative candidates are now made by the MALAEAC based on the opinion of the Committee for Safeguarding National Security of the MASAR (MANSC) and disqualified candidates cannot challenge these decisions in court.[174] This provision makes the MANSC[175] the de facto ultimate arbiter of the candidates' political loyalty. Since the opinions of the MALAEAC and MANSC are not disclosed to the public and

173 '創建民生力量交名單政綱 Macau Create People's Livelihood Force Submits Electoral List and Manifesto' *Macau Daily* (24 June 2025) <www.macaodaily.com/html/2025-06/24/content_1840745.htm> last accessed 3 January 2026; '傳新力量交參選名單政綱 Synergy of Macau Submits Electoral List and Manifesto' *Macau Daily* (24 June 2025) <www.macaodaily.com/html/2025-06/24/content_1840746.htm> last accessed 3 January 2026.

174 Art 33(2) of the Law on the Election of the Legislative Assembly of the MASAR stipulates 'For the application of the preceding paragraph, the Committee for Safeguarding National Security of the Macau SAR shall assess whether a candidate upholds the Basic Law and bears allegiance to the Macau SAR of the PRC, and shall issue a *binding* opinion to the Legislative Assembly Electoral Affairs Commission regarding any candidate who does not meet these requirements' (in Chinese 為適用上款的規定，由澳門特別行政區維護國家安全委員會就候選人是否擁護《基本法》和效忠中華人民共和國澳門特別行政區作出判斷，並就不符合者向立法會選舉管理委員會發出具約束力的審查意見書。).
Art 33(3) of the Law on the Election of the Legislative Assembly of the MASAR stipulates 'No objection or judicial appeal may be lodged against a decision of the Legislative Assembly Electoral Affairs Commission disqualifying a candidate based on the opinion referred to in the preceding paragraph' (in Chinese 針對立法會選舉管理委員會基於上款所指意見書而作出候選人不符合候選人資格的決定，不得提起聲明異議或司法上訴。). Art 5 of the HKBL Annex II (as amended in 2021) stipulates a similar candidate eligibility review mechanism, under which the Candidate Eligibility Review Committee of the HKSAR confirms the eligibility of candidates based on the opinion of the Committee for Safeguarding National Security of the HKSAR (HKNSC). Similarly, in Hong Kong, no legal proceeding can be brought against the decision made by the Candidate Eligibility Review Committee. Although Article 5 does not explicitly state that the HKNSC's opinion is binding on its Candidate Eligibility Review Committee – as is the case in the corresponding Macau legislation – it is highly unlikely that the HKSAR's Candidate Eligibility Review Committee would depart from adverse opinions given by its HKNSC.

175 The Committee for Safeguarding National Security of the Macau SAR (MANSC) was established in 2018 pursuant to AR No. 22/2018. It is chaired by the CE and is composed of nine government department members appointed by the CE: (1) The Secretary for Administration and Justice; (2) The Secretary for Security, who shall serve as Vice-Chair; (3) The Commissioner General of Police; (4) The Director of the Office of the Chief Executive; (5) The Director of the Office of the Secretary for Security; (6) The Director of the Legal Affairs Bureau; (7) The Director of the Judiciary Police; (8) One Advisor to the Office of the CE; and (9) One Advisor to the Office of the Secretary for Security. Committee for Safeguarding National Security of the Macau SAR (澳門特別行政區維護國家安全委員會) (AR 22/2018), art 4. In 2021, the CE amended AR No. 22/2018 and added one National Security Advisor and three National Security Technical

TABLE 2.7 Seats Held by Pro-Democracy Political Parties in the Macau Legislative Assembly (2001–2029)

Legislative Term	*Party Affiliation of Pro-Democracy Lawmakers*	*Seats in the Legislative Assembly*
2001–2005	New Macau Association	2/27
2005–2009	New Macau Association	2/29
2009–2013	New Macau Association	3/29
2013–2017	New Macau Association	2/33
2017–2021	New Macau Association	1/33
	New Democratic Macau Association	2/33
2021–2025	NA	0/33
2025–2029	NA	0/33

are not appealable,[176] it is unclear why the 12 candidates were deemed disloyal to Macau and China. But their disqualification clearly demonstrates that Beijing and Macau are even less tolerant of and more eager to purge non-establishment political groups now[177] (see Table 2.7).

Turning to Hong Kong, its elected lawmakers also serve a term of four years (except for the first term which lasted two years) and there are no term limits.[178] There are currently 90 seats in the Legislative Council, and they are constituted by three types of elections: GC election; FC election; and EC constituency election. They will be explained in turn.

Unlike Macau, Hong Kong does not have appointed lawmakers. But 40 out of 90 seats in the Legislative Council (LegCo) are now constituted by the same EC that picks the Hong Kong CE. The EC used to constitute 10 out of 60 seats in the first Hong Kong LegCo held in 1998, but EC legislators were completely phased out from the Legislative Council in 2004.[179] Nevertheless, in 2021, Beijing

Advisors to the MANSC. All advisors are appointed by the Central Government. Amendment to AR 22/2018 on Committee for Safeguarding National Security of the Macau SAR (修改第22/2018 號行政法規《澳門特別行政區維護國家安全委員會》) (AR 47/2021), art 1. For a comparison of Hong Kong and Macau's NSCs, see Chapter 4.

176 '選管會公佈維護國家安全委員會審查意見書，直選兩組別12人被 DQ Legislative Assembly Electoral Affairs Commission Follows the Review Report of the Committee for Safeguarding National Security, 12 Candidates from 2 Direct Election Groups Disqualified.' *星報 Sengpou* (16 July 2025) <https://sengpou.com/news_detail.php?news_id=14287&element_index=0> last accessed 3 January 2026.

177 '澳門立法會換屆：選民和學者如何看待一場「零中間派」選舉？ Macau Legislative Assembly Election: How Voters and Scholars View a "Zero-Centrist" Election?' *BBC* (11 September 2025) <www.bbc.com/zhongwen/articles/cvgnyp5r54xo/trad> last accessed 3 January 2026.

178 HKBL, art 69.

179 Annex II to the Basic Law of the HKSAR of the People's Republic of China: Method for the Formation of the Legislative Council of the HKSAR and its Voting Procedures, art 1(1) (Adopted at the Third Session of the Seventh National People's Congress on 4 April 1990).

reinstated the EC with a vengeance by allowing it to constitute the largest segment of the Hong Kong legislature, and only the 1500 EC members are allowed to vote in the EC constituency of the LegCo election.[180] Every Hong Kong EC member can vote for 40 election candidates,[181] and the 40 candidates with the highest number of votes will be elected as EC lawmakers.[182] But one does not need to be an EC member to run for these seats;[183] voting is merely limited to these EC members. Furthermore, to even contest these EC seats, each aspiring candidate must be first "subscribed" by at least ten EC members, with at least two EC members drawn from each of the five EC sectors[184] (see Table 2.2 for the composition of the EC).

Direct elections now constitute 20 out of 90 seats in the Hong Kong Legislative Council.[185] (As indicated in Table 2.4, direct elections currently constitute 14 out of 33 seats in the Macau Legislative Assembly). Directly elected seats in Hong Kong are known as GC seats as these lawmakers are directly elected from and represent different geographical areas in Hong Kong. Before Beijing overhauled Hong Kong's electoral system in 2021, GC seats comprised 35 out of 70 seats in the Legislative Council.[186] By decimating the number of directly elected seats in Hong Kong, Beijing is effectively undermining the constitutional promise that

180 Decision of the National People's Congress on Improving the Electoral System of the HKSAR, para. 4 (Adopted at the Fourth Session of the 13th National People's Congress on 11 March 2021); Annex II to the Basic Law of the HKSAR of the People's Republic of China: Method for the Formation of the Legislative Council of the HKSAR and its Voting Procedures, art 1 (Amended at the 27th Meeting of the Standing Committee of the 13th National People's Congress on 30 March 2021); Legislative Council Ordinance (LCO), s 48(3D). Ian Scott and Joan Y. H. Leung, 'Dysfunctional Elections and the Political System in Hong Kong' (2004) 12(2) *Asian Journal of Political Science* 1, 20.

181 LCO, s 52A(2).

182 LCO, s 52A(5).

183 LCO, s 37(3A).

184 Legislative Council (Subscribers and Election Deposit for Nomination) Regulation, s 7(3).

185 Annex II to the Basic Law of the HKSAR of the People's Republic of China: Method for the Formation of the Legislative Council of the HKSAR and its Voting Procedures, art 1 (Amended at the 27th Meeting of the Standing Committee of the 13th National People's Congress on 30 March 2021).

186 From 1998 to 2012, the LegCo of the HKSAR comprised 60 members. The number of LegCo members returned by GCs was 20 in the first term (1998–2000). See Decision of the National People's Congress on the Method for the Formation of the First Government and the First Legislative Council of the HKSAR, para. 6 (Adopted at the Third Session of the Seventh National People's Congress on 4 April 1990). The number of LegCo members returned by GCs was increased from 20 to 24 in the second term (2000–2004). See Annex II to the Basic Law of the HKSAR of the People's Republic of China: Method for the Formation of the Legislative Council of the HKSAR and its Voting Procedures, art 1 (Adopted at the Third Session of the Seventh National People's Congress on 4 April 1990). It was further increased and reached 30 in the Third and Fourth terms (2004–2012). See Decision of the Standing Committee of the National People's Congress on Issues Relating to the Methods for Selecting the CE of the HKSAR in the Year 2007 and for Forming the Legislative Council of the HKSAR in the Year 2008 (Adopted at the Ninth Session of the Standing Committee of the Tenth National People's Congress on 26 April 2004).

the "ultimate aim is the election of all the members of the Legislative Council by universal suffrage".[187]

Previously, before the electoral overhaul of 2021, GC elections were conducted in the HKSAR using the "list system of proportional representation",[188] which was only introduced in 1998 to replace the first-past-the-post system Governor Patten introduced in 1995.[189] Similar to Macau's direct elections, under the party-list proportional representation (PR) system, each voter in Hong Kong chose their preferred list of candidates put forward by the respective political parties rather than vote for specific individual candidates.[190] In the first stage, legislators were returned using the "quota".[191] The quota was a threshold of votes that guaranteed the election of a candidate. The quota was calculated by dividing the number of valid votes in a constituency by the number of seats in the same constituency, disregarding fractions.[192] If a list had enough votes to match or exceed the quota, the top-listed candidate was elected; if the list had excess votes which also matched or exceeded the quota, the next-listed candidate was also elected, and so on. If there were still vacancies in the constituency after using the quota, the remaining members would be returned using the "largest remainder formula".[193] Under this method, whichever list had the largest remaining number of votes (after deducting the votes belonging to candidates already elected) would return one candidate.[194] This stage continued for each round of remaining votes until all vacancies in the constituency were filled.[195]

The use of PR to allocate seats in the Hong Kong Legislative Council was part of Beijing's strategy to reverse the Patten reforms and shore up the legislative seats that the pro-establishment camp could win in the GC elections. As the pro-democracy camp consistently won 55%–65% of the popular vote for those GC seats,[196] the continued use of the first-past-the-post system would result in the decimation of the pro-Beijing camp for those seats, and Beijing would not accept this. But the introduction of PR had an unintended consequence – excessive political fragmentation in the legislature.[197] PR allows smaller political parties and

187 HKBL, art 68.

188 Section 49(2) of the pre-2021 LCO.

189 Chung Fun Steven Hung, 'Reviewing and Evaluating the Direct Elections to the Legislative Council and the Transformation of Political Parties in Hong Kong, 1991–2016' (2016) 13(8) *Journal of US-China Public Administration* 499, 505.

190 Section 49(3) of the pre-2021 LCO.

191 Section 49(5) of the pre-2021 LCO. The number is also known as the Hare quota.

192 Section 49(6) of the pre-2021 LCO.

193 Section 49(7) of the pre-2021 LCO.

194 Section 49(8)(b) of the pre-2021 LCO.

195 Section 49(8)(c) of the pre-2021 LCO.

196 Ngok Ma, 'Party Underdevelopment in Hong Kong: Hybrid Constraints and Value Changes' (2018) 58(3) *Asian Survey* 416, 422.

197 John M. Carey, 'Electoral Formula and Fragmentation in Hong Kong', (2017) 17 *Journal of East Asian Studies* 215.

independents to gain seats, so there was never a strong political party – pro-Beijing or otherwise – to command a majority in the house. The largest political party in the HKSAR is the DAB (Democratic Alliance for the Betterment and Progress of Hong Kong), but prior to the electoral overhaul of 2021, it had never won more than 13 seats in the Legislative Council. The "governing" legislative partnership in Hong Kong also includes an uneasy coalition of pro-Beijing business parties and pro-Beijing trade unionists. Even the pro-democracy camp was splintered into different factions, which made it difficult to achieve *intra*-camp consensus, let alone *inter*-camp consensus. As the number of elected seats in the Legislative Council *increased* after the constitutional reform of 2010,[198] the percentage of votes, which an aspiring candidate needed to win to gain a seat in the legislature via PR, *decreased.* In turn, the political incentives for a lawmaker to be more mainstream and compromising to win votes were reduced. Instead of broadening the political tent and bridging the ideological divide across the legislative aisle, aspiring or incumbent lawmakers would simply need to agitate and bring out their narrow base to vote. Pre-2021, for fear of losing seats in the GC elections, even the pro-establishment lawmakers abandoned the HKSAR government not just on controversial bills concerning national security,[199] but even those relating to copyright reform.[200] The legislative success rates of the first three CEs – Tung Chee-hwa, Donald Tsang, and Leung Chun-ying – were 55.33%, 57.47%, and 57.41%, respectively,[201] with the HKSAR government shelving or postponing 39.84% of its legislative initiatives that were originally planned in its annual Policy Address and Legislative Programme.[202] The legislative success rate of the 4th CE Carrie Lam's administration was equally abysmal as the city was roiled by months of relentless street protests in 2019 and the Legislative Council was even closed for weeks after it was besieged, stormed and vandalised by protestors.

198 In 2010, a bipartisan constitutional amendment was passed which increased the GC seats from 30 to 35 and added a new functional constituency – DC (Second) – with 5 legislative members. These five legislative members would be elected by universal suffrage from the pool of existing DC members. All these DC seats were removed in the 2021 electoral overhaul. Amendment to Annex II to the Basic Law of the HKSAR of the People's Republic of China Concerning the Method for the Formation of the Legislative Council of the HKSAR and its Voting Procedures (Recorded at the Sixteenth Session of the Standing Committee of the Eleventh National People's Congress on 28 August 2010); Legislative Council (Amendment) Ordinance 2011 (2 of 2011), ss 11, 12(3) and 15(3).

199 National Security (Legislative Provisions) Bill 2003.

200 Copyright (Amendment) Bill 2014.

201 Brian C. H. Fong, 'Executive-Legislative Disconnection in the HKSAR: Uneasy Partnership between Chief Executives and Pro-Government Parties, 1997–2016' in Brian C. H. Fong and Tai-Lok Lui (eds), *Hong Kong 20 Years after the Handover: Emerging Social and Institutional Fractures After 1997*(Palgrave Macmillan 2018) 55.

202 Brian C. H. Fong, 'Executive-Legislative Disconnection in the HKSAR: Uneasy Partnership between Chief Executives and Pro-Government Parties, 1997–2016' in Brian C. H. Fong and Tai-Lok Lui (eds), *Hong Kong 20 Years after the Handover: Emerging Social and Institutional Fractures After 1997* (Palgrave Macmillan 2018) 55, 56.

Therefore in 2021, Beijing decided to end the PR system once and for all. Now, all GCs use a modified "first-past-the-post" electoral system: each voter picks only one person amongst all the candidates contesting in their GC and the *two* legislative candidates with the highest number of votes in each GC will be duly elected.[203] And as discussed above, GC seats now only constitute 20 out of 90 seats. Furthermore, to even run for the GC seats, each candidate must be "subscribed" by at least ten EC members, with at least two EC members drawn from each of the five EC sectors mentioned above,[204] thereby ensuring that only candidates acceptable to the political establishment can even be on the ballot.

30 out of 90 seats in Hong Kong are constituted by FC elections.[205] FCs are similar to Macau's indirect seats and they are supposed to represent "the economic and professional sectors which are substantial and of importance in the community"[206]. Notably in 1997, as part of China's reversal of the Patten reforms, corporate voting was restored,[207] resulting in a significant reduction of eligible voters by almost 90%, from over 1.1 million in 1995 to fewer than 140,000 in the then upcoming 1998 election.[208] There were 28 FCs in 1998: Labour FC had three seats, while all others had one seat each.[209] While two new FCs were added in the 1998 election – Information Technology; Sports, Performing Arts, Culture and Publication[210] – three FCs were abolished: Community, Social, and Personal Services; Hotels and Catering; and Manufacturing.[211] Additionally, Insurance replaced Financing, Insurance, Real Estate, and Business Services; and Agriculture and Fisheries replaced Primary Production, Power, and Construction.[212] It is notable that all five

203 Section 49(1) and 49(2) of the LCO.

204 Section 7(1) of the Legislative Council (Subscribers and Election Deposit for Nomination) Regulation.

205 Annex II to the Basic Law of the HKSAR of the People's Republic of China: Method for the Formation of the Legislative Council of the HKSAR and its Voting Procedures, art 1 (Amended at the Twenty-Seventh Meeting of the Standing Committee of the 13th National People's Congress on 30 March 2021).

206 Constitutional Affairs Bureau, 'Administration's Responses to Points raised on 7 May by Members of the Bills Committee on the Legislative Council (Amendment) Bill 1999' <www.legco.gov.hk/yr98-99/english/bc/bc66/papers/b662151a.htm> last accessed 3 January 2026.

207 Schedule 1 on Functional Constituencies of the then-operative LCO enacted by the prevailing Provisional Legislative Council (PLC) on 3 October 1997.

208 See *A Companion to the history, rules and practices of the Legislative Council of the Hong Kong Special Administrative Region, Appendix 3-A Composition of the Legislative Council of Hong Kong (from October 1985 to June 1997) and the Legislative Council of HKSAR (from July 1997 onwards)*, pages 4–5, <www.legco.gov.hk/general/english/procedur/companion/chapter3_toc.html> last accessed 3 January 2026.

209 Section 21 of the then-operative LCO enacted by PLC on 3 October 1997.

210 Part 3 of Schedule 1 on Functional Constituencies of the then-operative LCO enacted by the PLC on 3 October 1997.

211 Schedule 1 on Functional Constituencies of the then-operative LCO enacted by the PLC on 3 October 1997.

212 Schedule 1 on Functional Constituencies of the then-operative LCO enacted by the PLC on 3 October 1997.

FCs abolished or reconfigured were FCs introduced by Governor Chris Patten for the 1995 election. This resulted in the pro-Beijing politicians winning 25 seats in the 1998 FC election, compared to only 20 FC seats in 1995.[213]

There are currently 28 FCs in Hong Kong,[214] and they include Heung Yee Kuk;[215] Commercial (First); Commercial (Second); Industrial (First); Insurance; Finance; Legal, etc. Prior to the 2021 electoral overhaul there were also two DC FCs in the LegCo. But after the pro-democracy lawmakers swept 17 out of 18 DCs in the 2019 DC elections, Beijing decided to remove all DC representation from the LegCo and add a new pro-Beijing FC seat – FC for the Hong Kong deputies to the National People's Congress, Hong Kong members of the CPPCC National Committee and representatives of relevant national organisations.[216]

Furthermore, despite the use of sectoral representation, not everyone working in their sector can vote for their sectoral candidate. For example, in the Commercial (First), Commercial (Second), and Industrial (First) FCs, only members, who are allowed to vote at the general meetings of the respective FC's constituent organisations, can participate in the FC elections.[217] The rank-and-file workers in these FCs are excluded. Others like the Finance and Insurance FCs limit voting to only *companies/bodies* operating in these sectors.[218] Even for the Labour FC, voting is restricted to the registered trade unions, and not individual employees.[219] Where FC membership is limited to corporate electors, each company will pick an authorised representative to vote on its behalf in the FC election.[220] Individual voting is allowed for the Legal, Accountancy, and the Medical and Health Services FCs, but voting is limited to the recognised professionals working in that relevant sector.[221] Since 2021, each aspiring FC candidate must also be "subscribed" by at least ten EC members, with at least two EC members drawn from each of those five EC sectors again,[222] thereby ensuring that political "outliers" can be excluded from the contest.

213 Tiansheng Ye 葉天生, *香港選舉資料匯編：1996年-2000年 Compendium of Hong Kong Election Materials: 1996–2000* (香港中文大學香港亞太研究所 Hong Kong Institute of Asia-Pacific Studies, CUHK 2001) 31–34.

214 Annex II to the Basic Law of the HKSAR of the People's Republic of China: Method for the Formation of the Legislative Council of the HKSAR and its Voting Procedures, art 3 (Amended at the 27th Meeting of the Standing Committee of the 13th National People's Congress on 30 March 2021).

215 Heung Yee Kuk is a pro-Beijing statutory body that represents the indigenous inhabitants of the New Territories in advising the government on socio-economic matters pertaining to their welfare.

216 Annex II to the Basic Law of the HKSAR of the People's Republic of China: Method for the Formation of the Legislative Council of the HKSAR and its Voting Procedures, art 3 (Amended at the 27th Meeting of the Standing Committee of the 13th National People's Congress on 30 March 2021).

217 LCO, ss 20P, 20Q, and 20R.

218 LCO, ss 20T and 20C.

219 LCO, s 20L.

220 LCO, s 26.

221 LCO, ss 20F, 20G, and 20IA.

222 Legislative Council (Subscribers and Election Deposit for Nomination) Regulation, s 7(2).

Unlike Macau's indirect elections, FC elections in Hong Kong use the first-past-the-post system.[223] Each eligible FC elector votes for one candidate in their sector, and the candidate with the highest vote in each sector is elected. The only exception is the Labour FC. Since the Labour FC is represented by three seats in LegCo, each FC elector has three votes, and the top three candidates are elected.[224] Unlike Macau, Hong Kong expressly requires the FC legislative candidates to have "a substantial connection with the constituency"[225] they are contesting in.

In essence, the FC system excludes the rank-and-file from voting.[226] Only companies, professionals, and the cherry-picked pro-Beijing constituents can be electors. The use of corporate voting in FCs had been challenged in court on the ground that Article 26[227] of the Hong Kong Basic Law only vests the right to vote on permanent residents and not on corporate entities. However, the Hong Kong Court of Appeal in 2010 flatly rejected this argument on the basis that "functional constituencies, embracing corporate voting, have played a central role"[228] in Hong Kong's electoral development since 1985; and while Article 26 confers the right to vote on permanent residents, it does not preclude the concurrent vesting of this right on corporations.[229]

Leaving aside corporate voting, the disparity of relative voting power between individual electors is another grave concern. The size of the constituency base in each FC differs such that an *individual* elector in a small FC would have far greater relative voting power vis-à-vis another *individual* elector in a large FC. The FC with the smallest electoral base is Heung Yee Kuk and it had an electoral base of 161 registered individual electors in 2021.[230] On the other hand, there were 85,117 registered individual electors in the Education FC in 2021.[231] The variation in constituency size invariably affects the relative weight that each vote carries in determining the voter's preferred candidate in the relevant FC.

To top off all the electoral gerrymandering instituted in 2021, any person seeking to be a candidate for any of the GC, FC, or EC seats must be pre-screened by a new Candidate Eligibility Review Committee comprising top government

223 LCO, s 51.

224 LCO, s 51(4).

225 LCO, s 37(2)(b)(ii) read with s 3(2).

226 For a critique on the FC system, see Simon N. M. Young and Anthony Law, 'Privileged to Vote: Inequalities and Anomalies of the FC System' in Christine Loh (ed), *Functional Constituencies: A Unique Feature of the Hong Kong Legislative Council* (HKU Press 2006) 59.

227 Article 26 of the Hong Kong Basic Law: 'Permanent residents of the Hong Kong Special Administrative Region shall have the right to vote and the right to stand for election in accordance with law.'

228 *Chan Yu Nam v Secretary for Justice* (CACV 2/2010, unreported, 7 December 2010), at [81].

229 *Chan Yu Nam v Secretary for Justice* (CACV 2/2010, unreported, 7 December 2010), at [93].

230 Voter Turnout Rate <www.elections.gov.hk/legco2021/eng/tt_fc_HYK.html> last accessed 3 January 2026.

231 Voter Turnout Rate <www.elections.gov.hk/legco2021/eng/tt_fc_EDU.html> last accessed 3 January 2026.

officials and government-appointed personnel[232] and the Committee's decision on the candidate's eligibility is non-justiciable.[233] The mandate from Beijing is crystal clear: only "patriots" can run Hong Kong.

With all these electoral reconfigurations, the pro-democracy camp in Hong Kong was decimated. Prior to the 2021 Legislative Council election, the pro-democracy camp would typically hold 33% to 40% of all the seats in the Hong Kong LegCo.[234] After the electoral overhaul, only *one* "non-establishment" candidate – Tik Chi-yuen – was elected into LegCo in 2021. In the 2025 elections, only two "non-establishment" candidates contested, but they were not elected, resulting in the pro-Beijing camp completely sweeping the Legislative Council.[235] (As discussed earlier, there are no "non-establishment" candidates left in Macau's Legislative Assembly.) Beijing's domination over the legislatures of both cities is now complete.

Constitutional Powers of the SAR Legislatures and CEs

The constitutional powers of the Macau and Hong Kong legislatures are similar. They are both vested with the powers to pass legislation, approve budgets and taxation, and debate issues of public interest.[236] As for the CEs, the CE in each SAR is constitutionally empowered to implement the laws of their SARs, sign bills and budgets passed by the respective legislatures, issue executive orders, appoint and remove judges, etc.[237] In fact, their constitutional powers are identical except for one. The Macau CE has the power to formulate and promulgate Administrative Regulations (ARs) (行政法規) for implementation,[238] while the Hong Kong CE does not.

232 LCO, s 42(A).

233 HKBL, Annex II, art 5 (as amended in 2021).

234 Chung Fun Steven Hung, 'Reviewing and Evaluating the Direct Elections to the Legislative Council and the Transformation of Political Parties in Hong Kong, 1991–2016' (2016) 13(8) *Journal of US-China Public Administration* 499, 509.

235 Jeffrey Chan Chun-hung and Allan Wong Wing-ho are members of the PoD Research Institute, a local think tank previously known as Path of Democracy, which is unaligned with the main pro-establishment parties. Third Side, the political party with which then-incumbent Tik Chi-yuen is affiliated, fielded three candidates but failed to receive enough "subscribers" from the EC to contest the election. See Hillary Leung, 'Hong Kong Centrist, Moderate Groups Hit Brick Wall in Securing Candidate Nominations for the "Patriots-Only" Elections' *HKFP* (10 November 2025) <https://hongkongfp.com/2025/11/16/hong-kong-centrist-moderate-groups-nominations-legislative-council-elections/> last accessed 3 January 2026.

236 HKBL, art 73; MABL, art 71. But there is a notable difference. The Hong Kong LegCo is constitutionally empowered to endorse the appointment and removal of HKCFA judges (Article 73(7) of HKBL), but the Macau Legislative Assembly has no role in the appointment of judges as this power is vested alone in the CE (Article 87(1) of the MABL).

237 MABL, art 50; HKBL, art 48.

238 MABL, art 50(5).

ARs[239] are a new source of law in the MASAR. They did not exist in colonial Macau but originated from Mainland China where the State Council, headed by the Chinese Premier, is empowered to enact ARs alongside the laws passed by the National People's Congress and its Standing Committee.[240] The use of ARs in Macau has engendered controversy because they are the primary source of law in Macau instead of legislation enacted by the Legislative Assembly. Between 1999 and 2025, 882 ARs (around 35.3 pieces per year)[241] were promulgated by the Macau CE, which is more than double the number of laws passed by the Macau Legislative Assembly over the same period (422 laws passed).[242] More controversially, ARs are not even subject to *ex post* vetting or approval by the Legislative Assembly.[243]

The extent of the Macau CE's power to promulgate ARs was not undisputed and was challenged in 2006. Macau CE Edmund Ho Hau Wah had promulgated AR No. 17/2004, which imposed a new set of administrative penalties on illegal workers, in addition to the pre-existing criminal sanctions provided in Law No. 2/90/M passed by the Legislative Assembly. The MACFA ultimately ruled for the government, affirming that the CE had the power to make ARs even if there was no delegation from the legislature,[244] so long as the AR in question does not restrict constitutional rights or violate international human rights treaties codified in the Macau Basic Law (MABL).[245] For the above two restrictions, the derogations must be prescribed by legislation enacted by the Macau Legislative Assembly.[246] After the lawsuit, a new law entitled Legal Framework of Internal Regulatory Norms (關於訂定內部規範的法律制度)[247] was passed in 2009 to demarcate more clearly the legislative subject-matter competence of both branches of government. Article 6 lists 19 subject-matter categories for which the Legislative Assembly has exclusive legislative power, and these include fundamental rights, electoral system,

239 MABL, art 50(5). Executive Orders (EOs) are also a new source of law in the MASAR (MABL, art 50(4)). But while EOs are new in theory, in practice they have been used by the Macau CE to replace *portaria* that were previously issued by the colonial governor (Organic Statute of Macau of 1976, art 15(2)) and EOs in the MASAR like their colonial predecessor usually relate to the appointment and removal of government officials, delegation of power to officials and institutes, and the conferral of honours and awards. See Jinyao Zheng 鄭錦耀, '各行政規章的位階及各自的規範範圍研究 Study on the Hierarchy of Administrative Rules and Their Respective Regulatory Scope' (2019) 42 *"一國兩制"研究 Journal of "One Country Two Systems" Studies* 72–73.

240 PRC Constitution, art 89(1).

241 The statistics are available at the website of the Press Office of the MASAR <www.io.gov.mo/cn/legis/list/a/?d=59> last accessed 10 March 2026.

242 Statistics are compiled from the Legislative Assembly Activity Reports <www.al.gov.mo/zh/work-file> last accessed 10 March 2026.

243 Hu Chang 常湝, '澳門特區行政法規制定權限爭議及其解決 The Dispute over the Administrative Regulation-making Power in the Macau SAR and the Resolution' (2010) 9 *"一國兩制"研究 Journal of "One Country Two Systems" Studies* 44, 62.

244 Case 28/2006, at 100–101 (18 July 2007). See Chapter 3 for a fuller discussion of this case.

245 Case 28/2006, at 108 (18 July 2007).

246 Case 28/2006, at 108 (18 July 2007).

247 Law on Internal Norms (關於訂定內部規範的法律制度) (Law No. 13/2009).

criminal law, administrative offences and penalties, Civil Code, Commercial Code, Code of Administrative Procedure, arbitration rules, government budget and tax system, as well as monetary and financial systems.[248] On the other hand, the Macau CE may promulgate independent ARs (獨立行政法規) and complementary ARs (補充性行政法規).[249] Independent ARs are rules for implementing government policies; rules concerning public affairs management; and rules pertaining to the organisation, operation and staffing of the government.[250] Complementary ARs are intended to provide detailed rules for enforcing the legislation passed by the Legislative Assembly of Macau.[251] Although Article 3 of the Legal Framework of Internal Regulatory Norms stipulates that legislation enacted by the Legislative Assembly is of a higher legal hierarchy than ARs,[252] there are still no legal provisions that allow the Legislative Assembly to supervise, veto, or scrutinise the legality of ARs.[253]

The lack of legislative oversight over subsidiary legislation in Macau is unlike Hong Kong where subsidiary legislation – known in Hong Kong as Regulations – is always subject to scrutiny and approval by its Legislative Council, either through a negative or positive vetting procedure.[254] This legislative override applies even for the emergency Regulations made by the Hong Kong CE, despite the primary legislation – Emergency Regulations Ordinance (ERO) – expressly providing that any Regulations made pursuant to the ERO by the Chief Executive in Council (CEIC) "shall continue in force until repealed"[255] by the CEIC.[256]

Both SARs subscribe to a model of an "executive-led government" (行政主導)[257] with the CE as the core (以行政長官為核心的行政主導),[258] and the

248 Law on Internal Norms (關於訂定內部規範的法律制度) (Law No. 13/2009), art 6.

249 Law on Internal Norms (關於訂定內部規範的法律制度) (Law No. 13/2009), art 4.

250 Law on Internal Norms (關於訂定內部規範的法律制度) (Law No. 13/2009), art 7(1).

251 Law on Internal Norms (關於訂定內部規範的法律制度) (Law No. 13/2009), art 7 (2). In Chinese "補充性行政法規可就具體執行相關法律訂定的事宜作出規定。"

252 Law on Internal Norms (關於訂定內部規範的法律制度) (Law No. 13/2009), art 3.

253 Hu Chang 常湝, '澳門特區行政法規制定權限爭議及其解決 The Dispute over the Administrative Regulation-making Power in the Macau SAR and the Resolution' (2010) 9 *"一國兩制"研究 Journal of "One Country Two Systems" Studies* 44, 62.

254 Interpretation and General Clauses Ordinance, ss 34–35.

255 Emergency Regulations Ordinance, s 2(3).

256 *Kwok Wing Hang v Chief Executive in Council* (2020) 23 HKCFAR 518, [62]–[65]. See Chapter 3 for a discussion of this case.

257 Wang Shuwen 王叔文 (ed), *香港特别行政区基本法导论 Introduction to the Basic Law of the Hong Kong Special Administrative Region* (2nd edn, 法律出版社和三联书店 Law Press China and Joint Publishing HK 2009) 345–350; Xiao Weiyun 肖蔚云, *论香港基本法 On the Hong Kong Basic Law* (北京大学出版社 Peking University Press 2003) 640–644.

258 Wu Bangguo, '香港政治体制的最大特点是行政主导 The Principal Feature of Hong Kong's Political System is that it is Executive-led', speech on 6 June 2007 <www.npc.gov.cn/zgrdw/npc/wbgwyz/hyhd/2007-06/06/content_366599.htm> last accessed 3 January 2026; Qingwei Li 李清偉, '澳門特別行政區行政主導體制的法理基礎 Juridical Basis of the Executive-led System of the Macau Special Administrative Region' (2014) 19 *"一國兩制"研究 Journal of "One Country Two Systems" Studies* 25–28.

legislative powers of their legislatures are significantly truncated. In both Hong Kong and Macau, legislators are prohibited from introducing private bills relating to public expenditure, political structure, or government operations; and bills relating to government policies may only be introduced with the respective CE's consent.[259] However, Macau differs from Hong Kong in the way legislation is passed. Typically in Macau, the passage of most bills and motions only requires a majority vote of all Legislative Assembly members.[260] In contrast, for Hong Kong, bills introduced by the *government* require a simple majority vote of all members present to pass, but bills introduced by *individual* members need a majority vote of the EC members present in the Legislative Council, plus a majority vote amongst FC and GC members present.[261] (Prior to the electoral overhaul in 2021, bills introduced by individual lawmakers needed a majority vote of FC members present and a majority vote of GC members present.) Given that pro-democracy lawmakers used to dominate the GC elections, split-voting in the Hong Kong Legislative Council for *private* bills was introduced as a "safeguard" by Beijing to prevent pro-democracy legislative voices from "hijacking" the legislative agenda. This "safeguard" was further entrenched in 2021 with the requirement of having the pro-Beijing EC members approve any private bill. In this way, even if a private bill is supported by an overall majority of the Hong Kong Legislative Council members, it would still fail without the support of the EC lawmakers.

In practice, the legislative success of an "executive-led" government in the SAR depends on the support of a coalition of various pro-China political parties and independent legislators. In Macau, this has never been an issue: opposition lawmakers were few – no more than three have ever been elected at any one time – and had little public support; the pro-Beijing politicians in turn would simply fall in line and lawmaking in Macau has almost always been uneventful.[262] (The only exception was in 2014 when the Macau government was forced to withdraw a legislative bill, which would have granted the CE and his senior government officials an exorbitant retirement package, after the bill engendered massive public discontent.[263])

259 HKBL, art 74; MABL, art 75.

260 MABL, art 77; Rules of Procedure of the Legislative Assembly of the Macau Special Administrative Region (澳門特別行政區立法會議事規則) (Resolution No. 1/1999), arts 56, 81, 155–158. A two-thirds majority vote is needed when (1) the CE vetoes the original bill (Articles 51, 52, 54 of the MABL); (2) changes to the CE and Legislative Council electoral method (MABL Annex I, art 7; and Annex II, art 3).

261 Annex II to the HKBL, art 7.

262 Jinhyeok Jang, 'Parliamentary Representation in the Macau Special Administrative Region: A Quantitative Analysis of Roll Call Voting Behavior in the 5th Legislative Assembly, 2013–2017' (2018) 4(2) *Contemporary Chinese Political Economy and Strategic Relations: An International Journal* 513, 525. See also Daina Chiba, Meng U Ieong, and Jiying Jiang, 'Legislative Politics under "One Country, Two Systems": Evidence from Macau, 2013–2021' (2025) 264 *The China Quarterly* 1071, 1078.

263 Meng U Ieong, 'Macao and Hong Kong, Convergence or Divergence?: The 2014 Retirement Package Bill Protest and Macao's Governance Crisis' (2017) 57(3) *Asian Survey* 504–527.

But for pre-2021 Hong Kong, with pan-democrats typically occupying 35% of the legislative seats in Hong Kong – and 55%–65% of the general public in support of them – the HKSAR government's performance was subject to intense scrutiny in the legislative chambers. Given that these pan-democrat lawmakers were constitutionally disempowered from introducing any significant bills, and they lacked the numbers to block legislative bills for which the pro-Beijing coalition was in agreement, coordinated filibustering became the common tactic used by the pan-democrats to delay the passage of legislative bills they disagreed with.[264] Notably in 2012 when the Hong Kong government tried to pass a law that banned any legislator who resigned from their legislative seat from contesting any by-election held within six months to fill that vacancy, opposition lawmakers filibustered by proposing a staggering 1306 amendments to the legislative bill and the legislative debate on this bill alone dragged on for seven days.[265] But now, with the institution of the "patriots-only" legislature and the decimation of the political opposition in Hong Kong after 2021, lawmaking in Hong Kong has become "smooth sailing" for the HKSAR government. Lawmakers are now reminded to be "cautious" when criticising the government and Beijing directly evaluates the lawmakers' performance based on their public engagement and publicly-made constructive suggestions on policies.[266] Notably, Hong Kong's Safeguarding National Security Ordinance was passed unanimously in 2024 after a swift 12-day legislative debate.[267] From the start of the public consultation to the passage of the law, the entire process took less than 50 days – which makes it the fastest Bill passed in the history of the HKSAR.[268] In fact, since the electoral overhaul of 2021, the first and only time a government bill failed to get the Legislative Council's green light was when the lawmakers in 2025 overwhelmingly vetoed a registration of same-sex partnership bill, which was intended to give same-sex

264 See Eric Chan, 'The Legislative Council of Hong Kong' in Po Jen Yap and Rehan Abeyratne (eds), *Routledge Handbook of Asian Parliaments* (Routledge 2023) 167–168.

265 Eric Chan, 'The Legislative Council of Hong Kong' in Po Jen Yap and Rehan Abeyratne (eds), *Routledge Handbook of Asian Parliaments* (Routledge 2023) 167.

266 Willa Wu, Edith Lin and Natalie Wong, 'Is Hong Kong's Legislature Becoming too Timid, too Tame? A Year in Review' *SCMP* (13 August 2025) <www.scmp.com/news/hong-kong/politics/article/3321636/hong-kongs-legislature-becoming-too-timid-too-tame-year-review> last accessed 3 January 2026.

267 For a full and detailed account of the legislative process of Hong Kong's Article 23 legislation, see Mercedes Hutton, 'Timeline: Hong Kong's New Security Law – From Public Consultation to Passage in 48 Days, after "27 Years" in the Making' *HKFP* (23 March 2024) <https://hongkongfp.com/2024/03/23/a-timeline-of-hong-kongs-new-security-law-from-public-consultation-to-passage-in-48-days-after-27-years-in-the-making/> last accessed 3 January 2026; also see '香港立法會三讀通過《基本法》23條立法 Hong Kong LegCo Passes Article 23 Legislation after Three Readings' *端傳媒 Initium Media* (19 March 2024) <https://theinitium.com/zh-Hans/article/20240319-whatsnew-hongkong-basic-law-article-23> last accessed 3 January 2026.

268 See Chapter 4 for a full discussion of this law.

couples legally married overseas limited rights concerning their partners' medical and funeral arrangements.[269]

Conclusion

China never wanted a strong ruling party to take root or a powerful CE to emerge in Hong Kong and Macau. A ruling party or a CE with mass public or elite support in the Regions would be more effective in resisting control from the Central Authorities[270] – a predicament Beijing would avoid at all costs. This is why the CEs of both Regions are prohibited from being members of any political parties.[271] The Central Government's strategy – through its Liaison Offices in Hong Kong and Macau – was to always divide power among its own allies, and to support and coordinate amongst the pro-China camp.[272] This in turn allows Beijing to play the kingmaker for all crucial personnel and policy decisions.

Moreover, with universal suffrage constituting part of the legislative seats in Hong Kong and Macau, Beijing had to ensure that the pro-Beijing parties in both cities were not electorally excluded by the masses. Therefore, upon the establishment of both SARs, proportional representation was used – instead of the first-past-the-post system – to constitute these seats. Alongside these freely elected seats, both Hong Kong and Macau also retained sectoral representation (known as FCs in Hong Kong and Indirect Seats in Macau) in the legislature, which allowed for pro-Beijing businesses and associations to directly impact lawmaking. In this way, the coalition of pro-Beijing parties and politicians always occupied a majority of legislative seats in both SARs.

Despite the similar political set-up in both Macau and Hong Kong upon establishment, Beijing's deliberate fragmentation of political power led to legislative gridlock in Hong Kong (prior to the electoral overhaul of 2021), while the Macau CEs' legislative agenda has proceeded largely without significant opposition.[273]

269 Willa Wu and Edith Lin, 'Hong Kong Lawmakers Vote Down Bill Recognising Same-Sex Partnerships' *SCMP* (11 September 2025) <www.scmp.com/news/hong-kong/politics/article/3325049/hong-kong-lawmakers-vote-down-bill-recognising-same-sex-partnerships> last accessed 3 January 2026.

270 Ngok Ma, 'Party Underdevelopment in Hong Kong: Hybrid Constraints and Value Changes' (2018) 58(3) *Asian Survey* 416, 419.

271 Chief Executive Election Ordinance (Hong Kong), s 31; Law on Chief Executive Election (Macau), art 36(3).

272 See Eliza W. Y. Lee, 'United Front, Clientelism, and Indirect Rule: Theorizing the Role of the "Liaison Office" in Hong Kong' (2020) 29 *Journal of Contemporary China* 763; Bill Chou, 'Local Autonomy in Action: Beijing's Hong Kong and Macau Policies' (2013) 42(3) *Journal of Current Chinese Affairs* 29, 33.

273 Ying-ho Kwong, 'Ruling Coalition Reconstruction under Macao's Hybrid Regime' (2017) 17(3) *The China Review* 111, 131.

What explains this divergence in Macau and Hong Kong? Pre-2021, 55%–65 % of the Hong Kong electorate typically voted for the pro-democracy camp.[274] With the inclusion of the FC legislators, the pro-democracy lawmakers may be outnumbered in the Hong Kong Legislative Council, but they still formed a sizable minority – typically 35% – in the legislature that could check or disrupt the government's legislative agenda. With the expansion of "universal suffrage" GC seats in the 2012 Legislative Council election, pro-democracy GC lawmakers could even win seats under the PR system with fewer votes. Political moderation became less necessary as even moderate pro-democracy lawmakers realised by 2015 that filibustering and the pursuit of a more radical political platform were a vote-winning strategy, for such messaging and theatrics drew out their invigorated electoral base.[275] It is therefore unsurprising that the rise of nativism in local politics coincided with the escalating confrontations and tensions within the fragmented legislature and the polarised society at large.

To compound the pre-2021 governance crisis for Beijing in Hong Kong, the CEs of Hong Kong were generally unpopular. According to surveys conducted by the Hong Kong Public Opinion Research Institute – an independent pollster – the approval ratings for CE Leung Chun-ying ranged between 37 and 53 out of 100 (over his term of office from July 2012 to June 2017), and the approval ratings for CE Carrie Lam ranged between 19 and 61 out of 100 (over her term of office from July 2017 to June 2022).[276] This contrasted sharply with the generally satisfactory job approval ratings of the Macau CEs.[277]

Unlike Hong Kong, the pro-democracy groups in Macau do not enjoy strong electoral appeal. Macau has a tiny population (688,300 by the end of December 2024)[278] compared to Hong Kong's 7,524,100 by mid-2024,[279] and 43.8% of the Macau population were born in the Mainland.[280] Macau is not an international

274 Ngok Ma, 'Party Underdevelopment in Hong Kong: Hybrid Constraints and Value Changes' (2018) 58(3) *Asian Survey* 416, 422.

275 Ngok Ma, 'From Executive Dominance to Fragmented Authority: An Institutional and Political Analysis' in Brian C. H. Fong and Tai-Lok Lui (eds), *Hong Kong 20 Years after the Handover: Emerging Social and Institutional Fractures After 1997* (Palgrave Macmillan 2018) 39.

276 'Comparison between Ratings of Chris Patten, Tung Chee-hwa, Donald Tsang Yam-kuen, Leung Chun-ying, Carrie Lam and John Lee' *PORI* (20 December 2024) <www.pori.hk/research-result/a-rating-combined> last accessed 4 January 2026.

277 The approval ratings for the first CE Edmund Ho Hau Wah were 6.68 (out of 10) according to the survey conducted by the "One Country, Two Systems" Research Centre at Macau Polytechnic University in 2009. <https://my.org.mo/zh_tw/news_before_2020_detail/article/kzzavecx.html> last accessed 3 January 2026. The approval rating of the 2nd CE Fernando Chui Sai On was 58.41 (out of 100) according to the survey conducted between 2009 and 2018 by Hong Kong Public Opinion Research Institute, an independent institution. <www.pori.hk/research-result/chui-sai-on-rating> last accessed 3 January 2026.

278 Macau Yearbook 2025. <https://yearbook.gcs.gov.mo/books?1&lang=en> last accessed 3 January 2026.

279 Hong Kong Yearbook 2024. <www.yearbook.gov.hk/2024/en/> last accessed 3 January 2026.

280 Macau Yearbook 2025. <https://yearbook.gcs.gov.mo/books?1&lang=en> last accessed 3 January 2026.

financial centre like Hong Kong, and the former's economy is more closely integrated with the Mainland.[281] The political orientation of the Macau residents is more homogeneously conservative;[282] civil society groups in Macau are weak,[283] and people prefer to focus on livelihood issues,[284] which in tandem impact the ability of the pro-democracy camp to raise funds to contest and win elections.

Before Beijing foisted a bespoke National Security Law on Hong Kong in 2020, pro-democracy civil society and bottom-up protests flourished in Hong Kong with a groundswell of local support. The Hong Kong youths used to be passionate about politics, and they drove many bottom-up initiatives on democracy and civil liberties. Notably, in 2012, the Hong Kong government was forced to shelve the introduction of a national education curriculum in primary and secondary schools after a mass protest led by student activists besieged the Government Headquarters for days.[285] Civil society and social movements in Macau, on the other hand, lack manpower and funding[286] because the Macau people are more consensus-driven and prefer to focus on livelihood issues.[287] Unlike Hong Kong, national education and patriotism had always been a compulsory component of Macau's school curriculum.[288] All these variables in Macau coalesced into a general public apathy about electing pro-democracy lawmakers. As discussed previously, there have never been more than three pro-democracy lawmakers in Macau, and they simply did not have the numbers in the legislature to unilaterally forestall the MASAR government's agenda.

This is not to say there were no protests in Macau. There were, but they were simply not of the magnitude we saw in pre-2020 Hong Kong. The largest protest in Macau occurred in 2014 when 20,000 demonstrators rallied against the Macau government's attempt to pass an exorbitant retirement package for its CE and principal officials.[289] Typically, protests in Macau focus on labour and employment

281 Richard Louis Edmonds, 'Land Use in Macau: Changes between 1973 and 1983' (1986) 3(1) *Land Use Policy* 47–63; Bill K. P. Chou, 'Interest Group Politics in Macau after Handover' (2005) 14(43) *Journal of Contemporary China* 191, 194.

282 Eilo Yu Wing-yat and Natalie Chin Ka-man, 'The Political Opposition and Democracy in Macao: Revolutionaries or Loyalists' (2012) 46 *Government and Opposition* 97, 102.

283 Shiu-Hing Lo, 'Consultative Governance, Legitimacy Problem and Democracy Deficit in Macau' (2011) 7 *Academic Journal of One Country Two Systems* 90, 94.

284 C. S. Bryan Ho, 'Political Culture, Social Movements, and Governability in Macao' (2011) 38(2) *Asian Affairs: An American Review* 59, 62.

285 Wai-Chung Ho, 'The Influence of Politics in Hong Kong's Education System 23 Years after Its Handover from the United Kingdom to China' (2020) 19(2) *International Education Journal: Comparative Perspectives* 36, 45.

286 Victor Zheng and others, 'Young People's Sense of Fairness and Social Action: A Survey Analysis of Taiwan, Hong Kong, and Macao' (2020) 5(3) *Asian Journal of Comparative Politics* 270–287.

287 C. S. Bryan Ho, 'Political Culture, Social Movements, and Governability in Macao' (2011) 38(2) *Asian Affairs: An American Review* 59, 62.

288 Shiu-Hing Lo, *Casino Capitalism, Society and Politics in China's Macau* (Cambridge Scholars Publishing 2020) 238–239.

289 Zhongxuan Lin, 'Contextualized Emotional Mobilization: Playful Protests and Resentful Protest in Macau in the Internet Age' in Meng U Ieong (ed), *Macau 20 Years after the Handover: Changes*

issues.[290] In contrast, half a million people in Hong Kong rallied in 2003 against the National Security bill; the financial district was partially blockaded for 79 days during the Occupy Central movement in 2014 over the political stalemate on democratic reform; and protests rocked Hong Kong for months in 2019 over the extradition bill, which saw at one point close to two million people taking to the streets, public facilities vandalised, and the legislature ransacked. In all these watershed events in Hong Kong, the pro-democracy lawmakers featured front and centre in the rallies, rousing the crowd and disrupting legislative proceedings to reflect public sentiments.

By 2020, Beijing's patience with Hong Kong ran out. First, the Central Authorities foisted the National Security Law on Hong Kong.[291] But this was not enough to appease Beijing; it had to further "improve"[292] the Hong Kong electoral system in 2021 and terminate the constant filibuster in the legislature and frequent anti-China mobilisation by opposition lawmakers once and for all. The "universal suffrage" GC seats were slashed, the EC seats were reinstituted, and only "patriots" as certified by the Hong Kong SAR government could run for office. Beijing defended this new model as a harbinger of a new era of "democracy with Hong Kong characteristics",[293] so that only those with a "correct understanding"[294] of the Basic Law can assume political office.

The local Hong Kong population was less impressed. The 2021 Legislative Council Election saw a record low turnout with only 30.2%[295] of the electorate casting their votes for this patriots-only legislature. While the 2025 election saw a slight increase in the turnout rate with 31.9% of the registered voters having voted, the actual total number of voters declined by 2.4% and the total number of invalid votes cast also increased by 1% in 2025 compared to 2021.[296]

and Challenges under "One Country, Two Systems" (Routledge 2020) 68–69; Meng U Ieong, 'Macao and Hong Kong, Convergence or Divergence?: The 2014 Retirement Package Bill Protest and Macao's Governance Crisis' (2017) 57(3) *Asian Survey* 504–527.

290 Lio Chi Fai and Meng U Ieong, 'Labour Protests in Macau (2000–2017)' in Meng U Ieong (ed), *Macau 20 Years after the Handover: Changes and Challenges under "One Country, Two Systems"* (Routledge 2020) 75–89.

291 Law of the People's Republic of China on Safeguarding National Security in the HKSAR (30 June 2020).

292 Decision of the National People's Congress on Improving the Electoral System of the HKSAR (Adopted at the Fourth Session of the 13th National People's Congress on 11 March 2021).

293 State Council Information Office White Paper, *Hong Kong Democratic Progress Under the Framework of One Country Two Systems* (December 2021).

294 '新华时评：坚决落实"爱国者治港"确保"一国两制"行稳致远 Xinhua Commentary: "Patriots Rule Hong Kong" to Ensure "One Country, Two Systems" Stable and Far-Reaching' *新华网 Xinhuanet* (31 January 2021) <www.xinhuanet.com/politics/2021-01/31/c_1127047646.htm> last accessed 3 January 2026.

295 Jeffie Lam, '5 Takeaways (and 1 surprise) from the Hong Kong Legislative Council Election 2021: An Unheeded Call, a Clean Sweep and Rising Forces' *SCMP* (20 December 2021) <www.scmp.com/news/hong-kong/politics/article/3160392/5-takeaways-and-1-surprise-hong-kong-legislative-council> last accessed 3 January 2026.

296 Edith Lin, 'Deadly Tai Po Blaze Affected Hong Kong Legco Election Voter Turnout, Minister Says' *SCMP* (21 December 2025) <www.scmp.com/news/hong-kong/politics/article/3337216/deadly-tai-po-blaze-affected-hong-kong-legco-election-voter-turnout-minister-says> last accessed 3 January 2026.

Beijing left Macau alone. But not to be outshone by its Hong Kong counterpart, the Macau government of its own accord barred all pro-democracy candidates from contesting its 2021 Legislative Assembly election and even disqualified all centrist candidates in the 2025 election.[297] As it stands, only pro-Beijing politicians are left in the Hong Kong and Macau legislatures. The "arrested democratisation"[298] of Hong Kong and Macau is now complete and political homogeneity is assured.

References

Baum, Richard, 'Democracy Deformed: Hong Kong's 1998 Legislative Elections – and Beyond' (2000) 162 *The China Quarterly* 439.

Beja, Jean-Philippe, Fu Hualing and Eva Pils (eds), *Liu Xiaobo, Charter 08 and the Challenges of Political Reform in China* (Hong Kong, Hong Kong University Press 2012).

Buhi, Jason, *Global Constitutional Narratives of Autonomous Regions: The Constitutional History of Macau* (Oxford, Routledge 2021).

Cardinal, Paulo, 'Macau: Transformation of an Historic Autonomy' in Yash Ghai and Sophia Woodman (eds), *Practising Self-Government: A Comparative Study of Autonomous Regions* (Cambridge, Cambridge University Press 2013) 383.

Cardinal, Paulo and Luís Pessanha, 'Macau' in David S. Law and others (eds), *Oxford Handbook of Constitutional Law in Asia* (Oxford, Oxford University Press forthcoming).

Carey, John M, 'Electoral Formula and Fragmentation in Hong Kong' (2017) 17 *Journal of East Asian Studies* 215.

Chan, Chan U 陳震宇, '比例代表制與澳門立法機關的直接選舉 Proportional Representation and the Direct Election of the Legislature of Macau' (2021) 4 *澳門研究 Journal of Macau Studies* 23.

Chan, Eric, 'The Legislative Council of Hong Kong' in Po Jen Yap and Rehan Abeyratne (eds), *Routledge Handbook of Asian Parliaments* (Oxford, Routledge 2023) 158.

Chang, Hu 常滸, '澳門特區行政法規制定權限爭議及其解決 The Dispute over the Administrative Regulation-Making Power in the Macau SAR and the Resolution' (2010) 9 *"一國兩制"研究 Journal of "One Country Two Systems" Studies* 44.

Chen, Jie 陈杰, '中葡两国关于澳门回归时间问题的外交博弈及其历史经验 The Diplomatic Bargain between China and Portugal over the Time of Macao's Handover and Its Historical Experience' (2022) 1 *统一战线学研究 Journal of United Frontier Science* 28.

Chiba, Daina, Meng U Ieong, and Jiying Jiang, 'Legislative Politics under "One Country, Two Systems": Evidence from Macau, 2013–2021' (2025) 264 *The China Quarterly* 1071.

Chou, Bill K P, 'Interest Group Politics in Macau after Handover' (2005) 14(43) *Journal of Contemporary China* 191.

297 '澳门立法会选举：政府大力动员，投票人数创新高，白票废票破万 Macau Legislative Assembly Election: Government Mobilises Heavily, Voter Turnout Hits Record High, Over 10,000 Blank and Invalid Ballots Cast' *BBC* (15 September 2025) <www.bbc.com/zhongwen/articles/cq657nnj29vo/simp> last accessed 3 January 2026.

298 Ngok Ma, 'Party Underdevelopment in Hong Kong: Hybrid Constraints and Value Changes' (2018) 58(3) *Asian Survey* 416, 416.

Chou, Bill K P, 'Local Autonomy in Action: Beijing's Hong Kong and Macau Policies' (2013) 42(3) *Journal of Current Chinese Affairs* 29.

Chou, Bill K P, 'Politics and Social Organisations in Macao: A Historical Institutionalist Analysis' (2015) 12(1) *China: An International Journal* 22.

Edmonds, Richard Louis, 'Land Use in Macau: Changes between 1973 and 1983' (1986) 3(1) *Land Use Policy* 47.

Edmonds, Richard Louis and Herbert S Yee, 'Macau: From Portuguese Autonomous Territory to Chinese Special Administrative Region' (1999) 160 *The China Quarterly* 801.

Fong, Brian C H, 'Executive-Legislative Disconnection in the HKSAR: Uneasy Partnership between Chief Executives and Pro-Government Parties, 1997–2016' in Brian C H Fong and Tai-Lok Lui (eds), *Hong Kong 20 Years after the Handover: Emerging Social and Institutional Fractures after 1997* (Cham, Palgrave Macmillan 2018) 45.

Fung, Wing K, 'The Last Legislative Election of Hong Kong under British Rule, 1995' (1996) 15(1) *Electoral Studies* 119.

Ghai, Yash, *Hong Kong's New Constitutional Order: The Resumption of Chinese Sovereignty and the Basic Law* (2nd edn, Hong Kong, Hong Kong University Press 1999).

Hao, Yufan, Li Sheng and Guanjin Pan, *Political Economy of Macao since 1999: The Dilemma of Success* (Singapore, Palgrave Macmillan 2017).

He, Zhihui 何志辉, *澳门法制史新编 A New Study on the Legal History of Macau* (Beijing, 社会科学文献出版社 Social Sciences Academic Press 2019).

Ho, C S Bryan, 'Political Culture, Social Movements, and Governability in Macao' (2011) 38(2) *Asian Affairs: An American Review* 59.

Ho, Wai-Chung, 'The Influence of Politics in Hong Kong's Education System 23 Years after Its Handover from the United Kingdom to China' (2020) 19(2) *International Education Journal: Comparative Perspectives* 36.

Holbig, Heike, 'Be Water, My Friend: Hong Kong's 2019 Anti-Extradition Protests' (2020) 50(4) *International Journal of Sociology* 325.

Hook, Brian, 'The Government of Hong Kong: Change within Tradition' (1983) 95 *The China Quarterly* 491.

Hung, Chung Fun Steven, 'Reviewing and Evaluating the Direct Elections to the Legislative Council and the Transformation of Political Parties in Hong Kong, 1991–2016' (2016) 13(8) *Journal of US-China Public Administration* 499.

Ieong, Meng U, 'Macao and Hong Kong, Convergence or Divergence?: The 2014 Retirement Package Bill Protest and Macao's Governance Crisis' (2017) 57(3) *Asian Survey* 504.

Jang, Jinhyeok, 'Parliamentary Representation in the Macau Special Administrative Region: A Quantitative Analysis of Roll Call Voting Behavior in the 5th Legislative Assembly, 2013–2017' (2018) 4(2) *Contemporary Chinese Political Economy and Strategic Relations: An International Journal* 513.

Kwong, Ying-Ho, 'Ruling Coalition Reconstruction under Macao's Hybrid Regime' (2017) 17(3) *The China Review* 111.

Lee, Eliza W Y, 'United Front, Clientelism, and Indirect Rule: Theorizing the Role of the "Liaison Office" in Hong Kong' (2020) 29 *Journal of Contemporary China* 763.

Lei, Jingxuan 雷競璇 and Guoxiang Shen 沈國祥, *香港選舉資料匯編：1982年–1994年 Compendium of Hong Kong Election Materials: From 1982 to 1994* (Hong Kong, 香港中文大學香港亞太研究所 Hong Kong Institute of Asia-Pacific Studies, CUHK 1995).

Lei, Jingxuan 雷競璇 and Guoxiang Shen 沈國祥, *香港選舉資料匯編：1995年 Compendium of Hong Kong Election Materials: 1995* (Hong Kong, 香港中文大學香港亞太研究所 Hong Kong Institute of Asia-Pacific Studies, CUHK 1996).

Li, Qingwei 李清偉, '澳門特別行政區行政主導體制的法理基礎 Juridical Basis of the Executive-Led System of the Macau Special Administrative Region' (2014) 19 *"一國兩制"研究 Journal of "One Country Two Systems" Studies* 25.

Lin, Zhongxuan, 'Contextualized Emotional Mobilization: Playful Protests and Resentful Protest in Macau in the Internet Age' in Meng U Ieong (ed), *Macau 20 Years after the Handover: Changes and Challenges under "One Country, Two Systems"* (Oxford, Routledge 2020) 57.

Lio, Chi Fai and Meng U Ieong, 'Labour Protests in Macau (2000–2017)' in Meng U Ieong (ed), *Macau 20 Years after the Handover: Changes and Challenges under "One Country, Two Systems"* (Oxford, Routledge 2020) 75.

Lo, Shiu-Hing, *Political Development in Macau* (Hong Kong, The Chinese University of Hong Kong Press 1995).

Lo, Shiu-Hing, *Political Change in Macao* (Oxford, Routledge 2009).

Lo, Shiu-Hing, 'Consultative Governance, Legitimacy Problem and Democracy Deficit in Macau' (2011) 7 *Academic Journal of One Country Two Systems* 90.

Lo, Shiu-Hing, *Casino Capitalism, Society and Politics in China's Macau* (Newcastle, Cambridge Scholars Publishing 2020).

Lo, Shiu-Hing and Yu Wing-Yat, 'The Politics of Electoral Reform in Hong Kong' (2001) 39(2) *Commonwealth & Comparative Politics* 98.

Lo, Shiu-Hing and Eric King-Man Chong, 'Casino Interests, Fujian Tongxianghui and Electoral Politics in Macao' (2016) 46 *Journal of Contemporary Asia* 286.

Lou, Shenghua 婁勝華, '競爭性與認受性辨析：以第四任行政長官選舉為中心 Debate about Competitiveness and Recognition – Focus on the Election of the Fourth Chief Executive' (2014) 22 *"一國兩制"研究 Journal of "One Country Two Systems" Studies* 21.

Lou, Shenghua 婁勝華 and Chan U Chan 陳震宇, *澳門行政 Administration of Macau* (Macau, 三聯書店和澳門基金會 Joint Publishing HK and Macau Foundation 2013).

Ma, Ngok, 'Party Underdevelopment in Hong Kong: Hybrid Constraints and Value Changes' (2018) 58(3) *Asian Survey* 416.

Ma, Ngok, 'From Executive Dominance to Fragmented Authority: An Institutional and Political Analysis' in Brian C H Fong and Tai-Lok Lui (eds), *Hong Kong 20 Years after the Handover: Emerging Social and Institutional Fractures after 1997* (Cham, Palgrave Macmillan 2018) 21.

Miners, Norman, 'The Transformation of the Hong Kong Legislative Council 1970–1994: From Consensus to Confrontation' (1994) 16(2) *Asian Journal of Public Administration* 224.

Rosa, Avelino, '澳門市政廳的前途 The Future of Macau Municipal Council' (1997) 3 *澳門公共行政雜誌 Macau Public Administration Journal* 967.

Scott, Ian and Joan Y H Leung, 'Dysfunctional Elections and the Political System in Hong Kong' (2004) 12(2) *Asian Journal of Political Science* 1.

Tang, Kaijian 湯開建, '澳門議事會的起源、發展與衰落 The Origin, Development and Decline of Macau Senate' (2016) 2 *澳門研究 Journal of Macau Studies* 81.

Wang, Chao, 'Hong Kong in the Age of the PRC's Alienation from the International System: In Search of Normative Consensus' (2024) 13(1) *Global Constitutionalism* 53.

Wang, Juxin 王巨新 and Xin Wang 王欣, *明清澳门涉外法律研究 A Research on Foreign-Related Laws in Macao of the Ming and Early Qing Dynasties* (Beijing, 社会科学文献出版社 Social Sciences Academic Press 2010).

Wang, Shuwen 王叔文 (ed), *香港特别行政区基本法导论 Introduction to the Basic Law of the Hong Kong Special Administrative Region* (2nd edn, Beijing, 法律出版社和三联书店 Law Press China and Joint Publishing HK 2009).

Wang, Yu 王禹 and Ran Shen 沈然, *澳门特别行政区立法会产生办法研究 A Study on the Method for the Formation of the Legislative Assembly of the Macau Special Administrative Region* (Beijing, 社会科学文献出版社和澳门基金会 Social Sciences Academic Press and Macau Foundation 2017).

Xiao, Weiyun 肖蔚云, *论香港基本法 On the Hong Kong Basic Law* (Beijing, 北京大学出版社 Peking University Press 2003).

Ye, Tiansheng 葉天生, *香港選舉資料匯編：1996年-2000年 Compendium of Hong Kong Election Materials: 1996–2000* (Hong Kong, 香港中文大學香港亞太研究所 Hong Kong Institute of Asia-Pacific Studies, CUHK 2001).

Yip, Paul S F and Christopher J Lloyd, 'Statistical Analysis of the 1995 Hong Kong Legislative Council Election Results' (1996) 18(1) *Asian Journal of Public Administration* 119.

Young, Simon N M and Anthony Law, 'Privileged to Vote: Inequalities and Anomalies of the FC System' in Christine Loh (ed), *Functional Constituencies: A Unique Feature of the Hong Kong Legislative Council* (Hong Kong, Hong Kong University Press 2006) 59.

Yu, Eilo Wing-Yat and Natalie Chin Ka-Man, 'The Political Opposition and Democracy in Macao: Revolutionaries or Loyalists' (2012) 46 *Government and Opposition* 97.

Zhai, Xiaobo, 'Macao's Constitutional Founding' in Kevin Y L Tan and Michael Ng (eds), *Constitutional Founding in Northeast Asia* (Oxford, Hart 2022) 73.

Zhang, Lianxing 張連興, *香港二十八總督 Hong Kong's 28 Governors* (2nd edn, Hong Kong, 三聯書店 Joint Publishing HK 2022).

Zheng, Jinyao 鄭錦耀, '各行政規章的位階及各自的規範範圍研究 Study on the Hierarchy of Administrative Rules and Their Respective Regulatory Scope' (2019) 42 *"一國兩制"研究 Journal of "One Country Two Systems" Studies* 72.

Zheng, Victor and others, 'Young People's Sense of Fairness and Social Action: A Survey Analysis of Taiwan, Hong Kong, and Macao' (2020) 5(3) *Asian Journal of Comparative Politics* 270.

3

JUDICIARIES OF HONG KONG AND MACAU

Introduction

At this time of writing, Hong Kong has a respected judiciary, especially its Court of Final Appeal. Although the city's reputation for respecting human rights took a beating after Beijing imposed a National Security Law in 2020 and instituted a "patriots-only" legislature in 2021, the territory in 2025 is still ranked 24th in the world according to the leading global rule of law index, ahead of the United States at 27th and the rest of the People's Republic of China (PRC) at 92nd.[1] Macau, on the other hand, has always been unranked and presumably lumped with the rest of the PRC.

While both Special Administrative Regions (SARs) are conferred with "independent judicial power"[2], and Macau's Basic Law (MABL) codifies even *more* constitutional rights for its people than its Hong Kong counterpart,[3] in practice the Macau Court of Final Appeal (MACFA) has significantly under-performed on rights-protection. Notably, the Hong Kong Court of Final Appeal (HKCFA) decisively exercised the powers of constitutional review and nullified legislation in its very first constitutional decision.[4] And to date, the HKCFA has declared laws unconstitutional on 27 occasions.[5] Notably, in 2023, the HKCFA unanimously ruled that it was unconstitutional for the government to require transgender persons to undergo full sex-reassignment surgery before they can alter their gender

1 WJP Rule of Law Index <https://worldjusticeproject.org/rule-of-law-index/global> last accessed 3 January 2026.

2 MABL, art 2; HKBL, art 2.

3 See MABL, Ch 3; HKBL, Ch 3. See also the comparisons in Chapter 1 of this book.

4 *Ng Ka Ling v Director of Immigration* (1999) 2 HKCFAR 4.

5 See Appendix 1 of this chapter.

DOI: 10.4324/9781003683872-3

markers on the government-issued identity cards,[6] thereby allowing the affected transgender persons to legally access public bathrooms that align with their gender identity. Later in that year, the Court declared that the local government's *failure* to provide an alternative legal framework for protecting the core rights of same-sex partnerships was unconstitutional, and the HKCFA gave the government until 2025 to enact requisite remedial legislation.[7] In contrast, the MACFA has only declared laws unconstitutional in three cases,[8] none since 2011, and in all three cases, the unconstitutional laws were only inapplicable vis-à-vis the successful claimants but remain operative otherwise.

Eric Ip in an important monograph published in April 2019 argued that the HKCFA's power and independence were secured by the political fragmentation within the local legislature, a sizable elected pro-democracy camp in opposition, and a rambunctious civil society, which collectively hampered the Hong Kong government's ability to effectively rein in the courts or its people.[9] But civil society has been decimated after the PRC government foisted a National Security Law on Hong Kong in 2020, and political opposition has been neutralised with the imposition of a "patriots-only" legislature in 2021. Oddly, despite these seismic political shifts, the HKCFA's post-2020 constitutional jurisprudence remains sufficiently distinct from its Macau counterpart, especially on LGBT rights.

In this chapter, we identify two additional variables still *extant* in Hong Kong that explain the dissimilar judicial records of both courts on constitutional review and rights-protection: (1) different appointment systems, backgrounds, and compositions of their top courts; and (2) divergent economic dynamics of the two cities.

Both BLs provide that their judges shall be chosen by an independent judicial commission,[10] but Macau's "Independent" Judicial Officers Nomination Commission (推薦法官的獨立委員會) is chaired by a local high-ranking pro-Beijing lawmaker[11] and practically the entire Commission is stacked with members with explicit pro-Beijing political affiliations, with very few members possessing legal training.[12] Notably, Macau's Chief Justice Sam Hou Fai – the SAR's first

6 *Q and Tse Henry Edward v Commissioner of Registration* (2023) 26 HKCFAR 25.

7 *Sham Tsz Kit v Secretary for Justice* (2023) 26 HKCFAR 385.

8 See Appendix 2 of this chapter.

9 Eric Ip, *Hybrid Constitutionalism: The Politics of Constitutional Review in the Chinese Special Administrative Regions* (CUP 2019).

10 HKBL, art 88; MABL, art 87.

11 Since the handover in 1999, Macau's Commission has been chaired by Lau Cheok Va, who concurrently served as vice president (1999–2009) and president (2009–2013) of the Macau Legislative Assembly, and he was a Macau delegate to the 10th and 11th National People's Congress (2003–2013).

12 Unlike Hong Kong, there have been only five legally trained persons serving on the Commission since the handover on 20 December 1999. Mr. Sam Hou Fai (岑浩輝), the first Chief Justice of the MACFA, was a member from December 1999 to August 2024. Philip Xavier (許輝年), a lawyer, served as a member of the Commission from 1999 to 2025 and he was a Macau delegate to the 10th National People's Congress (2003–2008). Mr. Wang Yu (王禹), a professor of public law at

Chief Justice – received Beijing's blessing to resign in August 2024 and ran unopposed to become the current Chief Executive (CE),[13] thereby demonstrating the Central Government's full confidence in his political loyalty. Conversely, Hong Kong's Judicial Officers Recommendation Commission (JORC) is chaired by its non-partisan Chief Justice and the Commission is dominated by serving appellate judges and lawyers. As we will explore in this chapter, this crucial difference in judicial appointment directly impacts the composition of the bench and results in judges of different backgrounds being appointed to the territories' highest courts.

Second, Hong Kong is an international financial hub, unlike Macau. As of 2025, Hong Kong is the world's third leading global financial centre.[14] With capital controls firmly in place within Mainland China, Hong Kong's Stock Exchange (SE) – with its advanced infrastructure and access to international capital – is the gateway through which Chinese state-owned enterprises, state-supported transnational corporations, and private enterprises raise capital to enter global markets.[15] The Hong Kong SE is dominated by the listing of red chip companies (PRC government-controlled companies incorporated outside China, e.g. China Mobile) and PRC government-controlled H-share companies (PRC companies incorporated in Mainland China, e.g. Bank of China, China Construction Bank, Ping An Insurance). Most overseas initial public offerings (IPOs) of Chinese private behemoths, e.g. Tencent and Xiaomi are also transacted in Hong Kong.[16] All these PRC companies primarily do business outside Hong Kong, but they all use the reputable Hong Kong SE to raise capital internationally, constituting more than 80% of the market capitalisation on the Hong Kong SE in 2024.[17]

China's connection to the global economy hinges on Hong Kong, which maintains a "semi-porous and heavily regulated economic border"[18] with Mainland China but a free financial border with the rest of the world. In this way, China gets the best of both worlds: capping capital flight *from* the Mainland, while attracting *foreign* capital through Hong Kong. It is noteworthy that 68.1% of Mainland

the University of Macau, has served as a member of the Commission since 2021. Chief Justice Song Man Lei (宋敏莉) was appointed to the Commission in 2025 in place of Mr. Sam Hou Fai. Mr. António José Dias Azedo, a lawyer of Portuguese descent, was appointed in 2025 in place of Philip Xavier.

13 'Sam Hou-fai elected as next Macau leader; Beijing lauds him as unifier and reformer' *SCMP* (13 Oct 2024) <www.scmp.com/news/hong-kong/politics/article/3282151/voting-starts-macau-leadership-election-ex-judge-sam-hou-fai-runs-uncontested> last accessed 4 January 2026.

14 'The Global Financial Centres Index 38' (September 2025) <www.longfinance.net/media/documents/GFCI_38_Report_2025.09.25_v1.0.pdf> last accessed 3 January 2026.

15 Yan-leung Cheung, Yuk-shing Cheng, and Chi-keung Woo, *Hong Kong's Global Financial Centre and China's Development: Changing Roles and Future Prospects* (Routledge 2017) 4–7.

16 Chris Bartoli, Ivy Wong, and Nick O'Donnell, 'The Battle for Listings' (2019) 6 *International Financial Law Review* 40, 41.

17 The Hong Kong Trade Development Council, *Economic and Trade Information on Hong Kong* <https://research.hktdc.com/en/article/MzIwNjkzNTY5> last accessed 3 January 2026.

18 Ho-fung Hung, *City on the Edge: Hong Kong under Chinese Rule* (CUP 2022) 51.

China's inward Foreign Direct Investments (FDI) originated from Hong Kong in 2024.[19] Furthermore, by expanding the circulation of "offshore" Renminbi (RMB) in Hong Kong, China succeeded in getting the International Monetary Fund to include the RMB in its Special Drawing Rights currency basket (alongside the freely convertible US dollar, UK pound sterling, Euro, Japanese yen) in 2016, while keeping the PRC currency capital account largely closed to the world.[20] "Free market constitutionalism"[21] was codified in Hong Kong's Basic Law (HKBL) to serve China's economic interests. With Beijing's tightening grip over Hong Kong since 2014,[22] and especially after 2020, the HKCFA is obviously no longer as confrontational as it used to be, especially on national security issues. But so long as the Hong Kong and Central Governments still want the city to remain a top international financial centre attractive to *overseas* financial and human capital, the politicians understand that the rule of law undergirded by an independent judiciary must remain a cornerstone of the city's governance, and they therefore cannot neuter the courts or overrule the HKCFA at every turn. China has other Free Trade Zones too – Shanghai and Shenzhen in particular – but none can replicate Hong Kong's economic success in attracting foreign capital without having an independent judiciary, freedom of information, and internationally recognised separate customs status. Macau shares many of Hong Kong's economic freedoms, but it is not an international financial centre upon which the Central Government can rely for attracting foreign capital; Macau's economy is wholly dependent on Mainland China, and the economic reliance is one-way. This fundamental difference in Hong Kong's political economy in turn provides the HKCFA with some capacity to chart a path less taken from the rest of communist China, especially on LGBT rights.

This chapter begins by examining the historical origins of the courts of Macau and Hong Kong, tracing their development from their colonial days to the establishment of the SARs. Next, we will contrast the judicial appointment, background, and

19 National Bureau of Statistics of China, *2025 China Statistical Yearbook*, section 11–14 (FDI by Country (Region)) <www.stats.gov.cn/sj/ndsj/2025/indexch.htm> last accessed 3 January 2026; 'Hong Kong is China's Financial Gateway to the World' *Forbes* (13 September 2022) <www.forbes.com/sites/hongkong/2021/11/01/hong-kong-is-chinas-financial-gateway-to-the-world/> last accessed 3 January 2026.

20 Ho-fung Hung, *City on the Edge: Hong Kong under Chinese Rule* (CUP 2022) 65–67; Yan-leung Cheung, Yuk-shing Cheng, and Chi-keung Woo, *Hong Kong's Global Financial Centre and China's Development: Changing Roles and Future Prospects* (Routledge 2017) 39–50; 'IMF Adds Chinese Renminbi to Special Drawing Rights Basket' *IMF News* (30 September 2016) <www.imf.org/en/news/articles/2016/09/29/am16-na093016imf-adds-chinese-renminbi-to-special-drawing-rights-basket> last accessed 3 January 2026.

21 Gonzalo Villalta Puig and Eric Ip, *The Freest Market in the World: The Constitutional Logic of Economic Liberty in China's Hong Kong* (Routledge 2023).

22 The Information Office of the State Council 国务院新闻办公室, *《"一国两制"在香港特别行政区的实践》白皮书 White Paper on 'The Practice of "One Country, Two Systems" Policy in the Hong Kong Special Administrative Region'* <https://english.www.gov.cn/archive/white_paper/2014/08/23/content_281474982986578.htm> last accessed 3 January 2026.

composition of their top judges, and underscore how these institutional variables impact the development of constitutional review and rights-protection in Hong Kong and Macau. While the HKCFA has insisted that "the common law approach"[23] must be used to interpret legislation passed by the National People's Congress Standing Committee (NPCSC) for Hong Kong, the MACFA has wholeheartedly transplanted PRC Chinese laws, theories, and practices into its local constitutional jurisprudence. But as this chapter underscores, on core issues of the PRC, especially high-stakes elections, the two top courts converge in upholding their respective local governments' stance. The HKCFA implicitly understands that its ability to generate significant changes in other areas of constitutional law is contingent on its acquiescence to the regime's core interests. And in turn, because the PRC and the Hong Kong governments depend on continued Western investment in the country's only international financial centre without capital controls, they need to uphold business confidence in the city's rule of law, thereby giving some leverage to the HKCFA when it exercises its constitutionally guaranteed "independent judicial power".[24]

Courts in the Colonies

In 1557, the Emperor of China allowed Portuguese sailors and merchants to settle down in Macau in return for the payment of annual leases to China.[25] Despite remaining under Chinese sovereignty and authority, a "system of a mixed jurisdiction" or "duality" evolved and developed in Macau.[26] Both the Chinese and Portuguese authorities had jurisdiction over Macau – Chinese laws and customs applied to the Chinese community whilst Portuguese law applied to the Portuguese community;[27] for disputes arising between Chinese residents and non-Chinese residents, Chinese laws applied.[28]

After Hong Kong became a British colony in 1843, Portugal also tightened its grip on Macau.[29] In 1845, Portugal unilaterally declared that Macau was a free

23 *HKSAR v Lui Sai Yu* (2023) 26 HKCFAR 332 at [45].
24 HKBL, art 2.
25 Victor F. S. Sit, *Macau Through 500 Years: Emergence and Development of an Untypical Chinese City* (Enrich Professional Publishing 2013) 23.
26 Paulo Cardinal, 'Macau: Transformation of an Historic Autonomy' in Yash Ghai and Sophia Woodman (eds), *Practising Self-Government: A Comparative Study of Autonomous Regions* (CUP 2013) 386.
27 Dan Wei, 'Macao's Legal System under Globalisation and Regional Integration: Between Tradition and Evolution' (2014) 9(2) *Frontiers of Law in China* 233, 234.
28 Dan Wei, 'Macao's Legal System under Globalisation and Regional Integration: Between Tradition and Evolution' (2014) 9(2) *Frontiers of Law in China* 233, 234.
29 Paulo Cardinal, 'Macau: Transformation of an Historic Autonomy' in Yash Ghai and Sophia Woodman (eds), *Practising Self-Government: A Comparative Study of Autonomous Regions* (CUP 2013) 386.

port open to commerce from all countries.[30] As discussed in Chapter 2, Portugal formally achieved perpetual occupation and governance of Macau when the Treaty of Friendship and Commerce was signed between Portugal and China in 1887.[31] In 1866, Portugal promulgated the Judicial Statute for the Province of Mozambique, State of India, and the Province of Macau-Timor, which designated these territories as counties (*comarca*) within the Portuguese judicial system and established a court of county in each territory.[32] The court of county was Macau's court of first instance and appeals from this court went up to the court of second instance in Goa, with the possibility of further appeals to the Supreme Court in Lisbon.[33]

After the Sino-Portuguese Joint Declaration was signed in 1987, which established 20 December 1999 as the date of China's resumption of sovereignty, Portugal began reforming Macau's local judiciary to ensure a smooth transition of the judicial system. The Judicial Organisation Law (JOL) (司法組織綱要法) was enacted in 1991. Pursuant to the JOL of 1991, Macau's court system consisted of the courts of first instance, the audit court, and the High Court of Justice.[34] The High Court of Justice was established in 1993 to serve as Macau's apex court until the handover.[35] Additionally, Macau's courts were also vested with the power of judicial review. Article 41(1) of the Organic Statute of Macau provided that Macau's courts would not apply any laws that were in breach of the Portuguese Constitution or the Organic Statute of Macau.[36] The *recurso de amparo* (the writ of protection) was also introduced to Macau through Article 17 of the JOL.[37] According to Article 17 of the JOL, people could appeal to the High Court of Justice on the grounds that judgments rendered by the local courts or executive acts taken by the government had violated their fundamental rights and freedoms.[38] Notwithstanding these

30 Zhihui He 何志辉, *澳门法制史新编 A New Study on the Legal History of Macau* (社会科学文献出版社 Social Sciences Academic Press 2019) 111–112.

31 Zhihui He 何志辉, *澳门法制史新编 A New Study on the Legal History of Macau* (社会科学文献出版社 Social Sciences Academic Press 2019) 124–125.

32 Luis W. K. Wong, 'Constitutional Review of Colonial Macau: A Historical Study' (2023) 53(2) *Hong Kong Law Journal* 643, 651.

33 Jorge Godinho and Paulo Cardinal, 'Macau's Court of Final Appeal' in Simon N. M. Young and Yash Ghai (eds), *Hong Kong's Court of Final Appeal: The Development of the Law in China's Hong Kong* (CUP 2014) 610; António Manuel Hespanha, *澳門法制史概論 Introduction to Macau's Legal History* (澳門基金會 Macau Foundation 1996) 67. In practice, very few cases were appealed to the court of second instance in Goa and to the Supreme Court in Lisbon from Macau.

34 Judicial Organisation Law of Macau (澳門司法組織綱要法) (Law No. 112/91), art 6(1).

35 Judicial Organisation Law of Macau (澳門司法組織綱要法) (Law No. 112/91), arts 6(2) and 11.

36 Organic Statute of Macau (澳門組織章程) (Law No. 1/76, amended by Law No. 13-A/90), art 41(1).

37 Judicial Organisation Law of Macau (澳門司法組織綱要法) (Law No. 112/91), art 17.

38 Article 17 of the JOL stipulates:

> '1. From any decision rendered by a court of the region, an appeal may be lodged with the plenary session of the High Court on the ground of a violation of fundamental rights guaranteed by the Organic Statute of Macau. Such appeal shall be directly lodged to the High Court and limited to the issue of the alleged violation.

judicial reforms, the Portuguese Constitutional Court, Supreme Court, Supreme Administrative Court, and Audit Court retained the powers of final adjudication over Macau affairs.[39] Constitutional appeals against the rulings of Macau's High Court of Justice could directly go up to the Portuguese Constitutional Court.[40] The Supreme Administrative Court retained original jurisdiction over cases against the Macau Governor.[41] Appeals from the High Court of Justice would go up to the Supreme Court or the Supreme Administrative Court in Lisbon, depending on the subject matter of the disputes,[42] while appeals from Macau's Audit Court went up to the Audit Court in Lisbon.[43]

Turning to Hong Kong, its colonial Legislative Council (LegCo) enacted Ordinance No. 15 of 1844, commonly known as the Supreme Court Ordinance, which established the Supreme Court of Hong Kong in 1844.[44] Minor criminal cases in colonial Hong Kong were handled by the magistracy.[45] Decisions made

> 2. Without prejudice to the provisions of the preceding article, an appeal shall lie to the administrative courts against administrative acts or any acts carried out by public authorities on the ground of a violation of fundamental rights guaranteed by the Organic Statute of Macau.'
>
> '(一、對於當地法院作出之裁判，得以違反澳門組織章程所保障之基本權利為依據，向高等法院之全會上訴，此上訴應直接作出，並只限對於違反上述所保障之權利之事宜而提起。
>
> 二、在不影響上條規定之情況下，對於公權之行政行為或單純事實行徑，得以違反澳門組織章程所保障之基本權利為依據，向具有行政審判權之法院上訴。)'

The Organic Statute of Macau did not contain fundamental rights provisions. But Articles 2 and 41(1) of the Organic Statute of Macau integrated the bill of rights enshrined in the Constitution of Portugal. Article 2 of the Organic Statute of Macau stipulated that Macau's autonomy was subordinated to the principles of 'respecting rights, freedoms and guarantees, established in the Constitution of Portugal', and Article 41(1) of the Organic Statute of Macau provided that the courts shall not apply any rules that were in breach of the provisions and principles of the constitution of Portugal and the Organic Statute of Macau. Vitalino Canas, 'The General Regime of Fundamental Rights in the Basic Law and in the International Instruments' in Jorge Oliveira and Paulo Cardinal (eds), *One Country Two Systems, Three Legal Orders – Perspectives of Evolution* (Springer 2009) 663–664.

39 Judicial Organisation Law of Macau (澳門司法組織綱要法) (Law No. 112/91), arts 11 and 34.

40 Judicial Organisation Law of Macau (澳門司法組織綱要法) (Law No. 112/91), arts 11 and 34; Chao Wang 汪超, '澳門法院的司法審查制度作為個人自由的保障及其與香港司法審查制度比較的啓示 Judicial Review of Macau Courts as Protection of Individual Rights and Implication after a Comparison with Hong Kong's Judicial Review' (2021) 2 *澳門法學 Macau Law Review* 89, 94.

41 Judicial Organisation Law of Macau (澳門司法組織綱要法) (Law No. 112/91), art 16(1).

42 Chang Xu 许昌, '论澳门特别行政区法院设置及其特点 On the Court System and Features of the Macau Special Administrative Region' (1994) 1 *中外法学 Peking Law Journal* 65, 71.

43 Judicial Organisation Law of Macau (澳門司法組織綱要法) (Law No. 112/91), art 10(6).

44 Albert Chen 陳弘毅, Christopher Munn 文基賢, and Michael Ng 吳海傑, '殖民地時代香港的法治與司法 The Rule of Law and the Administration of Justice in Colonial Hong Kong' in Wang Gungwu 王賡武 (ed), *香港史新編 Hong Kong History: New Perspectives* (三聯書店 Joint Publishing HK 2017) 447.

45 Albert Chen 陳弘毅, Christopher Munn 文基賢, and Michael Ng 吳海傑, '殖民地時代香港的法治與司法 The Rule of Law and the Administration of Justice in Colonial Hong Kong' in Wang Gungwu 王賡武 (ed), *香港史新編 Hong Kong History: New Perspectives* (三聯書店 Joint Publishing HK 2017) 461; Albert Chen 陳弘毅, '香港法律制度的現狀及前景 Hong Kong Legal

by the magistracy could be appealed to the Supreme Court. The Supreme Court was responsible for adjudicating serious criminal cases and most civil disputes. Decisions of the Supreme Court of Hong Kong could be appealed to the Privy Council based in London, which served as the court of final resort for all appeals from the British colonies.

After World War II, the significant population growth in Hong Kong presented considerable challenges for the caseload of the Supreme Court. Recognising the need for an intermediate court, the colonial government established the District Court in 1953.[46] But unlike the Supreme Court, jury trials were never used in the District Court. In 1976, the Supreme Court was reorganised as the High Court of Justice and the Court of Appeal.[47] The High Court of Justice handled cases at first instance,[48] and the Court of Appeal dealt with appeals from the High Court and the District Court.[49] This bifurcation of responsibility continued after Hong Kong was returned to China in 1997.

Structure and Jurisdiction of the SARs Courts

On 20 December 1999, Portugal formally returned Macau to China and the MABL – the "mini-constitution" of the Macau Special Administrative Region (MASAR) – came into force,[50] thereby abolishing the jurisdiction of Portuguese courts over Macau. On the same day, a new Judicial Organisation Law (司法組織綱要法) was promulgated and came into force. The MASAR judiciary now comprises the courts of first instance[51] (第一審法院), the Court of Second Instance (中級法院), and the MACFA;[52] and the MACFA shall exercise the power of final adjudication.[53]

System: Status Quo and Prospects' in Yushuo Zheng 鄭宇碩 (ed), *過渡時期的香港 Hong Kong in the Transitional Period* (三聯書店 Joint Publishing HK 1989) 79.

46 District Court Ordinance of 1953, s 3.

47 Supreme Court Ordinance of 1976, s 3.

48 Supreme Court Ordinance of 1976, s 12.

49 Supreme Court Ordinance of 1976, s 13.

50 Albert Chen and P. Y. Lo, 'The Constitutional Orders of "One Country, Two Systems": A Comparative Study of the Visible and Invisible Bases of Constitutional Review and Proportionality Analysis in the Chinese Special Administrative Regions of Hong Kong and Macau' in Rosalind Dixon and Adrienne Stone (eds), *The Invisible Constitution in Comparative Perspective* (CUP 2018) 230.

51 MABL, arts 84–86. The courts of first instance in the MASAR comprise the Court of Preliminary Hearings (初級法院) and the Administrative Court (行政法院). Judicial Organisation Law (司法組織綱要法) (Law No. 9/1999), art 10(2). Both courts pre-existed in colonial Macau. The colonial courts of first instance comprised the Court of General Jurisdiction (普通管轄法院), the Criminal Pre-Trial Tribunal (刑事預審法庭), and the Administrative Court (行政法院). The Court of General Jurisdiction and the Administrative Court continued their operations, becoming the Court of Preliminary Hearings and Administrative Court of the MASAR. The Criminal Pre-Trial Tribunal was merged into the Court of Preliminary Hearings.

52 MABL, arts 84–86; Judicial Organisation Law (司法組織綱要法) (Law No. 9/1999), art 10, which provides that (in Chinese) "一、設有第一審法院、中級法院及終審法院。二、第一審法院包括初級法院和行政法院。"

53 MABL, art 84(2); Judicial Organisation Law (司法組織綱要法) (Law No. 9/1999), art 10.

The MACFA was only established after the handover.[54] While the Court of Final Appeal was a new creation, the Court of Second Instance and the Courts of First Instance were grafted from their colonial equivalents. The Court of Second Instance took over the duties of the colonial High Court of Justice,[55] except for *habeas corpus* applications and the uniformisation of judicial decisions (統一司法見解). These two categories of cases are now within the original jurisdiction of the MACFA.[56] Appeals from the Court of Second Instance are heard by the MACFA.[57] The colonial Audit Court was replaced by the Commission of Audit established within the MASAR Government.[58]

Similar to Macau, the HKCFA sits at the apex of the Hong Kong judiciary and is also conferred with the power of final adjudication.[59] The HKCFA, which came into being after the Hong Kong Special Administrative Region (HKSAR) was established and replaced the Privy Council as Hong Kong's court of final resort.[60] Below the HKCFA in the judicial hierarchy is the High Court of Hong Kong, which comprises the Court of Appeal and the Court of First Instance, and the subordinate courts that include the District Court and Magistrates' Courts, all of which basically mirrored the pre-handover colonial practice.

However, it is noteworthy that *all* cases in Hong Kong can only go up to the HKCFA on *appeal* from its lower courts, while the MACFA is statutorily empowered to exercise *original* jurisdiction over the following matters:

1 Uniformisation of judicial decisions (統一司法見解).[61]

54 MABL, art 84; Jorge Godinho and Paulo Cardinal, 'Macau's Court of Final Appeal' in Simon N M Young and Yash Ghai (eds), *Hong Kong's Court of Final Appeal: The Development of the Law in China's Hong Kong* (CUP 2014) 611.

55 Judicial Organisation Law of Macau (澳門司法組織綱要法) (Law No. 112/91), arts 14 and 15; Judicial Organisation Law (司法組織綱要法) (Law No. 9/1999), art 36.

56 Judicial Organisation Law of Macau (澳門司法組織綱要法) (Law No. 112/91), art 14; Judicial Organisation Law (司法組織綱要法) (Law No. 9/1999), art 44.

57 Judicial Organisation Law (司法組織綱要法) (Law No. 9/1999), art 44.

58 Wanying Mi 米萬英, '澳門司法制度：延續與變革 Macau Judicial System: Continuity and Change' <www.macaudata.mo/macaubook/book262/html/0059001.htm> last accessed 4 January 2026.

59 HKBL, art 82; MABL, art 84.

60 'The Role of Hong Kong Court of Final Appeal' <www.hkcfa.hk/en/faqs/role_cfa/index.html> last accessed 4 January 2026.

61 Judicial Organisation Law (司法組織綱要法) (Law No. 9/1999), art 44(2)(1). Persons can petition the MACFA for a uniformisation of judicial decisions if a decision of the MACFA contradicts a previous MACFA decision or there are two conflicting decisions given by the Court of Second Instance, provided that the conflicting decisions pertain to the same issue under the same law. Such uniformisation decisions are binding on all courts in Macau. To date, the MACFA has issued 19 uniformisations of judicial decisions. They are Cases 108/2024, 40/2023, 94/2022, 69/2022, 19/2022, 160/2021, 50/2021, 130/2019, 84/2017, 15/2017, 7/2017, 128/2014, 126/2014, 57/2012, 69/2010, 23/2005, 17/2004, 4/2001, 1/2001. The case list is available here: <www.court.gov.mo/zh/subpage/casesearch> last accessed 4 January 2026.

The most notable public law uniformisation decision is Case 130/2019 where the MACFA ruled that the Court of Second Instance could directly impose a criminal sentence on an accused, after overturning his acquittal on appeal, and did not have to remand the case to the Court of First Instance for sentencing.

2 Acts, crimes and misdemeanours of the CE in connection to the discharge of his or her duties.[62]
3 Jurisdictional disputes between the Court of Second Instance (MACSI) and the courts of first instance and other administrative agencies.[63]
4 Writ of *habeas corpus*.[64]
5 Restrictions on notified public assemblies and demonstrations.[65]
6 Disputes arising from the election of the CE and the Legislative Assembly members.[66]

This absence of any *original* jurisdiction vested in the HKCFA has relieved – for better or worse – the Court of any responsibility in first-instance fact finding vis-à-vis politically divisive issues, giving time to the Court to duck the *immediacy* of an explosive issue. Criminal prosecutions brought against former Hong Kong CEs and principal officials for graft only came up to the HKCFA years after charges were first brought,[67] and the legality of *ex ante* governmental restrictions imposed on public assemblies was not litigated before the HKCFA until years after the planned demonstrations,[68] which we will discuss later in this chapter. On the other hand, in Macau, all cases of such nature were litigated in the *first* instance before the MACFA.[69]

62 Judicial Organisation Law (司法組織綱要法) (Law No. 9/1999, amended by Law No. 4/2019), art 44(2)(5) and 44(2)(6). The Judicial Organisation Law was amended in 2019. The following cases were heard by the MACFA but are now heard by the MACSI in first instance: administrative actions, crimes and misdemeanours committed by the President of the Legislative Assembly, the Secretaries of Government Departments, the judges of the MACFA and the MACSI, the Prosecutor General and assistant prosecutors general. See pre-2019 Judicial Organisation Law (司法組織綱要法) (Law No. 9/1999), art 44(2)(5) to 44(2)(8).
63 Judicial Organisation Law (司法組織綱要法) (Law No. 9/1999), arts 44(2)(14) and 44(2)(15).
64 Criminal Procedure Code (刑事訴訟法典) (Decree-Law No. 48/96/M), arts 204–207. In Hong Kong, an application for a writ of *habeas corpus* is made to the Court of First Instance and appeals from decisions of the Court of First Instance on an application for *habeas corpus* go to the Court of Appeal. High Court Ordinance, ss 22A and 24.
65 The Right to Assemble and Demonstrate (集會權及示威權) (Law No. 2/93/M, amended by Law No. 16/2008), art 12(1).
66 Law on the Election of the Chief Executive (行政長官選舉法) (Law No. 3/2004), art 97(1); Law on the Election of the Legislative Assembly (澳門特別行政區立法會選舉法) (Law No. 3/2001), arts 28A, 36, 47B and 138.
67 Donald Tsang – Hong Kong's Chief Executive (CE) from 2005 to 2012 – was convicted in 2017 for one count of misconduct in public office and sentenced by the High Court to 20 months imprisonment. The Hong Kong Court of Appeal reduced the sentence to one year, and the HKCFA quashed the conviction in 2019 – after Tsang had already served his prison term – on the ground that the trial judge's original directions to the jury were inadequate. Rafael Hui – Hong Kong's Chief Secretary from 2005 to 2007 – was convicted by the High Court in 2014 for misconduct in public office and sentenced to imprisonment for 7 years and 6 months. His appeal to the HKCFA was dismissed in June 2017.
68 *HKSAR v Chow Hang Tung* [2024] HKCFA 2.
69 Notably, in 2008, the MACFA, in exercise of its original jurisdiction, tried and convicted Ao Man Long – Macau's Secretary for Transport and Public Works between 1999 and 2006 – on 57 counts of corruption, money laundering, abuse of power, and possession of assets of unexplained sources.

Judicial Appointment, Background, and Composition

The MACFA comprises three judges[70] – the Chief Justice and two Permanent Judges. By convention, one Permanent Judge on the MACFA will be a Macau resident of Portuguese descent.[71] The MABL requires the Chief Justice of the MACFA to be a Chinese citizen[72] but not the other two Permanent Judges. Substantive appeals are typically adjudicated by this bench of three.[73]

Only six judges have been appointed to the MACFA since the handover. This low turnover is due to the relative youth of the first batch of MACFA judges.[74] The MACFA has only been led by two Chief Justices since the handover: Chief Justice Sam Hou Fai (岑浩輝) (December 1999–August 2024) and Chief Justice Song Man Lei (宋敏莉) since December 2024. Notably, Chief Justice Sam Hou Fai was appointed when he was only 37 years old, and he only resigned his judgeship in August 2024 – with Beijing's endorsement – to run for the Macau CE's position.[75]

The HKCFA comprises the Chief Justice and three Permanent Judges.[76] At this time of writing, there are also ten Non-Permanent Judges (NPJs) (both local and overseas)[77] who are rostered to hear substantive appeals with the permanent bench.[78] The Hong Kong Chief Justice must be a Chinese national,[79] but this is not a requirement for the other Permanent Judges and NPJs. Substantive appeals are heard on the HKCFA in panels of five. Hong Kong has seen three Chief Justices take office since the establishment of the SAR in 1997, and eight jurists who are former or incumbent Permanent Judges on the HKCFA.

After separate trials conducted in 2009 and 2012, the MACFA further convicted him on more counts of corruption and money laundering for new offences that were not previously tried in 2008. An overall prison sentence of 29 years was handed down at the end of the three trials. See Case 36/2007 (30 January 2008); Case 53/2008 (22 April 2009); Case 37/2011 (31 May 2012).

70 Judicial Organisation Law (司法組織綱要法) (Law No. 9/1999), art 46 and Annex 1, Table 3.

71 In 2019, Judge Viriato Lima reached the retirement age of 65 and he was replaced by José Maria Dias Azedo.

72 MABL, art 88(2).

73 Judicial Organisation Law (司法組織綱要法) (Law No. 9/1999), art 25(2). But a uniformisation of jurisprudence is made by five judges, including three judges of the MACFA, the president of the Court of Second Instance, and the most senior judge from the Court of Second Instance (art 46(2)).

74 Chu Kin (朱健) was 32 years old when he was first appointed; Song Man Lei (宋敏莉) was 46 years old when she was first appointed.

75 'Macau judge announces bid to lead world's biggest casino hub' *The Straits Times* (28 August 2024) <www.straitstimes.com/asia/macau-judge-announces-bid-to-lead-worlds-biggest-casino-hub> last accessed 4 January 2026; Song Man Lei was appointed as the next Chief Justice in December 2024 and subsequently in January 2026, Judge Ho Wai Neng (何偉寧) was appointed as a Permanent Judge of the MACFA. '法官就職儀式 Judicial swearing-in ceremony' (5 January 2026) <www.gov.mo/zh-hant/news/1210125/> last accessed 23 March 2026.

76 Court of Final Appeal Ordinance, s 5.

77 The list of Judges and Judicial Officers is available here: <www.judiciary.hk/en/about_us/judges.html> last accessed 4 January 2026.

78 Court of Final Appeal Ordinance, s 5.

79 HKBL, art 90(1).

Despite these notional differences between the MACFA and the HKCFA, there are additionally three distinctive differences between the two Courts which explain why the former is more conservative than the latter.

First, ethnic Chinese jurists on the MACFA have predominantly been born and trained in Mainland China. Sam Hou Fai (岑浩輝), Chu Kin (朱健), and Song Man Lei (宋敏莉) were born in the Mainland, and two out of three of them (Chief Justices Sam and Song) even obtained their bachelor's law degrees from Peking University. In contrast, no judge on the HKCFA graduated from a Mainland Chinese university. In fact, most judges who have served on the HKCFA completed their primary legal education in England, and only three out of 11 (past and present) justices completed their undergraduate law degree in Hong Kong.[80]

Second, Macau does not have Hong Kong's system of allowing *overseas* NPJs to sit on its CFA. In contrast, for Hong Kong, foreign judges based in other common law jurisdictions are authorised to sit on the HKCFA as NPJs,[81] and one overseas NPJ is typically rostered in every HKCFA case except national security ones. All the overseas NPJs appointed have been legal giants in the Western common law world, such as Sir Anthony Mason (Chief Justice of Australia), Justice Beverley McLachlin (Chief Justice of Canada), Lord Phillips (President of the Supreme Court of the United Kingdom). Interestingly, the overseas NPJs have only dissented on *three* occasions in Hong Kong,[82] and never once in a constitutional law dispute. But this near-unanimity in no way suggests that the overseas NPJs merely rubber-stamp the local judges' preferred policy agenda. Instead, the presence of an eminent jurist from a Western common law jurisdiction sitting on the HKCFA panel, and participating in internal deliberations, provides *ex ante* incentives for the HKCFA to ensure that its decisions are defensible to the wider Western common law world, and negotiations are made behind-the-scenes before a final, typically unanimous, decision is reached. (Dissents in the HKCFA are rare.[83])

Third, and the most important distinctive feature, pertains to the judicial appointment system. Both BLs require their judges to be appointed by their respective CE on the recommendation of an independent commission composed of local judges, lawyers, and eminent persons.[84] But the practically identical textual

80 The three justices are Justice Patrick Chan, Chief Justice Andrew Cheung, and Justice Johnson Lam.

81 HKBL, art 82.

82 The three cases are: *The Bank of East Asia Ltd v. Tsien Wui Marble Factory Ltd* (1999) 2 HKCFAR 349; *Next Magazine Publishing Ltd v. Ma Ching Fat* (2003) 6 HKCFAR 63; *Hong Kong Electric Co Ltd v. Commissioner of Rating and Valuation (No 3)* (2012) 15 HKCFAR 1.

83 By way of example, there was no dissent in the HKCFA in 2022 and dissenting opinions were issued in one HKCFA decision in 2023: *Sham Tsz Kit v Secretary for Justice* (2023) 26 HKCFAR 385.

84 MABL, art 87(1) stipulates

> Judges of the courts of the Macau Special Administrative Region at all levels shall be appointed by the Chief Executive on the recommendation of an independent commission composed of local judges, lawyers and eminent persons. Judges shall be chosen on the basis of their professional qualifications. Qualified judges of foreign nationality may also be employed.

mandate belies the substantive differences in the composition of their members. In Macau, the Chief Justice is the only judge on the 7-person Independent Judicial Officers Nomination Commission (推薦法官的獨立委員會),[85] and more importantly he does not chair the Commission. Furthermore, the fact that Chief Justice Sam – the MASAR's first Chief Justice – received Beijing's endorsement to become Macau's current CE is also a testament to his political reliability. Since the handover in 1999, Macau's Commission has been chaired by Lau Cheok Va, who concurrently served as vice president (1999–2009) and president (2009–2013) of the Macau Legislative Assembly, and he was a Macau delegate to the 10th and 11th National People's Congress (NPC) (2003–2013). Notably, practically all the current and past non-judicial members of the current Commission share an explicit pro-Beijing affiliation. By way of illustration, we can examine the other current members of this Commission:[86] Ho Teng Iat (appointed since 1999) was a member of the National Committee of the Chinese People's Political Consultative Conference (1993–2023) and is the sister of Ho Iat-seng, the former CE of Macau; Ieong Tou Hong (appointed since 2021) was a member of Macau's Executive Council between 2019 and 2024;[87] Chan Hong (appointed since 2021) was a member of the 13th National Committee of the Chinese People's Political Consultative Conference (2018–2023); Wang Yu has been a member of the Beijing-appointed Committee for the BL of the MASAR since December 2024.

When politicians have a significant role in the judicial appointment process, they will always seek to appoint judges who share their political ideology.[88] Where

HKBL, art 88 stipulates

> Judges of the courts of the Hong Kong Special Administrative Region shall be appointed by the Chief Executive on the recommendation of an independent commission composed of local judges, persons from the legal profession and eminent persons from other sectors.

But there is a notable difference. The Hong Kong Legislative Council is constitutionally empowered to endorse the appointment and removal of HKCFA judges [HKBL, art 73(7)], but the Macau Legislative Assembly has no role in the appointment of judges as this power is vested alone in the CE [MABL, art 87(1)]. However, the removal of the MACFA judges has to be decided by the CE based on the recommendation of a review committee consisting of five members of the Legislative Assembly. [Article 87(3) of the MABL read with Article 83(1) of the Law of Judicial Officers (司法官通則)]. But in practice, no appellate judge in either SAR has ever faced formal impeachment, and the Legislative Council of the Hong Kong SAR has endorsed every judicial appointment put forward.

85 Law of Judicial Officers (司法官通則) (Law No. 10/1999), art 91(3). But the law does not specify the background that the members of the Independent Judicial Officers Nomination Commission should be from. According to Article 91(3) of the Law of Judicial Officers (司法官通則), this Commission should comprise one judge, one lawyer, and five eminent persons from other sectors.

86 Members of the Independent Judicial Officers Nomination Commission <www.court.gov.mo/zh/subpage/ciij#tab_committeeList> last accessed 4 January 2026.

87 The members of the fifth Macau Executive Council can be viewed here <www.gov.mo/zh-hant/news/310827/ > last accessed 4 January 2026.

88 Robert Dahl, 'Decision-Making in a Democracy: The Supreme Court as a National Policy-Maker' (1957) 6 *Journal of Public Law* 279; Jeffrey A. Segal and Harold J. Spaeth, *The Supreme Court and the Attitudinal Model Revisited* (CUP 2002); Benjamin Alarie and Andrew J. Green, *Commitment and Cooperation in High Courts: A Cross Country Examination of Institutional Constraints on Judges* (OUP 2017) 83.

the same political party has a monopoly over the appointment process, it can continuously feed like-minded judicial agents into the constitutional system. This is so in Macau.

In contrast, for Hong Kong, its judges are *in substance* chosen[89] by the nine-member JORC chaired by the Chief Justice, and the Hong Kong JORC primarily comprises judges and lawyers, not pro-Beijing affiliates as we have seen in Macau. Therefore, the Hong Kong Chief Justice has great latitude in shaping the composition of the judiciary he commands, especially the crucial HKCFA.

Typically, the Hong Kong JORC comprises the Chief Justice (who chairs the JORC), the Secretary for Justice (SJ), two judges nominated by the Chief Justice, a barrister and a solicitor nominated, respectively, by the Bar Association and the Law Society, and three lay persons chosen by the CE. The presence of the SJ and the government appointees on the JORC would impose *ex ante* constraints on the Chief Justice to pursue candidates who are perceived by the HKSAR government to be in the political mainstream. But as all Permanent Judges of the HKCFA are in practice promoted from the Court of Appeal, and all Court of Appeal judges are drawn from the Court of First Instance, the Chief Justice who commands the entire Hong Kong judiciary occupies the vantage spot to recruit, evaluate, and expedite the promotion of his preferred candidates through the ranks. The lay persons on the Hong Kong JORC, whose membership is refreshed regularly, are usually drawn from the corporate world and academia (in disciplines other than law), and they would simply not have the in-depth knowledge of the Hong Kong judiciary to independently determine which Court of Appeal judges deserve promotion to the HKCFA. (There is a regular turn-over of the laypersons on the Hong Kong JORC, but as discussed above, the laypersons dominate Macau's Commission, and they serve lengthy terms.) The SJ – typically a barrister – only serves for a term coterminous with the CE who appoints them and returns to private practice thereafter. Unless the Chief Justice is seeking to promote an individual the government deems politically controversial, the SJ will be hard-pressed to openly block the promotion of the appellate judges the former wants, especially if the SJ will appear once again as mere counsel before these judges in a few years. Therefore, so long as the Chief Justice does not seek to promote any controversial personalities, he would in all probability get his preferred nominees approved. Furthermore, if the Permanent Judge, whom the Chief Justice is seeking to appoint, is 70 years old or older, the Chief Justice is not even statutorily required to consult the JORC; the Chief Justice alone decides, subject to the CE's formal approval.[90] Rather extraordinarily, in Hong Kong, a retiring Chief Justice also chairs the JORC that selects his successor. In view of the Hong Kong Chief Justice's extraordinary powers of appointing and promoting judges, unlike his Macau counterpart, the

89 Formally, all judges in Hong Kong are appointed by the CE of the HKSAR on the recommendation of the JORC. See HKBL, art 88. An equivalent provision applies in Macau. See MABL, art 87(1).
90 Court of Final Appeal Ordinance, s 14(2)(b).

former possesses greater autonomy in shaping his bench with more independent and less-partisan jurists. The only caveat is national security disputes – the CE of Hong Kong in consultation with the Chief Justice can designate specific judges to hear national security cases, but these judges must be selected from the pool of pre-existing Hong Kong judges.[91] To date, the Chief Justice and every Permanent Judge on the HKCFA are designated national security judges, but neither the judiciary nor the government has disclosed whether any *overseas* NPJ has been so designated.

Birth and Development of Constitutional Review in the SARs

It is important to note that neither the MABL nor the HKBL include any provision that expressly authorises their courts to exercise the power of constitutional review over legislation. But their BLs are identical in providing that laws previously in force in the territories shall not contravene their respective mini-constitutions,[92] and no law enacted by their SAR legislatures may contravene their respective BLs.[93]

This textual ambiguity over whether the SAR Courts were conferred with the power of constitutional review did not give the HKCFA any pause, and the Court in its *first* constitutional decision swiftly and emphatically claimed the power to invalidate local legislation. In *Ng Ka Ling v Director of Immigration,*[94] the HKCFA justified constitutional review in the following terms:

> [I]n exercising their judicial power conferred by the Basic Law, the courts of the Region have a duty to enforce and interpret that law [...] In exercising this jurisdiction, the courts perform their constitutional role under the Basic Law of acting as a constitutional check on the executive and legislative branches of government to ensure that they act in accordance with the Basic Law.[95]

In the HKCFA's view, the exercise of this constitutional jurisdiction is a matter of obligation, not of discretion.[96] On the facts, the HKCFA invalidated a series of local immigration provisions with great alacrity. These nullified legislative provisions include (1) rules passed on 10 July 1997 that required children – born in Mainland China to Hong Kong Permanent Residents – to first obtain one-way permits from the Mainland authorities before they could exercise their right of abode in Hong Kong; (2) a statutory provision that *retrospectively* applied the above rules and corresponding sanctions to 1 July 1997, and (3) a legislative provision that denied

91 NSL, art 44. See also the 'Statement by Chief Justice of Court of Final Appeal' on the implementation of art 44 <www.info.gov.hk/gia/general/202007/02/P2020070200414.htm> last accessed 4 January 2026.

92 MABL, art 8; HKBL, art 8.

93 MABL, art 11; HKBL, art 11.

94 (1999) 2 HKCFAR 4.

95 (1999) 2 HKCFAR 25.

96 (1999) 2 HKCFAR 25.

the right of abode to Mainland children born out of wedlock unless the child was subsequently legitimated by the parents' marriage. On the same day as *Ng Ka Ling*, in *Chan Kam Nga v Director of Immigration*,[97] the HKCFA also issued another judgment that invalidated a statutory bar that excluded a child – born *before* at least one of the parents acquired the right of permanent residency in Hong Kong – from claiming the right of abode by descent in Hong Kong.

What was even more extraordinary about *Ng Ka Ling* was that the HKCFA further asserted that the Court had a "duty to declare invalidity"[98] any act of the NPC or NPCSC that was inconsistent with the HKBL. As the HKCFA explained, the HKBL was enacted to implement China's commitment – under the Joint Declaration with the British – to preserve its basic policies regarding Hong Kong for 50 years. *A fortiori*, the courts' jurisdiction to interpret the HKBL "necessarily entails the jurisdiction stated above over acts of the National People's Congress and its Standing Committee to ensure their consistency with the Basic Law".[99]

This legal proposition is highly controversial as it poses a direct challenge to Beijing's sovereignty over the city and the Central Authorities' interpretive mandate in Hong Kong. By claiming the power to invalidate NPC and NPCSC legislative acts, the HKCFA was in essence claiming that the HKBL had the same constitutional status as the PRC Constitution, and the Hong Kong judiciary had the concomitant constitutional authority to superintend the legislative actions of the NPCSC. Notably, even the Supreme People's Court in China does not have such power of constitutional interpretation. This power resides exclusively with the NPCSC.[100] Furthermore, this judicial assertion was also gratuitous as there were no NPC or NPCSC legislative acts under challenge.

In the aftermath of *Ng Ka Ling*, the Hong Kong government swiftly proceeded with a request for the HKCFA to "clarify" its decision. While the HKCFA acceded to this request, the Court issued a very terse judgment that clarified little. In *Ng Ka Ling (No 2)*,[101] the HKCFA accepted that the NPCSC had the authority to issue a constitutional interpretation under Article 158 of the HKBL, and this Interpretation would have to be followed by the courts of the HKSAR. But more interestingly, the HKCFA followed this concession with a veiled reassertion of judicial power:

> [T]he Court accepts that it cannot question, the authority of the National People's Congress or the Standing Committee to do any act which is in accordance with the provisions of the Basic Law and the procedure therein.[102]

97 (1999) 2 HKCFAR 82.
98 (1999) 2 HKCFAR 26.
99 (1999) 2 HKCFAR 26.
100 Article 67 of the 1982 PRC constitution. See also Qianfan Zhang, *The Constitution of China: A Contextual Analysis* (Hart 2012) 135.
101 (1999) 2 HKCFAR 141.
102 (1999) 2 HKCFAR 142.

What the HKCFA left deliberately unspoken was the court's amenability to questioning acts of the NPC or the NPCSC that the Court deemed *not* to be in accordance with the HKBL. Oddly, Beijing was appeased by this "clarification", but the HKSAR government remained apprehensive about the practical and economic ramifications of granting the right of abode automatically to all Mainland-born children with at least one Hong Kong Permanent Resident parent. Within six months, the local government successfully sought an NPCSC Interpretation to reverse *Ng Ka Ling* and *Chan Kam Nga,* but parties in the original litigations were unaffected by this legislative reversal.[103] (This controversial obiter has however been quietly overruled by the HKCFA in 2024.)[104]

But in 1999, there was another landmark ruling handed down by the HKCFA that continues to have contemporary constitutional significance. This time, the HKCFA chose to uphold the constitutionality of Hong Kong laws prohibiting the desecration of the regional and national flags. The central issue in *HKSAR v Ng Kung Siu*[105] turned on whether the impugned restrictions were compatible with the freedom of expression entrenched under Article 27 of the HKBL and Article 16 of the Hong Kong Bill of Rights Ordinance (BORO). Both laws were upheld on the basis that there were legitimate societal interests in keeping the symbols of nationhood and sovereignty above the strife of politics;[106] and the Court also ruled that the penal prohibition against flag desecration was a limited restriction on free speech as only one mode of expression was banned, and the laws did not foreclose a person from expressing the same message by other means.[107]

What is perhaps more innocuous, and arguably more important, is the HKCFA's secondary pronouncement in this case. The Court also asserted that the BORO "in fact provides for the incorporation of the provisions of the [International Covenant on Civil and Political Rights (ICCPR)] into the laws of Hong Kong"[108], and to be compliant with Article 39 of the HKBL, any "restriction on either freedom [protected in the Basic Law or the BORO] cannot contravene the provisions of the ICCPR".[109] In other words, the HKCFA interpreted Article 39 to mean that the BORO has the same constitutional force as the HKBL itself and can override laws that are inconsistent with these rights-provisions.

This is a subtle but very significant declaration for the following reason. The HKBL duplicates most BORO rights, thereby expressly conferring constitutional

103 The Interpretation by the Standing Committee of the National People's Congress Regarding Paragraph 4 in Article 22 and Category (3) of Paragraph 2 in Article 24 of the BL of the HKSAR of the PRC (Adopted at the 10th Meeting of the Standing Committee of the Ninth National People's Congress on 26 June 1999).

104 *HKSAR v Ng Ngoi Yee Margaret* (2024) 27 HKCFAR 434 at [33].

105 (1999) 2 HKCFAR 442.

106 (1999) 2 HKCFAR 461.

107 (1999) 2 HKCFAR 456.

108 (1999) 2 HKCFAR 455.

109 (1999) 2 HKCFAR 455.

status on these statutory rights. Examples of these rights include the right to free expression, the right to assembly, the right to equality, the freedom of religious belief, and the right against arbitrary arrest and imprisonment. Vis-à-vis these rights concurrently and expressly protected in both the BORO and the HKBL, the invalidation of any rights-incompatible legislative provision is uncontroversial as it is expressly stated that HKBL rights prevail over conflicting legislative provisions.[110]

But there are several BORO rights that are *not* protected in the HKBL. The BORO expressly protects a person's right to a fair hearing in civil cases,[111] while this right is absent from the HKBL. Some BORO rights are more circumscribed in the HKBL. The BORO protects a person's right against torture and cruel, inhuman, or degrading treatment or punishment,[112] but the HKBL only prohibits torture;[113] there is a general right to privacy under the BORO,[114] but the HKBL only protects the privacy of one's communication.[115]

Originally, Section 3(2) of the BORO provided that "[a]ll pre-existing legislation that does not admit of a construction consistent with this Ordinance is, to the extent of the inconsistency, repealed" and Section 4 of the BORO stated that

> [a]ll legislation enacted on or after the commencement date [of the BORO] shall, to the extent that it admits of such a construction, be construed so as to be consistent with the International Covenant on Civil and Political Rights as applied to Hong Kong.

But, significantly, in February 1997, a few months before China resumed sovereignty over Hong Kong, the NPCSC decided that Sections 3 and 4 of the BORO would no longer be adopted as laws in Hong Kong after the handover on 1 July 1997.[116] This was an expression of China's unyielding resolve that only the HKBL could reign supreme over all Hong Kong laws.

Insofar as a BORO right is *concurrently* protected in the HKBL, *Ng Kung Siu*'s pronouncement is uncontroversial. On the other hand, if any legislative provision is invalidated because it violates rights found *exclusively* in the BORO, the HKCFA would in substance be rejecting the legislative repeal of Sections 3 and 4 of the

110 HKBL, arts 8 and 11.
111 BORO, art 10.
112 BORO, art 3.
113 HKBL, art 28.
114 BORO, art 14.
115 HKBL, art 30.
116 Decision of the Standing Committee of the National People's Congress on Treatment of the Laws Previously in Force in Hong Kong in accordance with Article 160 of the BL of the HKSAR of the PRC (Adopted at the 24th Session of the Standing Committee of the Eighth National People's Congress on February 23, 1997).

BORO; and the HKCFA would effectively be conferring quasi-constitutional status on these statutory rights too.[117]

Ostensibly, the HKCFA relied on Article 39 of the HKBL for this legal manoeuvre. Specifically, Paragraph 1 of Article 39 states that "[t]he provisions of the International Covenant on Civil and Political Rights … as applied to Hong Kong shall remain in force and shall be implemented through the laws of the Hong Kong Special Administrative Region". Paragraph 2 of Article 39 further provides that "[t]he rights and freedoms enjoyed by Hong Kong residents shall not be restricted unless as prescribed by law. Such restrictions shall not contravene the provisions of the preceding paragraph of this Article". But one should note that the text of Article 39 does not explicitly provide for the direct enforcement of ICCPR rights in Hong Kong or the concomitant judicial invalidation of any conflicting statutory provisions. Only those ICCPR rights *concurrently* protected in the HKBL enjoy that constitutional status – and only by virtue of Articles 8 and 11 of the HKBL which establish the supremacy of the HKBL over all other subordinate legal rules. For those ICCPR rights *not* found in the HKBL, Article 39 merely prohibits any restrictions from contravening any local implementation of the ICCPR, which in Hong Kong has been achieved through the BORO – an ordinary law. In the post-1997 legal regime, technically only BORO rights concurrently protected in the HKBL could prevail over local legislation; Beijing had unequivocally *removed* those judicial powers to invalidate pre-BORO legislation for violating exclusive BORO rights[118] and Beijing also repealed those judicial powers to interpret post-BORO legislation in a rights-friendly manner.[119]

Therefore, in *Ng Kung Siu*, with this expansive interpretation of Article 39, the HKCFA was clawing back power the judiciary lost with the statutory repeal. One should note that the repeal of these interpretative provisions in the BORO was passed by China *before* the handover and these legislative changes were timed to take effect when the HKBL came into force on the HKSAR's Establishment Day. Therefore, it is inconceivable that the HKCFA's reading of Article 39 would have reflected the original intentions of China when the latter framed the HKBL.

Nevertheless, on the facts, the HKCFA's judicial manoeuvre in *Ng Kung Siu* had little practical impact. Therein, the Court was addressing the freedom of expression, a right *concurrently* protected both in Article 16 of the BORO and Article 27 of the HKBL. But the HKCFA's expansive reading of Article 39 had momentous implications on another category of rights not at issue in this appeal, i.e. exclusive BORO rights – rights found *only* in the BORO and *not* in the HKBL – as this move implicitly reinstated Sections 3 and 4 of the BORO, which had been removed by the NPCSC in February 1997. Perhaps because all the impugned laws

117 See Po Jen Yap and Francis Chung, 'Statutory Rights and De Facto Constitutional Supremacy in Hong Kong?' (2019) 17(3) *International Journal of Constitutional Law* 836.

118 BORO, s 3(2), pre-Hong Kong handover.

119 BORO, s 4, pre-Hong Kong handover.

were upheld by the HKCFA in their entirety, the "subversive" potential of *Ng Kung Siu* went unnoticed by the HKSAR and Central Governments.

But, going forward, based on the HKCFA's expansive reading of Article 39 of the HKBL, lower courts went on to rely on this constitutional provision to strike down legislation that conflicted with exclusive BORO rights.[120] And this was also what the HKCFA did a decade later in *Lam Siu Po v Commissioner of Police*[121] when it invalidated a blanket ban on professional legal representation at a police officer's disciplinary hearing on the grounds that this exclusionary bar violated his right to a fair hearing in a civil case protected under Article 10 of the BORO – a right absent from the HKBL. Even though this statutory right is not found in the HKBL, the HKCFA explained that "Article 39 of the Basic Law gives constitutional force to Article 10 [of the BORO]".[122]

More remarkably in 2023, the HKCFA – in a very progressive ruling that post-dated the National Security Law of 2020 (hereinafter 2020 HKNSL) and the 2021 electoral overhaul – ruled that the Hong Kong government had violated Article 14 of the BORO – the right of privacy – in *failing* to establish an alternative statutory framework for legally recognising same-sex partnerships[123] and the Court gave the Government two years[124] to pass a new law that protects the "core"[125] rights of such same-sex relationships. Notably, the general right of privacy is only anchored in the BORO as the HKBL only enshrines the constitutional right to the privacy of one's communications.[126]

In contrast, the MACFA has been more cautious and circumspect when asserting the powers of constitutional review. On 20 December 1999 – the MASAR's Establishment Day – the Macau Legislative Assembly abolished the writ of amparo by amending the Judicial Organisation Law. As discussed earlier, the writ of amparo was an avenue for an individual pre-handover to challenge a Macau judgment or governmental decisions on the basis that it violated the fundamental rights protected by the Organic Statute of Macau. In 2000, in its first constitutional decision,[127] the MACFA dutifully affirmed that the MASAR courts may not rely on the writ of amparo post-handover, and all pending Macau appeals to the Constitutional Court of Portugal were terminated. But what was disconcerting was the MACFA's indication that under Macau law, there was no special mechanism or route of appeal which authorised the MASAR courts to engage in the constitutional

120 See *Chan Kin Sum v. Secretary for Justice* [2009] 2 HKLRD 166 (Hong Kong Court of First Instance); *Wong Hin Wai v. Secretary for Justice* [2012] 4 HKLRD 70 (Hong Kong Court of First Instance).
121 (2009) 12 HKCFAR 237.
122 (2009) 12 HKCFAR 237 at [60].
123 *Sham Tsz Kit v Secretary for Justice* (2023) 26 HKCFAR 385 at [214(2)].
124 *Sham Tsz Kit v Secretary for Justice* (2023) 26 HKCFAR 385 at [214(3)].
125 *Sham Tsz Kit v Secretary for Justice* (2023) 26 HKCFAR 385 at [181].
126 HKBL, art 30.
127 Case 1/2000 (16 February 2000).

review of legislation under the MABL,[128] thereby suggesting that the Macau courts are not empowered to declare local legislation unconstitutional – a position diametrically opposite to their Hong Kong counterpart.

But interestingly, in Case 2/2004, the MACFA ruled that several legislative provisions in the MASAR had no legal effect. The dispute concerned the interest rate applicable for a promissory note. The Macau Court of Second Instance (MACSI) had previously ruled that the interest rate payable should be 6% as this was specified in the Convention providing a Uniform Law for Bills of Exchange and Promissory Notes, an international agreement applicable in the MASAR. In doing so, the MACSI rejected the Applicant's argument that the company was entitled to an interest of 9.5% under two pieces of local legislation – Decree No 40/99/M read with Article 569 of the Commercial Code. According to the MACSI, Article 1(3) of the Civil Code provided that international agreements applicable to Macau shall prevail over ordinary laws, and the said Convention was one such applicable international agreement.[129] On appeal, the MACFA actually agreed with the MACSI that the chargeable interest rate should be 6%, but the MACFA ruled that it was not for the Civil Code to establish the precedence of international agreements over domestic law; this can only be achieved by a constitutional instrument like the MABL. Therefore, according to the MACFA, the said Convention should be enforced in preference to other ordinary laws in Macau because it had been made applicable in the SAR through Article 138 of the MABL[130] and Article 1(3) of the Civil Code consequently had no legal effect.[131] The other legal instruments that authorised a higher interest above the specified rate in the Convention were also deemed illegal.[132]

While the MACFA exercised constitutional review over legislation for the first time in Case 2/2004, the constitutional implication of that decision was limited as it was confined to the narrow holding that only the BL – and not domestic legislation – could establish the precedence of international agreements over ordinary laws. Hitherto, it remained unclear whether the Macau courts would declare domestic

128 Case 1/2000, at 3 (16 February 2000).
129 Case 2/2004, at 6 (2 June 2004).
130 Article 138 of the MABL reads:

> The application to the Macau Special Administrative Region of international agreements to which the People's Republic of China is a member or becomes a party shall be decided by the Central People's Government, in accordance with the circumstances and needs of the Region, and after seeking the views of the government of the Region. International agreements to which the People's Republic of China is not a party but which are implemented in Macau may continue to be implemented in the Macau Special Administrative Region. The Central People's Government shall, as necessary, authorise or assist the government of the Region to make appropriate arrangements for the application to the Region of other relevant international agreements.
> <www.cecc.gov/resources/legal-provisions/the-basic-law-of-the-macao-macau-special-administrative-region-of-the-prc> last accessed 4 January 2026.

131 Case 2/2004, at 7 (2 June 2004).
132 Case 2/2004, at 8 (2 June 2004).

laws unconstitutional for violating other provisions of the MABL, particularly constitutional rights.

Soon after, in Case 28/2006, the MACFA confirmed that it had the power to declare local laws unconstitutional if the impugned provisions violated *any* provision of the MABL.[133] In this case, the MACFA noted that Article 143 of the MABL (in *pari materia* with Article 158 of the HKBL) confers the local judiciary with the power of interpreting the BL on matters within the Region's autonomy. In exercising this power of constitutional interpretation, the MACFA emphasised that the judiciary would also have to observe Article 11, which requires that all laws in Macau not contravene the MABL.[134] *A fortiori,* laws that are judicially determined to be inconsistent with MABL can be declared unconstitutional. Most importantly, the MACFA buttressed its position by referencing academic writings by Professor Wang Zhenmin, who was a member of the Beijing-appointed Committee for the BL of the MASAR[135] at the time of the litigation. In other words, the MACFA only formally claimed this power of constitutional review after this position dovetailed with the official narrative. It is also noteworthy that the MACFA did *not* declare any laws unconstitutional on the facts.

Case 28/2006 raised a significant question concerning the division of legislative power between the Legislative Assembly and the CE.[136] In this landmark judgment, the MACFA resolutely accepted the MASAR Government's position that its CE possessed the requisite constitutional power to make Administrative Regulations (ARs) (行政法規) under Article 50(5) of the MABL.[137] But the Court also ruled that there are five subject matters for which the Legislative Assembly has *exclusive* legislative jurisdiction: protection of private property (art 6 of the MABL); protection of citizens' rights and freedoms (art 40(2) of the MABL); the composition, competence and operation of Macau courts and procuratorate (arts 84(3) and 90(4) of the MABL); crimes and punishment (art 29 of the MABL); and taxation (art 71 of the MABL).[138] The MACFA decided that these five subject matters are within the Legislative Assembly's exclusive jurisdiction because the MABL explicitly stipulates that such matters must be prescribed by law.[139] On top of that, the MACFA also acknowledged that there are other subject matters for

133 Case 28/2006, at 28 (18 July 2007).

134 Case 28/2006, at 29 (18 July 2007).

135 Case 28/2006, at 29 (18 July 2007). The Committee for the Basic Law of MASAR is a working committee under the NPCSC and was established in 1999 according to the Decision of the NPC on the Proposal by the Drafting Committee for the Basic Law of the MASAR on the Establishment of the Committee for the Basic Law of the MASAR under the NPCSC. The Committee's function is to advise the NPCSC on various matters concerning the MABL: See MABL, arts 17(3), 18(3), 143(4), and 144(3).

136 Case 28/2006, at 4–8 (18 July 2007).

137 Case 28/2006, at 92, 100–101 (18 July 2007).

138 Case 28/2006, at 96–97 (18 July 2007).

139 Case 28/2006, at 96 (18 July 2007).

which the Legislative Assembly has exclusive legislative jurisdiction, but the Court chose not to further elaborate on what these are.[140] As for the CE, the MACFA merely conceded that the MABL does not expressly stipulate subject matters for which the CE can legislate using ARs.[141] In short, the MACFA upheld the power of the CE to issue ARs, but largely left the legislative parameters of such ARs unaddressed.[142]

There are also two significant differences between the MACFA and the HKCFA vis-à-vis the binding effect of their judgments, which impact their constitutional powers. The first difference pertains to the binding effect of their Court's declaration of unconstitutionality. In Hong Kong, when the law is declared unconstitutional, the HKCFA has held that the impugned law would be "null and void".[143] In contrast, for Macau, if the law is declared unconstitutional in a "concrete" dispute, the MACFA has ruled that the unconstitutional legislative provision is merely disapplied in that *specific* case before the Court.[144] Disapplication of the impugned law does not affect its validity in other disputes.[145] As emphasised by the MACFA:

> The finding of unconstitutionality only applies to the specific case before the court and it does not bind other cases or other courts; the legal provision deemed unlawful also does not become invalid or unenforceable because of this judicial determination.[146]

It is noteworthy that there are no textual differences in the respective BLs or local legislation that justify this difference between Hong Kong and Macau. The divergence was purely a matter of judicial choices.[147]

However, the MACFA and the lower courts in Macau can render ARs null and void[148] when they engage in the "abstract" review of such laws under the Code

140 Case 28/2006, at 96, 98 (18 July 2007).

141 Case 28/2006, at 96–97 (18 July 2007).

142 In 2009, the Macau government passed a new law entitled Legal Framework of Internal Regulatory Norms (關於訂定內部規範的法律制度) (Law No. 13/2009), which outlined 19 subject matters for which the Legislative Assembly has exclusive legislative competence. See Chapter 2 of this book.

143 *Ng Ka Ling v Director of Immigration* (1999) 2 HKCFAR 46.

144 Case 8/2007, at 9 (30 April 2008).

145 Chao Wang 汪超, '澳門法院的司法審查制度作為個人自由的保障及其與香港司法審查制度比較的啓示 Judicial Review of Macau Courts as Protection of Individual Rights and Implication after a Comparison with Hong Kong's Judicial Review' (2021) 2 *澳門法學 Macau Law Review* 89, 94.

146 Case 8/2007, at 9 (30 April 2008) (Translation ours).

147 Chao Wang 汪超, '澳門法院的司法審查制度作為個人自由的保障及其與香港司法審查制度比較的啓示 Judicial Review of Macau Courts as Protection of Individual Rights and Implication after a Comparison with Hong Kong's Judicial Review' (2021) 2 *澳門法學 Macau Law Review* 89, 97.

148 Code of Administrative Litigation Procedure (行政訴訟法典) (Decree-Law No. 110/99/M), arts 88(1) and 89(1).

of Administrative Litigation Procedure (行政訴訟法典).[149] In contrast, like most common law courts in the world, the Hong Kong judiciary is not empowered to engage in the "abstract" review of any laws. In Macau, ARs that are declared illegal under this abstract review procedure can no longer be enforced against anyone.[150] (Conversely, as discussed above, when the MACFA engages in the "concrete" review of laws, a declaration of illegality or unconstitutionality only binds the parties in the dispute.) But the effectiveness of this "abstract" review as a mechanism of rights-protection in Macau is extremely limited. First, this review only applies to the legality of ARs, not legislation. Second, citizens may only request an "abstract" review of a disputed AR if the courts have previously ruled its application unlawful on three separate occasions when "concrete" review was exercised.[151] Third, the courts can only review whether a disputed AR is consistent with other legal rules and principles,[152] but "abstract" review cannot be used to assess whether the impugned AR violates the MABL or other international treaties applicable in Macau.[153] In view of this high threshold, the MACFA has only invalidated an AR *once* using "abstract" review. In Case 7/2007, the MACFA ruled that Resolution No. 154/CA of the Administrative Council of the Monetary Authority of Macau, which terminated the reimbursement of electricity, water, telephone, and parking expenses to eligible personnel, was invalid because the said AR contradicted provisions in another legally enforceable rule[154] that expressly authorised these payments.[155]

The second key difference between the MACFA and the HKCFA pertains to the jurisprudential weight of their respective judgments. As Macau is a civil law jurisdiction, the MACFA's decisions are not considered a source of law[156] and their rulings are less binding on lower courts. In contrast, in common law Hong Kong, lower courts always seek guidance from the legal reasoning and principles articulated in past HKCFA rulings to resolve current disputes that raise comparable

149 Code of Administrative Litigation Procedure (行政訴訟法典) (Decree-Law No. 110/99/M), arts 88–93.

150 Code of Administrative Litigation Procedure (行政訴訟法典) (Decree-Law No. 110/99/M), art 88(1).

151 Code of Administrative Litigation Procedure (行政訴訟法典) (Decree-Law No. 110/99/M), art 90(1). But if a regulation has an immediate effect on people's rights and interests, citizens can appeal to the court for abstract review without waiting for the regulation to be ruled unlawful on three separate occasions.

152 Code of Administrative Litigation Procedure (行政訴訟法典) (Decree-Law No. 110/99/M), arts 88(1) and 93(1).

153 Code of Administrative Litigation Procedure (行政訴訟法典) (Decree-Law No. 110/99/M), art 88(2).

154 Regulation for Staff of the Monetary Authority of Macau (澳門金融管理局人員專有通則).

155 Case 7/2007, at 31 (2 April 2008).

156 Jorge Godinho and Paulo Cardinal, 'Macau's Court of Final Appeal' in Simon N. M. Young and Yash Ghai (eds), *Hong Kong's Court of Final Appeal: The Development of the Law in China's Hong Kong* (CUP 2014) 609.

or even new controversies, even if those HKCFA principles were mere dicta. On the other hand, the MACSI has even flatly rejected legal principles articulated by the MACFA. The imbroglio over the constitutionality of AR 17/2004, which concerned the employment of non-locals in Macau, was one such dispute. In Case 28/2006, which we discussed above, the MACFA ruled that the Macau CE has the general constitutional power to independently promulgate ARs, even in the absence of any specific delegation from the legislature on the subject-matter at hand,[157] unless the subject-matter is one for which MABL reserves exclusively for the Legislative Assembly to prescribe by legislation[158] or when constitutional rights and international conventions are engaged.[159] For all other cases, the Macau CE must be conferred with greater rule-making powers to avoid legal vacuums.[160] This MACFA's decision essentially reversed the MACSI's earlier ruling[161] that the entire AR 17/2004 was illegal because the imposition of administrative penalties on the hiring of illegals was a matter for the Legislative Assembly alone to address by legislation.[162] After the MACFA remitted this case to the lower courts for reconsideration, the MACSI grudgingly accepted that the impugned AR 17/2004 was valid.[163] But the MACSI also ruled that only the MACFA's ruling on the legality of the impugned Regulation was legally binding and final, whilst the MACFA's pronouncement on the CE's general powers to formulate ARs was *not* binding and could be disregarded.[164] Furthermore, the MACSI also took the opportunity to openly chastise the MACFA, accusing the MACFA of altering the division of powers stipulated under the MABL, which had assigned legislative power exclusively to the Legislative Assembly.[165] Furthermore, the MACSI pointed out that Macau legislation has to be submitted to the NPCSC for review pursuant to Article 17 of MABL,[166] but this is not required for ARs.[167] Therefore, in the MACSI's view, this MACFA ruling would also compromise the NPCSC's supervision over ARs issued by the Macau CE that had *not* been specifically authorised by legislation.[168]

In sum, notwithstanding the identical textual mandates conferred by the respective BLs, the two Courts of Final Appeal from the get-go embarked on different paths to exercising their constitutional powers of review. Hong Kong

157 Case 28/2006, at 100–101 (18 July 2007).
158 Case 28/2006, at 37 (18 July 2007).
159 Case 28/2006, at 108 (18 July 2007).
160 Case 28/2006, at 100–101 (18 July 2007).
161 Case 223/2005 (I) (MACSI, 27 April 2006).
162 Case 223/2005 (I), at 21 (MACSI, 27 April 2006).
163 Case 223/2005 (II) (MACSI, 13 December 2007).
164 Case 223/2005 (II), at 63 (MACSI, 13 December 2007).
165 Case 223/2005 (II), at 64 (MACSI, 13 December 2007).
166 This provision is *in pari materia* with Article 17 of the HKBL.
167 Case 223/2005 (II), at 64 (MACSI, 13 December 2007).
168 Case 223/2005 (II), at 65 (MACSI, 13 December 2007).

exercised high-equilibrium judicial review, but Macau chose not to. Naturally, this difference impacted the level of rights-protection in both cities, which we will now turn to.

Rights Protection in Hong Kong and Macau

The HKCFA has declared laws unconstitutional on 27 occasions.[169] Among those notable rulings are the following groundbreaking ones: the HKCFA conferred the constitutional right of abode on *all* Mainland children born in Hong Kong even if none of their parents possessed Hong Kong permanent residency;[170] post-operative transgender persons have the constitutional right to marry in their acquired gender;[171] all persons who have resided in Hong Kong for at least one year are conferred with the constitutional right to social welfare;[172] same-sex expatriate couples have the same right as heterosexuals to bring into Hong Kong their spouses as dependants;[173] persons who are in same-sex marriages overseas are entitled to the same tax benefits in Hong Kong as those in opposite-sex marriages, and civil servants in same-sex marriages overseas are eligible for the same spousal benefits as their opposite-sex counterparts;[174] transgender persons are not required to undergo *full* sex reassignment surgery before they can alter their gender markers on Hong Kong Identity Cards;[175] and the HKSAR was required to pass legislation by 2025 to establish an alternative framework for the legal recognition of same-sex partnerships and to provide for appropriate core rights and obligations attendant on such recognition.[176] Soon after, in November 2024, as the clock ticked down to the judicially imposed deadline of 2025, the HKCFA granted same-sex couples legally married overseas equal access to local public rental housing[177] and equal inheritance rights if their spouses died intestate.[178]

In sharp contrast, the MACFA has done nothing to countermand similar legal restrictions operative in its territory. In fact, the MACFA has only declared laws

169 See Appendix 1 of this chapter.
170 *Director of Immigration v Chong Fung Yuen* (2001) 4 HKCFAR 211.
171 *W v Registrar of Marriages* (2013) 16 HKCFAR 112.
172 *Kong Yunming v Director of Social Welfare* (2013) 16 HKCFAR 950.
173 *QT v Director of Immigration* (2018) 21 HKCFAR 324.
174 *Leung Chun Kwong v Secretary for Civil Service* (2019) 22 HKCFAR 127.
175 *Q and Tse Henry Edward v Commissioner of Registration* (2023) 26 HKCFAR 25.
176 *Sham Tsz Kit v Secretary for Justice* (2023) 26 HKCFAR 385. As discussed in Chapter 2, the Legislative Council vetoed a government-sponsored Registration of Same-sex Partnerships bill tabled in 2025, but the government is now considering using administrative measures to protect these same-sex rights. Connor Mycroft and Matthew Cheng, 'Hong Kong to Seek Administrative Measures to Protect Same-Sex Couple Rights' *SCMP* (16 September 2025) <www.scmp.com/news/hong-kong/politics/article/3325687/hong-kong-seek-administrative-measures-protect-same-sex-couples-after-bill-defeat> last accessed 4 January 2026.
177 *Infinger, Nick v Hong Kong Housing Authority* [2024] HKCFA 29.
178 *Ng Hon Lam Edgar v Secretary for Justice* [2024] HKCFA 30.

unconstitutional thrice,[179] and only two cases pertain to a MABL rights-violation. In Case 5/2010, the MACFA ruled that a legislative scheme, which imposed differential contractual terms on teachers employed by Macau's Education and Youth Affairs Bureau and those teaching staff employed in public universities, violated the right to equality.[180] (For the former group of school teachers, medical leave that was less than 30 cumulative days annually would *not* count towards the staff's length of service). For the second case, in Case 25/2011, the MACFA ruled that it was unconstitutional for the Macau authorities to require a notified assembly to include the signatures of three organisers as this would effectively ban demonstrations with only one or two participants.[181] Therefore, the Court read down the requirements under the impugned law such that the signatures of "up to three"[182] organisers are now required on the requisite notification form.

On criminal justice, the HKCFA has interpreted penal legislation liberally to enhance safeguards for the accused. Where offence-creating penal provisions are silent or ambiguous as to the *mens rea* requirement, the HKCFA would avoid imposing absolute liability when severe penalties are involved.[183] Firearms offences that imposed a legal burden of proof on the accused to produce exculpatory evidence have been read down as an *evidential* burden to produce exculpatory evidence,[184] so as to better protect the accused's right to the presumption of innocence. Similarly, drug laws, which *presumed* that the accused knew the nature of the drugs found in his possession, were read down such that the law now only places an *evidential* onus – and not a legal burden of proof – on the accused to dispute possession or knowledge of the drug.[185]

In contrast, the MACFA has been unmoved by similar draconian drug laws in its territory. In Case 112/2018, the MACFA had to address the constitutionality of a statutory provision that allowed offenders to be convicted of drug trafficking if they were found in possession of drugs above a prescribed amount. Unlike the HKCFA, the MACFA ruled that the impugned law did not violate the constitutional right to the presumption of innocence[186] because the choice to impose a harsher penalty for larger quantities of drug possession fell within the discretion of the legislature, and it was not for the courts to interfere with such choices.[187] Furthermore, the MACFA

179 See Appendix 2 of this chapter.
180 Case 5/2010 (12 May 2010). On 20 August 2010, the Legislative Assembly complied and passed Law 12/2010 and standardised their service rules. Interestingly, in Case 9/2012 (9 May 2012), the MACFA has allowed the government to confer better employment benefits on nurses employed in the civil service compared to public-sector nurses hired as contract staff. On this occasion, the MACFA merely asserted that the differential terms were not manifestly intolerable.
181 Case 25/2011, at 6 (30 May 2011).
182 Case 25/2011, at 6 (30 May 2011).
183 *Kulemesin v HKSAR* (2013) 16 HKCFAR 195; *HKSAR v Choi Wai Lun* (2018) 21 HKCFAR 167.
184 *HKSAR v Lam Kwong Wai* (2006) 9 HKCFAR 574.
185 *HKSAR v Hung Chan Wa* (2006) 9 HKCFAR 614.
186 MABL, art 29.
187 Case 112/2018, at 13 (16 January 2019).

has even tightened the rules on reviewing sentences imposed by lower courts. Notwithstanding that Article 390(1)(g) of the Criminal Procedure Code expressly states that criminal sentences above 10 years can be appealed to the MACFA, the Court shockingly ruled that an appeal is only allowed if the sentence for *each individual* conviction exceeds 10 years.[188] In other words, even if an offender was sentenced to 11 years' imprisonment after trial, the MACFA would *not* entertain an appeal if this overall sentence was the consequence of combining two separate sentences of nine years and six years respectively. In line with this regrettable ruling, the MACFA later affirmed that it would only entertain appeals pursuant to this 10-year rule when the *actual* sentence exceeded 10 years, and not merely when the offence *authorised* a sentence above 10 years.[189] But the MACFA did draw a line in the sand by ruling that in the absence of any specific legislation authorising extradition to the Mainland, the local government's attempts to transfer fugitives to Mainland China were illegal.[190]

Central to the HKCFA's efforts to advance rights-protection in Hong Kong is its frequent use of the Proportionality Analysis (PA) in constitutional adjudication. In the 21st century, PA – in its varied manifestations and permutations – has emerged as the most ubiquitous legal doctrine relied upon by judges in rights-adjudication.[191] With its genesis in German law, this PA doctrinal device has diffused globally across Europe to the Anglophone common law jurisdictions (e.g. the UK, Canada, and New Zealand), mixed legal systems that are rooted in the common law (e.g. Israel and South Africa), parts of Latin America and Asia, including Hong Kong.[192]

In colonial Hong Kong,[193] and in the early days of the handover,[194] PA in Hong Kong lacked structure. This was a consequence of the Privy Council, in a case on appeal from Hong Kong, warning courts against following the PA doctrinal tests fashioned in Canada that are applied "rigidly or cumulatively".[195] But as the British Law Lords changed their minds on the matter,[196] the HKCFA also followed suit and soon endorsed a structured variant of PA for rights-adjudication.[197] Echoing contemporaneous developments in English law,[198] the HKCFA now

188 Case 34/2021, at 13 (24 September 2021).
189 Case 138/2021, at 13–17 (1 December 2021).
190 Case 3/2008 (12 February 2008); Case 12/2007 (20 March 2007).
191 Alec Stone Sweet and Jud Mathews, *Proportionality Balancing and Constitutional Governance: A Comparative and Global Approach* (OUP 2019).
192 Po Jen Yap (ed), *Proportionality in Asia* (CUP 2020).
193 *R v Sin Yau Ming* [1992] 1 HKCLR 127.
194 *HKSAR v Ng Kung Siu* (1999) 2 HKCFAR 442.
195 *Attorney General of Hong Kong v Lee Kwong-Kut* [1993] AC 951, [1993] 2 HKCLR 186, at 200.
196 *De Freitas v Permanent Secretary of Ministry of Agriculture, Fisheries, Lands and Housing* [1999] 1 AC 69.
197 *Leung Kwok Hung v HKSAR* (2005) 8 HKCFAR 229.
198 See *R (Aguilar Quila) v. Secretary of State for the Home Department* [2012] 1 AC 621, at [45]; *Bank Mellat v. Her Majesty's Treasury (No. 2)* [2014] AC 700, at [20] and [65]; *R (Lord Carlile of Berriew) v. Secretary of State for the Home Department* [2015] AC 945, at [19], [98], and [148].

applies a four-step PA in deciding whether rights have been violated by examining sequentially: (1) the "legitimacy" of the purpose for which the constitutional right is restricted; (2) the "rational connection" between such legitimate purpose and the means by which the right is restricted; (3) the "necessity" of the restriction; and (4) the "reasonable balance" struck between the societal benefits of the encroachment and the inroads made into the constitutionally protected rights of the individual.[199]

This is not to say that the HKCFA is always consistent in the way it applies PA in rights-adjudication.[200] Notably, the HKCFA regularly defers to the government on matters concerning "policy considerations" that include national security and election law.[201] In contrast to Hong Kong, the MACFA has not adopted PA in assessing the constitutionality of any type of rights-violations at all, insisting instead that it was not for judges to replace legislators in deciding what was reasonable or fair.[202] Interestingly, the MACFA has accepted the use of a structured and sequential PA (適度原則) under *administrative* law, but only for *non-constitutional* rights cases.[203]

Typically, the more progressive rulings issued by the MACFA were on lower stakes – administrative justice. In Case 11/2007, the MACFA ruled that a child's Macau permanent residency could not be revoked simply because a subsequent DNA test proved that the child was not genetically related to the father who was the sole Macau Permanent Resident in the child's family. The Court determined that such DNA reports may not override the child's parental records registered under the Macau Civil Registration Code.[204] In Case 21/2014, the MACFA also decided against the government and ruled that a foreigner was not precluded from acquiring the right of permanent residency in Macau simply because his spouse and children had *no* intentions of joining him in relocating to Macau.[205] More significantly, in Case 16/2021, the MACFA ruled that the principle against double jeopardy would

199 *Hysan Development v Town Planning Board* (2016) 19 HKCFAR 372, at [134]–[135].

200 For a critique on the inconsistency, see Rehan Abeyratne, 'More Structure, More Deference: Proportionality in Hong Kong' in Po Jen Yap (ed), *Proportionality in Asia* (CUP 2020) 25.

201 *Kwok Cheuk Kin v Secretary for Constitutional and Mainland Affairs* (2017) 20 HKCFAR 353, at [41]–[42].

202 Case 5/2010, at 34 (12 May 2010); Case 112/2018, at 13 (16 January 2019).

203 Referencing Art 5(2) of the Code of Administrative Procedure and Portuguese scholarship, the MACFA ruled that this proportionality principle comprised three elements: suitability, necessity and balance: the means should be suitable for achieving the governmental aims; the means chosen should be no more than necessary to achieve those stated aims; the costs imposed on the applicant's rights and interests must be acceptable and tolerable after they are balanced against the benefits of the regulatory measure (proportionality stricto sensu). See Case 6/2000 (27 April 2000), Case 9/2000 (3 May 2000), Case 8/2019 (27 March 2019); Case 11/2019 (4 April 2019); Case 59/2020 (31 July 2020).

204 Case 11/2007 (30 May 2008).

205 Case 21/2014 (7 January 2015).

bar a *second* disciplinary hearing from being brought against an applicant when an earlier disciplinary hearing based on the same facts had previously been instituted but terminated mid-way.[206] On the facts, after the first disciplinary hearing was discontinued, the applicant – a civil servant – was subsequently charged and sentenced for misconduct in public office. Based on this criminal sentence, the government attempted to re-institute a second disciplinary hearing against the errant civil servant. In rejecting the government's second bite at the cherry, the MACFA relied on the principle against double jeopardy. While this principle was *not* expressly enshrined in the MABL, the MACFA referenced Article 40 of the MABL which provides that the ICCPR shall remain in force in Macau and be implemented through the laws of the MASAR. Most importantly, the MACFA asserted that this principle against double jeopardy was implicitly embedded in Article 6 and Article 65(2) of the Macau Penal Code. But in truth, neither provision made any such reference: Article 6 governs when Macau's criminal laws may have extra-territorial effect and Article 65(2) merely lists factors judges should consider at sentencing. But with this sleight of hand, the MACFA was able to ground the principle of double jeopardy under Macau's criminal laws, and extend its application to disciplinary proceedings via Article 277 of the Statute of Public Administration Workers (澳門公共行政工作人員通則), which authorised criminal procedural processes and protections to be extended to disciplinary proceedings where appropriate. While the MACFA reached liberal results in all these cases, it is also worth noting that *no* laws were declared unconstitutional let alone invalidated by the Court.

Political Assemblies and Protests

Prior to Beijing's imposition of the 2020 HKNSL, large-scale public demonstrations in Hong Kong were a regular affair. Pre-2020, the Hong Kong police rarely *ex ante* prohibited assemblies from taking place and few cases percolated up to the HKCFA on appeal. In fact, back in 2005, the HKCFA in *Yeung May Wan v HKSAR*[207] even upheld the right of a small group of peaceful protestors to demonstrate outside the Liaison Office of the Central People's Government in Hong Kong. In view of the national security laws fully operative in Hong Kong now, it is unlikely that this case would have been decided the same way today.

After 2012, Hong Kong society became more polarised and political protests grew in scale. In 2014, the "Occupy Central" movement broke out and this mass street protest – with thousands of participants camping in the streets – partially shut down Hong Kong's financial district for 79 consecutive days and in its aftermath, the student leaders were charged for public order offences they committed in the lead-up to the road blockades. Notably, the Court of Appeal proceeded to

206 Case 16/2021 (3 June 2021).
207 (2005) 8 HKCFAR 137.

impose a custodial sentence on them, which ranged from six to eight months of imprisonment, by establishing an enhanced and more severe sentencing scheme for unlawful assemblies involving violence,[208] and ruled that community service orders or suspended prison sentences were manifestly inadequate. But in 2018 after the decision reached the HKCFA on appeal, the Court unilaterally forged a compromise. The HKCFA agreed that the Court of Appeal was right to issue a new sentencing guideline on unlawful assemblies involving violence, but since the custodial sentences imposed by the Court of Appeal on the offenders were significantly more severe than the range established by past judicial practice, the HKCFA held that these guidelines could not be retrospectively applied to the offenders,[209] thereby freeing the student leaders. In this way, the HKCFA stood up for a cardinal due process principle that an offender should not suffer a heavier punishment than was prescribed at the time the offence was committed and the government was equally appeased by the fact that future unlawful assemblies involving violence will be "subject to the new guidelines".[210]

By 2020, the political stakes were even higher. In *Kwok Wing Hang v Chief Executive in Council,*[211] the HKCFA had to decide on whether the Chief Executive in Council (CEIC) could invoke the Emergency Regulations Ordinance (ERO) to make regulations on any occasion of public danger, and whether the Prohibition on Face Covering Regulation (PFCR) – the subsidiary legislation enacted pursuant to the ERO – was constitutional. As discussed in Chapter 1, for most of 2019, Hong Kong was rocked by civil unrest. The protests originally arose in opposition to the government's attempt to pass an extradition law that would allow for Hong Kong residents to be extradited to other countries and jurisdictions, including Mainland China, Macau, and Taiwan, to face trial for alleged serious offences committed there. Even though the bill was eventually withdrawn, the unrest continued as protestors pressed on for other demands, including amnesty for arrested protestors and an independent inquiry into alleged police brutality. Notably, many protestors wore masks during the protests to prevent identification and to shield themselves from the effects of tear gas and pepper spray used regularly by the police. In response to the escalating street violence, the CEIC invoked the ERO to enact the PFCR, which banned facial covering in all public assemblies. When the constitutionality of the ERO and the PFCR came before the HKCFA, the Court forged another strategic compromise. Both the ERO and the PFCR were upheld as constitutional in their *entirety,* but the Court also read down the ERO such that the ERO – and any subsidiary legislation made pursuant – cannot be used to "override the [BORO]"[212]. In other words, the courts retain an independent role in

208 *Secretary for Justice v Wong Chi Fung* [2018] 2 HKLRD 699, at [135].
209 *Secretary for Justice v Wong Chi Fung* (2018) 21 HKCFAR 35, at [126].
210 *Secretary for Justice v Wong Chi Fung* (2018) 21 HKCFAR 35, at [135].
211 (2020) 23 HKCFAR 518.
212 (2020) 23 HKCFAR 518, at [73].

examining the proportionality of any rights-infringing regulations passed under the ERO, even though the law on its face expressly allows for emergency laws to override all legislation, including the BORO.[213] The draconian effects of the ERO were mitigated, but the government also retained its powers to ban facial coverings at all assemblies, including peaceful ones.

After Beijing foisted the 2020 HKNSL on Hong Kong, public assemblies have become rare, tightly controlled, and carefully choreographed.[214] National security legislation now hangs like a Sword of Damocles over the city and civil society has been practically neutered, which we will explore more closely in Chapter 4.

To date, the HKCFA has weighed in on the tightened rules once. In 2024, in *HKSAR v Chow Hang Tung*,[215] by a majority of 3 to 2, the HKCFA ruled that a defendant who was charged for taking part in an unauthorised assembly under the Public Order Ordinance (POO) was allowed to challenge the lawfulness of the prohibition by way of defence in her criminal proceedings,[216] without having to separately challenge the lawfulness of that prohibition in a judicial review proceeding, and the prosecution bore the burden of proof of proving the legality of the prohibition order.[217] But the Court also unanimously *upheld* the lawfulness of the prohibition order on the facts, as it decided that the police did *not* have a positive duty to proactively propose measures to enable the public assembly to proceed; instead, the police are merely obliged to give genuine and reasonable consideration to proposals suggested by the organisers, and assess their workability and likely effectiveness in light of the organisers' resources and capabilities.[218] Notably, the intended public assembly related to a proposed Tiananmen Square commemoration – an annual feature in Hong Kong pre-COVID – on 4 June 2021. The HKCFA adroitly avoided having to rule whether memorials of such nature are still lawful in Hong Kong, by focusing merely on the "public health concerns"[219] of the ongoing COVID-19 pandemic at that time.

Turning to Macau, its MACFA resolves far more cases on public assemblies. This is because in Macau, organisers of public assemblies can directly appeal[220] to

213 Section 2(4) of the ERO reads:

> A regulation […] shall have effect notwithstanding anything inconsistent therewith contained in any enactment; and any provision of an enactment which may be inconsistent with any regulation […] shall […] have no effect so long as such regulation […] remain in force.

214 Chris Lau, 'Hong Kong's First Protest in 3 Years Shows How the City Has Changed' *CNN* (28 March 2023) <https://edition.cnn.com/2023/03/28/asia/hong-kong-first-protest-in-years-intl-hnk/index.html> last accessed 4 January 2026.

215 [2024] HKCFA 2.

216 [2024] HKCFA 2, at [158].

217 [2024] HKCFA 2, at [182].

218 [2024] HKCFA 2, at [170].

219 [2024] HKCFA 2, at [171].

220 Art 12(1) of Law No. 2/93/M (The Right to Assemble and Demonstrate 集會權及示威權).

the MACFA when they receive an adverse decision from the police.[221] The police must submit their reply within forty-eight hours, and the MACFA has to resolve the case within five days upon receiving their response.[222] By contrast, cases in Hong Kong only reach the HKCFA via the ordinary appellate process which takes years.

Unlike the HKCFA, the MACFA had upheld a prohibition on demonstrations outside the Liaison Office of the Central People's Government in Macau. For the MACFA, the ban was necessary to ensure that the Office facilities were not damaged, and their operations were not impeded.[223] The MACFA had also regularly upheld bans on public assemblies that were planned in the vicinity of crowded roads with high foot traffic,[224] even if the planned demonstration was limited to only three people.[225] But the MACFA had allowed a planned demonstration to proceed when it was confined to a public park, and the Court had also overridden attempts by the government to simply select[226] or shortlist[227] *specific* venues for the organisers. As asserted by the MACFA, venues for public gatherings were for the applicants themselves to choose, subject to approval on public order grounds.

The MACFA has also liberalised the *notification* requirements imposed on planned demonstrations and assemblies. As discussed earlier, in 2011, the MACFA ruled that it would be unconstitutional for the government to require a notified assembly to include the signatures of three organisers as this would mean that demonstrations with only one or two persons would be effectively barred.[228] Therefore, the Court read down the law to mean that the signatures of "up to three"[229] organisers would be needed on the requisite notification form. But prohibitions on public assemblies are more commonly quashed in Macau on procedural grounds. The MACFA has ruled that it would not suffice for the Government to merely state the ban would be in the interest of public order or public safety without further elaboration;[230] or if the Government did not provide adequate reasons[231] or concrete explanations[232] for the ban.

221 Before August 2018, a notification of one's intention to hold an assembly and demonstration had to be submitted to the Municipal Affairs Bureau, which could reject or impose restrictions on proposed assemblies and demonstrations. At the same time, Article 8 of Law No. 2/93/M also empowered the police to impose conditions or ban the proposed demonstration. On 30 July 2018, an amendment to Law No. 2/93/M was passed, which removed the Municipal Affairs Bureau's role from the law. Now, any such notifications would be submitted directly to the police.

222 Art 12(3) of Law No. 2/93/M (The Right to Assemble and Demonstrate 集會權及示威權).

223 Case 6/2011, at 6 (24 February 2011).

224 Case 31/2011, at 11 (25 June 2011).

225 Case 34/2011, at 2 (11 July 2011).

226 Case 16/2010, at 10 (29 April 2010).

227 Case 21/2010, at 7 (4 May 2010).

228 Case 25/2011, at 6 (30 May 2011).

229 Case 25/2011, at 6 (30 May 2011).

230 Case 2/2011 (12 January 2011).

231 Case 33/2014 (4 June 2014); Case 34/2014 (4 June 2014).

232 Case 37/2018 (3 May 2018).

Unsurprisingly, the MACFA is in complete lockstep with the government vis-à-vis the most politically sensitive public gatherings occurring in Macau. Influenced by their Hong Kong counterparts, pro-democracy politicians in Macau attempted to organise a non-binding civic referendum for their own CE Election in August 2014. While Hong Kong's "referendum" was allowed to proceed and drew over 700,000 voters in June 2014,[233] the Macau authorities barred a similar event from taking place in their territory. When the Macau pro-democracy politicians appealed against the governmental ban, the MACFA farcically ruled the "referendum" was a mere "opinion poll"[234] and not an "assembly", and therefore the Court did not have any jurisdiction to hear the case.[235]

In late 2019, as the Hong Kong protests were boiling over, the Macau pro-democracy politicians wanted to jump into the fray and show their support by organising a 15-person assembly in Macau to urge the Hong Kong police to abide by the *Convention against Torture and Other Cruel, Inhuman or Degrading Treatment or Punishment.* The MASAR government swiftly banned the assembly and the MACFA upheld the prohibition on the flimsy pretext that such a demonstration in Macau would violate the "One Country, Two Systems" constitutional framework by interfering with how the Hong Kong government managed its own internal affairs.[236] The MACFA equally justified the police ban on the June 4 candlelight vigil in 2020 – a hitherto regular feature in Macau – ostensibly because of public health concerns relating to COVID-19, but it is also noteworthy that at the time of the court's ruling, not a single COVID-19 transmission had surfaced in Macau for months.[237] In 2021, the MACFA, by a 2–1 majority, decided to just rule outright that such June 4 candlelight vigils were illegal. As the CFA reasoned, these vigils were intended to disseminate information that incited disaffection against the PRC government, harmed national security and the country's reputation, and were inconsistent with the Central Government's own "factual" account.[238] In response to the argument that pre-COVID-19, the vigils had been going on in Macau for decades, the MACFA merely provided a pithy reply that the repetition of an unlawful act did not legalise it, nor bar subsequent sanctions.[239]

233 'Hong Kong democracy "referendum" draws nearly 800,000' *BBC* (30 June 2014) <www.bbc.com/news/world-asia-china-28076566> last accessed 4 January 2026.

234 Case 95/2014, at 7 (30 July 2014).

235 Case 95/2014, at 8–9 (30 July 2014).

236 Case 94/2019, at 16 (27 September 2019).

237 Case 58/2020, at 22–23 (29 May 2020).

238 Case 81/2021, at 50 (3 June 2021).

239 Case 81/2021, at 61–62 (3 June 2021). Interestingly, Justice José Maria Dias Azedo (司徒民正) dissented, arguing that the candlelight vigil should be allowed to proceed if the organisers excised "all defamatory and insulting elements" from their event.

Application of Chinese Law in the Constitutional Context

As discussed above, the HKCFA ruled in *Ng Ka Ling* that it had a "duty to declare invalidity"[240] any act of the NPC or NPCSC that was inconsistent with the HKBL. When this decision was partially reversed by the NPCSC via an Interpretation pursuant to Article 158 of the HKBL, the HKCFA in *Lau Kong Yung*[241] accepted that the NPCSC's power of Interpretation was "binding on the courts of the HKSAR"[242] and it would take effect retrospectively from the date the HKBL came into effect.[243]

But notably in *Lau Kong Yung*, the HKCFA kept silent on whether other types of legislative acts issued by the NPCSC and NPC e.g. NPC and NPCSC Decisions[244] – also commonly applied by Beijing in Hong Kong but without any constitutional basis in the HKBL – were equally binding on Hong Kong courts. Furthermore, the HKCFA would construe the NPCSC Interpretation strictly such that those parts of the HKCFA judgment which were not explicitly reversed by the Interpretation would still be legally operative. Specifically, in *Ng Ka Ling*, the HKCFA had also ruled that criminal sanctions imposed by the impugned immigration legislation were unconstitutional insofar as they were applied retrospectively to events predating the law's passage.[245] Given that this legal ruling was "not affected by the Interpretation",[246] the HKCFA decided in *Lau Kong Yung* that the retrospective statutory provision in the immigration law remained invalid.[247] Furthermore, in *Chong Fung Yuen*, the HKCFA decided that the NPCSC Interpretation would only be a "binding interpretation"[248] of the specific clause of the HKBL targeted by the Interpretation; statements made in the Interpretation about other BL clauses not expressly subject to Interpretation would not be binding on Hong Kong courts.[249] Since the Interpretation was specifically about the right of abode of Chinese children *born in the Mainland* to Hong Kong parents, the HKCFA ignored statements made in the Interpretation about Chinese children *born in Hong Kong* but whose parents were not Hong Kong Permanent Residents. By doing so, the HKCFA in *Chong Fung Yuen* ruled that all Mainland children born in Hong Kong had the constitutional right of Hong Kong permanent residency, even though the Interpretation in fact suggested otherwise.[250]

240 *Ng Ka Ling v Director of Immigration* (1999) 2 HKCFAR 26.
241 *Lau Kong Yung v Director of Immigration* (1999) 2 HKCFAR 300.
242 *Lau Kong Yung v Director of Immigration* (1999) 2 HKCFAR 324.
243 *Lau Kong Yung v Director of Immigration* (1999) 2 HKCFAR 326.
244 See Chapter 5 of this book for a discussion on the different types of PRC laws operative in Hong Kong.
245 *Ng Ka Ling v Director of Immigration* (1999) 2 HKCFAR 38–40.
246 *Lau Kong Yung v Director of Immigration* (1999) 2 HKCFAR 327.
247 *Lau Kong Yung v Director of Immigration* (1999) 2 HKCFAR 327.
248 *Director of Immigration v Chong Fung Yuen* (2001) 4 HKCFAR 223.
249 *Director of Immigration v Chong Fung Yuen* (2001) 4 HKCFAR 223.
250 *Director of Immigration v Chong Fung Yuen* (2001) 4 HKCFAR 223.

To date, Beijing's passage of the bespoke 2020 HKNSL poses the greatest challenge to the independence of the Court and its international standing. In our view, there had been some missteps by the HKCFA insofar as the Court tightened the rules for granting bail to the accused charged with any national security offence,[251] including national security offences that were committed prior to the passage of 2020 HKNSL.[252] We will examine these cases more closely in Chapter 4, but suffice to say here, the HKCFA nevertheless drew a line in the sand by ruling that the Hong Kong courts must only apply "the common law approach"[253] when interpreting the 2020 HKNSL, even though this PRC law was wholly drafted and enacted by the NPCSC. The HKCFA emphasised that the Hong Kong courts may *not* "search for and consider as possible aids to construction, similarly-worded Mainland laws".[254] In this way, the HKCFA was firewalling the HKSAR from the more *draconian* PRC Criminal Law whose similarly-worded language has influenced the 2020 HKNSL's PRC drafters when they crafted the city's own offence-creating provisions.[255] Equally significantly, the HKCFA ruled in 2025 that if the accused were alleged to be a "foreign agent" under the 2020 NSL Implementation Rules, the burden was on the Prosecution to prove this status beyond a reasonable doubt. Furthermore, insofar as the Prosecution had not disclosed to the accused why or how they were construed by the government to be foreign agents, the latter's right to a fair trial had been violated and their convictions by the lower courts were all quashed.[256]

In contrast, the MACFA has openly applied Chinese law in cases of constitutional significance, relying on Chinese laws, NPCSC Decisions, Mainland judicial opinions, and academic writings of Chinese scholars to underpin its arguments. In Case 28/2006, which we discussed above, when the MACFA ruled that the CE was constitutionally empowered to promulgate independent ARs without any specific delegation from the Legislative Assembly, the MACFA asserted that it must consider the PRC constitutional provisions, theories, and practice in understanding ARs and their relationship with statutory law.[257] This reference was justified on the basis that MABL was passed by the NPC, drafted by the MABL Drafting Committee which comprised eminent persons from the Chinese legal sector, and influenced by the PRC Constitution and relevant theories.[258] Since ARs were derived from the PRC State Council's AR-making power,[259] and did not exist in Macau before the handover, the MACFA drew parallels and adopted

251 *HKSAR v Lai Chee Ying* (2021) 24 HKCFAR 33.
252 *HKSAR v Ng Hau Yi* (2021) 24 HKCFAR 417.
253 *HKSAR v Lui Sai Yu* (2023) 26 HKCFAR 332, at [45].
254 *HKSAR v Lui Sai Yu* (2023) 26 HKCFAR 332, at [47].
255 See discussion in Chapter 4 of this book.
256 *HKSAR v Tang Ngok Kwan* [2025] HKCFA 3.
257 Case 28/2006, at 103 (18 July 2007).
258 Case 28/2006, at 103–104 (18 July 2007).
259 Constitution of the PRC, art 89.

the interrelationship between the State Council's AR-making power and the legislative power of the NPC/NPCSC.[260]

In Case 81/2021, when the MACFA upheld the government's ban on a candlelight vigil to commemorate the victims of the Tiananmen Square military crackdown, the Court expressly cited the *Resolution of the NPCSC on Stopping Riots and Quelling Anti-Revolution Unrest* (全国人民代表大会常务委员会关于制止动乱和平息反革命暴乱的决议) (6 July 1989), which labelled the June 4th 1989 crackdown as "disturbances aimed at overthrowing the leadership of the CCP, overthrowing the Central Government, and subverting the PRC".[261] In Case 113/2021, when the MACFA upheld the government's disqualification of *all* pro-democracy political parties from the then-upcoming 2021 Legislative Assembly election, the MACFA once again endorsed the above Resolution of the NPCSC, and also Article 1 of the PRC Constitution, which stipulates that "the leadership of the CCP is the defining feature of Chinese socialism".[262] The candidates' disqualification was premised on the basis that they had organised and participated in the June 4 vigils and assemblies held in Macau to commemorate Chinese dissident Liu Xiaobo and the pro-democracy manifesto Charter 08.[263] The MACFA viewed the participation in all these assemblies as challenges to the CCP's leadership,[264] referencing Liu Xiaobo's conviction in a closed-door judicial hearing in Beijing[265] as support.[266]

High Stakes Election Cases

But there is one notable point of convergence between the two top courts. Both Courts of Final Appeal are highly deferential to their governments on high-stakes elections. In 2012, after CY Leung was elected as Hong Kong CE, an election petition[267]

260 Case 28/2006, at 39–58 (18 July 2007).

261 Case 81/2021, at 50 (3 June 2021). The NPCSC Resolution stated in Chinese '他们的目的就是要推翻中国共产党的领导，推翻中央人民政府，颠覆社会主义的中华人民共和国。'

262 Case 113/2021, at 208–209 (31 July 2021).

263 Case 113/2021, at 204–209 (31 July 2021). Liu Xiaobo was one of China's most prominent dissidents and well-known human rights activists. He was arrested in December 2008 and was imprisoned for inciting subversion of state power in December 2009. His alleged crime was the public criticism of the Chinese government and being one of the main drafters of Charter 08, a manifesto calling for democracy, respect for human rights and the rule of law in China. See Jean-Philippe Beja, Fu Hualing, and Eva Pils (eds), *Liu Xiaobo, Charter 08 and the Challenges of Political Reform in China* (Hong Kong University Press, 2012).

264 Case 113/2021, at 208–209 (31 July 2021).

265 The judgment of the Beijing High Court is not released to the public. According to news reports, the First Intermediate Court of Beijing convicted Liu Xiaobo for inciting subversion of state power in December 2009. The Beijing High Court dismissed Liu Xiaobo's appeal in February 2010. '北京高级法院驳回刘晓波上诉 The Beijing High Court dismissed Liu Xiaobo's appeal' *BBC* (11 February 2010) <www.bbc.com/zhongwen/simp/china/2010/02/100211_liuxiaobo> last accessed 4 January 2026.

266 Case 113/2021, at 209–210 (31 July 2021).

267 In Hong Kong, under Section 32 of the Chief Executive Election Ordinance (CEEO), the election can be questioned if the winner "engaged in corrupt conduct or illegal conduct at the election".

was brought by Albert Ho – the only pro-democracy election candidate in the CE race. Ho challenged the election result on the basis that CY Leung had violated the Elections (Corrupt and Illegal Conduct) Ordinance (ECICO)[268] when the latter allegedly made two materially false and misleading statements prior to the election. In the first statement, CY Leung allegedly told journalists that he did not have any unauthorised building structures in his home. In the second statement, CY Leung had publicly accused Henry Tang – another CE candidate in the race – of concealing from the public the existence of illegal structures at the latter's residence. One may note that Henry Tang was another pro-Beijing candidate, and he was widely tipped to be the next CE. But when the local press reported that Tang had unauthorised structures built in his basement, public opinion turned against him. It was believed that Beijing – heeding public opinion – influenced the Election Committee delegates to switch their vote to CY Leung. In an interesting twist to the tale, *after* CY Leung was elected as CE, the local press uncovered that Leung too had unauthorised structures in his home.

The HKCFA in *Re Ho Chun Yan Albert*[269] swiftly rejected this electoral challenge. In the HKCFA's view, the first statement was allegedly made by CY Leung before he had publicly declared his candidacy for CE, and the ECICO only regulated statements made by persons who had been nominated or had publicly declared their candidacy.[270] Therefore, while the first statement was untrue, there was no violation of the electoral law at issue. In the Court's view, there was also no legal duty on the candidate to publicly retract any false statements he made prior to his candidacy.[271] As for the second statement, the CFA ruled that the statement was *not* materially false or misleading merely because "Mr CY Leung was susceptible to the very same attack which he was making on Mr Tang".[272] In short, hypocrisy is not misleading and hence not a crime.

A few years later, the HKCFA had to wade into greater political turmoil over the LegCo elections. In 2016, a slew of young pro-democracy activists was elected to the Hong Kong LegCo. Less compromising and more confrontational than "pan-democrats" of the past, two (Sixtus Leung and Yau Wai-ching) of these lawmakers openly derided China at their swearing-in ceremony on 12 October 2016 and they even referred to China as "Sheen-na" – a derogatory term used by the Japanese

268 Section 26(2) of the ECICO reads:

> A candidate engages in illegal conduct at an election if the candidate publishes a materially false or misleading statement of fact about the candidate or candidates with whom the candidate is associated, or about another candidate or other candidates, for the purpose of—
> (a) promoting the election of the candidate or candidates with whom the candidate is associated; or
> (b) prejudicing the election of the other candidate or candidates.

269 (2012) 15 HKCFAR 686.
270 (2012) 15 HKCFAR 686, at [20].
271 (2012) 15 HKCFAR 686, at [23]–[24].
272 (2012) 15 HKCFAR 686, at [39].

on the Chinese during the Second World War – and displayed banners advocating Hong Kong's independence. Naturally, the President of the LegCo did not accept the validity of the pair's oaths, but he nevertheless allowed them to retake their oaths at the next LegCo meeting. However, before Leung and Yau could retake their oaths, the Hong Kong government swiftly went to court and sought a declaration that the pair had been disqualified from their office by operation of law on 12 October 2016 when they declined to take the requisite oath of office, and the LegCo President was therefore disempowered from re-administering their oaths. Days after the Court of First Instance (HKCFI) finished hearing this case but before the court delivered judgment, the NPCSC issued an Interpretation of Article 104 of the HKBL.[273] The Interpretation *inter alia* provides that: "If the oath taken is determined as invalid, no arrangement shall be made for retaking the oath." Consequently, both the HKCFI[274] and the Hong Kong Court of Appeal[275] concluded that the errant legislators-elect had been automatically disqualified from assuming their offices when they declined to take their oath properly.[276] And the Appeal Committee of the HKCFA in *Yau Wai Ching* subsequently refused their leave to appeal. According to the HKCFA, the Interpretation can apply to events predating its announcement as it "declares what the law is and has always been since the coming into effect of the Basic Law on 1 July 1997"[277] and "there is no warrant for revisiting"[278] this proposition.

The *retrospective* application of the Interpretation to events that predated its announcement is deeply troubling. No Hong Kong law requires this. One should note that even under PRC law, there is no categorical rule that legislative interpretations by the NPCSC have retrospective effect. Article 50[279] of the PRC Law on Legislation simply stated that NPCSC Interpretations "have the same effect

273 Interpretation of Article 104 of the Basic Law of the Hong Kong Special Administrative Region of the People's Republic of China by the Standing Committee of the National People's Congress (Adopted by the Standing Committee of the 12th National People's Congress at its 24th Session on 7 November 2016). Article 104 of the HKBL reads:

> When assuming office, the Chief Executive, principal officials, members of the Executive Council and of the Legislative Council, judges of the courts at all levels and other members of the judiciary in the Hong Kong Special Administrative Region must, in accordance with law, swear to uphold the Basic Law of the Hong Kong Special Administrative Region of the People's Republic of China and swear allegiance to the Hong Kong Special Administrative Region of the People's Republic of China.

274 *Chief Executive of HKSAR v President of the Legislative Council* [2016] 6 HKC 417.

275 *Chief Executive of HKSAR v President of the Legislative Council* [2017] 1 HKLRD 460.

276 More importantly, one should note that the government's victory in the first case emboldened it to seek the removal of four additional pro-democracy lawmakers. See *Chief Executive of HKSAR v President of the Legislative Council* [2017] 4 HKLRD 115.

277 *Yau Wai Ching v Chief Executive of HKSAR* (2017) 20 HKCFAR 390, at [35].

278 *Yau Wai Ching v Chief Executive of HKSAR* (2017) 20 HKCFAR 390, at [36].

279 This Article 50 clause is now found in Article 53 of the PRC Law on Legislation after a revision in 2023.

as laws" but even this PRC Law does not expressly provide for the retrospective effect of NPCSC Interpretations.[280]

Given that an NPCSC Interpretation is a legislative act of a legislative body, a convincing case can be made that the presumption against retrospectivity of legislation should also apply. According to this common law presumption, unless a contrary intention appears, a legislative provision is presumed not to operate retrospectively,[281] that is, to impair vested rights acquired under then-existing laws or to create a new obligation, duty or disadvantage in relation to past events,[282] regardless of whether it is "penal in the sense of punishment".[283]

The HKCFA in *Lau Kong Yung*[284] has previously declared that an NPCSC Interpretation issued in 1999 applied retrospectively. As we discussed earlier, the 1999 NPCSC Interpretation was handed down to overrule a pair of HKCFA judgments – *Ng Ka Ling*[285] and *Chan Kam Nga*[286] – that conferred the constitutional right of abode on all Mainland-born children with at least one Hong Kong Permanent Resident parent. But we must note the central difference between the 1999 NPCSC Interpretation and the 2016 one: the 1999 Interpretation *expressly* states that it would have retrospective effect while the 2016 Interpretation is silent on its temporal effect. If the NPCSC was adamant about making the 2016 Interpretation retrospective, it could have easily expressed its intention clearly in the text as it did so in 1999. In contrast, the 2016 Interpretation simply makes no mention about its temporal effect. It is unclear why the Beijing officials chose not to do so in 2016. In light of this textual ambiguity, and since the 2016 Interpretation was passed by a legislative body and should be viewed as a piece of legislation, the presumption against retrospectivity should *not* be displaced. Ergo, the Interpretation should not operate retrospectively to events that predated its announcement.[287]

Unfortunately, in *Yau Wai Ching*, the Appeal Committee of the HKCFA simply deemed the legal distinction between the 1999 and 2016 NPCSC Interpretations "not reasonably arguable"[288] and refused leave to appeal. Interestingly, six months after *Yau Wai Ching* was decided, Robert Tang – a then-Permanent Judge of the

280 Han Zhu and Albert Chen, 'The Oath-taking Cases and the NPCSC Interpretation of 2016: Interface of Common Law and Chinese Law' (2019) 49(1) *Hong Kong Law Journal* 381, 403.

281 Francis Bennion and Oliver Jones (eds), *Bennion on Statutory Interpretation* (6th ed., Sweet and Maxwell 2013) 291; *Spread Trustee Co Ltd v Hutcheson* [2012] 2 AC 194 (Privy Council) at [65].

282 *Yew Bon Tew v Kenderaan Bas Mara* [1983] 1 AC 553 (Privy Council), 558–559.

283 *Re School Board Election for the Parish of Pulborough* [1894] 1 QB 725 (Court of Appeal), 737.

284 *Lau Kong Yung & Others v Director of Immigration* (1999) 2 HKCFAR 300.

285 *Ng Ka Ling & Others v Director of Immigration* (1999) 2 HKCFAR 4.

286 *Chan Kam Nga & Others v Director of Immigration* (1999) 2 HKCFAR 82.

287 Po Jen Yap and Eric Chan, 'Legislative Oaths and Judicial Intervention in Hong Kong' (2017) 47(1) *Hong Kong Law Journal* 1, 12–14.

288 *Yau Wai Ching v Chief Executive of HKSAR* (2017) 20 HKCFAR 390, at [36].

HKCFA – in an extra-judicial address at Oxford University voiced his disagreement with the HKCFA brethren on this issue:

> [T]he Court of Final Appeal may if it wishes to do so reconsider the point in a full court of five judges after full argument. The 2016 Interpretation may provide a good opportunity to do so.[289]

Notably, Robert Tang PJ (as he then was) was *not* assigned to the HKCFA's Appeal Committee panel that decided *Yau Wai Ching*.

While CE elections in Macau have always proceeded with little fanfare and controversy,[290] the Macau Legislative Assembly Election of 2021 was fraught with political tension. That year, the Macau Legislative Assembly Electoral Affairs Commission (立法會選舉管理委員會, MALAEAC) disqualified 21 people from contesting the 2021 Legislative Assembly, 15 of whom were from the pro-democracy political parties.[291] The MALAEAC asserted that these pro-democracy candidates had been disloyal to Macau and China, and therefore had failed to comply with the MABL and the Law on the Election of the Legislative Assembly of the MASAR (澳門特別行政區立法會選舉法).[292] On appeal to the MACFA, their disqualifications were all upheld.[293] The MACFA based its decision on the fact that many of these democrats had organised and participated in the candlelight vigils held annually in Macau on 4th June – the anniversary of the Tiananmen Square military crackdown.[294] Others were disqualified because they had organised and participated in public assemblies in Macau to commemorate Chinese dissident Liu Xiaobo and the pro-democracy manifesto Charter 08.[295]

289 Robert Tang, 'Dr Mok Hing Yiu Memorial Lecture: One Country, Two Systems: Basic Law, Common Law and the Rule of Law', 22 February 2018 (St Hugh's College, Oxford) [47].

290 Only one CE election petition has been lodged in Macau, but the dispute was uncontroversial as the applicant did not meet the minimum age requirement to be CE. The Macau CE must be at least 40 years old (MABL, art 46) but the applicant was only 30 years old at the time of the dispute.

291 The disqualified pro-democracy candidates were from three pro-democracy groups: the Macau Democratic Prosperity Association (民主昌澳門), the New Macau Progressives (學社前進), and the New Macau Progressive Association (新澳門進步協會). Besides the 15 candidates from pro-democracy parties, six were from labour and other groups. '澳門立法會候選人遭集體DQ,「愛國愛澳」面臨重新定義 Macau Legislative Assembly Candidates Face Mass Disqualification, 'Love the Motherland, Love Macau' Faces Redefinition' *BBC* (14 July 2021) <www.bbc.com/zhongwen/trad/chinese-news-57811700> last accessed 4 January 2026.

292 The loyalty requirement is codified in Article 6(8) of the Law on the Election of the Legislative Assembly of the MASAR (澳門特別行政區立法會選舉法).

293 Case 113/2021 (31 July 2021).

294 Case 113/2021, at 191 (31 July 2021).

295 Case 113/2021, at 204–209 (31 July 2021). Liu Xiaobo was one of China's most prominent dissidents and well-known human rights activists. He was arrested in December 2008 and was imprisoned for inciting subversion of state power in December 2009. His alleged crime was the public criticism of the Chinese government and being one of the main drafters of Charter 08, a manifesto calling for democracy, respect for human rights and the rule of law in China. Liu Xiaobo was awarded the Nobel Peace Prize on 8 October 2010, but he was absent from the ceremony and

The MACFA, echoing the PRC government's formal rhetoric, emphasised that the assemblies to commemorate the Tiananmen "Incident" were "well-planned and deliberate attack on and defamation of the official institutions and entities of the Central People's Government"[296] and "clearly contrary to Articles 1 and 5 of the Constitution of the People's Republic of China".[297] The MACFA equally endorsed the *Resolution of the NPCSC on Stopping Riots and Quelling Anti-Revolution Unrest*, which labelled the Tiananmen Square Protests as a premeditated political disturbance aimed at overthrowing the leadership of the CCP and subverting the PRC.[298] Additionally, the MACFA referred to Liu Xiaobo's conviction in a closed-door hearing in Beijing[299] for state subversion and emphatically asserted that the Macau electoral candidates' act of paying tribute to Liu Xiaobo and Charter 08 signified their disagreement with the constitutional order established by the PRC Constitution and evidenced their unwillingness to uphold the PRC Constitution and the MABL.[300]

Notably, when disqualifying the 21 candidates, the MALAEAC had relied on seven hitherto *undisclosed* criteria for assessing the candidates' eligibility: (1) candidates must safeguard the constitutional order established by the Constitution and the MABL; (2) candidates must safeguard national unity and territorial integrity; (3) candidates cannot collude with foreign countries or foreign forces in infiltrating the power bodies of the MASAR; (4) candidates must respect the political system established by the Constitution and the MABL, and may not denigrate the PRC and the MASAR; (5) candidates may not perform acts against the sovereignty and security of the State; (6) candidates must respect the competences delegated by the Constitution and the MABL to the NPC and the NPCSC; and (7) candidates cannot play a role in contradicting the above requirements.[301] Notably, the seven criteria were passed by the MALAEAC on 25 June 2021,[302] but they were not publicly

was represented by an empty chair. On 13 July 2017, Liu Xiaobo died of liver cancer in a hospital in Shenyang. Jean-Philippe Beja, Fu Hualing, and Eva Pils (eds), *Liu Xiaobo, Charter 08 and the Challenges of Political Reform in China* (HKU Press, 2012).

296 Case 113/2021, at 192 (31 July 2021).

297 Case 113/2021, at 202 (31 July 2021).

298 Case 113/2021, at 192 and 208 (31 July 2021). The Resolution of the Standing Committee of the National People's Congress on Stopping Riots and Quelling Anti-Revolution Unrest (全国人民代表大会常务委员会关于制止动乱和平息反革命暴乱的决议) (6 July 1989); In Chinese: '中央政府已将六四事件明确定性为有组织、有预谋的政治动乱，目的是推翻中国共产党的领导，推翻中央人民政府，颠覆中华人民共和国。'.

299 The judgment of the Beijing High Court is not released to the public. According to news reports, the First Intermediate Court of Beijing convicted Liu Xiaobo for inciting subversion of state power in December 2009. The Beijing High Court dismissed Liu Xiaobo's appeal in February 2010. 'Beijing High Court Dismisses Liu Xiaobo's Appeal 北京高级法院驳回刘晓波上诉' *BBC* (11 February 2010) <www.bbc.com/zhongwen/simp/china/2010/02/100211_liuxiaobo> last accessed 4 January 2026.

300 Case 113/2021, at 210 (31 July 2021).

301 Case 113/2021, at 179–180 (31 July 2021).

302 Case 113/2021, at 178 (31 July 2021).

disclosed until 12 July 2021, three days after the pro-democracy candidates were disqualified.[303] The disqualified applicants had therefore argued that these seven criteria were unlawful as they were not publicly disclosed when applied to restrict the people's rights. Shockingly, the MACFA dismissed this argument without giving any reason.[304]

Conclusion

This chapter has underscored how the HKCFA has displayed more activism, invalidated more laws, and disagreed more regularly with the SAR's political branches on public policy than its Macau counterpart. The "judicialisation"[305] of public law norms in Hong Kong has been facilitated by two key variables that are extant in Hong Kong but absent in Macau. First, Hong Kong is an international financial centre – third in the world as of 2025[306] – which Beijing relies on to link the Mainland economy to global capital and investments, and the preservation of an independent Hong Kong judiciary is essential to keeping Hong Kong attractive to foreign investors. Hong Kong is the only international financial centre in China with no capital controls. On the other hand, Macau is not an international financial centre and its economy for all practical purposes is conjoined with the Mainland. Second, HKCFA judges are largely picked by the non-partisan Chief Justice, while the MACFA judges are chosen by politicians with explicit pro-Beijing affiliations.

Pre-2021, judicialisation in Hong Kong was also fostered by a fragmentation of power within the HKSAR government,[307] which hampered the successful and efficacious pursuit of a unified legislative agenda. While judicialisation is more common in classic competitive dynamic democracies such as Taiwan and South Korea,[308] it is not exclusively so. Political fragmentation can occur too in some authoritarian democracies such as pre-2021 Hong Kong where the pro-Beijing politicians were splintered into multiple political parties and there was a sizable pro-democracy opposition that could delay the deliberation and passage of laws

303 Case 113/2021, at 22 (31 July 2021).

304 Case 113/2021, at 185–186 (31 July 2021).

305 For a comparative discussion of judicialisation see C. Neal Tate and Torbjorn Vallinder (eds), *The Global Expansion of Judicial Power* (NYU Press 1995); Alec Stone Sweet, *Governing with Judges: Constitutional Politics in Europe* (OUP 2000) 12–20; Ran Hirschl, *Towards Juristocracy* (Harvard University Press 2004) 211; Doreen Lustig and J. H. H. Weiler, 'Judicial Review in the Contemporary World – Retrospective and Prospective' (2018) 16(2) *International Journal of Constitutional Law* 315.

306 'The Global Financial Centres Index 38' (September 2025) <www.longfinance.net/media/documents/GFCI_38_Report_2025.09.25_v1.0.pdf> last accessed 3 January 2026.

307 C. Neal Tate, 'Why the Expansion of Judicial Power' in C. Neal Tate and Torbjorn Vallinder (eds), *The Global Expansion of Judicial Power* (NYU Press 1995) 30; John Ferejohn, 'Judicializing Politics, Politicizing Law' (2002) 65(3) *Law & Contemporary Problems* 41, 59.

308 Po Jen Yap, *Courts and Democracies in Asia* (CUP 2017) 94–124.

and veto constitutional amendments. As we have explored in Chapter 2, when the Geographical Constituencies (GCs) seats in the Hong Kong LegCo – 50% of the total LegCo seats – were elected by universal franchise, and the political opposition consistently controlled a majority of these GC seats, the pro-democracy camp possessed great leverage in the LegCo even if they did not control a numerical majority in the house. Furthermore, even the pro-Beijing lawmakers *pre-2021* would bow to public pressure – for fear of being punished at the polls – and break ranks with the HKSAR government, as seen with the aborted legislative attempts to pass national security legislation in 2003 and the infamous extradition law in 2019.[309] As the HKSAR judiciary was and still is traditionally viewed by the Hong Kong public as the branch of government most predisposed to defending constitutional rights, the presence of divided government in the Hong Kong legislature had raised the political transaction costs for overriding the courts,[310] such that the HKCFA would enjoy significant "policy" space to determine outcomes in a range of issues concerning criminal justice, social welfare, LGBT rights. The HKSAR government would usually not agree with these judicial rulings, but it would grudgingly accept the results because the political costs of overriding the HKCFA would be prohibitively high.

But since 2020, Hong Kong's new national security landscape has posed the greatest singular threat to the independence of its judiciary.[311] The city used to attract a long list of luminary judges from around the British Commonwealth to sit in every substantive decision decided by the HKCFA. At its peak, there were 15 such illustrious overseas NPJs serving on the HKCFA, which included legal giants such as Baroness Hale of Richmond (President of the UK Supreme Court), Beverley McLachlin (Chief Justice of Canada), Lord Reed of Allermuir (President of the UK Supreme Court), etc. The appointment of overseas judges on the city's highest court was intended to shore up business confidence in the city after the change of sovereignty in 1997.[312] Their presence on the HKCFA was meant to signal to international investors that Beijing remained committed to maintaining the rule of law in Hong Kong and upholding its status as an international financial centre. But following the Central Government's imposition of the 2020 HKNSL, at least five overseas judges have resigned from the HKCFA, explicitly citing their

309 Both epochal events are discussed in Chapters 1 and 4.

310 Eric Ip, *Hybrid Constitutionalism: The Politics of Constitutional Review in the Chinese Special Administrative Regions* (CUP 2019) 175–192.

311 Nikkei Asia has reported that the Hong Kong judiciary now faces significant challenges in recruiting new High Court judges as potential appointees are concerned about being sanctioned by Western governments for any future role in adjudicating national security cases, and one potential High Court appointee also failed a background check conducted by the Hong Kong government. <https://asia.nikkei.com/Spotlight/Hong-Kong-security-law/Hong-Kong-neglects-judicial-nominations-despite-case-backlog> last accessed 4 January 2026.

312 Yash Ghai, *Hong Kong's New Constitutional Order: The Resumption of Chinese Sovereignty and the Basic Law* (2nd edn, HKU Press 1999) 301–304, 323–324.

concerns about the political situation in Hong Kong or its national security laws.[313] The city is now left with 6 overseas judges, a precipitous decline from its peak of 15 in 2019.

Furthermore, following Beijing's overhaul of Hong Kong's electoral system in 2021 such that only pre-screened "patriots" can run for political office, the pro-democracy opposition in Hong Kong has been decimated and the HKSAR government now enjoys a free rein to pass legislation with little obstruction. With the neutering of the pro-democracy forces in the legislature and civil society, the courts have lost a vocal source of public support within Hong Kong society. But this does not mean the local judiciary has become constitutionally irrelevant. The HKCFA has built up a history of invalidating laws since 1997. Like all political practices, judicial practices are path-dependent,[314] such that Hong Kong judges can still appeal to history and stare decisis for continuing the practice of enforcing human rights against the Hong Kong government.

More importantly, the Central and HKSAR governments cannot and will not reverse every decision by the HKCFA as they do not want to appear to be rescinding their commitment to allow the HKSAR to "exercise a high degree of autonomy and enjoy … independent judicial power",[315] as this would adversely impact Hong Kong's long-term viability as an international financial centre. This is not some phantasm of hope. Hong Kong's continued viability as an international financial centre – undergirded by a respected independent judiciary – is indispensable to Beijing for linking the Mainland to the world economy so that China can generate capital in Hong Kong to fund its domestic and foreign policy ambitions. Socialism with Chinese Characteristics just means Capitalism *without* Democracy. And neo-capitalist China cannot afford an exodus of multinational companies and capital from Hong Kong to Singapore.

Certainly, China will not tolerate any judicial attempts to remove the Central Government's relentless chokehold on the city. National security, national

313 These five overseas NPJs were James Spigelman, Lord Reed, Lord Hodge, Lord Sumption and Lord Collins. Overseas NPJ Beverley McLachlin cited family reasons for retiring from the HKCFA, but interestingly she renewed her position as an international judge in Singapore for another 3 years a few months before leaving her post in Hong Kong. 'McLachlin renewed with Singapore court months before leaving Hong Kong court to be with family' *National Post* (17 June 2024) <https://nationalpost.com/news/canada/beverley-mclachlin-singapore-court-hong-kong-court> last accessed 4 January 2026. Interestingly, after Australian NPJ Robert French resigned from the HKCFA in 2025, while defending the Court's independence, he also argued that the role of the foreign judges in Hong Kong had become increasingly anachronistic and arguably cosmetic. See Edith Lin, 'Australian Judge Resigns from Hong Kong's Top Court, Sixth to Step Down in Year' *SCMP* (11 April 2025) <www.scmp.com/news/hong-kong/law-and-crime/article/3306246/australian-judge-resigns-hong-kongs-top-court-sixth-step-down-year> last accessed 4 January 2026.

314 Alec Stone Sweet, 'Path Dependence, Precedent, and Judicial Power' in Martin Shapiro and Alec Stone Sweet, *On Law, Politics, and Judicialization* (OUP 2002) 112.

315 HKBL, art 2.

sovereignty, and elections are core interests of the regime. With the NPCSC's plenary power to interpret the BL hanging like the Sword of Damocles over Hong Kong, the HKCFA implicitly understands that its ability to generate significant changes in other areas of constitutional law is contingent on its genuflection to Beijing on the communist regime's core concerns.

But where Beijing's core interests are *not* at stake, the HKCFA retains significant discretion to shape the law. As we have previously discussed in this Chapter, HKCFA judges are largely picked by the non-partisan Chief Justices and not by pro-Beijing politicians. Independent judges cherish their reputation.[316] In autocratic regimes, courts can only please their primary audience – the ruling government – for their institutional survival hinges on this.[317] On the other hand, where independent judges can be appointed and they possess a zone of adjudicatory discretion, non-partisan judges can "engage in self-presentation to other audiences whose esteem is important to them",[318] e.g. the public, lawyers, academia, the international community, and luminary judges from other leading courts of final resort. The six remaining overseas NPJs still participate in all types of cases that come before the HKCFA except national security ones. It is particularly noteworthy that it was the Australian judge – Patrick Keane – who cast the decisive tie-breaking vote when the HKCFA voted 3–2 in 2023 to require the Hong Kong government to establish a statutory framework by 2025 to legally recognise and protect the core rights of same-sex partnerships.[319] This groundbreaking progressive decision should give some pause to detractors who insist that the international members of the HKCFA are merely "lending prestige to persecution".[320]

On the other hand, Macau is starkly different. The MACFA judges are picked by Macau's Judicial Officers Nomination Commission that is chaired and dominated by politicians with explicit pro-Beijing affiliations; the MACFA judges have been primarily legally trained in Mainland China; the pro-democracy opposition has been practically non-existent from the MASAR's inception;[321] and the city is not an international financial centre for which the Mainland state-owned and state-linked enterprises are reliant upon for foreign capital and investments.

316 Nuno Garoupa and Tom Ginsburg, *Judicial Reputation: A Comparative Theory* (University of Chicago Press 2015).

317 Tamir Moustafa and Tom Ginsburg, 'Introduction: The Functions of Courts in Authoritarian Politics' in Tom Ginsburg and Tamir Moustafa (eds), *Rule by Law: The Politics of Courts in Authoritarian Regimes* (CUP 2008).

318 Lawrence Baum, *Judges and their Audiences: A Perspective on Judicial Behaviour* (Princeton 2008) 4.

319 *Sham Tsz Kit v Secretary for Justice* (2023) 26 HKCFAR 385.

320 'Lending Prestige to Persecution: How Foreign Judges are Undermining Hong Kong's Freedoms and Why They Should Quit' *The Committee for Freedom in Hong Kong* (14 May 2024) <www.thecfhk.org/post/lending-prestige-to-persecution-how-foreign-judges-are-undermining-hong-kong-s-freedoms-and-why-the> last accessed 4 January 2026.

321 As discussed in Chapter 2, there have never been more than three pro-democracy politicians elected to the Legislative Assembly of the MASAR.

Because of these differing exogenous and endogenous variables at play, the HKCFA has significant leverage that its Macau counterpart does not possess. Both the Central and HKSAR governments want to keep Hong Kong as a top international financial centre that is attractive to business investors and overseas talent. And to do that, the rule of law in Hong Kong must be perceived to be upheld, and the government cannot neuter its judiciary or overrule it at every turn. Therefore, while the HKCFA can do little to countermand Beijing's hegemony over core concerns, the Court can "dialogue" strategically with the government on policy prescriptions and rights-protection that are less objectionable to the regime,[322] as the HKSAR government will acquiesce to any calibrated judicial show-of-force to assuage international investors that the rule of law remains a cornerstone of Hong Kong's governance.

322 See chapter 6 of Albert Chen and Po Jen Yap, *The Constitutional System of the Hong Kong SAR: A Contextual Analysis* (Hart Publishing 2023).

Appendix 1

List of HKCFA Cases with Express Findings of Unconstitutionality (as of 1 March 2026)

Number	*Case Name*	*Legal Provision(s)/Policy*
1	*Ng Ka Ling v Director of Immigration* (1999) 2 HKCFAR 4	Immigration Ordinance: s 2A(1), s 2AA(1)(a), s 53D(3)(a), para 1(2)(b) of Sch 1 Immigration (Amendment) (No 3) Ordinance: s 1(2) Immigration Regulations: The second sentence in Form No 12 in Sch 1 Paragraphs A(1) and B of the Notice dated 11 July 1997 and published in the Gazette on 16 July 1997 (G No (E) 21 of 1997)
2	*Chan Kam Nga v Director of Immigration* (1999) 2 HKCFAR 82	Immigration Ordinance: para 2(c) in Sch 1 (introduced by the Immigration (Amendment) (No 2) Ordinance 1997)
3	*Director of Immigration v Chong Fung Yuen* (2001) 4 HKCFAR 211	Immigration Ordinance: para (2)(a) of Sch 1
4	*Gurung Kesh Bahadur v Director of Immigration* (2002) 5 HKCFAR 480	Immigration Ordinance: Application of Section 11(10) to non-permanent residents with valid permits
5	*Prem Singh v Director of Immigration* (2003) 6 HKCFAR 26	Immigration Ordinance: para 3(1)(c) in Sch 1, read with para 1(5)(b) of the said Sch.
6	*Solicitor v The Law Society of Hong Kong* (2003) 6 HKCFAR 570	Legal Practitioners Ordinance: s 13(1)
7	*Leung Kwok Hung and Others v HKSAR* (2005) 8 HKCFAR 229	Public Order Ordinance: ss 14(1), 14(5), 15(2)
8	*Koo Sze Yiu v Chief Executive of the HKSAR* (2006) 9 HKCFAR 441	Executive Order: Law Enforcement (Covert Surveillance Procedure) Order Telecommunications Ordinance: s 33
9	*Official Receiver v Chan Wing Hing* (2006) 9 HKCFAR 545	Bankruptcy Ordinance: s 30A(10)(b)(i)
10	*HKSAR v Lam Kwong Wai* (2006) 9 HKCFAR 574	Firearms and Ammunition Ordinance: s 20(1) read with s 20(3)(c)
11	*HKSAR v Hung Chan Wa* (2006) 9 HKCFAR 614	Dangerous Drugs Ordinance: ss 47(1) and 47(2)

(*Continued*)

Number	*Case Name*	*Legal Provision(s)/Policy*
12	*Secretary for Justice v Yau Yuk Lung* (2007) 10 HKCFAR 335	Crimes Ordinance: s 118F(1)
13	*HKSAR v Ng Po On* (2008) 11 HKCFAR 91	Prevention of Bribery Ordinance: s 14(4) read with s 24
14	*Koon Wing Yee v Insider Dealing Tribunal* (2008) 11 HKCFAR 170	Securities (Insider Dealing) Ordinance: s 23(1)(c)
15	*Lam Siu Po v Commissioner of Police* (2009) 12 HKCFAR 237	Police (Discipline) Regulations: Regulations 9(11) and 9(12)
16	*Mok Charles Peter v Tam Wai Ho* (2010) 13 HKCFAR 762	Legislative Council Ordinance: s 67(3)
17	*Lee To Nei v HKSAR* (2012) 15 HKCFAR 162	Trade Descriptions Ordinance: s 26(4)
18	*W v Registrar of Marriages* (2013) 16 HKCFAR 112	Matrimonial Causes Ordinance: s 20(1)(d) Marriage Ordinance: s 40
19	*Kong Yunming v Director of Social Welfare* (2013) 16 HKCFAR 950	Social Security Assistance Seven-year Residence Requirement
20	*Official Receiver v Zhi Charles* (2015) 18 HKCFAR 467	Bankruptcy Ordinance: s 30A(10)(a)
21	*QT v Director of Immigration* (2018) 21 HKCFAR 324	Immigration Policy on Spousal Dependant Visa: Exclusion of Same-sex Civil Partnerships
22	*Leung Chun Kwong v Secretary for Civil Service* (2019) 22 HKCFAR 127	Civil Service's Decision to Exclude Married Same-Sex Spouse from Spousal Benefits Inland Revenue Ordinance: ss 2 and 10
23	*Leung Kwok Hung v Commissioner of Correctional Services* (2020) 23 HKCFAR 456	Correctional Services Standing Order 41-05.
24	*Q and Tse Henry Edward v Commissioner of Registration* (2023) 26 HKCFAR 25	Commissioner of Registration's Guidelines on Amendment to the HKID Card Gender Marker
25	*Sham Tsz Kit v Secretary for Justice* (2023) 26 HKCFAR 385	Absence of a Statutory Framework for the Legal Recognition of Same-Sex Partnerships
26	*Infinger, Nick v Hong Kong Housing Authority* [2024] HKCFA 29	Policy of Excluding Same-Sex Couples as an "Ordinary Family" under the Public Rental Housing policies.
27	*Ng Hon Lam Edgar v Secretary for Justice* [2024] HKCFA 30	Intestates' Estates Ordinance: s 3(d) Inheritance (Provision for Family and Dependants) Ordinance: s 2

Notes: Appendix 1 excludes *Secretary for Justice v Chan Wah* (2000) 3 HKCFAR 459. In this case, the unconstitutional practice derives not from any governmental law or policy, but a customary practice within the villages.

Appendix 2

List of MACFA Cases with Express Findings of Unconstitutionality (as of 1 March 2026)

Number	*Case Name*	*Judgment Date*	*Legal Provision(s)/Policy*
1	*Case 2/2004*	2 June 2004	Article 1(3) of Decree No. 39/99/M – Civil Code
2	*Case 5/2010*	12 May 2010	Article 5(2)(b) of Decree No. 21/87/M
3	*Case 25/2011*	30 May 2011	Article 5(3) of Law No. 2/93/M – Right to Assembly and Demonstration

References

Abeyratne, Rehan, 'More Structure, More Deference: Proportionality in Hong Kong' in Po Jen Yap (ed), *Proportionality in Asia* (Cambridge, Cambridge University Press 2020) 25.

Alarie, Benjamin and Andrew J Green, *Commitment and Cooperation in High Courts: A Cross Country Examination of Institutional Constraints on Judges* (Oxford, Oxford University Press 2017).

Bartoli, Chris, Ivy Wong, and Nick O'Donnell, 'The Battle for Listings' (2019) 6 *International Financial Law Review* 40.

Baum, Lawrence, *Judges and their Audiences: A Perspective on Judicial Behaviour* (Princeton, Princeton University Press 2008).

Beja, Jean-Philippe, Fu Hualing and Eva Pils (eds), *Liu Xiaobo, Charter 08 and the Challenges of Political Reform in China* (Hong Kong, Hong Kong University Press 2012).

Bennion, Francis and Oliver Jones (eds), *Bennion on Statutory Interpretation* (6th edn, London, Sweet and Maxwell 2013).

Canas, Vitalino, 'The General Regime of Fundamental Rights in the Basic Law and in the International Instruments' in Jorge Oliveira and Paulo Cardinal (eds), *One Country Two Systems, Three Legal Orders – Perspectives of Evolution* (Berlin, Springer 2009) 655.

Cardinal, Paulo, 'Macau: Transformation of an Historic Autonomy' in Yash Ghai and Sophia Woodman (eds), *Practising Self-Government: A Comparative Study of Autonomous Regions* (Cambridge, Cambridge University Press 2013) 383.

Chen, Albert 陳弘毅, '香港法律制度的現狀及前景 Hong Kong Legal System: Status Quo and Prospects' in Yushuo Zheng 鄭宇碩 (ed), *過渡時期的香港 Hong Kong in the Transitional Period* (Hong Kong, 三聯書店 Joint Publishing HK 1989) 79.

Chen, Albert 陳弘毅, Christopher Munn 文基賢 and Michael Ng 吳海傑, '殖民地時代香港的法治與司法 The Rule of Law and the Administration of Justice in Colonial Hong Kong' in Wang Gungwu 王賡武 (ed), *香港史新編 Hong Kong History: New Perspectives* (Hong Kong, 三聯書店 Joint Publishing HK 2017) 445.

Chen, Albert and Pui Yin Lo, 'The Constitutional Orders of "One Country, Two Systems": A Comparative Study of the Visible and Invisible Bases of Constitutional Review and Proportionality Analysis in the Chinese Special Administrative Regions of Hong Kong and Macau' in Rosalind Dixon and Adrienne Stone (eds), *The Invisible Constitution in Comparative Perspective* (Cambridge, Cambridge University Press 2018) 230.

Chen, Albert and Po Jen Yap, *The Constitutional System of the Hong Kong SAR: A Contextual Analysis* (Oxford, Hart Publishing 2023).

Cheung, Yan-leung, Yuk-shing Cheng and Chi-keung Woo, *Hong Kong's Global Financial Centre and China's Development: Changing Roles and Future Prospects* (Oxford, Routledge 2017).

Dahl, Robert, 'Decision-Making in a Democracy: The Supreme Court as a National Policy-Maker' (1957) 6 *Journal of Public Law* 279.

Ferejohn, John, 'Judicializing Politics, Politicizing Law' (2002) 65(3) *Law & Contemporary Problems* 41.

Garoupa, Nuno and Tom Ginsburg, *Judicial Reputation: A Comparative Theory* (Chicago, The University of Chicago Press 2015).

Ghai, Yash, *Hong Kong's New Constitutional Order: The Resumption of Chinese Sovereignty and the Basic Law* (2nd edn, Hong Kong, Hong Kong University Press 1999).

Godinho, Jorge and Paulo Cardinal, 'Macau's Court of Final Appeal' in Simon N M Young and Yash Ghai (eds), *Hong Kong's Court of Final Appeal: The Development of the Law in China's Hong Kong* (Cambridge, Cambridge University Press 2014) 608.

Hespanha, António Manuel, *澳門法制史概論 Introduction to Macau's Legal History* (Macau, 澳門基金會 Macau Foundation 1996).

He, Zhihui 何志辉, *澳门法制史新编 A New Study on the Legal History of Macau* (Beijing, 社会科学文献出版社 Social Sciences Academic Press 2019).

Hirschl, Ran, *Towards Juristocracy* (Cambridge, Harvard University Press 2004).

Hung, Ho-fung, *City on the Edge: Hong Kong under Chinese Rule* (Cambridge, Cambridge University Press 2022).

Ip, Eric, *Hybrid Constitutionalism: The Politics of Constitutional Review in the Chinese Special Administrative Regions* (Cambridge, Cambridge University Press 2019).

Lustig, Doreen and Joseph Halevi Horowitz Weiler, 'Judicial Review in the Contemporary World – Retrospective and Prospective' (2018) 16(2) *International Journal of Constitutional Law* 315.

Moustafa, Tamir and Tom Ginsburg, 'Introduction: The Functions of Courts in Authoritarian Politics' in Tom Ginsburg and Tamir Moustafa (eds), *Rule by Law: The Politics of Courts in Authoritarian Regimes* (Cambridge, Cambridge University Press 2008).

Puig, Gonzalo Villalta and Eric Ip, *The Freest Market in the World: The Constitutional Logic of Economic Liberty in China's Hong Kong* (Oxford, Routledge 2023).

Segal, Jeffrey A and Harold J Spaeth, *The Supreme Court and the Attitudinal Model Revisited* (Cambridge, Cambridge University Press 2002).

Sit, Victor F S, *Macau Through 500 Years: Emergence and Development of an Untypical Chinese City* (Singapore, Enrich Professional Publishing 2013).

Stone Sweet, Alec, *Governing with Judges: Constitutional Politics in Europe* (Oxford, Oxford University Press 2000).

Stone Sweet, Alec, 'Path Dependence, Precedent, and Judicial Power' in Martin Shapiro and Alec Stone Sweet, *On Law, Politics, and Judicialization* (Oxford, Oxford University Press 2002) 112.

Stone Sweet, Alec and Jud Mathews, *Proportionality Balancing and Constitutional Governance: A Comparative and Global Approach* (Oxford, Oxford University Press 2019).

Tate, C Neal, 'Why the Expansion of Judicial Power' in C. Neal Tate and Torbjorn Vallinder (eds), *The Global Expansion of Judicial Power* (New York, New York University Press 1995) 30.

Tate, C Neal and Torbjorn Vallinder (eds), *The Global Expansion of Judicial Power* (New York, New York University Press 1995).

Wang, Chao 汪超, '澳門法院的司法審查制度作為個人自由的保障及其與香港司法審查制度比較的啓示 Judicial Review of Macau Courts as Protection of Individual Rights and Implication after a Comparison with Hong Kong's Judicial Review' (2021) 2 *澳門法學 Macau Law Review* 89.

Wei, Dan, 'Macao's Legal System under Globalisation and Regional Integration: Between Tradition and Evolution' (2014) 9(2) *Frontiers of Law in China* 233.

Wong, Luis W K, 'Constitutional Review of Colonial Macau: A Historical Study' (2023) 53(2) *Hong Kong Law Journal* 643.

Xu, Chang 许昌, '论澳门特别行政区法院设置及其特点 On the Court System and Features of the Macau Special Administrative Region' (1994) 1 *中外法学 Peking Law Journal* 65.

Yap, Po Jen, *Courts and Democracies in Asia* (Cambridge, Cambridge University Press 2017).

Yap, Po Jen (ed), *Proportionality in Asia* (Cambridge, Cambridge University Press 2020).

Yap, Po Jen and Eric Chan, 'Legislative Oaths and Judicial Intervention in Hong Kong' (2017) 47(1) *Hong Kong Law Journal* 1.

Yap, Po Jen and Francis Chung, 'Statutory Rights and De Facto Constitutional Supremacy in Hong Kong?' (2019) 17(3) *International Journal of Constitutional Law* 836.

Zhu, Han and Albert Chen, 'The Oath-Taking Cases and the NPCSC Interpretation of 2016: Interface of Common Law and Chinese Law' (2019) 49(1) *Hong Kong Law Journal* 381.

4

NATIONAL SECURITY LAWS OF HONG KONG AND MACAU

Introduction

National security has always been a central preoccupation of the PRC Central Government, and this is so even for the two Special Administrative Regions (SARs) it controls. Notably, the national security mandates for both SARs are codified in Article 23 of their respective Basic Laws (BLs) and the constitutional requirements are identical:

> The [...] Special Administrative Region shall enact laws on its own to prohibit any act of treason, secession, sedition, subversion against the Central People's Government, or theft of state secrets, to prohibit foreign political organisations or bodies from conducting political activities in the Region, and to prohibit political organisations or bodies of the Region from establishing ties with foreign political organisations or bodies.[1]

But as we will examine in this Chapter, both SARs took different paths to implementing this constitutional duty. Hong Kong's attempt to pass one in 2003 was aborted, while Macau successfully enacted one on its own in 2009.

Following President Xi Jinping's rise to power in 2012, and the escalation of geo-political tensions, state security has risen to the top of the country's priorities and agenda.[2] The Party State was securitised with the establishment of an all-powerful National Security Commission chaired by Xi in 2014, and a raft of new

1 Hong Kong Basic Law (HKBL), art 23; Macau Basic Law (MABL), art 23.

2 Hualing Fu, 'China's Imperatives for National Security Legislation' in Cora Chan and Fiona de Londras (eds), *China's National Security: Endangering Hong Kong's Rule of Law?* (Hart 2020) 41–60.

DOI: 10.4324/9781003683872-4

national security laws were soon passed in rapid-fire: Counter-Espionage Law (2014), National Security Law (2015), Counter-terrorism Law (2015), Law on the Administration of Activities of Overseas Nongovernmental Organisations in Mainland China (2016), Cybersecurity Law (2016), National Intelligence Law (2017), etc.

In Beijing's view, Hong Kong was a weak link in the country's path to national securitisation. The Central Authorities watched the 2014 Occupy Central movement and 2019 anti-extradition bill protests in Hong Kong – two epochal events discussed in Chapter 1 – play out with much anxiety and they feared the infiltration of hostile foreign forces that would use the city as a base to launch a "colour revolution" across the whole of China.[3] China simply would not allow its economic powerhouse to become a political contagion, and it therefore unilaterally "inoculated" Hong Kong with a bespoke National Security Law in 2020. Genuflecting to the national zeitgeist, Macau swiftly revised and strengthened its national security law in 2023 to demonstrate its own commitment to the country's cause. And the subjugated Hong Kong finally enacted its own home-grown national security law in 2024 to complement the Beijing-imposed one.

In this chapter, we shall first trace the developmental trajectories of national security legislation in Hong Kong and Macau. Next, we will contrast the national security laws currently applicable in both cities and examine their implementation by the local governments and their courts. Finally, we explore how the enactment of national security laws has reshaped constitutional practices in both SARs and reconstituted multiple aspects of their political and legal systems. In essence, the transcendent role that national security now plays in the SARs underscores the fragility of the so-called "high degree of autonomy"[4] granted under the "One Country, Two Systems" constitutional framework, and this tension will pose a significant stress-point in the relationship between the SARs and the Central Authorities for the years to come.

National Security Legislation in Hong Kong: Past and Present

Before Article 23 of Hong Kong's Basic Law (HKBL) took its current form, the clause underwent several rounds of revisions. The first version, released in April 1988, stipulated that Hong Kong "shall prohibit by law any act designed to undermine national unity or subvert the central government".[5] The phrase

3 See People's Daily Commentary, '坚决反对外部势力干预香港事务 Resolutely Opposing External Forces Interfering in Hong Kong Affairs' *人民日报People's Daily* (30 May 2020) <http://opinion.people.com.cn/n1/2020/0530/c1003-31729506.html> last accessed 1 January 2026; see also the State Council Information Office of the PRC, 'Hong Kong: Democratic Progress under the Framework of One Country, Two Systems' (20 December 2021) <http://english.scio.gov.cn/whitepapers/2021-12/20/content_77941455_8.htm> last accessed 1 January 2026.

4 HKBL, art 2; MABL, art 2.

5 HKBL Draft (April 1988), art 22 <https://sunzi1.lib.hku.hk/bldho/BL0084.pdf#page=40> last accessed 1 January 2026.

"undermine national unity" was widely criticised for being too vague and the term "subversion" – absent in English law – also caused great consternation in Hong Kong.[6] The second draft, published in February 1989, removed references to "subversion" and was more specific about the prohibited acts that the SAR had to criminalise. In this version, Hong Kong "shall enact laws on its own to prohibit any act of treason, secession, sedition or theft of state secrets".[7] The second version was clearly an improvement on the first, but it was superseded by events. On 4 June 1989, the Central Government unleashed its army on the student protestors at Tiananmen Square, and Hong Kong society coalesced against the brutality. This conflict deepened the mistrust between the Central Government and Hong Kong society, especially as the latter mobilised enormous moral and financial support for the student protestors during the demonstrations and after the crackdown.[8] The resistance reinforced Beijing's fear that Hong Kong would – in collusion with foreign forces – become a base for state subversion against the Central Government. Consequently, Article 23 of the HKBL was redrafted post-Tiananmen to impose a duty on the SAR to criminalise state subversion and prohibit political activities by foreign political organisations.[9]

After China's resumption of sovereignty over Hong Kong in 1997, local legislation implementing Article 23 HKBL was placed on the backburner for five years. It was not until 2002 that Hong Kong's first Chief Executive – Tung Chee-hwa – proceeded to enact local Article 23 legislation upon Beijing's prompting.[10] In September 2002, the Hong Kong government unveiled the Consultation Document[11] on the local government's various proposals to enact national security legislation. But after three months of public consultation, the National Security (Legislative Provisions) Bill ("the 2003 Bill") was swiftly tabled before the

6 Carole Petersen, 'National Security Offences and Civil Liberties in Hong Kong: A Critique of the Government's Consultation on Article 23 of the Basic Law' (2002) 32 *Hong Kong Law Journal* 457–470.

7 HKBL Draft (1989), art 23 <https://sunzi1.lib.hku.hk/bldho/BL0102.pdf#page=13> last accessed 1 January 2026.

8 See Joseph Cheng, 'The Tiananmen Incident and the Pro-democracy Movement in Hong Kong' in Jean-Philippe Beja (ed), *The Impact of China's 1989 Tiananmen Massacre* (Routledge 2011) 179–193.

9 For a detailed introduction on the history of Article 23 HKBL's drafting, see Carole Petersen, 'Hong Kong's Spring of Discontent: The Rise and Fall of the National Security Bill in 2003' in Hualing Fu, Carole Petersen and Simon Young (eds), *National Security and Fundamental Freedoms: Hong Kong's Article 23 under Scrutiny* (HKU Press 2005) 13–20.

10 In February 2002, Li Peng, Chairman of the National People's Congress Standing Committee announced that Article 23 legislation in Hong Kong should be enacted within Tung Chee-hwa's second term, and this was echoed by Qian Qichen, Vice Premier of the PRC, in June 2002. See Ngok Ma, 'Civil Society in Self-Defense: the Struggle against National Security Legislation in Hong Kong' (2005) 14(44) *Journal of Contemporary China* 465, 467; See also Wong Yiu-chung, ' "Super Paradox" or "Leninist Integration": the Politics of Legislating Article 23 of Hong Kong's Basic Law' (2006) 30(2) *Asian Perspective* 65, 71–78.

11 The full title of the document is 'Consultation Document on Proposals to Implement Article 23 of the Basic Law'.

Hong Kong Legislative Council in February 2003. While the Hong Kong Special Administrative Region (HKSAR) government undertook substantial research on comparative national security laws when drafting the legislation, the local Law Reform Commission was not consulted and the "white bill" – a final draft of the Bill – was not sent for another round of public consultation. The HKSAR government chose instead to campaign for a swift enactment of the 2003 Bill as law. But in the first quarter of 2003, Hong Kong was ravaged by the SARS pandemic and the economy was in a downspin. Economic anxieties dovetailed with public displeasure over the 2003 Bill, leading to more than half a million people rallying against the draft legislation on 1 July 2003, which hitherto marked the largest demonstration ever held in Hong Kong after the handover. Caving to public sentiments, the pro-establishment Liberal Party legislators withdrew their support of the 2003 Bill, and the law was shelved on 5th September after the government no longer had the requisite votes to get it passed.[12]

Despite the debacle over the 2003 Bill, and even before the Central Government imposed the National Security Law on Hong Kong in 2020, the city had several piecemeal national security laws in place. Upon the Central Government's instruction to implement the 2001 United Nations Security Council Resolution 1373 on combating terrorism,[13] the HKSAR government passed the United Nations (Anti-Terrorism Measures) Ordinance in 2002, which mainly addressed money laundering and the financing of terrorism. Annex III of the BL allows for some national laws to apply in Hong Kong, the most salient of which is the Garrison Law that stations the Chinese military in Hong Kong. Under Article 14 of the BL (HKBL14), the HKSAR government "may, when necessary, ask the Central People's Government for assistance from the garrison in the maintenance of public order and in disaster relief". Although HKBL14 has never been invoked in Hong Kong, the stationing of the military in the city has a deterrent value. Particularly, in the midst of the 2019 mass protests against the anti-extradition bill, there was chatter that the People's Liberation Army (PLA) garrison stationed in Hong Kong would intervene. Ultimately HKBL14 was not invoked, but at the height of the chaos, soldiers from the garrison emerged from their barracks in army fatigues to clear roadblocks – a gesture to demonstrate the garrison's capacity to mobilise if necessary.[14] And the Central Government – pursuant to Article 18(4) of HKBL – can apply National Laws in Hong Kong if the city is in a state of emergency by

12 For a detailed analysis of controversies surrounding 2003 Article 23 Legislation, see Albert Chen, 'The Consultation Document and the Bill: An Overview' in Hualing Fu, Carole Petersen and Simon Young (eds), *National Security and Fundamental Freedoms: Hong Kong's Article 23 under Scrutiny* (HKU Press 2005) 94–118.

13 See Security Bureau of the HKSAR, 'Legislative Council Brief: United Nations (Anti-Terrorism Measures) Bill (SBCR 2/16/1476/74)' (10 April 2002) <www.legco.gov.hk/yr01-02/english/bills/brief/b51_brf.pdf> last accessed 1 January 2026.

14 See 'LCQ21: Participation of Hong Kong Garrison in Voluntary Activity' (4 December 2019) <www.info.gov.hk/gia/general/201912/04/P2019120400372.htm> last accessed 1 January 2026.

reason of any turmoil within Hong Kong which endangers national unity or security and is beyond the control of the local government. In addition to these legal measures, Hong Kong pre-2024 retained a number of colonial laws concerning national and local security, such as the Crimes Ordinance (criminalising treason and sedition) and the Official Secrets Ordinance (protection of official documents and prohibition of spying). In particular, the sedition laws – introduced prior to World War II and hitherto unenforced since the 1970s – were only revived after the passage of the National Security Law in 2020, which we will discuss in the next part of this chapter.

2019 was the critical year in Hong Kong when everything changed. A young Hong Kong man Chan Tong-Kai murdered his girlfriend in Taiwan and fled back to Hong Kong. But there was no extradition agreement between Taiwan and Hong Kong, and he could not be prosecuted for murder extraterritorially in Hong Kong.[15] In the face of this legal lacuna, the Hong Kong government proposed an extradition bill,[16] which sought to create a statutory mechanism that authorised case-by-case transfer of fugitives to any jurisdiction with which Hong Kong lacked a formal extradition treaty. But the inclusion of Mainland China in this law caused a public ruckus as Hong Kong residents balked at the idea of being extradited to face criminal proceedings in Mainland China. Protests against the extradition bill surged, even after it was suspended by the government, with close to two million protestors out in the streets at one point.[17] The civil unrest continued for months and Hong Kong saw rampant vandalism of public properties including the Legislative Council, violent skirmishes between the police and demonstrators, and unprecedented unleashing of around 16,000 tear gas canisters by the police over the course of six months.[18] The radical uprising shocked Beijing and hardened its resolve to restore Hong Kong's political and societal stability. Behind the scenes, Beijing started work on a National Security Law it specially tailored for Hong Kong. On 28 May 2020, the National People's Congress (NPC) of the PRC issued its "Decision on Establishing and Improving the Legal System and Enforcement Mechanisms for the Hong Kong Special Administrative Region to Safeguard National Security" (the "2020 NPC Decision") and formally authorised the Standing Committee of the NPC (NPCSC) to enact a national security law for Hong Kong. On 30 June that

15 For a historical background to the saga, see Albert Chen, 'A Perfect Storm: Hong Kong-Mainland Rendition of Fugitive Offenders' (2019) 49(2) *Hong Kong Law Journal* 419–429.

16 The full title of the Bill is 'Fugitive Offenders and Mutual Legal Assistance in Criminal Matters Legislation (Amendment) Bill 2019'.

17 SCMP Reporters, '"Nearly 2 Million" People Take to Streets, Forcing Public Apology from Hong Kong Leader Carrie Lam as Suspension of Controversial Extradition Bill Fails to Appease Protesters' *SCMP* (17 June 2019) <www.scmp.com/news/hong-kong/politics/article/3014737/nearly-2-million-people-take-streets-forcing-public-apology> last accessed 1 January 2026.

18 Kris Cheng, 'Hong Kong Police Used Crowd Control Weapons 30,000 Times since June; over 6,000 Arrested' *HKFP* (10 December 2019) <https://hongkongfp.com/2019/12/10/hong-kong-police-used-crowd-control-weapons-30000-times-since-june-6000-arrests/> last accessed 1 January 2026.

same year, the NPCSC promulgated the *Law of the People's Republic of China on Safeguarding National Security in the Hong Kong Special Administrative Region* (hereinafter termed "2020 HKNSL") and added it to the list of National Laws applicable in the city.[19]

Unlike the aborted national security legislation in 2003, the Central Government dominated the entire legislative process this time in 2020, with little engagement with the HKSAR machinery. Fusing Chinese law with the Hong Kong common law, this hybrid instrument posed unprecedented challenges to Hong Kong's legal system. Since promulgation, the 2020 HKNSL has been enforced aggressively, and its enactment marks the reconstruction of a national security law regime in Hong Kong. The 2020 HKNSL criminalises four primary offences – secession, subversion, terrorism, and external collusion. But Article 7 of the 2020 HKNSL further requires the HKSAR government "to complete, as early as possible" its own national security legislation and prohibit other activities mandated under Article 23 of the BL, particularly theft of state secrets. In addition, many other local laws have since been amended to shore up national security imperatives. In 2021, the Film Censorship Ordinance was amended to allow the government to ban films deemed prejudicial to national security.[20] The Legal Practitioners Ordinance was amended in 2023 to prohibit the ad-hoc admission of overseas qualified counsel in national security cases, except in exceptional circumstances approved by the Hong Kong Chief Executive.[21]

On 30 January 2024, the Hong Kong government released a public consultation document on the domestic Article 23 legislation.[22] In the revamped Hong Kong, this legislative attempt faced little opposition in Hong Kong, and it was expedited through the legislative process at breakneck speed. The public consultation lasted 30 days, and 8 days after the "consultation" ended, the HKSAR government was

19 See 'National Laws to be Applied in the Hong Kong Special Administrative Region'<www.basiclaw.gov.hk/en/basiclaw/national-laws.html> last accessed 1 January 2026.

20 See 'Film Censorship (Amendment) Ordinance 2021 and Updated Guidelines Come into Effect' (5 November 2021) <www.info.gov.hk/gia/general/202111/05/P2021110500240.htm> last accessed 1 January 2026.

21 Section 27B(2) of the Legal Practitioners Ordinance now provides:

> The exceptional circumstance is that the Chief Executive has sufficient grounds for believing that the person's practising or acting as a barrister for the case does not involve national security or would not be contrary to the interests of national security.

Notably, Timothy Owen KC was denied admission to represent Jimmy Lai – a pro-democracy media mogul – when the latter was charged with external collusion and sedition. Ng Kang-chung, 'Committee Backs Hong Kong Government Bid to Ban Overseas Counsel from National Security Cases' *SCMP* (11 January 2023) <www.scmp.com/news/hong-kong/politics/article/3206468/committee-backs-hong-kong-government-bid-ban-overseas-counsel-national-security-cases> last accessed 1 January 2026.

22 Security Bureau of the HKSAR government, 'Safeguarding National Security: Basic Law Article 23 Legislation – Public Consultation Document' (30 January 2024) <www.sb.gov.hk/eng/bl23/consultation.html> last accessed 1 January 2026.

ready to reveal a full draft bill in the Legislative Council. After a swift 12 days of debate, the bill was passed unanimously by the "patriots-only" legislature and enacted into law amidst thunderous self-congratulatory cheers and applause within the legislative chambers.[23] The law, entitled "Safeguarding National Security Ordinance 維護國家安全條例" (hereinafter termed "2024 HKNSL") officially took effect on 23 March 2024.[24] From the start of the public consultation to the passage of the law, the entire process took less than 50 days – the fastest Bill passed in the history of the HKSAR.

National Security Legislation in Macau: Past and Present

In comparison with Hong Kong, Article 23 legislation in Macau proceeded relatively smoothly, largely due to the city's harmonious relations with the Central Authorities and the absence of a strong opposition and civil society in the city. At the outset, the drafters of the Macau Basic Law (MABL) simply adopted the final version of Hong Kong's Article 23 and there was no discussion of other drafts.[25]

During Portuguese colonial rule, the Portuguese Penal Code, which applied in Macau until 1995, had a special chapter that criminalised acts endangering national security, but they pertained to interests of the Portuguese State. As part of the localisation of the Macau legal system in the 1990s, the Portuguese Penal Code was replaced with the Macau Penal Code in 1995, and those provisions relating to national security offences against Portugal were removed and the Macau Penal Code only criminalised offences against the local government.[26]

After China's resumption of sovereignty over Macau in 1999, the 1995 Macau Penal Code was retained, but Macau had to enact a more comprehensive national security law as required under Article 23 of the MABL.[27] In 2002, following Hong Kong's lead in implementing Article 23, the Macau government also followed suit,

23 For a full and detailed account of the legislative process of Hong Kong's Article 23 legislation, see Mercedes Hutton, 'Timeline: Hong Kong's New Security Law – from Public Consultation to Passage in 48 Days, after "27 Years" in the Making' *HKFP* (23 March 2024) <https://hongkongfp.com/2024/03/23/a-timeline-of-hong-kongs-new-security-law-from-public-consultation-to-passage-in-48-days-after-27-years-in-the-making/> last accessed 1 January 2026; also see '香港立法會三讀通過《基本法》23條立法 Hong Kong LegCo Passes Article 23 Legislation after Three Readings' *端傳媒 Initium Media* (19 March 2024) <https://theinitium.com/zh-Hans/article/20240319-whatsnew-hongkong-basic-law-article-23> last accessed 1 January 2026.

24 The full text of the law is available at <www.elegislation.gov.hk/hk/a305> last accessed 1 January 2026.

25 Luo Weijian 骆伟建 et al., *澳门特别行政区基本法解析：立法背景和立法原意的探究 Analysing the Basic Law of the Macau Special Administrative Region: An Approach from Legislative Background and Intent* (社会科学文献出版社 Social Sciences Academic Press 2020) 90.

26 Part 5 (Articles 297–307) of the Macau 1995 Penal Code was on 'Offences against the Territory' (妨害本地區罪).

27 Jorge Godinho, 'The Regulation of Article 23 of the Macau Basic Law: A Commentary of the Draft Law on the Protection of State Security' (28 November 2008) <https://papers.ssrn.com/sol3/papers.cfm?abstract_id=1303245> last accessed 1 January 2026.

but the latter also abandoned this initiative after Hong Kong shelved its bill in 2003.[28] But unlike Hong Kong, Macau decided to restart work on its own national security legislation again in 2008,[29] and the Law on Safeguarding National Security (hereinafter termed 2009 MANSL) was passed in 2009.[30]

The 2009 MANSL was legislated at a different time in China's developmental history. Relations between the West and China were at an all-time high with Beijing successfully hosting the Summer Olympics of 2008 and Shanghai about to host the World Expo in 2010. And by taking charge of national security legislation of its own accord, the Macau government was able to exercise a high degree of autonomy in crafting this law.

The 2009 MANSL comprised only 15 articles, primarily codifying national security offences, penalties, and criminal jurisdiction, leaving other matters to be regulated under the Macau Penal Code and the Macau Criminal Procedure Code. Vis-à-vis the 2020 HKNSL and the PRC Criminal Law, the offences in the 2009 MANSL were also more narrowly defined. Secession[31] and subversion[32] in Macau required the prosecution to prove that the perpetrator had used "violence" or "grave unlawful means", and a lengthy definition of "grave unlawful means" was included to further limit the scope of the two offences.[33] For "theft of state secrets", "state secrets" referred only to "national secrets" (excluding "SAR secrets") that had to be pre-classified *ex ante*.[34] Sedition was limited to inciting treason, secession, subversion, and rebellion of the PLA garrison in Macau, and the incitement must be done "publicly and directly";[35] academic research or mere commentary was

28 Zhuang Jinfeng 莊金鋒, '從《維護國家安全法》的制定看澳門模式的基本特徵 The Legislation of Macau National Security Law Epitomises the Basic Features of Macau Model' (2010) 3 *一國兩制研究 Journal of 'One Country Two Systems' Studies* 12, 17–18.

29 Guo Tianwu 郭天武 and Zhu Ziqian 朱紫芊, '澳门特别行政区维护国家安全立法探析 A Legal Analysis of the Law of the Macau SAR on Safeguarding National Security' (2021) 3 *上海政法学院学报(法治论丛) Journal of Shanghai University of Political Science & Law (The Rule of Law Forum)* 58, 59.

30 Hereinafter, the MANSLs enacted in 2009 and 2023 will be referred to as "2009 MANSL" and "2023 MANSL" respectively.

31 2009 MANSL, art 2.

32 2009 MANSL, art 3.

33 Under Article 2 (3) of the 2009 MANSL, "grave unlawful means" referred to (1) Crimes against the life, physical integrity and personal freedom of another person; (2) Acts that damage or threaten the security of public infrastructure facilities; (3) Arson and other acts that endanger public safety or health; or (4) Crimes involving the use of nuclear energy, firearms and other dangerous devices or substances.

34 Article 5(5) of the 2009 MANSL stipulated that:

> state secrets refer to documents, communication or objects that must be kept secret and have been classified as such, in the fields of national defence, foreign relations and other issues concerning the relationship between the Central Authorities and the MASAR as set out in the Basic Law of the MASAR of the PRC.

35 2009 MANSL, art 4.

not deemed "direct incitement".[36] The prohibition on foreign political bodies conducting political activities in Macau and the prohibition on the establishment of ties between local and foreign political bodies were both limited to activities that implicated the five crimes prescribed by the 2009 MANSL (i.e. treason, secession, subversion, sedition, and theft of state secrets).[37] The five crimes also had extra-territorial effect on Macau residents, but for treason the Macau resident in question must concurrently be a Chinese national;[38] foreigners were liable under the 2009 MANSL only if the crimes were committed within Macau.[39] Notably, after the 2009 MANSL was passed, the law was never invoked to charge any individual.

After the passage of the 2020 HKNSL, and the shift in national conditions and geopolitics, the Macau government decided to revise and "strengthen" its own NSL, so that its local law could better align with the Hong Kong and Mainland counterparts. But even before the revised law was passed in 2023,[40] Macau had made incremental changes to its national security regime.

Political events in Hong Kong are always closely watched in Macau as the local authorities are concerned about any potential spill-over effects. For instance, there were criticisms that the foreign judges in Hong Kong were sympathetic to protestors[41] who took part in the 2014 Occupy Central movement and the Fish-ball riot[42] in Hong Kong. While the Hong Kong government did not address the issue of foreign judges, the Macau government quickly responded by adding Article 19-A to the Judicial Organisation Law (司法組織綱要法) in 2019 to exclude foreign judges and prosecutors from handling national security cases.

After Beijing foisted the 2020 NSL on Hong Kong, Macau decided to revise and toughen its MANSL. In crafting Macau's 2023 Law on Safeguarding National Security (維護國家安全法) (hereinafter termed "2023 MANSL"), the local government explicitly cited the 2020 HKNSL as an important reference point,

36 See MASAR Government, '《維護國家安全法》(草案)諮詢文件The Law on Safeguarding National Security (Consultation Documents)' (22 Oct 2008). Document on file with the authors.

37 2009 MANSL, arts 6 and 7.

38 2009 MANSL, art 10(2).

39 2009 MANSL, art 10(1).

40 A bilingual (Chinese and Portuguese) version of the law is available at <https://images.io.gov.mo/bo/i/2023/24/despce-79-2023.pdf> last accessed 1 January 2026.

41 A non-ethnic Chinese Hong Kong District Court judge was harshly criticised by the pro-Beijing camp in Hong Kong when he sentenced seven police officers to two years imprisonment for assaulting protestors during the Occupy Central protests. Criticisms were directed at the foreign judges, questioning whether their foreign nationality should disqualify them from handling politically sensitive cases or protest cases. See Stuart Hargreaves, 'Canaries or Colonials? The Reduced Prominence of the "Overseas Judges" on Hong Kong's Court of Final Appeal' (2021) 16 *Asian Journal of Comparative Law* 187, 210–211.

42 The Fish-ball riot was triggered by the police's crackdown on unlicensed street hawkers during the Chinese New Year holiday in 2016. Violent clashes broke out between the police and a few hundred protestors, marking the worst outbreak of riots hitherto in Hong Kong since the 1960s. See Ying-ho Kwong, 'State-Society Conflict Radicalization in Hong Kong: The Rise of "Anti-China" Sentiment and Radical Localism' (2016) 47(3) *Asian Affairs* 428–442.

particularly with respect to the offences, criminal procedures, and police powers.[43] In addition to revising the MANSL, the Macau government also amended and added other local laws to enhance the safeguarding of national and local security, including cybersecurity and state secrets.[44] When Beijing imposed a "patriots-only" legislature on Hong Kong in 2021, the Macau government on its own initiative also toughened its own screening of electoral candidates for public office. As we discussed more fully in Chapter 2, the Macau Legislative Assembly Electoral Affairs Commission disqualified *all* pro-democracy candidates from running in the then-upcoming 2021 Legislative Assembly election, ensuring that only "patriots" could govern Macau.

Comparison of Hong Kong and Macau National Security Laws

In hindsight, by delaying the passage of a national security law on its own before the city was rocked by turmoil in 2019, Hong Kong missed a golden opportunity of enacting a national security law within its control that was more consistent with its common law traditions. In contrast, Macau's efforts to enact a national security law on its own initiative in 2009 and the drama-free nature of its Central-SAR relations allowed the local government to craft legislation that was more circumscribed and autonomous from the Mainland legal infrastructure. Ironically, for Hong Kong, the social unrest of 2019 – with protestors using both peaceful and violent actions to campaign for more democracy and governmental accountability – ultimately backfired and led to the sinification of its national security law regime.[45] Unfortunately for Macau, and due to no fault of its own, the local government felt it had to revise and toughen its own NSL in 2023 after the Central Authorities imposed one on Hong Kong that was far more stringent than its pre-existing 2009 version. With Chinese patriots fully in control of the Hong Kong legislature after 2021,[46] the home-grown 2024 HKNSL also draws freely from and incorporates key concepts from Chinese law, such as PRC definitions of "central authorities",[47] "national

43 See MASAR Government, '澳門特別行政區修改《維護國家安全法》諮詢文本 Consultation Document on Amendment to the Law of the Macau SAR on Safeguarding National Security' (22 August 2022) 8, 11–13 <www.gov.mo/zh-hant/wp-content/uploads/sites/4/2022/08/修改《維護國家安全法》諮詢文本_中文.pdf> last accessed 1 January 2026.

44 E.g., Macau Cybersecurity Law 網絡安全法 (2019), Legal Framework for Interception and Protection of Communications 通訊截取及保障法律制度 (2022), and State Secret Protection Law 保守國家秘密法 (2023). Also see Leng Tiexun 冷铁勋, '切实维护国家安全是澳门成功实践"一国两制"的宝贵经验 Effectively Maintaining National Security is a Valuable Lesson from Macau's Successful Practice of "One Country, Two Systems"' (25 March 2019) <www.basiclaw.org.mo/index.php?p=5_1&art_id=2145&lang=1> last accessed 1 January 2026.

45 Albert Chen and Po Jen Yap, *The Constitutional System of the Hong Kong SAR: A Contextual Analysis* (Hart 2023) 105.

46 See Chapter 2 of this book.

47 2024 HKNSL, Section 3(1); also see Legislative Affairs Commission of the NPCSC, '關於香港特別行政區《維護國家安全條例草案》就"中央"一詞作出釋義有關問題的答覆'(The Response

security",[48] and "state secrets".[49]

Now, we will proceed to draw parallels and note key differences between the national security laws of Hong Kong and Macau.

Nature and Status of the Laws

The 2020 HKNSL is a national law enacted by the Standing Committee of the National People's Congress of the PRC (NPCSC) and annexed directly into HKBL.[50] In those rare serious cases where foreign governments are involved or the Hong Kong government is unable to enforce the law effectively, the Chinese procuratorate and courts are legally empowered to take over from local counterparts.[51] The law opens up the chilling possibility that for these exceptional cases, the offenders, if in Hong Kong, can be extradited to the Mainland to face trial. The power of interpreting this national security law lies with the NPCSC,[52] which expressly allows Mainland officials to overrule the Hong Kong judiciary's interpretation of the 2020 HKNSL. The 2020 HKNSL also overrides all Hong Kong local laws if there is any inconsistency.[53] On the other hand, the 2024 HKNSL is a locally enacted law that complements the Beijing-imposed 2020 HKNSL.

In contrast to the 2020 HKNSL, the 2023 MANSL is a local law enacted by the Macau Special Administrative Region (MASAR); it does not hold a higher status than other local laws, and Macau authorities retain jurisdiction over all its national security cases.

Legislative Process

The 2020 HKNSL was drafted secretly in Mainland China and foisted onto Hong Kong. The Chinese Communist Party's Central Committee first announced that it would establish a "national security legal system" for Hong Kong in October 2019,[54] with no further details provided. On 28 May 2020, the NPC passed a

regarding the Interpretation of the Term 'Central Authorities' in the Safeguarding National Security Bill of the HKSAR) (9 March 2024) <www.npc.gov.cn/npc/c2/c30834/202403/t20240309_435704.html> last accessed 1 January 2026.

48 2024 HKNSL, Section 4.

49 2024 HKNSL, Section 29; also see Security Bureau of the HKSAR government, 'Safeguarding National Security: Basic Law Article 23 Legislation – Public Consultation Document', 5.5–5.8 (30 January 2024) <www.sb.gov.hk/eng/bl23/consultation.html> last accessed 1 January 2026.

50 HKBL, Annex III.

51 2020 HKNSL, art 55.

52 2020 HKNSL, art 65.

53 2020 HKNSL, art 62.

54 Decision of the Central Committee of the Chinese Communist Party on Major Issues Concerning Upholding and Improving the System of Socialism with Chinese Characteristics and Advancing the Modernisation of China's System and Capacity for Governance (中共中央关于坚持和完善中国特色社会主义制度推进国家治理体系和治理能力现代化若干重大问题的决定) (31 October 2019) <www.gov.cn/zhengce/2019-11/05/content_5449023.htm> last accessed 1 January 2026.

Decision authorising the NPCSC to draft a National Security Law for Hong Kong that would be annexed directly to the city's BL.[55] This news shocked Hong Kong and the international community. Within five weeks of this announcement, the law was swiftly passed by the NPCSC on 30 June 2020 with not a single draft of the bill released for public viewing – let alone consultation – until the law was formally promulgated, which is even exceptional for the passage of National Laws in the Mainland.[56] The entire legislative process of the HKNSL was completely controlled by Beijing, with fewer than 10 Hong Kong officials involved in the process.[57]

The passage of the 2024 HKNSL was also swift as it was rushed through the Hong Kong Legislative Council at unprecedented speed. While this 2024 version was primarily a locally driven effort, Beijing closely monitored the legislative process.[58] More significantly, the HKSAR government sought a legal opinion from the NPCSC on the definition of "Central Authorities (中央)" which they intended to use in the offence-creating provisions of the 2024 HKNSL.[59] In March 2024, the Legislative Affairs Commission of the NPCSC publicly issued a "legal inquiry

55 Decision of the National People's Congress on Establishing and Improving the Legal System and Enforcement Mechanisms for the Hong Kong Special Administrative Region to Safeguard National Security (Adopted at the Third Session of the 13th National People's Congress on 28 May 2020).

56 Articles 32 and 40 of the PRC Legislation Law require, as a general rule, that a bill go through deliberation at three sessions of the NPCSC and that the draft law, together with an explanation of the draft, shall be released to the public to solicit opinions for no less than 30 days. For a detailed introduction on the HKNSL legislative process, see Albert Chen, 'The National Security Law of the HKSAR: A Contextual and Legal Study' in Hualing Fu and Michael Hor (eds), *The National Security Law of Hong Kong: Restoration and Transformation* (HKU Press 2022) 20, 24–26.

57 Hong Kong Chief Executive Carrie Lam revealed this piece of information in an interview one year after the promulgation of the HKNSL, and she also emphasised that she had to type out documents herself in order to prevent information leakage. See '林鄭月娥：特區的定海神針 Carrie Lam: The Stabiliser of the SAR' in *香港國安法立法一週年：國安法下的香港 The 1st Anniversary of Hong Kong National Security Law: Hong Kong under the HKNSL* (星島雜誌集團 Sing Tao Magazine Group Limited 2021) 14, 16.

58 On 22 February 2024, Xia Baolong, Director of the Hong Kong and Macau Affairs Office of the State Council, visited Hong Kong and met with various officials in Hong Kong before the law was passed. See Chen Qingqing, 'Top Official's Visit to Hong Kong Demonstrates Central Govt's Position on Article 23 Legislation, Clears Doubts: Experts' *Global Times* (22 February 2024) <www.globaltimes.cn/page/202402/1307538.shtml> last accessed 1 January 2026; On 21 March 2024, just two days after the passage of the 2024 HKNSL, Xia met with Hong Kong's Chief Executive, the LegCo president, and other senior officials and lawmakers, in Shenzhen to hear their reports on the law. See Lilian Cheng et al., 'Beijing's Point Man on Hong Kong Affairs Tells City Leader he's "Very Satisfied" with Quick Passage of Article 23 National Security Law' *SCMP* (21 March 2024) <www.scmp.com/news/article/3256209/hong-kong-leader-john-lee-meets-beijings-point-man-xia-baolong-shenzhen-2-days-after-delivering> last accessed 1 January 2026.

59 For example, Section 23 of the 2024 HKNSL criminalises inter alia sedition against the offices of the Central Authorities in Hong Kong, Section 49 criminalises inter alia the sabotage of any public infrastructure belonging to the Central Authorities in Hong Kong, and Sections 52 and 53 criminalise inter alia any external interference by improper means that prejudices the relationship between the Central Authorities and any region in China.

response (法律询问答复)" and defined the term "Central Authorities (中央)" for the HKSAR government.[60] This marked the first publicly disclosed occasion in which the legal inquiry response mechanism was invoked for any Hong Kong local legislation. Notably, while such a mechanism is available for Mainland laws under the PRC Legislation Law,[61] neither the HKBL nor any local legislation provides for this. Furthermore, in defining "national security"[62] within the 2024 HKNSL, the Hong Kong government simply "copy-and-pasted" the PRC's definition of "national security", which not only includes the state's political regime, sovereignty, unity, and territorial integrity, but also all-encompassing and nebulous terms such as "welfare of the people, sustainable economic and social development, and other major interests of the state".[63]

While the entire legislative process of the 2024 HKNSL took less than 50 days – from the commencement of its public consultation to the passage of the law – there was relatively more transparency and less haste in Macau's enactment of the 2023 MANSL. Without the historical baggage of Hong Kong's experience with national security law enactment, Macau had less reason to rush. On 22 August 2022, the Macau government released the "Consultation Document on Amendment to the Law of the Macau SAR on Safeguarding National Security"[64] for a 45-day public consultation. Two drafts of the proposed law and the review opinion of the Legislative Assembly were all released online.[65] After two readings in the Macau Legislative Assembly, the amendment was passed on 18 May 2023.[66]

60 Legislative Affairs Commission of the NPCSC, '關於香港特別行政區《維護國家安全條例草案》就"中央"一詞作出釋義有關問題的答覆 The Response regarding the Interpretation of the Term "Central Authorities" in the Safeguarding National Security Bill of the HKSAR' (9 March 2024) <www.npc.gov.cn/npc/c2/c30834/202403/t20240309_435704.html> last accessed 1 January 2026. The Reply specifies that "Central Authorities" and "the body of central power" include: (1) the NPC and its Standing Committee; (2) the PRC President; (3) the Central People's Government; (4) the PRC Central Military Commission; and (5) [any] other body of central power of the PRC. See Section 3(1) of the 2024 HKNSL.

61 Article 69 of the PRC Legislation Law stipulates that:

> The working bodies of the Standing Committee of the National People's Congress may, after research, respond to legal inquiries regarding specific issues and report thereon to the Standing Committee for the record (全國人民代表大會常務委員會工作機構可以對有關具體問題的法律詢問進行研究予以答覆，並報常務委員會備案).

62 2024 HKNSL, Section 4.

63 2024 HKNSL, Section 4; PRC National Security Law, art 2.

64 MASAR Government, '澳門特別行政區修改《維護國家安全法》諮詢文本 Consultation Document on Amendment to the Law of the Macau SAR on Safeguarding National Security' (22 August 2022) 8, 11–13 <www.gov.mo/zh-hant/wp-content/uploads/sites/4/2022/08/修改《維護國家安全法》諮詢文本_中文.pdf> last accessed 1 January 2026.

65 These documents are available at <www.al.gov.mo/zh/law/lawcase/553> last accessed 1 January 2026.

66 A bilingual version of the law is available at <https://images.io.gov.mo/bo/i/2023/24/despce-79-2023.pdf> last accessed 1 January 2026.

Criminal Offences

The 2020 HKNSL was drafted by Beijing, and it is therefore unsurprising that its substantive offences were modelled after the PRC Criminal Law[67] even though this reference was not explicitly spelt out in the local legislation. Only four substantive crimes are prohibited under the 2020 HKNSL – secession, subversion, terrorism, and collusion with external forces. But notably *terrorism* is not an offence mandated under Article 23, and the offence of *collusion* sweeps more broadly than what Article 23 of the HKBL requires, as we discuss later in this chapter.

The 2024 HKNSL legislates against five main offences in five different parts of the legislation, including "treason";[68] "insurrection"[69] and "acts with seditious intention";[70] "offences in connection with state secrets and espionage";[71] "sabotage";[72] and "external interference".[73] Several of these offences are not wholly new as they existed as colonial relics that were kept on Hong Kong's lawbooks after the handover. Such colonial offences included treason;[74] sedition;[75] crimes relating to the unauthorised use of official documents;[76] and spying.[77]

Like its 2009 version, the 2023 MANSL is comprehensive insofar as it legislates on all seven offences required by Article 23 of the MABL – treason; secession; sedition; subversion of the Central People's Government; theft of state secrets; conduct of political activities by foreign political organisations; and the establishment of ties between foreign and local political organisations. In addition, the 2023 MANSL introduces a new inchoate offence of "instigating or supporting insurrection",[78] which criminalises acts that encourage or support persons who commit the primary offences of treason, secession and subversion.

Both Hong Kong's and Macau's national security laws have alarming extra-territorial effects – they are applicable even if the putative acts are committed *outside* the respective SARs by *non-residents*.[79]

67 See Part II, Chapter 1 of the PRC Criminal Law. For a comparative study on the HKNSL's substantive offences and their Mainland equivalent, see also Albert Chen, 'The National Security Law of the HKSAR: A Contextual and Legal Study' in Hualing Fu and Michael Hor (eds), *The National Security Law of Hong Kong: Restoration and Transformation* (Hong Kong University Press 2022) 20, 26–42.

68 2024 HKNSL, Part 2.

69 2024 HKNSL, Part 3.

70 2024 HKNSL, Part 3.

71 2024 HKNSL, Part 4.

72 2024 HKNSL, Part 5.

73 2024 HKNSL, Part 6.

74 Sections 2 and 3 (now-repealed) of the Crimes Ordinance.

75 Sections 9 and 10 (now-repealed) of the Crimes Ordinance.

76 Section 6 (now-repealed) of the Official Secrets Ordinance.

77 Section 3 (now-repealed) of the Official Secrets Ordinance.

78 2023 MANSL, art 10.

79 2020 HKNSL, art 38; 2023 MANSL, art 3(3). For the 2024 HKNSL, the law only applies extra-territorially to non-residents for offences such as espionage and sabotage endangering national security. See 2024 HKNSL Sections 9, 40(2), 48, and 51.

Secession

Both the 2020 HKNSL and the 2023 MANSL criminalise secession. Notably, the Chinese version of HKNSL Article 20 criminalises "secession or undermining national unification" (分裂國家、破壞國家統一), and this phrase is largely identical to its equivalent in the PRC Criminal Law.[80] But unlike the Mainland criminal law, the 2020 HKNSL specifically spells out the relevant prohibited secessionist acts: (1) separating the HKSAR or any part of the PRC from China; (2) altering the legal status of Hong Kong or other parts of the PRC by "*unlawful* means"; or (3) surrendering Hong Kong or any part of the PRC to a foreign country.[81] To be liable for secession, offenders must act "whether or not by force or threat of force", with "a view to committing secession or undermining national unification".[82] Even though the 2020 HKNSL only criminalises the altering of Hong Kong's legal status by *unlawful* means, the phrase "unlawful means" is not defined.

In *pari materia* with the 2020 HKNSL, the 2023 MANSL also spells out the same three prohibited acts that would constitute secession, but with reference to the MASAR. But in Macau, all the punishable acts must additionally be committed by "unlawful means".[83] Therefore, while the peaceful chanting of pro-Hong Kong independence slogans will be a crime under the 2020 HKNSL, the peaceful chanting of pro-Macau independence slogans may *not* necessarily be prohibited under the 2023 MANSL. Notably, the 2023 MANSL also does not define "unlawful means".[84]

Subversion

Both Macau and Hong Kong criminalise subversive acts by "unlawful means",[85] but this phrase is again left undefined. Questions have been raised as to whether the "unlawful means" are limited to penal offences or whether they also include civil wrongs.[86]

Both the 2020 HKNSL and the 2023 MANSL criminalise as subversive acts that undermine the basic system of the PRC established by the PRC Constitution, overthrow the body of the central power of the PRC, or seriously interfere in the

80 PRC Criminal Law, art 103.
81 2020 HKNSL, art 20.
82 2020 HKNSL, art 20.
83 2023 MANSL, art 8.
84 Under the 2009 MANSL, Macau previously only criminalised secessionist acts using "violence" or "grave unlawful means". See 2009 MANSL, art 2.
85 2023 MANSL, art 9; 2020 HKNSL, art 22.
86 Michael Jackson, 'Two Years On: Reviewing the Implementation of the National Security Law in the HKSAR' (2023) 52(3) *Hong Kong Law Journal* 875, 901. In *HKSAR v Ng Gordon Ching-hang* [2024] HKCFI 1468, [42], the Court left the question open on whether civil wrongs can constitute an "unlawful means" under Article 22 of the 2020 HKNSL.

discharge of their duties. Notably, the specific prohibition against undermining the basic system of the PRC established by the PRC Constitution is an oblique reference to acts that undermine "the leadership of the Chinese Communist Party" – a phrase that was only added to the main articles of the PRC Constitution in 2018.[87] This particular prohibition was absent from the 2009 MANSL subversion law.[88]

The primary distinction between the 2020 HKNSL and the 2023 MANSL is that the latter criminalises subversive acts targeting only the central government, omitting any reference to the MASAR government. But one should note that Macau's Penal Code already criminalises subversive acts undertaken against the local authority.[89] In contrast, the 2020 HKNSL additionally criminalises acts that overthrow or seriously interfere with the performance of functions of the HKSAR government.[90] Notably, Article 23 of the HKBL makes no mention of, nor requires, any legislation prohibiting subversive acts against the local authorities. Furthermore, in response to the illegal occupation and vandalism of the Legislative Council by protestors in 2019, the 2020 HKNSL also expressly criminalises as subversion any attack or damage to premises used by the HKSAR government that renders them incapable of performing their normal functions.[91]

Terrorism and Sabotage

The 2020 HKNSL criminalises terrorism,[92] but terrorism is simply not an offence for which either SAR is constitutionally required under Article 23 of its BL to enact laws on, but Beijing enacted one for Hong Kong anyway. Terrorist activities in Hong Kong are defined to include not only serious violence against persons, but also the "sabotage of means of transport, transport facilities"[93] and "serious interruption or sabotage of electronic control systems"[94] that manage the provision

87 Article 1 of the PRC Constitution, as amended in 2018. Before 2018, Article 1 of the PRC Constitution only provided: "The socialist system is the basic system of the People's Republic of China". In 2018, the PRC Constitution was revised and an additional sentence was added: "The defining feature of socialism with Chinese characteristics is the leadership of the Communist Party of China".

88 2009 MANSL, art 3. The 2009 MANSL also required the offender to have used violence or "grave unlawful means".

89 Articles 297–304 of the Macau Penal Code, including offences of "violent alteration of the established system 暴力變更已確立之制度" (Article 297); "incitement to violent alteration of the established system 煽動以暴力變更已確立之制度" (Article 298); "sabotage 破壞" (Article 299); "incitement to collective disobedience 煽動集體違令" (Article 300); "external collusion 通謀外地" (Article 301); "insulting the symbols of the territory 侮辱本地區象徵" (Article 302); "coercion against organs of the territory 脅迫本地區之機關" (Article 303); and "disrupting the functioning of the territory's organs 擾亂本地區機關之運作" (Article 304).

90 2020 HKNSL, arts 22(2) and 22(3).

91 2020 HKNSL, art 22(4).

92 2020 HKNSL, Part 3.

93 2020 HKNSL, art 24(3).

94 2020 HKNSL, art 24(4).

of water, electricity, gas, transport, telecommunications, and internet. The offenders are liable so long as they commit the abovementioned acts with a view to coercing the Central People's Government/HKSAR government or intimidating the public "in order to pursue a political agenda".[95]

Not content with the "sabotage" offence in the 2020 HKNSL, the 2024 HKNSL further codifies a separate offence on sabotage that imposes criminal liability on any person who intentionally or recklessly endangers national security and "damages or weakens a public infrastructure".[96]

The 2023 MANSL does not include offences against terrorism or sabotage. But the city has a separate counter-terrorism law[97] that is comparable to Hong Kong's terrorism offence under the 2020 HKNSL, and the Macau Penal Code also criminalises acts that damage public facilities, with the requisite intent to endanger the SAR's political and social systems.[98]

External Collusion and External Interference

It is important to point out that Article 23 of both BLs also does not require the SAR governments to enact a law on external collusion per se. All Article 23 does is to require a law prohibiting local political organisations from establishing ties with foreign political organisations. But with the 2020 HKNSL, Beijing has crafted a specific provision on external collusion for Hong Kong that is more expansive than what Article 23 HKBL requires. Notably, the collusion offence under the 2020 HKNSL applies even to foreign individuals and non-political bodies,[99] as is the case under the PRC Criminal Law.[100] But while PRC Criminal Law does not define what constitutes external collusion, Article 29 of the 2020 HKNSL spells out the specific scenarios in which external collusion would be established, cataloguing up to 16 different acts that are punishable by law.[101]

95 2020 HKNSL, art 24.
96 2024 HKNSL, Section 49.
97 Act of Prevention and Suppression of Terrorism Crimes 防止及遏止恐怖主義犯罪 (2017), arts 4–8.
98 Macau Penal Code, art 299.
99 2020 HKNSL, art 29.
100 PRC Criminal Law, art 102.
101 See Albert Chen and Simon Young, 'Liability for Imposing Sanctions under Hong Kong's National Security Law' (2020) 50(2) *Hong Kong Law Journal* 353, 354–355. Chen and Young's parsing of Article 29 reveals that it consists of at least sixteen criminal acts, including (1), (2)(a–e), (3)(a–e), and (4)(a–e), as shown below:

1 stealing, spying, obtaining with payment, or unlawfully providing state secrets or intelligence concerning national security for outsiders;
2 requesting outsiders;
3 conspiring with outsiders; or
4 directly or indirectly receiving instructions, control, funding, or other types of support from outsiders, to commit any of the following acts:

Although the 2023 MANSL does not prescribe a separate collusion offence, it criminalises three offences – "violation of state secrets",[102] "acts contrary to national security committed by organisations outside the MASAR",[103] and the "establishment of ties with organisations and individuals outside the MASAR for the purpose of committing acts against national security",[104] which overlap to some extent with the collusion offence under the 2020 HKNSL.

The 2023 MANSL prohibits anyone from establishing links with individuals or groups outside the MASAR for the purpose of committing acts against national security. Such acts include the unlawful disruption to the implementation of laws in the SAR, the undermining of elections in the MASAR, the imposition of sanctions on China or the MASAR, and the provocation of hatred by unlawful means among local residents against the Central Government.[105] These acts are prohibited under Hong Kong's collusion offence too. However Macau not only targets foreign individuals and non-political bodies, as Hong Kong has done, Macau also includes links with Mainland Chinese organisations,[106] which is excluded from the 2020 HKNSL.[107] On the other hand, Hong Kong's collusion offence includes the prohibition on external collusive links that provoke hatred by unlawful means against the local SAR government,[108] which is absent in Macau.

Not content with the external collusion offence provided under the 2020 HKNSL, the Hong Kong government tacked on an additional offence of "external interference" in the 2024 HKNSL. It is now an offence for a person, with intent to bring about an interference effect, to collaborate with an "external force" to do an act by "improper means".[109] "External force" is defined so widely as to include all non-Hong Kong governments, political parties, organisations pursuing political ends,

a waging a war against the PRC, or using or threatening to use force to seriously undermine the sovereignty, unification and territorial integrity of the PRC;
b seriously disrupting the formulation and implementation of laws or policies by the Government of the HKSAR or by the Central People's Government, which is likely to cause serious consequences;
c rigging or undermining an election in the HKSAR, which is likely to cause serious consequences;
d imposing sanctions or blockade, or engaging in other hostile activities against the HKSAR or the PRC; or
e provoking, by unlawful means, hatred among Hong Kong residents towards the Central People's Government or the Government of the Region, which is likely to cause serious consequences.

102 2023 MANSL, art 12. 2023 MANSL changes the offence name from "theft of state secrets" under the 2009 MANSL to "violation of state secrets".
103 2023 MANSL, art 15.
104 2023 MANSL, art 13.
105 2023 MANSL, art 13(1). Previously under Article 7 of 2009 MANSL, the prohibition on the establishment of ties between local and foreign political bodies was only limited to activities that implicated five crimes prescribed under 2009 MANSL: treason; secession; subversion; sedition; and theft of state secrets.
106 2023 MANSL, art 13(1).
107 2020 HKNSL, art 29.
108 2020 HKNSL, art 29(5).
109 2024 HKNSL, Section 52.

and individuals related to them.[110] Given that the influence on "the formulation or execution of any policy"[111] of the Chinese or HKSAR government will constitute "interference", the only real constraint on this law is that the offender must have used "improper means", i.e. knowingly making material misrepresentations, using or threatening the use of force against persons or property, causing or threatening financial, psychological, or reputational harm on other persons.[112] This law renders hardball economic bargaining involving Chinese state-owned enterprises potentially a crime.

State Secrets and Espionage

As the 2020 HKNSL's collusion offence only applies when there is an external party involved, the 2024 HKNSL further enacts a general prohibition against the unlawful acquisition, possession, and disclosure of state secrets.[113] The 2023 MANSL has a similar prohibition.[114]

For Macau, "state secrets" is defined in its Macau State Secrets Protection Law (保守國家秘密法),[115] which closely mirrors the PRC Law on Guarding State Secrets[116] (中华人民共和国保守国家秘密法). The definition of "state secrets"[117] in the 2024 HKNSL is also inspired by the same PRC law. Both the Macau State Secrets Protection Law[118] and the 2024 HKNSL[119] cover six similar areas of matters that are also protected in the PRC:[120] (1) major policy decisions, (2) national defence, (3) diplomatic and foreign affairs, (4) socio-economic development, (5) science and technology, and (6) activities for safeguarding national security and criminal investigations.

Both SARs also introduced a seventh category of state secrets not found in the PRC Law – state secrets pertaining to the relationship between the Central Authorities and the SAR. For Macau, this is limited to activities carried out by its Chief Executive when executing directives of the Central People's Government,[121] while Hong Kong covers all secrets concerning the Central Authorities–HKSAR relationship.[122] But the Macau State Secrets Protection Law – echoing Article 13

110 2024 HKNSL, Section 6.
111 2024 HKNSL, Section 53(1)(a)(i).
112 2024 HKNSL, Section 55.
113 2024 HKNSL, Sections 32–37.
114 2023 MANSL, art 12.
115 Macau State Secrets Protection Law, arts 2(1)(1) and 10.
116 PRC Law on Guarding State Secrets, arts 2 and 13.
117 2024 HKNSL, Section 29.
118 Macau State Secrets Protection Law, art 10 read with art 2(1)(1).
119 2024 HKNSL, Section 29.
120 PRC Law on Guarding State Secrets, art 13.
121 Article 10(7) of the Macau State Secrets Protection Law covers "Secretive matters in the activities carried out by the Chief Executive in executing directives issued by the Central People's Government in accordance with the Macau Basic Law".
122 Subsection (g) within the definition of 'state secret' in Section 29 of the 2024 HKNSL.

of the PRC Law on Guarding State Secrets – has an eighth catch-all category that covers *other* matters occurring within or originating from the MASAR that are significant to national security and should be classified as state secrets.[123] This catch-all category is absent from the 2024 HKNSL.

However, unlike the PRC equivalent,[124] both Macau and Hong Kong omit from their respective definitions of "state secrets" any references to "secrets of political parties" and "other secrets determined by the state secrecy administration". Nevertheless, it is self-evident that what remain in both cities' definitions of "state secrets" are still overly broad and have sparked particular public concern in Hong Kong.[125]

It is also notable that while Macau establishes specific procedures for the classification, declassification, extension of classification, and archiving of state secrets[126] – the period of classification as state secrets in Macau shall not exceed 30 years except in exceptional circumstances[127] – all such procedural safeguards are absent from Hong Kong's law.[128]

On the other hand, the 2024 HKNSL provides a limited "public interest" defence for an unauthorised "specified disclosure"[129] of state secrets, but it is incredibly narrow in application. To benefit from this defence, there must be a serious threat to public order, public safety or public health; the disclosure must not exceed what is necessary; and the public interest served by the disclosure must manifestly outweigh any public interest served by non-disclosure. Basically, only a whistle-blower like Dr Li Wenliang[130] – the Chinese doctor who tried to raise the alarm on

123 Macau State Secrets Protection Law, art 10(8).

124 PRC Law on Guarding State Secrets, art 13.

125 E.g., see Ezra Cheung, 'Hong Kong's Article 23 Law: Auditors Call for Clarity amid Fears over Handling Confidential Information Linked to Possible State Secrets' *SCMP* (17 March 2024) <www.scmp.com/news/hong-kong/society/article/3255706/hong-kongs-article-23-law-auditors-call-clarity-amid-fears-over-handling-confidential-information> last accessed 1 January 2026; Lo Hoi-ying and Harvey Kong, 'More Clarity needed on Hong Kong's Article 23 Domestic Security Law to Reassure Investors, Say Legal Experts and Business Chambers' *SCMP* (31 January 2024) <www.scmp.com/news/hong-kong/politics/article/3250409/more-clarity-needed-hong-kongs-article-23-domestic-security-law-reassure-investors-financial-hub> last accessed 1 January 2026.

126 Macau State Secrets Protection Law, Chapters 2–4.

127 Macau State Secrets Protection Law, art 12.

128 Unlike Macau, Hong Kong does not have any specific legislation governing the procedures for classifying secrets and the management of public archives. The Hong Kong government has issued guidelines, such as the Records Management Manual of the Government of the HKSAR and the Code on Access to Information, which regulate the classification of archives and public access to information. However, these documents are not legally binding and government agencies possess the discretion to classify their documents and determine the length of the confidentiality period.

129 2024 HKNSL, Section 30.

130 Stephanie Hegarty, 'The Chinese Doctor who Tried to Warn Others about Coronavirus' *BBC* (7 February 2020) <www.bbc.com/news/world-asia-china-51364382> last accessed 1 January 2026.

the coronavirus spreading in Wuhan – would be able to benefit from such a defence in the future. This public interest defence is absent in Macau.

The 2024 HKNSL also establishes an espionage offence,[131] expanding upon the spying activities outlawed by the colonial Official Secrets Ordinance.[132] Notably, the new espionage offence not only targets typical espionage activities such as the accessing of prohibited places or the collection of information useful to external forces,[133] the espionage law even criminalises the dissemination of fake news – it is a crime to collude with an external force to knowingly publish a statement of fact that is false or misleading if the offender has the intent to endanger national security.[134] In Macau, such "fake" news is criminalised under its Penal Code,[135] but the perpetrator must possess the intention of "using violence" to undermine Macau's established system.

Treason and Insurrection

Under the 2023 MANSL, the treason offence specifically prohibits Chinese citizens from joining a foreign army that is in an armed conflict with China, colluding with a foreign organisation or government to provoke war with China, or assisting a foreign state against China in times of war.[136]

The 2024 HKNSL criminalises treason in similar ways, but the substantive elements of treason in Hong Kong differ from Macau in one key area. In Hong Kong, a Chinese citizen who intends to endanger the sovereignty, unity or territorial integrity of China, and uses force, is liable for treason,[137] *regardless of any external party involvement*; Macau's treason law does not have this specific clarification.

As the treason offences apply only to Chinese citizens, the Hong Kong government decided to tack on an insurrection offence in the 2024 HKNSL that criminalises the abovementioned acts when undertaken by any "person",[138] thereby including non-nationals operating in Hong Kong. On the other hand, the insurrection offence in Macau exists as an inchoate offence that criminalises the encouragement or support of treason, secession, and subversion.[139] Furthermore, the 2024 HKNSL also codifies the defunct colonial common law offence of misprision of treason, by legally requiring Chinese citizens to inform the police if they have knowledge that any other Chinese citizen has or is about to commit treason[140] – this offence is omitted by Macau.

131 2024 HKNSL, Section 43.
132 Official Secrets Ordinance, Section 3 (now-repealed).
133 2024 HKNSL, Section 43(1) and Section 43(2).
134 2024 HKNSL, Section 43(3).
135 Macau Penal Code, art 301.
136 2023 MANSL, art 7.
137 2024 HKNSL, Section 10(1)(e).
138 2024 HKNSL, Section 15.
139 2023 MANSL, art 10.
140 2024 HKNSL, Section 12.

Sedition

Article 11 of the 2023 MANSL criminalises sedition, which is defined as the incitement of treason, secession, or subversion, or the incitement of others to take part in disturbances that endanger the internal or external security interests of the State.

For Hong Kong, the incitement of secession and subversion are criminalised under the respective secession[141] and subversion[142] offences of the 2020 HKNSL. The 2024 HKNSL further consolidates the substantive elements of the colonial-era sedition offences found in Sections 9 and 10 of the Crimes Ordinance, which had inter alia prohibited acts, words, or publications that bring into hatred or contempt or excite disaffection against the government or the administration of justice in Hong Kong; or promote feelings of ill-will and enmity between different classes of the population of Hong Kong. But two major revisions to the colonial sedition law were made by the 2024 HKNSL. First, under the colonial-era law, sedition prohibited acts that *inter alia* bring into hatred or contempt or excite disaffection against the Hong Kong and Central governments.[143] Now, under the 2024 HKNSL, the sedition offence expands its coverage to include "the fundamental system of the State established by the Constitution of the PRC" (an oblique reference to the Chinese Communist Party), any state institutions under the PRC Constitution, the Liaison Office in Hong Kong, the Office for Safeguarding National Security in Hong Kong, the Office of the Commissioner of the Ministry of Foreign Affairs, and even the Hong Kong Garrison of the PLA.[144] Second, previously under the Crimes Ordinance, prosecution for sedition had to be brought within 6 months of the offence's commission or it was time-barred;[145] this time-bar has been repealed by the 2024 HKNSL.[146]

What distinguishes the sedition offence in Macau from Hong Kong is that the former sets a relatively higher threshold for criminalisation – the incitement must be done "publicly and directly".[147] Academic research or mere commentary is excluded from "direct incitement" in Macau.[148] But the 2024 HKNSL largely

141 2020 HKNSL, art 21.

142 2020 HKNSL, art 23.

143 Sections 9 and 10 (now-repealed) of the Crimes Ordinance read with Schedule 8 of the Interpretation and General Clauses Ordinance on "Her Majesty".

144 2024 HKNSL, Section 23(2).

145 Crimes Ordinance, Section 11 (now-repealed).

146 2024 HKNSL, Section 139.

147 2023 MANSL, art 11.

148 MASAR Government, '《維護國家安全法》(草案)諮詢總結報告 Summary Report on the Public Consultation for the MANSL' (2008) 19–20. The Macau government emphasised in the Summary Report that:

> the term "inciting directly" does not include mere suggestions or advice, nor does it include purely academic research or commentaries (這裏所指的直接煽動不包括單純的建議或勸告，亦不包括單純的學術研究或評論).

maintains the statutory defences provided in the colonial era law insofar as opinions are not deemed seditious "only"[149] if they are given "with a view to improving"[150] the system, constitutional order, relevant institution or authority; or to persuade any person to procure alterations by lawful means.[151] Furthermore, the 2024 legislation also clarifies that the incitement of public disorder or violence is not necessary for a sedition conviction, thereby preserving a prior Hong Kong Court of Appeal's legal position on the past colonial-era sedition law.[152]

Hong Kong's colonial-era sedition law had a long chequered history since it was first passed in 1914.[153] During colonial rule, the sedition laws were frequently enforced by the British against leftist newspapers and individuals.[154] But from the 1970s onwards, the British shelved the use of this law, and it was only revived by the HKSAR government after the passage of the 2020 HKNSL to supplement the Beijing-imposed law.[155] Opposition activist Tam Tak Chi, who was arrested for uttering seditious words two months after the enactment of the 2020 HKNSL, became the first person charged with sedition in over half a century.[156] And the HKSAR government continues to aggressively prosecute offenders for sedition under the 2024 HKNSL.[157] At the time of writing, at least one in five arrests by Hong Kong's national security police are for sedition,[158] and there are 54 convictions under both laws.[159]

149 2024 HKNSL, Section 23(3).
150 2024 HKNSL, Section 23(4).
151 2024 HKNSL, Section 23(4)(c).
152 *HKSAR v Tam Tak Chi* [2024] HKCA 231. The Hong Kong Court of Appeal's position was later affirmed by the HKCFA in *HKSAR v Tam Tak Chi* [2025] HKCFA 4.
153 The Seditious Publications Ordinance and the Sedition Ordinance were passed in 1914 and 1938, respectively. They were incorporated into the Crimes Ordinance in 1972. See Hualing Fu, 'Past and Future Offences of Sedition in Hong Kong' in Hualing Fu, Carole Petersen and Simon Young (eds), *National Security and Fundamental Freedoms: Hong Kong's Article 23 under Scrutiny* (HKU Press 2005) 217, 219–231.
154 Michael Ng, *Political Censorship in British Hong Kong: Freedom of Expression and the Law (1842–1997)* (CUP 2022).
155 See Pui-yin Lo, 'Reactivated and Re-energised: the Sedition Offences in "New Era" Hong Kong' (2022) 52(3) *Hong Kong Law Journal* 913, 914–916.
156 Eric Lai, 'Hong Kong's Sedition Law is Back' *The Diplomat* (3 September 2021) <https://thediplomat.com/2021/09/hong-kongs-sedition-law-is-back/> last accessed 1 January 2026.
157 See Appendix 2 and Appendix 3 of Chapter 4.
158 Data on file with authors based on Chinese and English news reports; Also see 'Tracking the Impact of Hong Kong's National Security Law' *China File* (14 November 2024) <www.chinafile.com/tracking-impact-of-hong-kongs-national-security-law> last accessed 1 January 2026.
159 See Appendices 2 and 3 of this chapter. Two individuals, Chu Kai-pong and Au Kin-wai, were convicted twice for sedition – each person was convicted once under the Crimes Ordinance and a second time for a separate sedition offence under the 2024 HKNSL.

Penalties

The maximum sentence for all four 2020 HKNSL offences – secession, subversion, terrorism, and external collusion – is life imprisonment.[160] Vis-à-vis the 2024 HKNSL, life imprisonment is also applicable for treason, insurrection, and sabotage.[161] The maximum sentence for external interference is 14 years of imprisonment,[162] while the unlawful disclosure of state secrets and espionage carry a maximum prison sentence of 10 years[163] and 20 years,[164] respectively. The 2024 HKNSL raises the maximum prison term for sedition to seven years,[165] and ten years if the accused has colluded with an "external force".[166] Previously under the colonial-era sedition law, the prison term was capped at two years for a first-time offender.[167] In contrast, the 2023 MANSL caps imprisonment at 25 years for treason, secession, and state subversion,[168] 8 years for sedition and insurrection,[169] 15 years for violating state secrets,[170] and 10 years for the establishment of links with non-Macau entities that jeopardise national security.[171]

Imitating the PRC Criminal Law, the 2020 HKNSL categorises offenders as "principal offenders",[172] "active participants",[173] or "other participants",[174] with principal offenders subjected to the harshest penalties, but all three terms are left undefined. In contrast, the 2023 MANSL does not categorise offenders, but persons convicted of "preparatory acts" for all offences can be imprisoned up to three years.[175]

The 2023 MANSL imposes *minimum prison* sentences for the violation of all the *primary* offences: ten years[176] for treason, secession, and subversion; one year[177] for insurrection, sedition, and violation of state secrets; and three years[178] for establishing links with non-Macau entities that jeopardise national security. For the offences of secession, subversion, and terrorism under the 2020 HKNSL,

160 2020 HKNSL, arts 20, 22, 24, 29.
161 2024 HKNSL, Sections 10, 15, 49.
162 2024 HKNSL, Section 52.
163 2024 HKNSL, Section 35.
164 2024 HKNSL, Section 43.
165 2024 HKNSL, Section 24(1).
166 2024 HKNSL, Section 24(2).
167 Section 10 (now-repealed) of the Crimes Ordinance.
168 2023 MANSL, arts 7, 8, and 9.
169 2023 MANSL, arts 10 and 11.
170 2023 MANSL, art 12(4)(ii) and art 12(5)(ii).
171 2023 MANSL, art 13.
172 2020 HKNSL, arts 20 and 22.
173 2020 HKNSL, arts 20, 22 and 25.
174 2020 HKNSL, arts 20, 22 and 25.
175 2023 MANSL, art 14.
176 2023 MANSL, arts 7, 8, 9.
177 2023 MANSL, arts 10, 11, 12.
178 2023 MANSL, art 13.

the *minimum* sentence is ten years for principal offenders[179] or organisers;[180] three years for active participants;[181] and a prison sentence is not mandatory for "other participants".[182] For external collusion under the 2020 HKNSL, the minimum prison sentence is ten years for grave violations and three years for other convictions.[183] There are no minimum sentences for offences in the 2024 HKNSL.

National Security Committee

Macau first established a National Security Committee (MANSC) in 2018 via an administrative regulation.[184] The Committee comprised senior local officials and was chaired by the Macau Chief Executive, and its main function was to formulate and coordinate national security policies across the various local organs. But there were criticisms from the Mainland that Macau lacked the presence of Central Authorities law enforcement institutions in the MASAR to assist in national security affairs.[185]

These criticisms were taken on board when the 2020 HKNSL was drafted. The 2020 HKNSL not only establishes a National Security Committee (HKNSC) chaired by the Hong Kong Chief Executive,[186] but it also adds a National Security Advisor designated by the Central Government to provide advice on national security matters and to sit in on the Committee meetings.[187] In this way, the HKNSC is transformed from a purely SAR institution in charge of coordinating local agencies into an institution that facilitates cross-border national security interactions between the Central and SAR governments. Not to be outdone by Hong Kong, the MASAR government swiftly requested the Central Government to appoint a National Security Advisor in Macau too. This request was approved by the PRC State Council in 2021.[188] Technical Advisors – dispatched by the

179 2020 HKNSL, arts 20, 22.

180 2020 HKNSL, art 25.

181 2020 HKNSL, arts 20, 22, 25.

182 2020 HKNSL, arts 20, 22, 25.

183 2020 HKNSL, art 29.

184 澳門特別行政區維護國家安全委員會 Committee for Safeguarding National Security of the MASAR (Administrative Regulation No. 22/2018).

185 Wu Wei 吴为, Li Donghua 李东华 and Li Taishan李泰山，'澳门《维护国家安全法》解读 An Analysis of Macau National Security Law' (2016) 18(4) *江南社会学院学报 Journal of Jiangnan Social University* 14, 17.

186 2020 HKNSL, art 13.

187 2020 HKNSL, art 15.

188 '国务院关于同意在澳门特别行政区维护国家安全委员会设立国家安全事务顾问和国家安全技术顾问的批复 Official Reply of the State Council to Approve the Appointment of a National Security Affairs Advisor and National Security Technical Advisors to the Committee for Safeguarding National Security of the Macao SAR' (30 November 2021). It is common practice for the State Council to reply to requests submitted by governments at lower levels regarding a specific issue. The legal effect of the State Council's reply is unclear as it is not expressly covered or authorised under the PRC Legislation Law. Generally, the State Council's Reply is deemed a "normative document" (规范性文件) that is binding internally on the administration. See Huang

Central Government – are also appointed to assist the Macau National Security Advisor and the MANSC.[189] In both Hong Kong and Macau, the current National Security Advisor is also the Director of the Liaison Office of the Central People's Government in the respective SAR – Beijing's top representative in the SAR. The 2020 HKNSL does not explicitly stipulate who shall be the National Security Advisor, while the PRC State Council in 2021 explicitly stated that the Director of the Liaison Office in Macau shall be its Advisor.[190]

Notably, in Hong Kong, all decisions made by the HKNSC shall "not be amenable to judicial review".[191] This ouster clause is absent from the 2023 MANSL. However, in 2026 Macau authorities enacted a new law entitled "Committee for Safeguarding National Security of the Macao Special Administrative Region 澳門特別行政區維護國家安全委員會" (hereinafter termed "2026 MANSC Law"). This law incorporates provisions drawn from Hong Kong's national security laws, stipulating that the MANSC's operations are not subject to disclosure or judicial review,[192] and the MANSC is empowered to vet the qualifications of candidates for public office.[193]

Office for Safeguarding National Security of the Central People's Government

Alongside the HKNSC, the 2020 HKNSL also creates an Office for Safeguarding National Security of the Central People's Government in the HKSAR (NSO)[194]— an even more controversial institution. The NSO is established and staffed by personnel dispatched from the Central People's Government, and is empowered to engage in intelligence collection, policy formulation, and "handling cases"[195] concerning national security in Hong Kong. The NSO must abide by Hong Kong laws,[196] but acts performed in the course of duty are not subject to HKSAR's jurisdiction.[197] Premises of the NSO are "prohibited places"[198] and persons are prohibited from

Jinrong 黄金荣, '"规范性文件"的法律界定及效力 Legal Definition and Effect of "Normative Documents"'(2014) 7 *Law Science* 法学10–20.

189 See Official Reply of the State Council to Approve the Appointment of a National Security Affairs Advisor and National Security Technical Advisors to the Committee for Safeguarding National Security of the Macao SAR (30 November 2021).

190 See Official Reply of the State Council to Approve the Appointment of a National Security Affairs Advisor and National Security Technical Advisors to the Committee for Safeguarding National Security of the Macao SAR (30 November 2021).

191 2020 HKNSL, art 14.

192 2026 MANSC Law, arts 3(4) and 3(5). The full text of the MANSC Law is available at https://bo.dsaj.gov.mo/bo/i/2026/12/lei02_cn.asp.

193 2026 MANSC Law, art 3(3).

194 2020 HKNSL, art 48.

195 2020 HKNSL, art 49(4).

196 2020 HKNSL, art 50.

197 2020 HKNSL, art 60.

198 維護國家安全(禁地宣佈)令 Safeguarding National Security (Declaration of Prohibited Places) Order (issued by the Acting Chief Executive in Council on 13 May 2025).

disclosing their investigations without lawful authority.[199] Remarkably, the NSO is even allowed to exercise jurisdiction over a Hong Kong national security case if the case is complex due to the involvement of a foreign or external element; the HKSAR government is unable to effectively enforce the 2020 HKNSL; or a major and imminent threat to national security occurs.[200] In such circumstances, these offenders can be removed to Mainland China and face trial under PRC laws.[201] Notably, in 2025, the first publicly known joint operation took place between the Hong Kong national security police and the NSO: the residences and office of six unidentified individuals were searched on the basis that they were involved in a "complex collusion case".[202] Although no extradition to Mainland China has occurred, this case demonstrated the increasing routinisation and visibility of the NSO in Hong Kong.

In contrast, Macau does not have an equivalent NSO and the MASAR exercises jurisdiction over all national security cases in the city. Despite the absence of an institutionalised Central Government agency operating in Macau, Alvin Chau Cheok-wa – the biggest junket operator in Macau – was arrested by Macau authorities within 12 hours after the Mainland police issued an arrest warrant for him on money laundering and illegal gambling charges in 2021,[203] thereby underscoring the formidable informal influence Mainland law enforcement wields in Macau.

Judiciary and Prosecution

As discussed previously, Macau revised its Judicial Organisation Law (司法組織綱要法) in 2019 to require all judges and prosecutors handling national security cases to be Chinese nationals.[204] The 2026 MANSC Law discussed previously further extends this Chinese nationality requirement to all proceedings where there is a need to protect national security,[205] including civil ones. Macau's national security judges and prosecutors are, respectively, appointed by the Judges Committee[206]

199 維護國家安全(中央人民政府駐香港特別行政區維護國家安全公署)規例 (Safeguarding National Security (Office for Safeguarding National Security of the Central People's Government in the HKSAR) Regulation), art 8.

200 2020 HKNSL, art 55.

201 2020 HKNSL, arts 56 and 57.

202 Natalie Wong, 'Beijing-Hong Kong Operation May be First Step in "Complex National Security Case"' *SCMP* (13 June 2025) <www.scmp.com/news/hong-kong/politics/article/3314403/beijing-hong-kong-operation-may-be-first-step-complex-national-security-case> last accessed 1 January 2026.

203 Ng Kang-chung and Jeffie Lam, 'Macau Police Arrest Casino Junket Boss Alvin Chau, 10 Other over Alleged Gambling Offences' *SCMP* (28 November 2021) <www.scmp.com/news/hong-kong/law-and-crime/article/3157657/macau-police-arrest-casino-junket-boss-alvin-chau-10> last accessed 1 January 2026.

204 Judicial Organisation Law, art 19-A.

205 2026 MANSC Law, art 19.

206 Judicial Organisation Law, art 19-A (1).

(法官委員會) and the Chief Procurator;[207] national security judges serve for a renewable term of two years.[208]

Hong Kong does not exclude foreign judges from hearing national security cases. But national security cases can only be heard by designated judges chosen by the Hong Kong Chief Executive from the pre-existing bench of judges, and the designated judges serve for a renewable term of one year.[209] This mechanism allows the Hong Kong Chief Executive to cherry-pick pro-establishment judges to hear national security cases and remove them after one year if they are deemed unsuitable after appointment. Notably, no overseas Non-Permanent Judges of the Hong Kong Court of Final Appeal (HKCFA) have been assigned to hear national security cases. For prosecutors in Hong Kong national security cases, they can only be appointed by the Secretary for Justice upon the consent of the HKNSC.[210]

Pre-trial and Trial Procedures

The 2020 HKNSL denies bail to criminal suspects unless the judge has sufficient grounds for believing that they will "not continue to commit acts endangering national security."[211] The HKCFA has extended this high threshold for bail to all national security laws,[212] which include the sedition offence under the Crimes Ordinance and the now-operative 2024 HKNSL. The Hong Kong government routinely opposes bail, with defendants languishing in pre-trial detention for more than a year.[213] But the 2023 MANSL is even harsher in this regard. No bail is provided under the 2023 MANSL and pre-trial detention is required for all persons charged under the offences.[214]

In Hong Kong, an accused typically has to be charged within 48 hours of their arrest. But the 2024 HKNSL now allows pre-charge detention for any "offence endangering national security" – thereby including both the 2020 HKNSL and 2024 HKNSL offences – to be extended by another 14 days, subject to judicial approval.[215] Moreover, the police can apply to a magistrate to restrict a suspect's access to legal representation if the legal consultation will endanger national security or obstruct the course of justice.[216] There are no such restrictions on

207 Judicial Organisation Law, art 19-A (2).
208 Judicial Organisation Law, art 19-A (1).
209 2020 HKNSL, art 44; 2024 HKNSL, Section 100.
210 2020 HKNSL, art 18; 2024 HKNSL, Section 99.
211 2020 HKNSL, art 42.
212 *HKSAR v Ng Hau Yi* (2021) 24 HKCFAR 417.
213 Carole Petersen, 'National Security Law in Hong Kong: Transforming "One Country, Two Systems" as a Model of Regional Autonomy' in Ngoc Son Bui, Stuart Hargreaves and Ryan Mitchell (eds), *Routledge Handbook of Constitutional Law in Greater China* (Routledge 2023) 187, 193.
214 2023 MANSL, art 25.
215 2024 HKNSL, Sections 76–78.
216 2024 HKNSL, Sections 79 and 80.

legal representation under the 2023 MANSL, but the 2026 MANSC Law requires legal representatives to obtain special permission from the court in cases where the judicial authority reasonably believes that there is a need to protect national security.[217]

Furthermore, under Article 47 of the 2020 HKNSL, the Hong Kong courts are required to obtain a certificate from the Chief Executive to certify whether an act involves national security or whether any relevant evidence arising during adjudication involves state secrets. This certificate is binding on the Hong Kong judiciary.[218] In 2022, the NPCSC – in its first Interpretation of the 2020 HKNSL[219] – ruled that the issue of whether overseas-qualified lawyers could legally represent persons charged with national security offences was an act that required the Chief Executive's certification under Article 47. Relying on this Interpretation, the HKNSC barred Timothy Owen KC from representing Jimmy Lai – the publisher of now-defunct *Apple Daily* (Hong Kong's hitherto largest and most successful anti-establishment newspaper) – in his national security proceedings,[220] a move that overturned the permission previously granted by the local courts.[221] Under the 2023 MANSL, the Macau judiciary *may* seek a similar certificate from its Chief Executive on whether a particular information or object is state secret, but the legislation does not expressly state that such certificates are binding on the courts.[222]

Trials under the 2020 HKNSL shall be conducted in an open court. But if the case "involve[s] state secrets or public order"[223] – all left undefined – all or part of the trial may be closed. The 2020 HKNSL is silent on whether it is the judge, prosecution, or the HKNSC who decides whether the hearings should be closed to the public. For national security proceedings tried in the Court of First Instance (CFI) of the High Court, the Secretary for Justice is empowered to replace jury trials with a bench trial of three judges.[224] The 2024 HKNSL explicitly stipulates that the pre-trial and trial procedures provided in the 2020 HKNSL would equally apply to offences under the 2024 HKNSL.[225]

217 2026 MANSC Law, art 20.

218 2020 HKNSL, art 47.

219 Interpretation by the Standing Committee of the National People's Congress of Article 14 and Article 47 of the PRC Law on Safeguarding National Security in the Hong Kong Special Administrative Region (Adopted at the 38th Session of the Standing Committee of the 13th National People's Congress on 30 December 2022).

220 Brian Wong, 'Hong Kong Appeal Court Blocks Jimmy Lai from Challenging Foreign Counsel Ban' *SCMP* (29 April 2024) <www.scmp.com/news/hong-kong/law-and-crime/article/3260826/hong-kong-appeal-court-blocks-jimmy-lai-challenging-foreign-counsel-ban> last accessed 1 January 2026.

221 *Re Timothy Wynn Owen KC* [2022] HKCFI 3233; *Secretary for Justice v Timothy Wynn Owen KC* (2022) 25 HKCFAR 288.

222 2023 MANSL, art 23.

223 2020 HKNSL, art 41(4).

224 2020 HKNSL, art 46.

225 2024 HKNSL, Section 99.

Under the 2023 MANSL, it is for the judge to decide if certain proceedings shall be *in camera.* Closed hearings are only allowed for the "violation of state secrets" offence and the certification of state secrets, and only if open hearings would be detrimental to national security.[226] But it is noteworthy that the 2026 MANSC Law now allows for a closed-door trial for *any* case if the presiding judge concludes that an open hearing will adversely affect national security.[227] There are no jury trials in Macau as that has never been a feature of the city's legal system.

Implementation of National Security Laws in Hong Kong and Macau

The greatest difference between Hong Kong and Macau's national security laws has been in their implementation. While both the 2020 and 2024 HKNSL have been rigorously enforced from the outset, no one was charged in Macau until 2025. Au Kam San, a former Macau Legislative Assembly member and long-term pro-democracy activist, was charged in July 2025 with the offence of "establishment of ties with organisations and individuals outside the MASAR for the purpose of committing acts against national security".[228] Specifically, it was alleged that he had provided seditious and false information to unnamed foreign groups since 2022, in order to stir up hatred against the Macau and Central governments, disrupt the city's 2024 Chief Executive election, and cause foreign countries to take hostile actions against Macau.[229] He remains in detention pending trial.[230]

On the other hand, as of 1 December 2025, 365 people have been arrested in national security cases.[231] As of 1 March 2026, 95 persons have been charged under the 2020 HKNSL and 13 individuals charged under the 2024 HKNSL.[232] After the passage of the 2020 HKNSL, but prior to the enactment of the 2024 HKNSL, the Hong Kong government also revived the use of the colonial-era sedition law under the Crimes Ordinance, with 53 persons charged under this British relic until its

226 2023 MANSL, art 22.

227 2026 MANSC Law, art 19.

228 2023 MANSL, art 13.

229 Macau Judiciary Police, '一居民涉勾结境外敌对势力危害国家安全被捕 A Resident Arrested for Allegedly Colluding with Foreign Hostile Forces to Endanger National Security' (31 July 2025) <www.gov.mo/zh-hans/news/840967/> last accessed 1 January 2026; also see 'Macau Ex-lawmaker Arrested in City's First Nat. Security Law Action' *HKFP* (31 July 2025) <https://hongkongfp.com/2025/07/31/macau-ex-lawmaker-arrested-in-citys-first-nat-security-law-action/> last accessed 1 January 2026.

230 'Macao: Ex-Lawmaker Held on National Security Charge' *Human Rights Watch* (6 August 2025) <www.hrw.org/news/2025/08/06/macao-ex-lawmaker-held-on-national-security-charge> last accessed 1 January 2026.

231 'Explainer: Hong Kong's National Security Crackdown – Month 65' *HKFP* (14 December 2025) <https://hongkongfp.com/2025/12/14/explainer-hong-kongs-national-security-crackdown-month-65/> last accessed 1 January 2026.

232 Data on file with authors based on Chinese and English news reports.

repeal in 2024.[233] There are currently 75 convictions under the 2020 HKNSL and the Implementation Rules;[234] and their prison sentences range between 3 months and 20 years. In addition, there are 46 convictions under the colonial-era sedition law[235] and 9 convictions under the 2024 HKNSL.[236] Thus far, the conviction rate for all the abovementioned national security offences is close to 100%. The government has also dispensed with jury trials for all national security proceedings – hitherto available for all criminal proceedings before the CFI. Million-dollar bounties have also been placed on dissidents who fled the territory.[237]

Jimmy Lai is the most prominent person targeted under Hong Kong national security laws. A media mogul and fierce critic of the Communist Party of China, he was accused of colluding with foreign forces, including calling for sanctions against China and Hong Kong officials, and using his now-shuttered *Apple Daily* newspaper to disseminate allegedly seditious materials.[238] A frequent bugbear of the local and Mainland authorities, he had been a strident supporter of Hong Kong's pro-democracy movement and was on the frontlines of the city's protests from Occupy Central 2014 to the anti-extradition bill movement of 2019. The newsroom of *Apple Daily* was raided, its top executives arrested, the company assets frozen,[239] and the daily eventually shuttered in June 2021.[240] Jimmy Lai himself was convicted by the CFI on all counts of his national security charges and sentenced in 2026 to 20 years imprisonment.[241]

Hong Kong Alliance in Support of Patriotic Democratic Movements of China – the primary organiser of the city's hitherto annual candlelight vigil commemorating victims of the June 4th Tiananmen Square military crackdown – was forced to

233 Data on file with authors based on Chinese and English news reports. 13 of the 53 persons charged under the Crimes Ordinance were concurrently charged under the 2020 HKNSL.

234 See Appendix 1 of this chapter.

235 See Appendix 2 of this chapter.

236 See Appendix 3 of this chapter.

237 Hong Kong Police Force, 'Wanted Persons and Reward Notices of National Security Cases' <www.police.gov.hk/ppp_en/06_appeals_public/nsc/index.html> last accessed 1 January 2026; also see Clifford Lo et al., 'Hong Kong National Security Police Offer HK$1 million Bounties on Another 5 Fugitive Opposition Figures' *SCMP* (14 December 2023) <www.scmp.com/news/hong-kong/law-and-crime/article/3245087/hong-kong-national-security-police-offer-hk1-million-bounties-another-5-fugitive-opposition-figures> last accessed 1 January 2026; 'Hong Kong Police Issue Bounties for Six more Overseas Activists' *The Guardian* (24 December 2024) <www.theguardian.com/world/2024/dec/24/hong-kong-police-bounties-pro-democracy-activists-overseas> last accessed 1 January 2026.

238 Jessie Pang and Edward Cho, 'Overseas Figures Reject Prosecution Accusations in Hong Kong Trial of Jimmy Lai' Reuters (3 January 2024) <www.reuters.com/world/china/overseas-figures-refute-allegations-hong-kong-security-trial-jimmy-lai-2024-01-03/> last accessed 1 January 2026.

239 Austin Ramzy and Tiffany May, 'Hong Kong Cracks Down on a Pro-Democracy Newspaper' *The New York Times* (16 June 2021) < www.nytimes.com/2021/06/16/world/asia/hong-kong-apple-daily.html > last accessed 1 January 2026.

240 Another pro-democracy news outlet – Stand News – was forced to close in December 2021 after the police also raided its premises and arrested its senior staff.

241 *HKSAR v Lai Chee Ying* [2026] HKCFI 854.

disband in September 2021 after several leaders were arrested under the 2020 HKNSL.[242] Prior to the onslaught of the COVID-19 pandemic, the vigil used to draw tens of thousands of people – the largest June 4th commemoration on Chinese soil. Five members were jailed for between three and five months as they refused to hand over information on the Alliance's activities as required under the 2020 HKNSL Implementation Rules,[243] and the Chair and Vice-Chairs of the Alliance are being tried for state subversion and have been on remand for over four years.

The largest crackdown under the 2020 HKNSL has been the arrest and prosecution of 47 pro-democracy activists and legislators on charges of conspiracy to commit subversion.[244] Their alleged crime rested on the mere fact that they had participated in the organisation of an unofficial election primary in July 2020 to select the most electable pro-democracy candidates who could win a majority of seats in the Legislative Council, and subsequently use this legislative majority to veto budgetary bills and force the Chief Executive to resign.[245] In 2024, the Hong Kong CFI convicted 14 out of 16 of these activists, while 31 defendants had pleaded guilty before trial.[246] The Hong Kong CFI ruled that the *indiscriminate* vetoing of governmental budgets to bring down the government was a breach of the legislators' constitutional duty under Article 73 of the HKBL,[247] and such a

242 Tom Grundy, 'Hong Kong Tiananmen Massacre Vigil Group Disbands Following Pressure from Authorities' (26 September 2021) <https://hongkongfp.com/2021/09/25/breaking-hong-kong-tiananmen-massacre-vigil-group-disbands-following-pressure-from-authorities/> last accessed 1 January 2026.

243 Schedule 5 of the Implementation Rules for Article 43 of the Law of the People's Republic of China on Safeguarding National Security in the Hong Kong Special Administrative Region. See Appendix 1 for the relevant cases. But notably in 2025, the HKCFA in *HKSAR v Tang Ngok Kwan* [2025] HKCFA 3 quashed their criminal convictions under this charge as the Prosecution failed to prove the accused were foreign agents and the non-disclosure of the relevant redacted facts in the Prosecution's case deprived the accused of a fair trial.

244 'Hong Kong 47: Who are the Key Defendants in National Security Trial over Legco Primary and What do They Claim?' *SCMP* (10 December 2023) <www.scmp.com/news/hong-kong/law-and-crime/article/3244511/hong-kong-47-who-are-key-defendants-national-security-trial-over-legco-primary-and-what-do-they> last accessed 1 January 2026.

245 Chris Lau and Brian Wong, 'Hong Kong National Security Trial: Prosecutors Accuse 47 Opposition Figures of Plotting to Turn Legislature into "Lethal Constitutional Weapon" against Beijing' *SCMP* (6 February 2023) <www.scmp.com/news/hong-kong/politics/article/3209209/national-security-law-16-47-hong-kong-opposition-figures-contest-subversion-charge-major-trial> last accessed 1 January 2026.

246 See 'As It Happened: Hong Kong 47–14 Found Guilty of Subversion and 2 Acquitted under National Security Law over Election Plot to Overthrow Government' *SCMP* (30 May 2024) <www.scmp.com/news/hong-kong/law-and-crime/article/3264620/hong-kong-47-16-defendants-learn-fate-after-being-charged-landmark-national-security-case#> last accessed 1 January 2026.

247 Article 73 of the HKBL reads:

> The Legislative Council of the Hong Kong Special Administrative Region shall exercise the following powers and functions: (1) To enact, amend or repeal laws in accordance with the provisions of this Law and legal procedures; (2) To examine and approve budgets introduced by the government; (3) To approve taxation and public expenditure.

breach would constitute an "unlawful means" by which subversion under the 2020 HKNSL could be established.[248] The 45 defendants have been sentenced to prison terms ranging between four and ten years.[249] Unfortunately, the Court of Appeal has also upheld the CFI's findings that such a breach of Article 73 of the HKBL would be unlawful and constitute subversion.[250]

After the passage of the 2024 HKNSL, several persons were also arrested under sedition for their social media posts commemorating victims of the June 4th Tiananmen Square military crackdown.[251] Today, with intense public policing in Hong Kong on all June 4th anniversaries, such commemorations can now only be marked privately off-line at home.[252] When a fatal blaze at a Hong Kong apartment complex claimed the lives of over 160 people in 2025, two individuals who circulated online petitions for more governmental accountability were arrested by the national security police for inciting hatred against the authorities.[253] At the heart of this controversy is the authorities' paranoia that demands for governmental accountability would spiral once again into political mobilisation reminiscent of the 2019 social unrest.[254]

The top court in Hong Kong has yet to weigh in on most of these national security disputes. But, notably, and perhaps unsurprisingly, the HKCFA has cursorily accepted the constitutionality of the 2020 HKNSL[255] and the colonial-era sedition law.[256] Nevertheless, the HKCFA has also handed down several landmark decisions that would shape the implementation of Hong Kong's national security laws for the years to come.

248 *HKSAR v Ng Gordon Ching-hang & 15 others* [2024] HKCFI 1468.

249 *HKSAR v Ng Gordon Ching-hang & 44 others* [2024] HKCFI 3298; see Appendix 1.

250 *HKSAR v Yeung Suet-ying Clarisse* [2026] HKCA 284 at [137]–[159].

251 Clifford Lo, 'Hong Kong Police Arrest Seventh Suspect in First Sedition Case under Article 23 Law' *SCMP* (29 May 2024) <www.scmp.com/news/hong-kong/law-and-crime/article/3264597/hong-kong-police-arrest-seventh-suspect-sedition-case-under-article-23-law> last accessed 1 January 2026.

252 Oscar Liu, 'Hongkongers can Mark Tiananmen Square Crackdown in Private without Breaching Article 23 National Security Law, Government Advisers Say' *SCMP* (2 June 2024) <www.scmp.com/news/hong-kong/politics/article/3265076/hongkongers-can-mark-tiananmen-square-crackdown-private-without-breaching-article-23-national> last accessed 1 January 2026.

253 Hillary Leung, 'Tai Po Fire: Ex-local Councillor and Volunteer Arrested for Allegedly Inciting Hatred of Gov't-Reports' *HKFP* (1 December 2025) <https://hongkongfp.com/2025/12/01/tai-po-fire-ex-local-councillor-and-volunteer-arrested-for-allegedly-inciting-hatred-of-govt-reports/> last accessed 1 January 2026.

254 Bang Xiao, 'One Fire, Two Systems: Hong Kong's Grief Meets Beijing's Red Lines' *ABC* (1 December 2025) <www.abc.net.au/news/2025-12-02/tai-po-fire-hong-kong-mainland-grief-red-lines/106087732> last accessed 1 January 2026.

255 *HKSAR v Ng Ngoi Yee Margaret* [2024] HKCFA 24 at [33]; *HKSAR v Lai Chee Ying* (2021) 24 HKCFAR 33 at [37].

256 *HKSAR v Tam Tak Chi* [2024] HKCFA 25 (denied leave to appeal the constitutionality of the sedition law).

In its first substantive ruling on the 2020 HKNSL, the HKCFA ruled that Article 42(2)[257] has introduced "a considerably more stringent threshold requirement"[258] for bail which statutorily reversed the presumption of bail commonly granted for other criminal law cases. But the HKCFA did accept that the trial judge, when deciding whether to grant bail, is entitled to examine whether bail conditions – in lieu of pre-trial detention – would suffice to ensure that the accused would not continue to commit acts endangering national security pending trial.[259] With the heightened conditions for granting bail, almost half of the suspects arrested under the 2020 HKNSL had languished in pre-trial detention,[260] with some defendants like Jimmy Lai and the Hong Kong 47 arrestees having to wait more than 2 years behind bars for their national security trials to commence.

Furthermore, in *HKSAR v Ng Hau Yi,*[261] the HKCFA also confirmed that the sedition offence under the Crimes Ordinance also qualified as an offence endangering national security, and therefore the more stringent threshold for granting bail under the 2020 HKNSL would equally apply to this offence. Furthermore, in 2025, the HKCFA also decided that for the sedition offence under the Crimes Ordinance to be established, the prosecution was not required to prove that the accused intended to incite violence or public disorder.[262]

But there are some glimmers of hope. In *HKSAR v Lo Kin Man,*[263] the HKCFA unanimously decided that the common law doctrine of joint enterprise cannot be used to impose liability on a defendant as a principal offender for the offences of unlawful assembly or rioting, if the defendant was not physically present at the unlawful or riotous assembly. Next, in *HKSAR v Chan Chun Kit,*[264] the HKCFA also ruled unanimously that a 6-inch plastic cable tie is not an "instrument fit for unlawful purposes" that is prohibited under the Summary Offences Ordinance. As the penal legislation expressly lists "crowbar, picklock, skeleton key"[265] as statutory examples, the CFA ruled that the *ejusdem generis* common law rule of statutory interpretation would limit an "instrument fit for unlawful purposes" to only instruments fit for gaining unlawful access to premises, vehicles, or objects.[266]

257 Article 42(2) of the 2020 HKNSL reads:

> No bail shall be granted to a criminal suspect or defendant unless the judge has sufficient grounds for believing that the criminal suspect or defendant will not continue to commit acts endangering national security.

258 *HKSAR v Lai Chee Ying* (2021) 24 HKCFAR 33 at [53b].

259 *HKSAR v Lai Chee Ying* (2021) 24 HKCFAR 33 at [57].

260 Han Zhu, 'A Chinese Law Wedge into the Hong Kong Common Law System: A Legal Appraisal of the Hong Kong National Security Law' (2023) 21(1) *Northwestern Journal of Human Rights* 43, 82.

261 (2021) 24 HKCFAR 417.

262 *HKSAR v Tam Tak Chi* [2025] HKCFA 4.

263 (2021) 24 HKCFAR 302.

264 (2022) 25 HKCFAR 191.

265 Section 17 of the Summary Offences Ordinance.

266 *Chan Chun Kit* (2022) 25 HKCFAR 191 at [28].

Plastic cable ties are simply not used for such purposes and therefore fall outside the coverage of the penal law. Both cases pertain to the prosecution of the protestors in Hong Kong's 2019 social unrest, and the HKCFA did not capitulate on its *common law* interpretation of Hong Kong's ordinary criminal laws, even if such interpretation may have national security or political implications.

In *HKSAR v Lui Sai Yu*,[267] the HKCFA ruled that for an offence – and corresponding punishment – under the 2020 HKNSL to be reduced from "serious" to "minor", the mitigating factors found in Article 33[268] are exhaustive. But what is equally important is another significant pronouncement of the Court. The lower courts have held that in interpreting the 2020 HKNSL, "regard may properly be had to the relevant Mainland Law in aid of its construction".[269] This would in effect allow the Prosecution to import PRC Criminal Law concepts and sentencing procedures into Hong Kong as many phrases from the 2020 HKNSL are grafted from its Mainland counterpart, as we have discussed above. But the HKCFA resolutely rejected such transplants. The HKCFA emphasised that the common law will be used to interpret the 2020 HKNSL[270] and there will be no convergence between the 2020 HKNSL and "any unrelated Mainland law which employs concepts using similar language".[271] Ergo, the Court ruled that there is no need for Hong Kong courts "to search for and consider as possible aids to construction similarly-worded Mainland laws".[272]

Perhaps the greatest rebuke of the Hong Kong authorities from the HKCFA would be its landmark ruling in *HKSAR v Tang Ngok Kwan*.[273] In 2025, the Court unanimously ruled that if the accused were alleged to be a "foreign agent" under the 2020 NSL Implementation Rules,[274] the burden was on the Prosecution to prove this status beyond reasonable doubt.[275] Furthermore, insofar as the Prosecution had

267 *HKSAR v Lui Sai Yu* [2023] HKCFA 26.

268 Article 33 of the 2020 HKNSL reads:

> A lighter penalty may be imposed, or the penalty may be reduced or, in the case of a minor offence, exempted, if an offender, criminal suspect, or defendant: (1) in the process of committing an offence, voluntarily discontinues the commission of the offence or voluntarily and effectively forestalls its consequences; (2) voluntarily surrenders himself or herself and gives a truthful account of the offence; or (3) reports on the offence committed by other person, which is verified to be true, or provides material information which assists in solving other criminal case.

269 *HKSAR v Lui Sai Yu* [2022] HKCA 1780 at [88].

270 *HKSAR v Lui Sai Yu* [2023] HKCFA 26 at [45]

271 *HKSAR v Lui Sai Yu* [2023] HKCFA 26 at [47].

272 *HKSAR v Lui Sai Yu* [2023] HKCFA 26 at [47].

273 *HKSAR v Tang Ngok Kwan* [2025] HKCFA 3.

274 See Schedule 5, Section 3(3) of the Pre-2026 Implementation Rules made under Article 43 of the 2020 HKNSL. But it is noteworthy that the Hong Kong government in 2026 amended Section 3 of the said Implementation Rules to allow the Commissioner of Police to impose the related regulations so long as he "reasonably believes" the regulated person/ organisation is an "agent of an external force".

275 *HKSAR v Tang Ngok Kwan* [2025] HKCFA 3 at [45].

redacted all the relevant information such that the accused had no knowledge of why or how they were construed by the government to be foreign agents, their right to a fair trial had been violated and their convictions by the lower courts were all quashed.[276]

In the coming years, as more national security cases snake their way through the appellate process, the HKCFA would face an interpretive dilemma: How can the Judiciary preserve its autonomy whilst quelling Beijing's concerns that Hong Kong courts, if left unleashed, would turn the city into another "renegade province" in the south?[277] Understandably, with the NPCSC poised to retaliate against any abrasive ruling with an Interpretation that clips its wings, the HKCFA cannot hollow out either of Hong Kong's national security laws. But the Court can and it must fire-wall the application of the common law in Hong Kong. As we discussed in Chapter 3, this is not some phantasm of hope. Hong Kong's continued viability as an international financial centre – undergirded by a respected *independent* judiciary applying the *common law* – is indispensable to Beijing for linking the Mainland to the world economy so that China can generate capital in Hong Kong to fund its domestic and foreign policy ambitions. To preserve Hong Kong as China's gateway to international capital, Beijing will overlook occasional contretemps with the HKCFA on the national security laws, especially if the Court is seeking to apply well-established common law principles. Therefore, the Court must equally seize upon this leverage it possesses and not uncritically capitulate on all national security controversies such that these national security laws become the Trojan horse that turns Hong Kong into Shenzhen South.[278]

Conclusion

The promulgation of the 2020 HKNSL was a constitutional moment that reshaped the practice of "One Country, Two Systems" in Hong Kong. When the National People's Congress issued its "Decision on Establishing and Improving the Legal System and Enforcement Mechanisms for the Hong Kong Special Administrative Region to Safeguard National Security" in 2020, only the specific provisions in the PRC Constitution[279] were referenced. When the NPC overhauled Hong Kong's political system a year later, only specific provisions of the PRC Constitution[280] were used as legal justification once again. In both instances, the HKBL was

276 *HKSAR v Tang Ngok Kwan* [2025] HKCFA 3 at [97]–[98].

277 See Po Jen Yap, 'Judging Hong Kong's National Security Law' in Hualing Fu and Michael Hor (eds), *The National Security Law of Hong Kong: Restoration and Transformation* (HKU Press 2022) 166.

278 See Po Jen Yap, 'Judging Hong Kong's National Security Law' in Hualing Fu and Michael Hor (eds), *The National Security Law of Hong Kong: Restoration and Transformation* (HKU Press 2022) 166.

279 PRC Constitution, arts 31, 62(2), 62(14), 62(16).

280 PRC Constitution, arts 31, 62(2), 62(14), 62(16).

cursorily mentioned but no attempt was made to identify the specific HKBL provisions that the Mainland authorities were relying upon for their actions. The PRC Constitution, which used to operate behind-the-scenes, has emerged front and centre of Hong Kong's constitutional development and the HKBL's relevance has beaten a hasty retreat.

With the establishment of the NSO, Mainland law enforcement can now operate legally and openly in Hong Kong.[281] Given that national security is impacted by the city's policies on education, culture, financial regulation, technological development and even immigration, the potential of the NSO operating as a shadow source of power in Hong Kong – intervening in every aspect of the city's socio-economic life – cannot be underestimated.

The state–society relationship in Hong Kong has dramatically changed in the aftermath of the 2020 HKNSL. While law and order have been restored, civil society has been decimated. Alongside the prosecutions of pro-democracy politicians and activists, 66 pro-democracy social movement groups, news outlets, and labour unions have disbanded.[282] International human rights NGOs, such as Amnesty International, have shuttered their Hong Kong offices.[283] Aside from *Apple Daily*, several other independent media outlets – *Stand News*, *Citizen News*, *FactWire*, and *Transit Jam* – have all ceased operations. Those that remain are subjected to intensive tax probes,[284] and these audits have extended to independent publishers and bookstores.[285] All the major pro-democracy political parties – the Civic Party, the Democratic Party and the League of Social Democrats – have folded.[286] Films and exhibitions face stricter

281 2020 HKNSL, chapter V.

282 For example, the Hong Kong Confederation of Trade Unions (the largest pro-democracy coalition of trade unions), the Hong Kong Alliance (the organiser of the annual June 4th vigil), the Hong Kong Professional Teachers' Union (the 47-year-old largest teachers' organisation), and the Civil Human Rights Front (the organiser of the annual 1st July rallies). See 'Timeline: Over 60 Hong Kong Civil Society Groups Disband Following the Onset of the Security Law' *HKFP* (30 June 2022) <https://hongkongfp.com/2022/06/30/explainer-over-50-groups-gone-in-11-months-how-hong-kongs-pro-democracy-forces-crumbled/> last accessed 1 January 2026.

283 James Pomfret, 'Amnesty to Shut Hong Kong Offices Given National Security Law Risks' *Reuters* (25 October 2021) <www.reuters.com/world/asia-pacific/amnesty-shut-hong-kong-offices-given-national-security-law-risks-2021-10-25/> last accessed 1 January 2026.

284 '"Unreasonable" Tax Audit of Some Hong Kong Media: Press Union' *The Straits Times* (22 May 2025) <www.straitstimes.com/asia/east-asia/unreasonable-tax-audit-of-some-hong-kong-media-press-union> last accessed 1 January 2026.

285 '"Is it a Coincidence?" – Hong Kong Independent Bookstores, Publishers Face Simultaneous Tax Probes' *HKFP* (20 July 2025) <https://hongkongfp.com/2025/07/20/is-it-a-coincidence-hong-kong-independent-bookstores-publishers-face-simultaneous-tax-probes/> last accessed 1 January 2026.

286 Emily Hung and Oscar Liu, 'Hong Kong Opposition Party Folds, Citing "Immense Political Pressure", "Safety Fears"' *SCMP* (29 June 2025) <www.scmp.com/news/hong-kong/politics/article/3316276/hong-kongs-opposition-party-folds-citing-immense-political-pressure-and-safety-fears> last accessed 1 January 2026.

scrutiny,[287] with "problematic" content all purged from schools and libraries[288] and public universities tearing down longstanding public memorials on the Tiananmen bloodshed.[289] The Hong Kong government has also successfully obtained an injunction against internet platforms like Google and YouTube to ban the dissemination of the protest anthem "Glory to Hong Kong" – hitherto popular amongst the pro-democracy movement during the 2019 social unrest – from Hong Kong internet search results and content sharing platforms.[290] Even video games have been banned in the name of national security.[291] "Soft resistance"[292] – subtler expressions of discontent and defiance – are also targeted: teachers and students are warned against attending the US Consulate's 4th July Independence Day festivities and fringe bookfairs face police investigations.[293] Even the private sector has piled on with democracy-leaning organisations having their fundraising events cancelled at the last minute by restaurants and hotels due to "technical" glitches.[294]

All these developments are perhaps unsurprising as public officials in Hong Kong are now statutorily required to "regard national security as the most important factor"[295] when making any decision.[296] The "protest

287 13 films have been banned from screening in Hong Kong on national security grounds since 2021. Kelly Ho, 'Hong Kong Bars 13 Films from Screening on National Security Grounds since 2021 Censorship Law' *HKFP* (8 October 2025) <https://hongkongfp.com/2025/10/08/hong-kong-bars-13-films-from-screening-on-national-security-grounds-since-2021-censorship-law/> last accessed 1 January 2026.

288 '"Not Recommended" Reading: The Books Hong Kong is Purging from Public Libraries' *HKFP* (3 June 2023) <https://hongkongfp.com/2023/05/26/not-recommended-reading-the-books-hong-kong-is-purging-from-public-libraries/> last accessed 1 January 2026.

289 'Hong Kong Universities Remove More Monuments Marking Tiananmen' *BBC* (23 December 2021) <www.bbc.com/news/world-asia-china-59752089> last accessed 1 January 2026.

290 *Secretary for Justice v Persons Conducting Themselves in any Acts Prohibited under Paragraph 1(a), (b), (c) or (d) of the Indorsement of Claim* [2024] HKCA 442; Jessie Pang, 'Hong Kong Court Bans Protest Anthem, Says it Can be Used as Weapon' *Reuters* (8 May 2024) <www.reuters.com/world/china/hong-kong-court-bans-protest-anthem-glory-hong-kong-2024-05-08/> last accessed 1 January 2026.

291 Tiffany May and Amy Chang Chien, 'Hong Kong Outlaws a Video Game, Saying it Promotes "Armed Revolution"' *The New York Times* (11 June 2025) <www.nytimes.com/2025/06/11/world/asia/hong-kong-bans-taiwan-game.html> last accessed 1 January 2026.

292 Joy Dong, 'Hong Kong Officials Harden Their Stance on "Soft Resistance"' *The New York Times* (20 August 2025) <www.nytimes.com/2025/08/20/world/asia/hong-kong-soft-resistance.html> last accessed 1 January 2026.

293 Chen Qingqing, 'HK Police to Follow Up with Investigations into "Soft Resistance" Case in Local Book Fair' *Global Times* (22 July 2025) <www.globaltimes.cn/page/202507/1339002.shtml> last accessed 1 January 2026.

294 Tim Hamlett, 'Catering Cancel Culture: Why Do Mystery Hotel Breakdowns Plague Hong Kong Fundraising Events' *HKFP* (22 February 2025) <https://hongkongfp.com/2025/02/22/catering-cancel-culture-why-do-mystery-hotel-breakdowns-plague-hong-kong-fundraising-events/> last accessed 1 January 2026.

295 Section 8(3) of the 2024 HKNSL.

296 For a critique, see Trevor Wan, 'Where Proportionality Meets the "Most Important Factor" of National Security' (2025) *Public Law* 442.

city"[297] is no more; public demonstrations are now few and far between, and authorised ones are subject to robust police scrutiny and regulation.[298] Hong Kong's press freedom now ranks 140th in the world – a precipitous plummet from its high of 18th in the world in 2002 – and is fast closing the gap with the rest of China which ranks at 178th.[299]

The passage of the 2020 HKNSL prompted Macau to enact a more robust MANSL in 2023, but only one person has been charged under this law. While there is no National Security Office established by the Central People's Government in Macau, the role of the NSO is *informally* played by the dispatch of the Beijing-appointed National Security Advisor and Technical Advisors to Macau since 2021.

The casino industry – the bedrock of Macau's economy – has been reconstituted in light of China's rising concerns about national security. Traditionally, the casino industry is a huge revenue source for the city, but it is also a major source of triad-related crimes and cross-border money laundering,[300] especially via the use of the junket system that connects VIP guests discreetly to Macau casinos. Concerns over the casinos posing national security threats heightened when a public trial in the USA[301] revealed that Sands Macau – the Macau flagship of Las Vegas Sands Corp. – had allegedly spied on Macau's top officials in attempts to dig up "dirt" that could be used by the casino as bargaining leverage with local authorities. The secret investigation included gathering information on Macau's then Chief Executive Fernando Chui to identify any weaknesses that might compromise his loyalty to Beijing.[302] The entire gaming industry model was subsequently overhauled in Macau. Macau's Gaming Law[303] has been amended to explicitly

297 Antony Dapiran, *City of Protest: A Recent History of Dissent in Hong Kong* (Penguin Australia 2017).

298 Oscar Liu, 'Security Chief Says Public Must Wear Numbered Lanyards or Special T-shirts to March in Hong Kong to Prevent Rallies from being "Hijacked"' *SCMP* (2 April 2023) <www.scmp.com/news/hong-kong/politics/article/3215753/security-chief-says-public-must-wear-numbered-tags-or-special-t-shirts-march-hong-kong-prevent> last accessed 1 January 2026.

299 'RSF World Press Freedom Index 2025: Economic Fragility a Leading Threat to Press Freedom' *Reporters without Borders* <https://rsf.org/en/rsf-world-press-freedom-index-2025-economic-fragility-leading-threat-press-freedom> last accessed 1 January 2026.

300 Lo Shiu Hing, 'Casino Politics, Organized Crime and the Post-Colonial State in Macau' (2005) 14(43) *Journal of Contemporary China* 207–224.

301 *Steve Jacobs v. Las Vegas Sands Corp.*, No. A627691-B (Nev. Dist. Ct. Clark Cnty.). In 2016, Las Vegas Sands Corp. settled the lawsuit with Jacobs, see Kate O'Keeffe and Alexandra Berzon, 'Las Vegas Sands to Pay More Than $75 Million to Settle Suit Filed by Former Macau CEO' *The Wall Street Journal* (1 June 2016) <www.wsj.com/articles/las-vegas-sands-to-pay-more-than-75-million-to-settle-suit-filed-by-former-macau-ceo-1464752315> last accessed 1 January 2026.

302 Yufan Hao, Li Sheng and Guanjin Pan, *Political Economy of Macao since 1999: The Dilemma of Success* (Palgrave Macmillan 2017) 86.

303 The full title of the law is '娛樂場幸運博彩經營法律制度 Legal Framework for the Operations of Casino Games of Fortune'.

"safeguard the national security of the PRC".[304] Passed in 2022, the new Gaming Law added a national security clause that grants the Chief Executive the power to terminate a concessionaire's contract on the grounds of national security and the security of the MASAR.[305] The new law also tightens oversight over the junket and casino operations. Under the new law, each junket operator is only allowed to partner with one casino concessionaire, and junket operators are prohibited from sharing gaming revenue with concessionaires or from entering into contracts for the exclusive use of a casino gaming area.[306] Junkets are now also banned from accepting "player deposits" or sharing commissions on revenues with any third party.[307] These restrictions put an end to the practice of junkets operating their own private VIP clubs in casinos, thereby cutting off a significant channel of cross-border capital flow. Following the gaming overhaul, junket operators have also been targeted in major sting operations. Leading junket operators, Alvin Chau Cheok-wa and Levo Chan Weng-lin, were arrested in late 2021 and early 2022 respectively for money laundering and illegal cross-border gambling, signifying China and the MASAR's crackdown on the junket system.

The Hong Kong and Macau SARs were poles apart in the first two decades of their establishment. The younger sibling was docile and obedient, while the older one was always tugging at its leash. But as Hong Kong careened towards civil war in 2019, Beijing lost all patience and overhauled the entire system, with national security placed at the forefront of the city's future development. Critics were aghast and believed that Beijing's disproportionate actions eroded Hong Kong's high degree of autonomy and threatened the long-term sustainability of the "One Country, Two Systems" project.[308] Residents who agreed with this view left the city by tens of thousands.[309] Hong Kong's regression prompted Macau to take similar actions and "update" its national security law in 2023.

304 Macau Gaming Law, art 1(A)(1); also see 'Summary Report on the Public Consultation for the Revision of the Legal Framework for the Operations of Casino Games of Fortune' (23 December 2021) 36–7<www.gov.mo/zh-hant/wp-content/uploads/sites/4/2021/09/修改博彩法公開諮詢總結報告-中文版本.pdf> last accessed 1 January 2026.

305 Macau Gaming Law, art 45(1)(1).

306 Macau Gaming Law, art 23.

307 Macau Gaming Law, art 22(17).

308 Michael Pompeo, 'On Beijing's Imposition of National Security Legislation on Hong Kong' (30 June 2020) <https://2017-2021-translations.state.gov/2020/06/30/on-beijings-imposition-of-national-security-legislation-on-hong-kong/> last accessed 1 January 2026; Secretary of State for Foreign, Commonwealth and Development Affairs, 'The Six-Monthly Report on Hong Kong 1 July to 31 December 2020' (10 June 2021) <https://assets.publishing.service.gov.uk/media/60c1fb908fa8f57ce4614fbe/hong-kong-six-monthly-report-48-jul-dec-2020.pdf> last accessed 1 January 2026; U.S. Department of State, 'Hong Kong's Proposed Article 23 Legislation Further Undermines "One Country, Two Systems" Framework' (28 Feb 2024) <https://china.usembassy-china.org.cn/hong-kongs-proposed-article-23-legislation-further-undermines-one-country-two-systems-framework/> last accessed 1 January 2026.

309 Irene Chan, 'Over 27,000 Hong Kong Students Left City's Schools Last Year amid Emigration Wave' *HKFP* (12 July 2023) <https://hongkongfp.com/2023/07/12/over-27000-hong-kong-students-left-citys-schools-last-year-amid-emigration-wave/> last accessed 1 January 2026; Peter Lee, 'Over 144,000 Hong Kongers Move to UK in 2 Years since Launch of BNO Visa Scheme' *HKFP*

Hong Kong's vaunted judicial system has taken a beating and international observers remain sceptical about whether the common law can survive Hong Kong's twin national security laws. Since 2020, five overseas judges have resigned from the HKCFA, explicitly citing their concerns with the political situation in Hong Kong or its national security laws.[310] Specifically, after the Hong Kong CFI convicted 14 of the Hong Kong-47 arrestees for subversion, Lord Sumption resigned as an overseas judge from the HKCFA and explained his decision in a hard-hitting op-ed published in the *Financial Times*. Lord Sumption lamented that this lower-court "decision is symptomatic of a growing malaise in the Hong Kong judiciary"[311] where judges have to "operate in an impossible political environment created by China".[312] To no one's surprise, the Hong Kong Chief Justice swiftly refuted this accusation in a press statement, asserting that his "Court of Final Appeal will continue to act with integrity and professionalism in handling any appeals".[313] Time will tell who is proven right.

(1 February 2023) <https://hongkongfp.com/2023/02/01/over-144000-hongkongers-move-to-uk-in-2-years-since-launch-of-bno-visa-scheme/> last accessed 1 January 2026.

310 See Chapter 3 of this book on the constitutional role of the HKCFA's overseas Non-Permanent Judges and the background to some of their departures since 2020.

311 Jonathan Sumption, 'The Rule of Law in Hong Kong is in Grave Danger' *Financial Times* (10 June 2024) <www.ft.com/content/60c825be-b70a-4152-895f-f6127974570a> last accessed 1 January 2026.

312 Jonathan Sumption, 'The Rule of Law in Hong Kong is in Grave Danger' *Financial Times* (10 June 2024) <www.ft.com/content/60c825be-b70a-4152-895f-f6127974570a> last accessed 1 January 2026.

313 'Statement of Chief Justice of Court of Final Appeal' (11 June 2024) <www.hkcfa.hk/filemanager/PressRelease/en/upload/129/press_release_20240611_01en.pdf> last accessed 1 January 2026.

Appendix 1

Persons Convicted under the 2020 HKNSL & 2020 IR43 (as of 1 March 2026)

Date	*No.*	*Names*	*Judgment*	*Offence*	*Sentence*
30 July 2021	1	Tong Ying-Kit	[2021] HKCFI 2239	Inciting secession (Art 21) & terrorism (Art 24)	9-years imprisonment
22 Dec 2021	2	Leung Kam-wai	WKCC 3633/ 2021[314]	Refusal to provide information (Sch. 5, IR43)	3-months imprisonment
11 Nov 2021 3 Aug 2022	3	Ma Chun-Man	[2021] HKDC 1406 [2022] HKCA 1151[315]	Inciting secession (Art 21)	5-years imprisonment
23 Nov 2021	4	Tony Chung Hon Lam	[2021] HKDC 1484	Secession (Art 20)	40-months imprisonment[316]
29 Apr 2022 30 Nov 2022 22 Aug 2023	5	Lui Sai Yu	[2022] HKDC 384 [2022] HKCA 1780 [2023] HKCFA 26	Inciting secession (Art 21)	5-years imprisonment
11 May 2022	6	Chan To-wai	WKCC 3633/ 2021[317]	Refusal to provide information (Sch. 5, IR43)	3-months imprisonment
8 Oct 2022	7	Yuen Ka-him	[2022] HKDC 1147	Conspiracy to incite subversion (Art 23)	Sentenced to a training centre for all
	8	Wan Chung-wai			
	9	Leung Yung-wan			

314 This is an unreported judgment. See Brian Wong, '3 Tiananmen Square Vigil Group Members Jailed for 4½ Months over Refusal to Assist Hong Kong Police in Probe' *SCMP* (11 Mar 2023) <www.scmp.com/news/hong-kong/law-and-crime/article/3213176/3-tiananmen-square-vigil-group-members-jailed-4-1/2-months-over-refusal-assist-hong-kong-police> last accessed 1 January 2026.

315 The District Court initially imposed a prison sentence of five years and nine months; however, the High Court reduced the sentence to five years.

316 The offender received a combined 43-months prison sentence for secession and money laundering. The sentence for secession alone was 40-months imprisonment.

317 This is an unreported judgment. See Brian Wong, '3 Tiananmen Square Vigil Group Members Jailed for 4½ Months over Refusal to Assist Hong Kong Police in Probe' *SCMP* (11 Mar 2023) <www.scmp.com/news/hong-kong/law-and-crime/article/3213176/3-tiananmen-square-vigil-group-members-jailed-4-1/2-months-over-refusal-assist-hong-kong-police> last accessed 1 January 2026.

Date	*No.*	*Names*	*Judgment*	*Offence*	*Sentence*
	10	Tseung Chau Ching-yu			
	11	Kwok Man-hei			
22 Oct 2022	12	Wong Yat-chin	[2022] HKDC 1210	Conspiracy to incite subversion (Art 23)	36-months imprisonment
	13	Chan Chi-sum			34-months imprisonment
	14	Chu Wai-ying			30-months imprisonment
	15	Wong Yuen-lam			Sentenced to a training centre
9 Feb 2023	16 17	Choi Wing-kit Chan Yau-tsun	[2023] HKDC 214	Conspiracy to incite subversion (Arts 22 and 23)	5-years imprisonment for both[318]
24 Feb 2023	18	Wong Denis Tak Keung	[2023] HKDC 168	Inciting subversion (Arts 22 and 23)	5-years imprisonment
28 Dec 2023	19	Ho Yu-wang[319]	[2024] HKCFI 280	Conspiracy to commit terrorism (Art 24)	6-years imprisonment
11 Apr 2024	20	John Joseph	[2024] HKDC 640	Conspiracy to incite secession (Arts 20 and 21)	5-years imprisonment
19 Nov 2024	21	Ng Gordon Ching-hang	[2024] HKCFI 3298 (19 Nov 2024)[320] [2026] HKCA 284 (23 Feb 2026)[321]	Conspiracy to commit subversion (Art 22(3))	87-months imprisonment
	22	Cheng Tat-hung			78-months imprisonment
	23	Yeung Suet-ying Clarisse			78-months imprisonment

318 Choi Wing-kit received a combined prison sentence of five years and three months for conspiracy to incite subversion and another non-national security offence. The sentence for conspiracy to incite subversion alone was 5-years imprisonment.

319 Two other defendants in this case, Kwok Man-hei and Cheung Ho-yeung, pleaded guilty to the alternative charge of "conspiracy to cause explosions likely to endanger life or property", instead of "conspiracy to commit terrorism". They were sentenced to 30-months and 6-years in prison, respectively.

320 All the 45 defendants (no. 21–65) were sentenced to imprisonment on 19 November 2024. The duration of their sentences ranged between four and ten years.

321 The Court of Appeal dismissed the appeals of 12 defendants and upheld the acquittal of Lawrence Lau Wai-chung.

Date	No.	Names	Judgment	Offence	Sentence
	24	Pang Cheuk-kei			78-months imprisonment
	25	Ho Kai-ming Kalvin			79-months imprisonment
	26	Wong Pik-wan			78-months imprisonment
	27	Sze Tak-loy			79-months imprisonment
	28	Ho Kwai-lam			7-years imprisonment
	29	Chan Chi-chuen Raymond			78-months imprisonment
	30	Chow Ka-shing			93-months imprisonment
	31	Lam Cheuk-ting			81-months imprisonment
	32	Leung Kwok-hung			81-months imprisonment
	33	Or Yiu-lam Ricky			79-months imprisonment
	34	Yu Wai-ming Winnie			81-months imprisonment
	35	Tai Yiu-ting			10-years imprisonment
	36	Au Nok-hin			81-months imprisonment
	37	Chiu Ka-yin Andrew			7-years imprisonment
	38	Chung Kam-lun			73-months imprisonment
	39	Yuen Ka-wai Tiffany			51-months imprisonment
	40	Leung Fong-wai Fergus			59-months imprisonment
	41	Chui Chi-kin			50-months imprisonment
	42	Sham Tsz-kit			51-months imprisonment
	43	Mo Man-ching Claudia			50-months imprisonment
	44	Fung Tat-chun Frankie			53-months imprisonment
	45	Lau Chak-fung			53-months imprisonment
	46	Wong Chi-fung			56-months imprisonment

Date	*No.*	*Names*	*Judgment*	*Offence*	*Sentence*
	47	Tam Man-ho Jeremy Jansen			50-months imprisonment
	48	Li Ka-tat			51-months imprisonment
	49	Tam Tak-chi			53-months imprisonment
	50	Wu Chi-wai			53-months imprisonment
	51	Chu Hoi-dick Eddie			53-months imprisonment
	52	Cheung Ho-sum			59-months imprisonment
	53	Wong Ji-yuet			53-months imprisonment
	54	Ng Kin-wai			67-months imprisonment
	55	Wan Siu-kin Andrew			56-months imprisonment
	56	Kwok Ka-ki			50-months imprisonment
	57	Ng Man-yee Carol			53-months imprisonment
	58	Tam Hoi-pong			51-months imprisonment
	59	Lau Wing-hong			53-months imprisonment
	60	Yeung Alvin Ngok-kiu			61-months imprisonment
	61	Fan Gary Kwok-wai			50-months imprisonment
	62	Lui Chi-hang Hendrick			51-months imprisonment
	63	Lam King-nam			62-months imprisonment
	64	Shum Lester			54-months imprisonment
	65	Wong Pak-yu			51-months imprisonment
15 Dec 2025	66	Wong Chi Lok	[2025] HKDC 1986	Conspiracy to commit secession (Art 20)	42-months imprisonment
9 Feb 2026	67	Jimmy Lai Chee-ying	[2026] HKCFI 854	Conspiracy to commit collusion (Art 29(4))	20-years imprisonment[322]

322 The court imposed a combined sentence of 20-years imprisonment on Jimmy Lai Chee-ying for conspiracy to commit collusion and sedition. See [2026] HKCFI 854 at [78].

Date	*No.*	*Names*	*Judgment*	*Offence*	*Sentence*
	68	Cheung Kim-hung		Conspiracy to commit collusion (Art 29(4))	81-months imprisonment
	69	Law Wai-kwong		Conspiracy to commit collusion (Art 29(4))	10-years imprisonment
	70	Chan Pui-man		Conspiracy to commit collusion (Art 29(4))	7-years imprisonment
	71	Lam Man-chung		Conspiracy to commit collusion (Art 29(4))	10-years imprisonment
	72	Fung Wai-kong		Conspiracy to commit collusion (Art 29(4))	10-years imprisonment
	73	Yeung Ching-kee		Conspiracy to commit collusion (Art 29(4))	87-months imprisonment
	74	Andy Li Yu-hin		Conspiracy to commit collusion (Art 29(4))	87-months imprisonment
	75	Chan Tsz-wah		Conspiracy to commit collusion (Art 29(4))	75-months imprisonment

Appendix 2

Persons Convicted for Sedition under the Hong Kong Crimes Ordinance (as of 1 March 2026)

Date	*No.*	*Names*	*Judgment*	*Offence*	*Sentence*
20 Apr 2021	1	Hui Pui Yee	[2021] HKDC 504	Conspiracy to do an act with a seditious intention (Section 10(1)(a), Crimes Ordinance)	15-months imprisonment[323]
31 Jan 2022	2	Cho Suet-sum Chloe	[2022] HKDC 119	Conspiracy to print, publish, distribute, display or reproduce seditious publications (Sections 10(1)(c), 159A and 159C, Crimes Ordinance)	13½ months imprisonment
	3	Wong Chun-wai			Sentenced to Rehabilitation Centre
31 Jan 2022	4	Kim Chiang Chung-sang	WKCC 3129/ 2021[324]	Displaying seditious publication & possessing seditious publication (Sections 10(1)(a) and 10(2), Crimes Ordinance)	8-months imprisonment
20 Apr 2022 7 Mar 2024	5	Tam Tak Chi	[2022] HKDC 343 [2024] HKCA 231	Uttering seditious words (Section 10(1)(b), Crimes Ordinance)	21-months imprisonment[325]
28 Jun 2022	6	Hau Wing-yan	WKCC 699/ 2022[326]	Doing an act with seditious intention (Section 10(1)(a), Crimes Ordinance)	7-months imprisonment
	7	Lam Yuen-yi			6-months imprisonment

323 The offender received a combined 3-years prison sentence for sedition and another non-national security offence. The sentence for sedition alone was 15-months imprisonment.

324 This is an unreported judgment. See Selina Cheng, 'Hong Kong Man Jailed for 8 Months in First Sedition Sentencing since 1967 Leftist Riots' *HKFP* (1 February 2022) <https://hongkongfp.com/2022/02/01/hong-kong-man-jailed-for-8-months-in-first-sedition-sentencing-since-1967-leftist-riots/> last accessed 1 January 2026.

325 The offender received a combined 40-months prison sentence for sedition and another four non-national security offences. The sentence for sedition alone was 21-months imprisonment.

326 This is an unreported judgment. See Hillary Leung, 'Hong Kong Tea Shop Owners Jailed for 6 and 7 Months over Anti-Vaccine Posts' *HKFP* (29 June 2022) <https://hongkongfp.com/2022/06/29/hong-kong-tea-shop-owners-jailed-for-6-and-7-months-over-anti-vaccine-posts/> last accessed 1 January 2026.

Date	*No.*	*Names*	*Judgment*	*Offence*	*Sentence*
12 July 2022	8	Koo Sze Yiu	[2022] HKMagC 5	Attempting to do or making any preparation to do an act with seditious intention (Section 10(1)(a), Crimes Ordinance)	9-months imprisonment
10 Sep 2022	9 10 11 12 13	Lai Man Ling Yeung Yat-yee Melody Ng Hau Yi Sidney Chan Yuen-sum Samuel Fong Tsz-ho	[2022] HKDC 1004	Conspiracy to print, publish, distribute, display and/or reproduce seditious publications (Sections 10(1)(c), 159A and 159C, Crimes Ordinance)	19-months imprisonment for all
15 Sep 2022	14	Raymond Chen	[2022] HKMagC 6	Doing an act with seditious intention (Section 10(1)(a), Crimes Ordinance)	4-months imprisonment
16 Sep 2022	15	Chan Kwun-yuk	[2022] HKMagC 7	Doing an act with seditious intention (Section 10(1)(a), Crimes Ordinance)	5-months imprisonment
27 Sep 2022	16	Chan Wai-lun	[2022] HKMagC 8	Doing an act with seditious intention (Section 10(1)(a), Crimes Ordinance)	16-weeks imprisonment
7 Oct 2022	17	Wan Yiu Sing Edmund	[2022] HKDC 958	Conspiracy to do an act with a seditious intention (Section 10(1)(a), Crimes Ordinance)	14-months imprisonment[327]
25 Oct 2022	18	Luk Ting-fung	[2022] HKMagC 10	Doing an act with seditious intention (Section 10(1)(a), Crimes Ordinance)	6-months imprisonment
27 Oct 2022	19	Pang Moon-yuen Garry	[2022] HKMagC 11	Doing an act with seditious intention and uttering seditious words (Sections 10(1)(a)(b), Crimes Ordinance)	12-months imprisonment

327 The offender received a combined 32-months prison sentence for sedition and another non-national security offence. The sentence for sedition alone was 14-months imprisonment.

Date	*No.*	*Names*	*Judgment*	*Offence*	*Sentence*
	20	Chiu Mei-ying		Uttering seditious words (Section 10(1)(b), Crimes Ordinance)	3-months imprisonment
15 Nov 2022	21	Chan Tai Sum	[2022] HKDC 1336	Doing an act with seditious intention (Section 10(1)(a), Crimes Ordinance) (along with another non-sedition offence)	8-months imprisonment[328]
14 Dec 2022	22	Chui Hoi-chun	[2022] HKMagC 13	Doing an act with seditious intention, (Section 10(1)(a), Crimes Ordinance)	Sentenced to a training centre
16 Dec 2022	23	Choi Chun-nok	[2022] HKMagC 14	Doing an act with seditious intention (Section 10(1)(a), Crimes Ordinance)	8-months imprisonment
5 Jan 2023	24	Wong Chun Kit	[2023] HKMagC 1	Doing an act with seditious intention (Section 10(1)(a), Crimes Ordinance)	8-months imprisonment
20 Mar 2023	25	Chui Chun-man	[2023] HKMagC 6	Doing an act with seditious intention (Section10(1)(a), Crimes Ordinance)	10-months imprisonment
20 Mar 2023	26	Alex Lee Lung-yin	[2023] HKMagC 5	Conspiracy to do an act with seditious intention (Section 10(1)(a), Crimes Ordinance)	5-months imprisonment
	27	Alan Keung Ka-wai			8-months imprisonment
	28	Cannis Chan Sheung-yan			10-months imprisonment
27 Mar 2023	29	Wong Ho-cheong	[2023] HKMagC 8	Doing an act with seditious intention (Section 10(1)(a), Crimes Ordinance)	5-months imprisonment
27 Apr 2023	30	Law Oi-wa	[2023] HKMagC 10	Doing an act with seditious intention (Section 10(1)(a), Crimes Ordinance)	4-months imprisonment
27 Jul 2023	31	Danny Kong Tat Kuen	[2023] HKMagC 11	Doing an act with seditious intention (Section 10(1)(a), Crimes Ordinance)	3-months imprisonment

328 The offender received a combined 12-months prison sentence for sedition and another non-national security offence. The sentence for sedition alone was 8-months imprisonment.

Date	*No.*	*Names*	*Judgment*	*Offence*	*Sentence*
31 Aug 2023	32	Tommy Yuen Man-on	[2023] HKDC 1218	Doing an act with seditious intention (Section 10(1)(a), Crimes Ordinance)	21-months imprisonment[329]
12 Sep 2023	33	Zeng Yuxuan	[2023] HKMagC 12	Attempting to do or making any preparation to do an act with seditious intention (Section 10(1)(a), Crimes Ordinance)	6-months imprisonment
6 Oct 2023	34	Kurt Leung Kui-ming	[2023] HKMagC 14	Importing seditious publication (Section 10(1)(d), Crimes Ordinance)	4-months imprisonment
3 Nov 2023	35	Yuen Ching-ting	[2023] HKMagC 13	Doing an act with seditious intention (Section 10(1)(a), Crimes Ordinance)	2-months imprisonment
23 Nov 2023	36	Chow Man-wai	[2023] HKMagC 15	Doing an act or acts with a seditious intention (Section 10(1)(a), Crimes Ordinance)	4-months imprisonment
14 Dec 2023	37	Au Kin-wai	[2023] HKMagC 16	Doing an act or acts with a seditious intention (Section 10(1)(a), Crimes Ordinance)	6-months imprisonment
10 Jan 2024	38	Chu Kai-pong	[2024] HKMagC 2	Doing an act with a seditious intention & possessing seditious publication (Sections 10(1)(a) and 10(2), Crimes Ordinance)	3-months imprisonment
16 Feb 2024	39	Koo Sze Yiu[330]	[2024] HKMagC 4	Attempting to do or making any preparation to do an act or acts with seditious intention (Section 10(1)(a), Crimes Ordinance)	9-months imprisonment

329 The offender received a combined 26-months prison sentence for sedition and another non-national security offence. The sentence for sedition alone was 21-months imprisonment.

330 This was Koo Sze Yiu's second conviction for sedition. See #8 in Appendix 2.

Date	*No.*	*Names*	*Judgment*	*Offence*	*Sentence*
29 Feb 2024	40	Chan Sze-lok	[2024] HKDC 438	Doing an act with a seditious intention (Section 10(1)(a), Crimes Ordinance)	15-months imprisonment[331]
	41	Lee Ho-yuen		Conspiracy to do an act with a seditious intention (Section 10(1)(a), Crimes Ordinance)	18-months imprisonment[332]
	42	Wong Yuu-ro		Conspiracy to do an act with a seditious intention (Section 10(1)(a), Crimes Ordinance)	15-months imprisonment[333]
10 Apr 2024	43	Tsang Kwok-hei	[2024] HKMagC 5	Doing an act with seditious intention (Section 10(1)(a), Crimes Ordinance)	5-months imprisonment
26 Sep 2024	44	Chung Pui-kuen	[2024] HKDC 1609	Conspiracy to publish and/or reproduce seditious publications (Section 10(1)(c), Crimes Ordinance)	21-months imprisonment
	45	Patrick Lam Shiu-tung			10-months and 9 days imprisonment[334]
9 Feb 2026	46	Jimmy Lai Chee-ying (convicted of collusion concurrently)	[2026] HKCFI 854	Conspiracy to publish and/or reproduce seditious publications (Section 10(1)(c), Crimes Ordinance)	22-months imprisonment[335]

331 The offender received a combined 38-months prison sentence for sedition and another non-national security offence. The sentence for sedition alone was 15-months imprisonment.

332 The offender received a combined 29-months prison sentence for sedition and another non-national security offence. The sentence for sedition alone was 18-months imprisonment.

333 The offender received a combined 24-months prison sentence for sedition and another three non-national security offences. The sentence for sedition alone was 15-months imprisonment.

334 Initially, the judge sentenced Lam to 11-months imprisonment. Considering Lam's health condition and the fact that he had already been remanded for a period of 10 months and 9 days, the judge further reduced his sentence so that Lam could be released immediately to receive medical treatment.

335 Jimmy Lai Chee-ying was sentenced to 20 years imprisonment for conspiracy to commit collusion and sedition. The sentence for sedition alone was 22-months imprisonment.

Appendix 3

Persons Convicted under the 2024 HKNSL (as of 1 March 2026)

Date	*No.*	*Names*	*Judgment*	*Offence*	*Sentence*
19 Sep 2024	1	Chu Kai-pong	[2024] HKMagC 6	Doing an act with seditious intention (Section 24(1)(a)(i))	14-months imprisonment
19 Sep 2024	2	Chung Man-kit	[2024] HKMagC 7	Doing an act with seditious intention (Section 24(1)(a)(i))	10-months imprisonment
20 Sep 2024	3	Au Kin-wai	[2024] HKMagC 8	Publishing seditious publication (Section 24(1)(b))	14-months imprisonment
1 Apr 2025	4	Ernest Lee	[2025] HKMagC 3	Doing an act with seditious intention (Section 24(1)(a)(i))	8-months imprisonment[336]
8 Apr 2025	5	Chow Kim-ho	[2025] HKMagC 4	Publishing seditious publication (Section 24(1)(b))	12-months imprisonment
8 May 2025	6	Li Chun-kit	[2025] HKMagC 5	Publishing seditious publication (Section 24(1)(b))	12-months imprisonment
13 Nov 2025	7	Lan Fei	[2025] HKMagC 6	Doing an act with seditious intention (Section 24(1)(a)(i))	12-months imprisonment
26 Feb 2026	8	Kwok Yin-sang	[2026] HKMagC 2	Attempting to deal with any funds or other financial assets or economic resources belonging to an absconder (Sections 90(2)(b) and 90(3))	8-months imprisonment
27 Feb 2026	9	Lam Chung-ming	[2026] HKMagC 3	Publishing seditious publication (Section 24(1)(b))	8-months imprisonment

336 The offender received a combined 10-months prison sentence for sedition and another non-national security offence. The sentence for sedition alone was 8-months imprisonment.

References

Chen, Albert, 'The National Security Law of the HKSAR: A Contextual and Legal Study' in Hualing Fu and Michael Hor (eds), *The National Security Law of Hong Kong: Restoration and Transformation* (Hong Kong, Hong Kong University Press 2022) 20–48.

Chen, Albert, 'A Perfect Storm: Hong Kong-Mainland Rendition of Fugitive Offenders' (2019) 49(2) *Hong Kong Law Journal* 419–429.

Chen, Albert, 'The Consultation Document and the Bill: An Overview' in Hualing Fu, Carole Petersen and Simon Young (eds), *National Security and Fundamental Freedoms: Hong Kong's Article 23 under Scrutiny* (Hong Kong, Hong Kong University Press 2005) 94–118.

Chen, Albert and Po Jen Yap, *The Constitutional System of the Hong Kong SAR: A Contextual Analysis* (Oxford, Hart 2023).

Chen, Albert and Simon Young, 'Liability for Imposing Sanctions under Hong Kong's National Security Law' (2020) 50(2) *Hong Kong Law Journal* 353–363.

Cheng, Joseph, 'The Tiananmen Incident and the Pro-democracy Movement in Hong Kong' in Jean-Philippe Beja (ed), *The Impact of China's 1989 Tiananmen Massacre* (Oxford, Routledge 2011) 179–193.

Fu, Hualing, 'China's Imperatives for National Security Legislation' in Cora Chan and Fiona de Londras (eds), *China's National Security: Endangering Hong Kong's Rule of Law?* (Oxford, Hart 2020) 41–60.

Fu, Hualing, 'Past and Future Offences of Sedition in Hong Kong' in Hualing Fu, Carole Petersen and Simon Young (eds), *National Security and Fundamental Freedoms: Hong Kong's Article 23 under Scrutiny* (Hong Kong, Hong Kong University Press 2005) 217–249.

Guo, Tianwu 郭天武 and Zhu Ziqian 朱紫芊, '澳门特别行政区维护国家安全立法探析 A Legal Analysis of the Law of the Macau SAR on Safeguarding National Security' (2021) 3 *上海政法学院学报(法治论丛) Journal of Shanghai University of Political Science & Law (The Rule of Law Forum)* 58–71.

Hao, Yufan, Li Sheng and Guanjin Pan, *Political Economy of Macao since 1999: The Dilemma of Success* (Singapore, Palgrave Macmillan 2017).

Hargreaves, Stuart, 'Canaries or Colonials? The Reduced Prominence of the "Overseas Judges" on Hong Kong's Court of Final Appeal' (2021) 16 *Asian Journal of Comparative Law* 187–217.

Huang, Jinrong 黄金荣, '"规范性文件"的法律界定及效力 Legal Definition and Effect of "Normative Documents"' (2014) 7 *法学 Law Science* 10–20.

Jackson, Michael, 'Two Years On: Reviewing the Implementation of the National Security Law in the HKSAR' (2023) 52(3) *Hong Kong Law Journal* 875–912.

Kwong, Ying-ho, 'State-Society Conflict Radicalization in Hong Kong: The Rise of "Anti-China" Sentiment and Radical Localism' (2016) 47(3) *Asian Affairs* 428–442.

Lo, Pui-yin, 'Reactivated and Re-energised: The Sedition Offences in "New Era" Hong Kong' (2022) 52(3) *Hong Kong Law Journal* 913–936.

Lo, Shiu Hing, 'Casino Politics, Organized Crime and the Post-Colonial State in Macau' (2005) 14(43) *Journal of Contemporary China* 207–224.

Luo, Weijian 骆伟建 et al, *澳门特别行政区基本法解析：立法背景和立法原意的探究 Analysing the Basic Law of the Macau Special Administrative Region: An Approach from Legislative Background and Intent* (Beijing, 社会科学文献出版社 Social Sciences Academic Press 2020).

Ma, Ngok, 'Civil Society in Self-Defense: the Struggle against National Security Legislation in Hong Kong' (2005) 14(44) *Journal of Contemporary China* 465–482.

Ng, Michael, *Political Censorship in British Hong Kong: Freedom of Expression and the Law (1842–1997)* (Cambridge, Cambridge University Press 2022).

Petersen, Carole, 'National Security Law in Hong Kong: Transforming "One Country, Two Systems" as a Model of Regional Autonomy' in Ngoc Son Bui, Stuart Hargreaves and Ryan Mitchell (eds), *Routledge Handbook of Constitutional Law in Greater China* (Oxford, Routledge 2023) 187–203.

Petersen, Carole, 'Hong Kong's Spring of Discontent: The Rise and Fall of the National Security Bill in 2003' in Hualing Fu, Carole Petersen and Simon Young (eds), *National Security and Fundamental Freedoms: Hong Kong's Article 23 under Scrutiny* (Hong Kong, Hong Kong University Press 2005) 13–62.

Petersen, Carole, 'National Security Offences and Civil Liberties in Hong Kong: A Critique of the Government's Consultation on Article 23 of the Basic Law' (2002) 32 *Hong Kong Law Journal* 457–470.

Wan, Trevor, 'Where Proportionality Meets the "Most Important Factor" of National Security' (2025) *Public Law* 442–451.

Wong, Yiu-chung, '"Super Paradox" or "Leninist Integration": the Politics of Legislating Article 23 of Hong Kong's Basic Law' (2006) 30(2) *Asian Perspective* 65–95.

Wu, Wei 吴为, Li Donghua 李东华and Li Taishan 李泰山, '澳门《维护国家安全法》解读 An Analysis of Macau National Security Law' (2016) 18(4) *江南社会学院学报 Journal of Jiangnan Social University* 14–18.

Yap, Po Jen, 'Judging Hong Kong's National Security Law' in Hualing Fu and Michael Hor (eds), *The National Security Law of Hong Kong: Restoration and Transformation* (Hong Kong, Hong Kong University Press 2022) 149–166.

Zhu, Han, 'A Chinese Law Wedge into the Hong Kong Common Law System: A Legal Appraisal of the Hong Kong National Security Law' (2023) 21(1) *Northwestern Journal of Human Rights* 43–108.

Zhuang, Jinfeng 莊金鋒, '從《維護國家安全法》的制定看澳門模式的基本特徵The Legislation of Macau National Security Law Epitomises the Basic Features of Macau Model' (2010) 3 *一國兩制研究 Journal of 'One Country Two Systems' Studies* 12–22.

5

CONSTITUTIONAL INTERFACE WITH MAINLAND CHINA

China is not a federal state. But Article 31[1] of the PRC Constitution authorises the establishment of Special Administrative Regions (SARs) within the country, thereby formally allowing the Central Government to devolve and delegate governmental powers to selected regions. Originally designed to entice Taiwan to return to the fold,[2] this "One Country, Two Systems" constitutional model was retrofitted for Hong Kong and Macau to ease the political transition of the two erstwhile European colonies.

Ostensibly, both SARs were formally conferred with a "high degree of autonomy"[3] under their respective Basic Laws. And in the early days of their establishment, Beijing did adopt a relatively more hands-off approach towards the two cities, especially vis-à-vis Hong Kong. But as this global financial hub tugged relentlessly at its leash, with political opposition gaining ground and street protests gaining traction over the years, the Central Government changed tack and asserted greater control over its two "autonomous" cities.

This chapter will begin by exploring the evolving relations between the Central Government and the two SARs, particularly how they were shaped by the "resistance" or protest movements in Hong Kong. Next, we will examine how PRC laws interface with the SAR systems, specifically the PRC Constitution,

1 Article 31 of the PRC Constitution stipulates that: 'The state may establish special administrative regions when necessary. The systems to be instituted in special administrative regions shall be prescribed by law enacted by the National People's Congress in light of the specific conditions.'

2 See Chapter 1 of this book.

3 Article 2 of the Hong Kong Basic Law (HKBL); Article 2 of the Macau Basic Law (MABL).

DOI: 10.4324/9781003683872-5

National Laws, Decisions of the National People's Congress (NPC) and its Standing Committee, and Interpretations of the Basic Laws by the National People's Congress Standing Committee (NPCSC). As Hong Kong "strayed" from the fold, these PRC legal instruments were foisted on the city with great ferocity to bring it back onto the "right track"[4]. Over two decades after the establishment of the SARs, the two cities have been constitutionally tamed and re-ordered, as they now embark on a new path of renewed economic and political integration with Mainland China. This chapter is an account of how both Hong Kong and Macau reached this inflection point.

Evolution of Central–SAR Relations in Hong Kong and Macau

After China's resumption of sovereignty over Hong Kong in 1997, three critical junctures in the city's history shaped and reshaped the relationship between Mainland China and Hong Kong: (1) the mass public protests on 1 July 2003 against the city government's first attempt to pass national security legislation; (2) the 2014 Occupy Central Movement (OCM) where the city's financial district was partially blockaded by pro-democracy activists for 79 days; and (3) the months-long street protests in 2019 against the city government's attempt to pass a bill that would have allowed offenders to be extradited to Mainland China to face trial. These episodes are discussed below.

From 1997 to 2003, the Central Government in Beijing largely stuck to a policy of mutual non-interference. In the words of Chinese President Jiang Zemin: "'the well water shall not intrude upon the river' (井水不犯河水)".[5] But as we have discussed more fully in Chapter 4, the Party leadership did nudge the Hong Kong government to fulfill its constitutional duty and enact national security legislation "on its own"[6] in 2003. But after half a million people rose in opposition against the local national security bill on 1 July 2003, and some pro-establishment lawmakers withdrew support for the bill, the legislative plan was aborted. After this political debacle, Beijing officials realised that the "Hong Kong people's hearts

4 Abigail Ng, 'Hong Kong's Leader Says National Security Law has City "Back on the Right Track"' *CNBC* (6 October 2021) <www.cnbc.com/2021/10/06/hong-kongs-carrie-lam-says-national-security-law-has-curbed-chaos.html> last accessed 1 January 2026.

5 Carole Petersen, 'Hong Kong's Spring of Discontent: The Rise and Fall of the National Security Bill in 2003' in Fu Hualing, Carole Petersen and Simon Young (eds), *National Security and Fundamental Freedoms: Hong Kong's Article 23 under Scrutiny* (Hong Kong University Press 2005) 13, 18.

6 Article 23 of HKBL reads:

> The Hong Kong Special Administrative Region shall enact laws *on its own* to prohibit any act of treason, secession, sedition, subversion against the Central People's Government, or theft of state secrets, to prohibit foreign political organisations or bodies from conducting political activities in the Region, and to prohibit political organisations or bodies of the Region from establishing ties with foreign political organisations or bodies.

haven't returned to the motherland"[7] and they were afraid that Hong Kong was slipping away.[8]

Consequently, the Central Government abandoned its self-restraint and adopted a policy euphemistically termed as "doing what should be done while leaving others alone (有所為有所不為)".[9] In 2003, the Central Coordination Group on Hong Kong and Macau Affairs (中央港澳工作協調小組) was set up and led by a senior Politburo Standing Committee member Zeng Qinghong.[10] The Politburo Standing Committee is the most powerful decision-making body within the Chinese Communist Party (CCP). In 2006, Hong Kong and Macau were also incorporated into the national economic planning framework outlined in the country's 11th Five-Year Plan for National Economic and Social Development (國民經濟和社會發展"十一五"規劃).[11] The intention was clear: Beijing would facilitate Hong Kong's economic integration with the Mainland. Within the political arena, both the Liaison Office in Hong Kong[12] and the United Front Work Department[13] increased their presence and capacity after

7 'The Past and Present of Hong Kong's "Article 23": Five Turning Points in the Thirty-Year Struggle Between Public Opinion and Authorities 香港「23條」的前世今生：三十年來民意與權力當局較量的五個節點' *BBC* (1 April 2024) <www.bbc.com/zhongwen/trad/chinese-news-68634200> last accessed 1 January 2026; also see Hai Huang (黃海), *Alienated Hearts: An Analysis of the Social Ethos in Hong Kong (疏離的人心：香港社會思潮評析)* (City University of Hong Kong Press 2019) 5.

8 Vivienne Chow, 'China and Hong Kong: "One Country Above All"' *The Interpreter* (4 July 2017) <www.lowyinstitute.org/the-interpreter/china-hong-kong-one-country-above-all> last accessed 1 January 2026.

9 'The Plenary Power to Govern: From Implicit to Blatant Expression Is It a Sign of Turning Tough or Positive? 全面管治權：從委婉到直接，是強硬是積極？' *HK01* (23 October 2017) <www.hk01.com/社會新聞/127752/十九大解讀-全面管治權-從委婉到直接-是強硬是積極> last accessed 1 January 2026.

10 Sonny Shiu-Hing Lo, 'The Mainlandization and Recolonization of Hong Kong: A Triumph of Convergence over Divergence with Mainland China' in Joseph Cheng (ed), *The Hong Kong Special Administrative Region in its First Decade* (City University of Hong Kong Press 2007) 179, 179; Yunna Huang (黃雲娜), ' From Past to Present: An Analysis of Why the Central Government Reformed the HKMAO Five Times 從港澳辦的前世今生看中央為什麼五度改革' *HK01* (26 March 2023) <www.hk01.com/深度報道/879777/中央港澳辦-從港澳辦的前世今生-看中央為什麼五度改革> last accessed 1 January 2026.

11 The Five-Year Plan was drafted by the PRC State Council and approved by the National People's Congress. See Xudong Cao (曹旭东)，'Application of the Constitution in the Hong Kong Special Administrative Region: Theoretical Review and Practical Reflection 宪法在香港特别行政区的适用:理论回顾与实践反思' (2018) 1 *Political Science and Law* (*政治与法律*) 85–87; also see Joseph Yu-shek Cheng, 'Beijing's Changing Hong Kong Policy: The Rise and Fall of Pragmatism' (2023) 53(4) *Journal of Contemporary Asia* 626, 635.

12 The full name of the institution is the 'Liaison Office of the Central People's Government in the Hong Kong Special Administrative Region'. This office serves as the representative office of the Central Government in Hong Kong, and it is responsible for liaising between the Central and local governments. A similar liaison office is established in the MASAR.

13 The United Front Work Department is an agency under the Central Committee of the Chinese Communist Party (CCP) responsible for 'united front work', which seeks to expand the Party's

2003,[14] and the Central Government also began reshaping political discourse in Hong Kong. From 2004, Beijing repeatedly emphasised that Hong Kong had an "executive-led government" (行政主導) – a phrase not found in the Basic Law. This phrase underscores the pivotal role that the Hong Kong Special Administrative Region (HKSAR)'s Chief Executive, who is directly appointed by and accountable to the Central People's Government, plays in the city's political system. Notably, in March 2004, Chen Zuoer, Deputy Director of the Hong Kong and Macau Affairs Office of the State Council (HKMAO), emphasised that only in an executive-led political structure could the SAR's Chief Executive be truly accountable to the Central Authorities.[15] In June 2007, Wu Bangguo, Chairman of the NPCSC, also stated that a key characteristic of the HKSAR's political system was its "executive-led government" with the Chief Executive as the core.[16] And the Hong Kong government swiftly incorporated this emphasis on an "executive-led government" into its official discourse for the first time in 2004.[17]

But Hong Kong civil society was undeterred and continued to grow restless at the lack of democratic progress in the city. In January 2013, legal scholar Benny Tai publicly flirted with the idea of a civil disobedience campaign whereby protestors would occupy the financial district to pressure the Central Government into granting genuine universal suffrage for electing the Chief Executive.[18] Beijing was unmoved and the PRC State Council instead asserted in a White Paper released in June 2014 that the Central Authorities had "comprehensive/overall jurisdiction" (全面管治權) over the HKSAR.[19] Doubling down further, the NPCSC issued a

influence over individuals and organisations outside the CCP, particularly the overseas Chinese community.

14 Peter Cheung, 'The Changing Relations between Hong Kong and the Mainland since 2003' in Lam Wai-man et al. (eds), *Contemporary Hong Kong Government and Politics* (Hong Kong University Press 2012) 325–347; Joseph Yu-shek Cheng, 'Beijing's Changing Hong Kong Policy: The Rise and Fall of Pragmatism' (2023) 53(4) *Journal of Contemporary Asia* 626, 631–632.

15 See Albert Chen, 'Executive-led Government, Strong and Weak Governments and "Consensus Democracy"' in Johannes Chan and Lison Harris (eds), *Hong Kong's Constitutional Debates* (Hong Kong Law Journal 2005) 9, 10.

16 Bangguo Wu (吴邦国), 'The Principal Feature of Hong Kong's Political System is that it is Executive-led 香港政治体制的最大特点是行政主导', speech on 6 June 2007 <www.npc.gov.cn/zgrdw/npc/wbgwyz/hyhd/2007-06/06/content_366599.htm> last accessed 1 January 2026.

17 In April 2004, the Chief Executive of the HKSAR submitted a report on Hong Kong's political reform to the NPCSC, emphasising that the existing political system in Hong Kong is an executive-led system headed by the Chief Executive and that any political reform proposals must consolidate this system. See Albert Chen (陳弘毅), 'The Executive and Legislative Organs in the Political System of the HKSAR 香港特別行政區政治體制中的行政與立法機關' (2014) 1 *Journal of 'One Country Two Systems' Studies* ('一國兩制'研究) 6, 10.

18 Benny Tai, 'The Most Lethal Weapon of Civil Disobedience (公民抗命的最大殺傷力武器)' *Hong Kong Economic Journal* (信報) (16 January 2013) <https://sparkpost.wordpress.com/2013/01/19/戴耀廷：公民抗命的最大殺傷力武器/> last accessed 1 January 2026.

19 The State Council, 'The Practice of the "One Country, Two Systems" Policy in the Hong Kong Special Administrative Region' (10 June 2014) <https://english.www.gov.cn/archive/white_paper/2014/08/23/content_281474982986578.htm> last accessed 1 January 2026.

Decision (commonly known as the "831 Decision")[20] on 31 August 2014, which allowed for universal suffrage elections in the 2017 Hong Kong Chief Executive election and beyond, but all the eligible candidates must first be pre-screened by a pro-Beijing nominating committee. Furthermore, no changes would be made for the legislative elections. Outraged by the perceived hard stance taken by the Central Government, the OCM broke out in the financial district on 28 September 2014 and the street protests lasted for 79 days.[21]

The failure of the civil disobedience movement to pressure Beijing into making any substantive concessions on democratic change hardened the resolve of the disenchanted youths and civil activists. In the aftermath of the OCM, a more radicalised group of civil activists emerged, openly advocating Hong Kong independence from the PRC. Their seething frustrations found an outlet when Chief Executive Carrie Lam in 2019 attempted to pass an extradition bill that would have allowed persons in Hong Kong to be extradited to Mainland China to face criminal trial. This epochal event has been discussed more fully in Chapters 1 and 4. Suffice to say here, the bill engendered mass opposition, which saw nearly 2 million people taking to the streets to oppose the bill at one point.[22] Even after the bill was suspended by the government, the street protests continued unabated for months; vandalism of public facilities and violent clashes between street protestors and the police were also common occurrences. Stunned by the deteriorating turn of events in Hong Kong, the Central Authorities secretly worked on a customised National Security Law for Hong Kong and foisted it on the city on 30 June 2020.[23] Doubling down further, the NPC overhauled the electoral system in 2021 such that only "patriots" can rule Hong Kong.[24]

Now, in the subdued and reconstituted Hong Kong, the Director of the HKMAO can openly make "inspection trips"[25] to Hong Kong, address its Legislative Council,[26] and even visit the Hong Kong Court of Final Appeal

20 Decision of the Standing Committee of the National People's Congress on Issues Relating to the Selection of the Chief Executive of the HKSAR by Universal Suffrage and on the Method for Forming the Legislative Council of the HKSAR in the Year 2016 (Adopted at the Tenth Session of the Standing Committee of the 12th National People's Congress on 31 August 2014).

21 Steven Chung Fun Hung, 'The Occupy Central Campaign in 2014 Hong Kong' (2016) 2(2) *Contemporary Chinese Political Economy and Strategic Relations* 669–734.

22 'Hong Kong Protest: "Nearly Two Million" Join Demonstration' *BBC* (16 June 2019) <www.bbc.com/news/world-asia-china-48656471> last accessed 1 January 2026.

23 Law of the PRC on Safeguarding National Security in the HKSAR《中華人民共和國香港特別行政區維護國家安全法》(30 June 2020).

24 Decision of the National People's Congress on Improving the Electoral System of the Hong Kong Special Administrative Region (Adopted at the Fourth Session of the 13th National People's Congress on 11 March 2021). See also Chapter 2 of this book.

25 'Xia Baolong Kicks off 7-day Hong Kong Inspection Tour' *China Daily* (23 February 2024) <www.chinadailyhk.com/hk/article/377585> last accessed 1 January 2026.

26 'Opposing Views doesn't Equal "quality democracy", Beijing's Point Man on Hong Kong Affairs Tells Legislators during "Historic" Legco Chamber Visit' *SCMP* (16 April 2023) <www.scmp.com/news/hong-kong/politics/article/3217255/opposition-doesnt-equal-quality-democracy-beijings-point-man-hong-kong-affairs-tells-legislators> last accessed 1 January 2026.

(HKCFA).[27] All these measures would have been political taboo in the past.[28] Now they are par for the course. Hong Kong has been successfully tamed.

In contrast to its boisterous sibling, Macau was the "well-behaved" child. Unlike Hong Kong, Macau never had a strong pro-democracy presence in the legislature – three "opposition" legislators were the most Macau ever had at any one time.[29] Macau's civil society was weak and the people focused mainly on livelihood issues.[30] Therefore, the Macau government had the political space to proactively address the Central Government's core concerns without the latter managing the former's local affairs directly.[31] For example, as early as 1999, Macau passed the Law on "The Use and Protection of the National Flag, Emblem, and Anthem" (國旗、國徽及國歌的使用及保護)[32] to protect and promote the use of the National Anthem in Macau, even though the PRC National Anthem Law was not even enacted at that time. This stands in stark contrast to the fierce debate in Hong Kong in 2019 when the local legislature sought to pass a similar law. Critics raised free speech concerns as the law criminalises acts that "insult the anthem"[33] and mandates broadcasters and schools to promote the anthem[34] as part of patriotic education.[35] Furthermore, as we have examined in Chapter 4, Macau passed a National Security Law[36] on its own in 2009, while Beijing had to foist one on Hong Kong in 2020.[37] Even with its constitutional duty on national security already fulfilled with the 2009 law, Macau again on its own initiative passed a second National Security Law[38] in 2023 (hereinafter termed 2023 MANSL) to toughen the

27 'Xia Baolong meets HK community' *News.gov.hk* (14 April 2023) <www.news.gov.hk/eng/2023/04/20230414/20230414_210738_631.html> last accessed 1 January 2026.

28 See Natalie Wong and Lilian Cheng, '28 Meetings in 6 Days: What Was Beijing's Point Man's Visit to Hong Kong All About?' *SCMP* (21 April 2023) <www.scmp.com/news/hong-kong/politics/article/3217773/28-meetings-6-days-what-was-beijings-point-mans-visit-hong-kong-all-about-cool-towards-politics-and> last accessed 1 January 2026.

29 See Chapter 2 of this book.

30 Bryan Ho, 'Political Culture, Social Movements, and Governability in Macao' (2011) 38(2) *Asian Affairs: An American Review* 59, 62.

31 Sonny Shiu-hing Lo, 'One Formula, Two Experiences: Political Divergence of Hong Kong and Macao since Retrocession' (2007) 16(52) *Journal of Contemporary China* 359, 383.

32 The full text of the law is available at <https://bo.io.gov.mo/bo/i/1999/01/lei05_cn.asp> last accessed 1 January 2026.

33 Section 7 of the National Anthem Ordinance.

34 Sections 9 and 10 of the National Anthem Ordinance.

35 For a full discussion on the context and debates surrounding the National Anthem Ordinance legislation in Hong Kong, see Brendan Clift, 'Mandating Symbolic Patriotism: China's Flag and Anthem in the Hong Kong Special Administrative Region' (2022) 9 *Asian Journal of Law and Society* 500–518.

36 Law on Safeguarding National Security《維護國家安全法》('2009 MANSL'). The full text of the law is available at <https://bo.io.gov.mo/bo/i/2009/09/lei02_cn.asp> last accessed 1 January 2026.

37 Law of the PRC on Safeguarding National Security in the HKSAR《中華人民共和國香港特別行政區維護國家安全法》(30 June 2020).

38 2023 Law on Safeguarding National Security《維護國家安全法》. A bilingual (Chinese and Portuguese) version of the law is available at <https://images.io.gov.mo/bo/i/2023/24/despce-79-2023.pdf> last accessed 1 January 2026.

original legislation. Even on electoral matters, Macau was always one step ahead. When the NPCSC issued an Interpretation in 2016[39] to require every incoming public office holder in Hong Kong to sincerely and solemnly take their oaths of office or face immediate disqualification, the Macau government swiftly brought its own electoral law in line with this Hong Kong Interpretation.[40] When Beijing overhauled Hong Kong's electoral system in 2021 such that only "patriots" can run for office,[41] the Macau government on its own also disqualified all pro-democracy candidates from contesting the 2021 Macau Legislative Assembly elections.[42]

After the overhaul of Hong Kong's electoral system in 2021, there has been a noticeable convergence between the two cities in how they echo developments in the Mainland. The Hong Kong government, like its Macau counterpart, is now very eager to openly display its political loyalty to the Communist Party leadership and the country's ideological agenda. After Chinese President Xi Jinping gave a speech in Hong Kong on 1 July 2022, over 60 study sessions were organised in the city, involving thousands of civil servants and a diverse range of community groups.[43] As Ivan Choy pointed out, "Hong Kong is following the mainland's political path as the new culture of 'political learning' starts taking off in the city".[44] When the 2023 PRC Patriotic Education Law was passed in the Mainland,[45] and even though this law does not apply to Hong Kong, the city government went all out to promote

39 Interpretation of Article 104 of the Basic Law of the Hong Kong Special Administrative Region of the People's Republic of China by the Standing Committee of the National People's Congress (Adopted by the Standing Committee of the 12th National People's Congress at its 24th Session on 7 November 2016).

40 Amendment to No. 3/2001 Law on the Election of the Legislative Assembly of the MASAR 《修改第3/2001號法律〈澳門特別行政區立法會選舉制度〉》(28 December 2016). See also Jason Buhi, 'Macau's Response to the November 2016 Interpretation of Hong Kong's Basic Law' *HKU Legal Scholarship Blog* (21 December 2016) <http://researchblog.law.hku.hk/2016/12/macaus-response-to-november-2016.html> last accessed 1 January 2026.

41 Decision of the National People's Congress On Improving the Electoral System of the Hong Kong Special Administrative Region (Adopted at the Fourth Session of the 13th National People's Congress on 11 March 2021).

42 See Chapter 3 of this book. See also 'Legislative Assembly Candidates in Macau Disqualified En Masse; "Patriots Governing Macau" Faces Redefinition 澳门立法会候选人遭集体DQ,「爱国爱澳」面临重新定义' *BBC* (14 July 2021) <www.bbc.com/zhongwen/trad/chinese-news-57811700> last accessed 1 January 2026.

43 Almond Li, 'Hong Kong Held Over 60 Seminars in a Month to Promote Speech by China's Xi Jinping' *HKFP* (27 July 2022) <https://hongkongfp.com/2022/07/27/hong-kong-held-over-60-seminars-in-a-month-to-promote-speech-by-chinas-xi-jinping/> last accessed 1 January 2026.

44 Almond Li, 'Hong Kong Held Over 60 Seminars in a Month to Promote Speech by China's Xi Jinping' *HKFP* (27 July 2022) <https://hongkongfp.com/2022/07/27/hong-kong-held-over-60-seminars-in-a-month-to-promote-speech-by-chinas-xi-jinping/> last accessed 1 January 2026.

45 Willa Wu and Lilian Cheng, 'Hong Kong to Set up "High-Level Unit to Promote Patriotic Education" in Response to New National Law Passed on Tuesday' *SCMP* (24 October 2023) <www.scmp.com/news/hong-kong/politics/article/3239049/hong-kong-set-high-level-unit-promote-patriotic-education-response-new-national-law-passed-tuesday> last accessed 1 January 2026.

and integrate patriotic education into the school curriculum.[46] Following the examples of other rich Mainland Chinese provinces, the Macau government, since 2023, has even participated in the country's National Rural Revitalisation Strategy and provided economic assistance to Xiushui County in Jiangxi Province.[47]

Application of the PRC Constitution in the SARs

Since the promulgation of the Basic Laws in both Hong Kong and Macau, there has been a longstanding debate on how the PRC Constitution applies in the SARs. There are primarily two schools of thought.[48] The first is the "overall applicability with exception" theory (總體適用、部分不適用), which posits that the PRC Constitution generally applies to the SARs, except for those provisions that expressly contradict the Basic Law. For instance, PRC constitutional provisions on sovereignty and national institutions are applicable to Hong Kong, but those relating to the Mainland's socialist systems are not.[49] On the other hand, the "application through the Basic Law" theory (憲法通過基本法適用) posits that the PRC Constitution applies to the SARs exclusively through the Basic Law.[50] This second theory essentially echoes the views of many Hong Kong legal scholars[51] who argue that the PRC Constitution is not directly applicable in the SAR as this would compromise the "high degree of autonomy"[52] constitutionally vested.

46 Willa Wu and Lilian Cheng, 'Hong Kong to Set up "High-Level Unit to Promote Patriotic Education" in Response to New National Law Passed on Tuesday' *SCMP* (24 October 2023) <www.scmp.com/news/hong-kong/politics/article/3239049/hong-kong-set-high-level-unit-promote-patriotic-education-response-new-national-law-passed-tuesday> last accessed 1 January 2026.

47 'Jiangxi Province, the MASAR Government, and the Macau Liaison Office Sign Tripartite Cooperation Framework Agreement 江西省与澳门特别行政区政府、澳门中联办签署三方合作框架协议' *People's Daily Online* (人民网) (19 March 2023) <https://news.cctv.com/2023/03/19/ARTIY899l89tPlT8r6aMqxdD230319.shtml> last accessed 1 January 2026.

48 For a detailed introduction on the two schools of thought, see Xudong Cao (曹旭东)，'Application of the Constitution in the Hong Kong Special Administrative Region: Theoretical Review and Practical Reflection 宪法在香港特别行政区的适用:理论回顾与实践反思' (2018) 1 *Political Science and Law* (政治与法律) 79–89.

49 Weiyun Xiao (肖蔚雲), *One Country Two Systems and the Hong Kong Basic Law System* (一國兩制與香港基本法制度) (Beijing University Press 1990) 94; Shuwen Wang (王叔文) (ed), *Introduction to the Hong Kong Special Administrative Region Basic Law* (香港特別行政區基本法導論) (Chinese Communist Party Central Party School Press 1997) 87–91.

50 Huanchun Ding (丁焕春), 'On the Legal Effect of the PRC Constitution on the Hong Kong Special Administrative Region 论我国宪法对香港特别行政区的法律效力' (1991) 3 *Law Review* (法学评论) 8–13; Chongde Xu (许崇德), *Hong Kong and Macau Basic Law Textbook* (港澳基本法教程) (China Renmin University Press 1994) 263.

51 Yash Ghai, *Hong Kong's New Constitutional Order: The Resumption of Chinese Sovereignty and the Basic Law* (Hong Kong University Press 1999) 218–219; Hualing Fu, 'Supremacy of a Different Kind: The Constitution, the NPC, and the Hong Kong SAR' in Johannes Chan et al. (eds), *Hong Kong's Constitutional Debate: Conflict Over Interpretation* (Hong Kong University Press 2000) 97–111.

52 Article 2 of the HKBL; Article 2 of the MABL.

According to the second theory, the Basic Law, enacted pursuant to Article 31 of the PRC Constitution, was designed to serve as a legal jurisdictional firewall to separate the SAR legal system from the PRC Constitution and other national laws.[53]

At their founding, and in the earlier years of the SARs, the "application through the Basic Law" theory was ostensibly the dominant operative theory. On 4 April 1990, the day on which the Hong Kong Basic Law (HKBL) was promulgated, the NPC issued a Decision to proclaim that: "The Basic Law is constitutional …[The] systems, policies and laws to be instituted after the establishment of the HKSAR shall be based on the Basic Law".[54] This Decision implicitly recognised the HKBL as the sole supreme legal authority within the HKSAR. In 1993, the NPC issued a similar Decision regarding the Macau Basic Law (MABL).[55] Even when the Provisional Legislative Council was established for Hong Kong in 1996 to reverse Governor Chris Patten's electoral reforms – as we discussed in Chapter 2 – the PRC Constitution was not invoked.[56] Up till 2014, official documents issued by Beijing officials – reports made by the General Secretary of the CCP to the National Congress of the CCP and the State Council's reports to the NPC – all stated that the Central Government would "act in strict accordance with the Basic Law"[57] when managing Hong Kong and Macau affairs, with no mention made of the PRC Constitution, thereby signalling that the respective Basic Laws would serve as the only supreme legal authority operating in the SARs. In essence, it was widely accepted hitherto in both Mainland China and the SARs that the PRC Constitution would apply in both cities through their respective Basic Laws, and it was unnecessary and undesirable to invoke specific provisions of the PRC Constitution as an additional source of legal authority.

However, in the aftermath of Hong Kong's OCM in 2014 and the accompanying rise of pro-Hong Kong independence activism, there was a dramatic shift in Mainland academic constitutional discourse on "One Country, Two Systems". The "application through the Basic Law" theory was largely jettisoned as Mainland

53 Hualing Fu, 'Supremacy of a Different Kind: The Constitution, the NPC, and the Hong Kong SAR' in Johannes Chan et al. (eds), *Hong Kong's Constitutional Debate: Conflict Over Interpretation* (Hong Kong University Press 2000) 97–111.

54 Decision of the National People's Congress on the Basic Law of the Hong Kong Special Administrative Region of the People's Republic of China (Adopted at the Third Session of the Seventh National People's Congress on 4 April 1990).

55 Decision of the National People's Congress on the Basic Law of the Macau Special Administrative Region of the People's Republic of China (Adopted at the First Session of the Eighth National People's Congress on 31 March 1993).

56 Qichen Qian (錢其琛), 'Working Report of the NPC Preparatory Committee for the HKSAR (10 Mar 1997) (全國人民代表大會香港特別行政區籌備委員會工作報告)' in Qiushi Yuan (袁求實) (ed), *Compilation of Important Documents During the Hong Kong Transition Period* (香港過渡時期重要文件彙編) (Joint Publishing 1997) 129, 133.

57 Bruce Lui, 'Constitution applies to Hong Kong automatically? Let Official Documents Say 憲法自動適用香港？讓官方報告來踢爆' *Ming Pao* (明報) (18 July 2018) A27.

Chinese and pro-Beijing scholars[58] started advocating for the "respect" (尊重) of the PRC Constitution in the SARs.[59] While the PRC Constitution may not directly apply in the SARs, the SARs should recognise its validity.[60] The shift in the academic winds largely reflected the change in the official constitutional narrative. In 2015, the State Council for the first time added the PRC Constitution as an explicit source of legal power in the management of the cities' affairs, whereby it was stressed that the Central Government would "act in strict accordance with the Constitution and the Basic Law".[61] This phrase has become a constant official refrain since 2015.[62]

This official reference to the PRC Constitution was not mere rhetorical flourish. In the aftermath of Hong Kong's 2019 street protests against the extradition bill, Beijing drafted a bespoke National Security Law for Hong Kong (2020 HKNSL) and foisted it on the city in 2020. While Hong Kong's Basic Law expressly stated that national security legislation was for the SAR government to enact "on its own"[63], Beijing decided to do so on Hong Kong's behalf. In the NPC's Decision in 2020[64] that authorised the imposition of this law in Hong Kong, the Central Government directly referenced two provisions of the PRC Constitution – Articles

58 Xudong Cao (曹旭东), 'Application of the Constitution in the Hong Kong Special Administrative Region: Theoretical Review and Practical Reflection 宪法在香港特别行政区的适用:理论回顾与实践反思' (2018) 1 *Political Science and Law* (政治与法律) 79, 83.

59 Dayuan Han (韩大元), 'On the Role of the Constitution in the Drafting Process of the Hong Kong Basic Law 论《宪法》在《香港特别行政区基本法》制定过程中的作用' (2017) 5 *Modern Law Science* (现代法学) 3–10; Pingxue Zou (邹平学), 'An Analysis of Article 31 of the 1982 Constitution and the Application of the Current Constitution in the SARs (1982年《宪法》第31条辩析——兼论现行《宪法》在特别行政区的适用)' (2013) 1 *Studies on Hong Kong and Macau* (当代港澳研究) 78–96.

60 Mei-fun Leung (梁美芬), 'Issues Regarding the Application of Chinese Constitution in Hong Kong (中國憲法在香港適用問題)' *Wen Wei Po* (文匯報) (2 February 2005) A18.

61 'Report on the Work of the Government' (delivered at the Third Session of the 12th National People's Congress on 5 March 2015) <http://english.www.gov.cn/archive/publications/2015/03/05/content_281475066179954.htm> last accessed 1 January 2026.

62 For instance, 'Xi Jinping's Speech at Meeting Marking Hong Kong's 20th Return Anniversary and Inaugural Ceremony of 5th-Term HKSAR Government' (1 July 2017) <www.xinhuanet.com/english/2017-07/01/c_136409940.htm> last accessed 1 January 2026; Xi Jinping's Report to the 20th National Congress of the Communist Party of China (16 October 2022) <www.idcpc.org.cn/english2023/tjzl/cpcjj/20thPartyCongrssReport/> last accessed 1 January 2026. Between 2015 and 2019, the State Council's annual Report on the Work of the Government all adopted the term 'acting in strict accordance with the Constitution and the Basic Law'. After the passage of the 2020 HKNSL, and since 2023, these Reports use the phrase 'governing Hong Kong and Macau in accordance with the law' (依法治港治澳), as an unspoken but collective reference to the PRC Constitution, the Basic Law, and the 2020 HKNSL.

63 Article 23 of the HKBL.

64 The full name of the decision is the 'Decision of the National People's Congress on Establishing and Improving the Legal System and Enforcement Mechanisms for the Hong Kong Special Administrative Region to Safeguard National Security' (Adopted at the Third Session of the 13th National People's Congress on 28 May 2020).

31[65] and 62[66] – as legal justification, and the Basic Law was merely mentioned without referencing any specific provisions. Notably, Article 31 of the PRC Constitution was previously viewed by legal experts as a firewall that separates the SAR legal systems from Mainland China, but it has now been reconstrued to justify legal intervention by the Central Government.[67] Five months after the 2020 HKNSL was foisted on Hong Kong, the NPCSC issued a Decision[68] that expelled any Hong Kong legislator who "supports 'Hong Kong independence', refuses to recognise the People's Republic of China's sovereignty over Hong Kong", or "carries out other activities endangering national security". Once again, the Central Authorities rested their Decision on specific provisions of the PRC Constitution – Article 52 (Citizen's Obligation to Safeguard National Unity); Article 54 (Citizen's Obligation to Safeguard National Security); and even Article 67(1), which empowers the NPCSC to supervise the implementation of the PRC Constitution. Notably, this was the first occasion after the establishment of the HKSAR where a specific PRC constitutional provision was invoked by the NPCSC on a matter specific to Hong Kong. Clearly, in the post- 2020 HKNSL era, the PRC Constitution no longer operates behind-the-scenes and it is now front and centre of the constitutional and legal discourse in the HKSAR.

In contrast, the Macau Special Administrative Region (MASAR) has always been more affirming of the transcendent role that the PRC Constitution plays in the city. Compared to Hong Kong, the Macau government since the establishment of the MASAR has been more proactive in "educating" its youth and civil servants about the PRC Constitution and national institutions.[69] As early as 2007, the

65 Article 31 of the PRC Constitution stipulates that: 'The state may establish special administrative regions when necessary. The systems to be instituted in special administrative regions shall be prescribed by law enacted by the National People's Congress in light of the specific conditions.'

66 Three subsections of Article 62 of the PRC Constitution were invoked in the NPC Decision of 2020. Article 62 of the PRC Constitution stipulates that the National People's Congress shall exercise the following functions and powers: (2) to supervise the enforcement of the Constitution; (14) to decide on the establishment of SARs and the systems to be instituted there; (16) to exercise such other functions and powers as the highest organ of state power should exercise.

67 For a detailed introduction on the constitutional and legal basis for the 2020 HKNSL, see Han Zhu, 'The Hong Kong National Security Law: The Shifted Grundnorm of Hong Kong's Legal Order and Its Implications' in Hualing Fu and Michael Hor (eds), *The National Security Law of Hong Kong: Restoration and Transformation* (Hong Kong University Press 2022) 49–66.

68 Decision of the Standing Committee of the National People's Congress on Issues Relating to the Qualification of the Members of the Legislative Council of the Hong Kong Special Administrative Region (Adopted at the 23rd Session of the Standing Committee of the 13th National People's Congress on 11 November 2020).

69 Jianzong He (何建宗), 'A Comparative Study on the Promotion of the Constitution and Basic Law among Public Servants and Youths in the Hong Kong and Macau SARs (對公職人員和青少年推廣憲法與基本法港澳特區的比較研究)' (2019) <https://octsyouth.hk/wp-content/uploads/promote-the-Constitution-and-the-Basic-Law-summary.pdf> last accessed 1 January 2026.

Macau Court of Final Appeal (MACFA) even referenced the PRC Constitution and Mainland legal norms when interpreting the MABL.[70]

Since 2020, there has been a noticeable increase in the invocation of the PRC Constitution by both Hong Kong and Macau lawmakers and senior government officials.[71] For instance, both local governments wrote into the respective national security laws[72] the citizens' constitutional obligations to safeguard national security under the PRC Constitution.[73] Since 2022, Hong Kong civil servants are required to take courses on the Chinese Constitution to pass probation;[74] mid to senior-level public servants are also provided with constitutional and national education by Mainland academic institutions.[75] Similar measures have been introduced in Macau since 2021.[76] Specifically for Hong Kong, Constitution Day is now a big affair in Hong Kong. Initially organised as an annual small-scale seminar by civic organisations, the event is now a gala event co-hosted by the Hong Kong government and the Liaison Office, with approximately 1000 participants in 2024,

70 Case 28/2006, 100–107 (18 July 2007). The MACFA relied on Mainland Chinese law to determine that Article 50(5) of the MABL authorises the Chief Executive to promulgate independent administrative regulations without the need for any specific authorisation from the Legislative Assembly. See Chapter 3 of this book.

71 Both the Chief Executives and senior officials in Hong Kong and Macau have explicitly acknowledged that the PRC Constitution and the Basic Law jointly formed the constitutional foundation of the respective SARs. See 'Ho Iat-Seng: Promoting a New Phase of "One Country, Two Systems" in Macau (賀一誠：推動澳門「一國兩制」開創新局面)' *Ta Kung Pao* (大公報) (2 April 2023) <www.tkww.hk/epaper/view/newsDetail/1642234759893618688.html> last accessed 1 January 2026; 'Chief Executive Attends and Delivers Speech at the 2024 "National Constitution Day" Seminar (行政長官出席二O二四年「國家憲法日」座談會致辭)' <www.info.gov.hk/gia/general/202412/04/P2024120400310p.htm> last accessed 1 January 2026.

72 Article 6(1) of the 2023 Macau National Security Law (2023 MANSL) and Preamble of the Safeguarding National Security Ordinance (hereinafter 2024 HKNSL).

73 See Articles 52, 54, and 55 of the PRC Constitution.

74 Tony Cheung, 'Hong Kong Civil Servants Must Take Courses on Chinese Constitution, National Security Law to Pass Work Probation, Gain Promotion' *SCMP* (9 February 2022) <www.scmp.com/news/hong-kong/politics/article/3166406/hong-kong-civil-servants-must-take-courses-chinese> last accessed 1 January 2026.

75 Irene Chan, 'Hong Kong Officials, Civil Servants Study Doctrine of Chinese Leader Xi Jinping and Communist Party Theories' *HKFP* (22 November 2023) <https://hongkongfp.com/2023/11/22/hong-kong-officials-civil-servants-study-doctrine-of-chinese-leader-xi-jinping-and-communist-party-theories/> last accessed 1 January 2026.

76 See 'Macau to Organise Civil Servant Training on the Constitution and Basic Law Next Year 澳门明年将组织公务人员参加宪法和基本法等培训' *People's Daily Overseas Edition* (25 November 2021) <https://paper.people.com.cn/rmrbhwb/html/2021-11/25/content_25890563.htm> last accessed 1 January 2026; also see 'Macau Civil Servant Federation Holds Seminar to Deepen Public Understanding of the Constitution and the Basic Law 團體辦座談會加深公務員憲法基本法認識' *Macau Broadcasting Television Limited* (2 July 2024) <www.tdm.com.mo/zh-hant/news-detail/981477> last accessed 1 January 2026.

with Central Government officials, the Chief Executive, lawmakers, and even the Chief Justice in attendance.[77]

Constitutional Interface between the Central Government and the SARs

Article 31 of the PRC Constitution empowers the NPC to enact laws to prescribe the systems instituted in the SARs. While the NPC is the country's "highest organ of state power",[78] it only convenes once a year.[79] Therefore, in practice, legislative power is primarily delegated to the Standing Committee of the NPC to exercise on the NPC's behalf.[80] This explains why since the establishment of the HKSAR and the MASAR, the NPC has only legislated twice on SAR affairs – notably both times over Hong Kong and none vis-à-vis Macau. As discussed above, the NPC issued a Decision in 2020 to empower the NPCSC to pass a National Security Law for Hong Kong.[81] And in 2021, the NPC authorised the NPCSC to amend the HKBL and overhaul the electoral system so that only "patriots" can govern the city.[82]

In essence, Beijing legislatively intervenes in SAR affairs primarily through the NPCSC. The NPCSC can interpret the Basic Laws,[83] propose bills to amend the Basic Laws,[84] and add/delete PRC National Laws to/from the Basic Laws.[85] Aside from these constitutional powers expressly conferred by their respective Basic Laws, the NPCSC has issued Decisions on SAR affairs, but it is notable that both Basic Laws make no mention of the legal validity of such Decisions. All these legal instruments will be explored in turn.

Application of National Laws in the SARs

PRC National Laws shall not be applied in the SARs unless they are listed in Annex III of their respective Basic Laws.[86] The NPCSC may add National Laws to those listed

77 'Hong Kong Holds Seminar on Constitution Day to Advance Law-Based Governance' *Xinhua News* (5 December 2024) <https://english.news.cn/20241205/ec83a1088cef4e6bb0e28c6893bc1518/c.html> last accessed 1 January 2026.

78 Article 57 of the PRC Constitution.

79 Article 61 of the PRC Constitution.

80 Article 67(2) of the PRC Constitution.

81 Decision of the National People's Congress On Establishing and Improving the Legal System and Enforcement Mechanisms for the Hong Kong Special Administrative Region to Safeguard National Security (Adopted at the Third Session of the 13th National People's Congress on 28 May 2020).

82 Decision of the National People's Congress On Improving the Electoral System of the Hong Kong Special Administrative Region (Adopted at the Fourth Session of the 13th National People's Congress on 11 March 2021).

83 Article 158 of the HKBL, Article 143 of the MABL.

84 Article 159 of the HKBL, Article 144 of the MABL.

85 Article 18 of the HKBL, Article 18 of the MABL.

86 Article 18 of the HKBL, Article 18 of the MABL. See Appendix 1 of this chapter for the List of National Laws applicable.

in Annex III, but they must be "confined to those relating to defence and foreign affairs as well as other matters outside the limits of the autonomy of the Region".[87]

To date, the NPC/NPCSC has listed 14[88] National Laws in Annex III of HKBL and 12[89] in MABL. Most of these National Laws listed under Annex III are uncontroversial, e.g. Resolution on the Capital, Calendar, National Anthem and National Flag of the People's Republic of China; Resolution on the National Day of the People's Republic of China; Nationality Law of the People's Republic of China, etc.

All the National Laws applicable in Macau equally apply in Hong Kong. But Hong Kong has two additional National Laws. The first is the "Declaration of the Government of the PRC on the Territorial Sea", which is only listed in the HKBL. This is because the HKSAR jurisdiction includes territorial seas,[90]while the MASAR territory at the time of its establishment did not cover any territorial waters.[91]

The second and hitherto most troubling National Law is the 2020 HKNSL that the NPCSC foisted on Hong Kong in 2020. While the 2020 HKNSL was passed by a national legislative organ, one of us has raised concerns about whether this legislation can be considered a National Law under Article 18.[92] Some scholars like Albert Chen take the view that "National Laws" under Article 18 refers to any "law made by the NPC or NPCSC (as legislative organs of the central authorities), which has the force of law in the PRC".[93] But one must note that in the Chinese text of Article 18 HKBL, the Chinese term used for "National Laws" is "全國性法律", which refers to laws that have nation-wide applications or effects. Notably, the 2020 HKNSL only applies to Hong Kong and not to Mainland China. And when there is a discrepancy between the Chinese text of the Basic Law and its English

87 The Central People's Government may also apply specific National Laws to the Region when that Region is in "a state of emergency", but this extraordinary emergency power has never been invoked in either city. See Article 18(4) of the HKBL and Article 18(4) of the MABL.

88 See Appendix 1 of this chapter.

89 See Appendix 1 of this chapter.

90 NPC Decision on the Establishment of the Hong Kong Special Administrative Region (全國人民代表大會關於設立香港特別行政區的決定) (4 April 1990) specifies that "The area of the Hong Kong Special Administrative Region covers the Hong Kong Island, the Kowloon Peninsula, and the islands and adjacent waters under its jurisdiction 香港特別行政區的區域包括香港島、九龍半島，以及所轄的島嶼和附近海域".

91 The Preamble of the Macau Basic Law refers to Macau as "including the Macau Peninsula, Taipa Island and Coloane Island". In 2015, the PRC State Council issued Order No.665, which adjusted Macau's territorial boundaries by adding an 85-square-kilometre sea area to its jurisdiction. See 中華人民共和國國務院令第665號 (Order No.665 of the State Council of the People's Republic of China) (20 December 2015).

92 Po Jen Yap, 'Judging Hong Kong's National Security Law' in Hualing Fu and Michael Hor (eds), *The National Security Law of Hong Kong: Restoration and Transformation* (Hong Kong University Press 2022) 149, 153–155.

93 Albert Chen, 'Constitutional Controversies in the Aftermath of the Anti-Extradition Movement of 2019' (2020) 50 *Hong Kong Law Journal* 609, 626. See also Shuwen Wang (王叔文), 'The Basic Law Is a National Law That Embodies the "One Country, Two Systems" Policy 基本法是体现"一国两制"方针的全国性法律' (1990) 2 *Chinese Journal of Law* (法学研究) 1–10.

translation, the Chinese version prevails.[94] Pre-empting this objection, Albert Chen points to the Garrison Law of the HKSAR, another Annex III law that only applies to Hong Kong.[95] But as Johannes Chan rightly points out, the Garrison Law does not concern or affect the rights of Hong Kong people in any tangible way[96] as it only regulates members of the Hong Kong Garrison who are "not… treated as ordinarily resident in Hong Kong".[97] On the other hand, the 2020 HKNSL subjects everyone in Hong Kong to penal liability. A broad reading of "National Law" under Article 18 HKBL would authorise the Central Authorities to enact any law specifically tailored for the SAR that they desire, and this would undercut Article 18's safeguard as a constitutional firewall that insulates Hong Kong residents from the application of PRC laws.[98]

Another controversy that erupted related to the HKSAR government's decision to implement Mainland Customs, Immigration, and Quarantine (CIQ) procedures at a high-speed train terminus in Hong Kong.[99] Pursuant to a Co-operation Arrangement signed between the People's Government of Guangdong Province and the HKSAR Government in November 2017,[100] a "Mainland Port Area" (MPA) was carved out in the West Kowloon Station in Hong Kong for Mainland immigration personnel to conduct CIQ procedures therein so that travellers can enjoy one-stop seamless travel into Mainland China. Notably, this MPA at

94 Decision of the Standing Committee of the National People's Congress on the English Text of the Basic Law of the Hong Kong Special Administrative Region of the People's Republic of China (Adopted on 28 June 1990).

95 Albert Chen, 'Constitutional Controversies in the Aftermath of the Anti-Extradition Movement of 2019' (2020) 50 *Hong Kong Law Journal* 609, 626.

96 Johannes Chan, 'Five Reasons to Question the Legality of a National Security Law for Hong Kong' *Verfassungsblog* (1 June 2020) <https://verfassungsblog.de/five-reasons-to-question-the-legality-of-a-national-security-law-for-hong-kong/> last accessed 1 January 2026.

97 Section 2(4)(a)(viii) of the Immigration Ordinance.

98 Carole Petersen, 'The Disappearing Firewall: International Consequences of Beijing's Decision to Impose a National Security Law and Operate National Security Institutions in Hong Kong' (2020) 50 *Hong Kong Law Journal* 633.

99 *See* Hong Kong Bar Association, 'Statement of the Hong Kong Bar Association on the Decision of the NPCSC of 27 December 2017 on the Co-operation Agreement Between the Mainland and the HKSAR on the Establishment of the Port at the West Kowloon Station of the Guangzhou-Shenzhen-Hong Kong Express Rail Link for Implementing Co-location Arrangement' (28 December 2017) <chrome-extension://efaidnbmnnnibpcajpcglclefindmkaj/https://www.hkba.org/uploads/20171228%20-%20Bar%20Co-Location%20Arrangement%20Statement%20(English)%20FINAL_0.pdf > last accessed 1 January 2026; Albert Chen, 'A Legal Analysis of the NPCSC Decision on Co-location (Part I)' *Ming Pao* (8 January 2018) A18; Albert Chen, 'A Legal Analysis of the NPCSC Decision on Co-location (Part II)', *Ming Pao* (9 January 2018) A27; Joyce Huang, 'Critics: Hong Kong Sets Bad Precedent with Mainland Police in Rail Station' *VOA* (28 July 2017) <www.voanews.com/a/hong-kong-mainland-police-high-speed-rail/3962653.html> last accessed 1 January 2026.

100 Co-operation Arrangement between the Mainland and the Hong Kong Special Administrative Region on the Establishment of the Port at the West Kowloon Station of the Guangzhou-Shenzhen-Hong Kong Express Rail Link for Implementing Co-location Arrangement (English Translation)

the train station would be subject to the jurisdiction and the laws of Mainland China.[101] This Co-location Arrangement was also approved by an NPCSC Decision.[102] Critics of this Co-location Arrangement argued that the application of Mainland immigration law in the MPA violated Article 18 of the HKBL.[103] But as one of us has argued, Article 18 HKBL was not violated herein because it was simply not engaged.[104] Under Co-location, the HKSAR Government had relinquished legal control of the land comprising the MPA, such that it was deemed part of the Mainland, and not in Hong Kong. Consequently, insofar as Article 18 HKBL provides that "[n]ational laws shall not be applied in the Hong Kong Special Administrative Region", this no longer applies to the MPA as for all practical purposes the land comprising the MPA would no longer be "in the [HKSAR]". The relinquishment of legal control over land in Hong Kong is also not unprecedented as the HKSAR Government – with consent from the Central People's Government – has also regularly relinquished legal control over land when foreign consulates are established in Hong Kong.[105]

More troubling, however, is how PRC National Laws have permeated local legislation in Hong Kong and Macau, especially those relating to national security.

(CB(4)441/17-18(04)) (18 November 2017) <www.legco.gov.hk/yr17-18/english/panels/tp/papers/tpcb4-441-4-e.pdf> last accessed 1 January 2026.

101 Co-operation Arrangement between the Mainland and the Hong Kong Special Administrative Region on the Establishment of the Port at the West Kowloon Station of the Guangzhou-Shenzhen-Hong Kong Express Rail Link for Implementing Co-location Arrangement (English Translation) (CB(4)441/17-18(04)) (18 November 2017), Art 1 provides:

> The West Kowloon Station Port comprises the Hong Kong Port Area and the Mainland Port Area. The Hong Kong Port Area is to be established by the HKSAR and be subject to its jurisdiction in accordance with the laws of the HKSAR and managed as a cross-boundary restricted area. The Mainland Port Area is to be established by the Mainland and be subject to its jurisdiction in accordance with this Co-operation Arrangement and the laws of the Mainland, and the port administration system is to be implemented thereat.

102 Decision of the Standing Committee of the National People's Congress on Approving the Co-operation Arrangement Between the Mainland and the Hong Kong Special Administrative Region on the Establishment of the Port at the West Kowloon Station of the Guangzhou-Shenzhen-Hong Kong Express Rail Link for Implementing Co-location Arrangement (English Translation) (27 December 2017) <www.elegislation.gov.hk/hk/a214> last accessed 1 January 2026.

103 E.g. Hong Kong Bar Association, 'Statement of the Hong Kong Bar Association on the Decision of the NPCSC of 27 December 2017 on the Co-operation Agreement Between the Mainland and the HKSAR on the Establishment of the Port at the West Kowloon Station of the Guangzhou-Shenzhen-Hong Kong Express Rail Link for Implementing Co-location Arrangement' (28 December 2017) < chrome-extension://efaidnbmnnnibpcajpcglclefindmkaj/https://www.hkba.org/uploads/20171228%20-%20Bar%20Co-Location%20Arrangement%20Statement%20(English)%20FINAL_0.pdf > last accessed 1 January 2026, paras 6, 9.

104 Po Jen Yap and Zixin Jiang, 'Co-location is Constitutional' (2018) 48 *Hong Kong Law Journal* 37–50.

105 For some examples, see Arts 3(1) and 3(3) of the Agreement Between the Government of the United Kingdom of Great Britain and Northern Ireland And the Government of the People's Republic of China on the Establishment of a British Consulate-General at Shanghai and a Chinese

In Macau's 2023 National Security Law, the city's definition of "national security"[106] now mirrors the broad definition of "national security" under the PRC National Security Law,[107] which includes nebulous and expansive concepts such as "welfare of the people [and] sustainable economic and social development" as facets of national security. Notably, Hong Kong's 2024 National Security Law also copied this PRC definition.[108] Furthermore, in the 2024 HKNSL, the local definition of state secrets not only covers matters of foreign policy and defence, but also includes any "secret concerning the economic or social development of China or the HKSAR"[109] and any "secret concerning the technological development or scientific technology of China or the HKSAR",[110] thereby aligning the city with the country's broad definition of state secrets.[111] Similarly, in the 2023 Macau State Secrets Protection Law (保守國家秘密法),[112] the city too aligned its definition of state secrets with the PRC Law on Guarding State Secrets.[113]

NPCSC Interpretations

The NPCSC is expressly constitutionally empowered to interpret the Basic Laws of Hong Kong[114] and Macau.[115] And it has exercised this power of interpretation five times in Hong Kong and only once in Macau.

The NPCSC's first Hong Kong Interpretation[116] was issued in 1999 to *overrule* a pair of HKCFA's decisions – both judgments were handed down on the same

Consulate-General at Manchester, as incorporated into the Agreement Constituted by Exchange of Notes Between the Government of the People's Republic of China And the Government of the United Kingdom of Great Britain and Northern Ireland Concerning the Establishment of a British Consulate-General in the Hong Kong Special Administrative Region of the People's Republic of China (signed 26 September 1996, entered into force 1 July 1997); Art 3(a) of the Agreement Between the Government of the People's Republic of China And the Government of the United States of America Regarding the Maintenance of the United States Consulate General in the Hong Kong Special Administrative Region (signed 25 March 1997, entered into force 1 July 1997); Arts 6(1) and 6(5) of the Agreement on Consular Relations Between the People's Republic of China And Japan (signed 24 October 2008, entered into force 16 February 2010).

106 Article 2(1) of the 2023 MANSL.

107 Article 2 of the PRC National Security Law (2015).

108 Section 4 of the 2024 HKNSL.

109 Section 29 of the 2024 HKNSL.

110 Section 29 of the 2024 HKNSL.

111 PRC Law on Guarding State Secrets, art 13.

112 Macau State Secrets Protection Law, arts 2(1)(1) and 10.

113 PRC Law on Guarding State Secrets, arts 2 and 13. See also Chapter 4 for a comparative analysis of state secrets in Hong Kong and Macau.

114 HKBL, Article 158.

115 MABL, Article 143.

116 The Interpretation by the Standing Committee of the National People's Congress Regarding Paragraph 4 in Article 22 and Category (3) of Paragraph 2 in Article 24 of the Basic Law of the Hong Kong Special Administrative Region of the People's Republic of China (Adopted at the Tenth Meeting of the Standing Committee of the Ninth National People's Congress on 26 June 1999).

day – which had conferred the constitutional right of abode in Hong Kong on all Mainland-born children with at least one parent who was a Hong Kong Permanent Resident,[117] regardless of whether the child was born before or after the parent obtained Hong Kong permanent residency.[118] This controversial saga was discussed in Chapter 3. Suffice to say here, the first NPCSC Interpretation on Hong Kong centred on the interpretation of Article 22(4)[119] – approval of entry for persons from Mainland China into Hong Kong – and Article 24(2)(3)[120] – right of abode of Chinese nationals born outside Hong Kong – of the HKBL. The NPCSC ruled herein that Mainland-born children of Hong Kong Permanent Residents must "hold valid documents issued by the relevant authorities"[121] before they can enter Hong Kong and for the child to be eligible for the right of abode by descent, the parent must be a Hong Kong Permanent Resident "at the time of [the child's] birth".[122]

The HKCFA has accepted that the NPCSC's power of interpreting the HKBL is "general and unqualified"[123] and these Interpretations are "binding on the courts of the HKSAR".[124] Furthermore, these Interpretations apply retrospectively from the date the Basic Law came into effect on 1 July 1997,[125] but these Interpretations would not affect judgments previously rendered by the courts.[126] The HKCFA has

117 *Ng Ka Ling v Director of Immigration* (1999) 2 HKCFAR 4.

118 *Chan Kam Nga v Director of Immigration* (1999) 2 HKCFAR 82.

119 Article 22(4) of the HKBL reads:

> For entry into the Hong Kong Special Administrative Region, people from other parts of China must apply for approval. Among them, the number of persons who enter the Region for the purpose of settlement shall be determined by the competent authorities of the Central People's Government after consulting the government of the Region.

120 Article 24(2) of the HKBL reads:

> The permanent residents of the Hong Kong Special Administrative Region shall be: (1) Chinese citizens born in Hong Kong before or after the establishment of the Hong Kong Special Administrative Region; (2) Chinese citizens who have ordinarily resided in Hong Kong for a continuous period of not less than seven years before or after the establishment of the Hong Kong Special Administrative Region; (3) Persons of Chinese nationality born outside Hong Kong of those residents listed in categories (1) and (2).

121 The Interpretation by the Standing Committee of the National People's Congress Regarding Paragraph 4 in Article 22 and Category (3) of Paragraph 2 in Article 24 of the Basic Law of the Hong Kong Special Administrative Region of the People's Republic of China (Adopted at the Tenth Meeting of the Standing Committee of the Ninth National People's Congress on 26 June 1999).

122 The Interpretation by the Standing Committee of the National People's Congress Regarding Paragraph 4 in Article 22 and Category (3) of Paragraph 2 in Article 24 of the Basic Law of the Hong Kong Special Administrative Region of the People's Republic of China (Adopted at the Tenth Meeting of the Standing Committee of the Ninth National People's Congress on 26 June 1999).

123 *Lau Kong Yung v Director of Immigration* (1999) 2 HKCFAR 323.

124 *Lau Kong Yung v Director of Immigration* (1999) 2 HKCFAR 324.

125 *Lau Kong Yung v Director of Immigration* (1999) 2 HKCFAR 326. *Yau Wai Ching v Chief Executive of the HKSAR* (2017) 20 HKCFAR 390 at [35].

126 Article 158(3) of the HKBL.

further ruled that statements made in an NPCSC Interpretation that do *not* pertain to the specific Basic Law provisions subject to Interpretation would "not amount to a binding interpretation",[127] and the Hong Kong courts can choose *not* to follow these pronouncements.

In 2004, the NPCSC issued its Second Interpretation on Hong Kong – Interpretation of Article 7, Annex I of the HKBL (Method for selecting the Hong Kong Chief Executive) and Article III, Annex II of the HKBL (Method for forming the Hong Kong Legislative Council).[128] Specifically, the NPCSC ruled that prior to any constitutional bills undertaken within the HKSAR to amend its electoral rules, the Chief Executive must first "make a report"[129] to the NPCSC, and it was for the NPCSC to "make a determination"[130] on whether "there is a need"[131] for such an amendment to proceed. Basically, the NPCSC – under the guise of constitutional interpretation – inserted new hurdles for the HKSAR to surmount before constitutional amendments on elections could be undertaken. As Johannes Chan pointed out, the Central Authorities were not content to merely have a veto power over any constitutional change in Hong Kong; they wanted full control over whether any change could be even "proposed in the first place".[132] In 2011, the NPCSC issued its first and thus far only Interpretation of the MABL since the handover, and imposed the same two additional hurdles for amending the MABL vis-à-vis electoral rules.[133]

127 *Director of Immigration v Chong Fung Yuen* (2001) 4 HKCFAR 223.

128 The Interpretation by the Standing Committee of the National People's Congress Regarding Annex I (7) and Annex II (III) to the Basic Law of the Hong Kong Special Administrative Region of the People's Republic of China (Adopted at the Eighth Meeting of the Standing Committee of the Tenth National People's Congress on 6 April 2004).

129 The Interpretation by the Standing Committee of the National People's Congress Regarding Annex I (7) and Annex II (III) to the Basic Law of the Hong Kong Special Administrative Region of the People's Republic of China (Adopted at the Eighth Meeting of the Standing Committee of the Tenth National People's Congress on 6 April 2004), para 3.

130 The Interpretation by the Standing Committee of the National People's Congress Regarding Annex I (7) and Annex II (III) to the Basic Law of the Hong Kong Special Administrative Region of the People's Republic of China (Adopted at the Eighth Meeting of the Standing Committee of the Tenth National People's Congress on 6 April 2004), para 3.

131 The Interpretation by the Standing Committee of the National People's Congress Regarding Annex I (7) and Annex II (III) to the Basic Law of the Hong Kong Special Administrative Region of the People's Republic of China (Adopted at the Eighth Meeting of the Standing Committee of the Tenth National People's Congress on 6 April 2004), para 3.

132 Johannes Chan, 'Hong Kong's Constitutional Journey, 1997–2011' in Albert Chen (ed), *Constitutionalism in Asia in the Early Twenty-First Century* (Cambridge University Press 2014) 169, 177.

133 The Interpretation by the Standing Committee of the National People's Congress Regarding Annex I (7) and Annex II (III) to the Basic Law of the MASAR (Adopted at the 24th Meeting of the Standing Committee of the 11th National People's Congress on 31 December 2011).

The Third NPCSC Interpretation concerning Hong Kong was less controversial. In 2005, Chief Executive Tung Chee-hwa resigned mid-term and the NPCSC issued an Interpretation of Article 53(2) of the HKBL[134] regarding vacancy in the Chief Executive office and decided that his successor would only "serve the remainder of the previous Chief Executive['s term of office]".[135]

The Fourth NPCSC Interpretation on Hong Kong resulted from a judicial reference initiated by the HKCFA. Pursuant to Article 158(3) of the HKBL, the HKCFA was required to refer Basic Law provisions, which relate to affairs within the responsibility of the Central People's Government or the relationship between the Central Authorities and the HKSAR, to the NPCSC if the interpretation of these clauses would affect the judgments of the cases before the Court. In *Democratic Republic of the Congo v FG Hemisphere Associates LLC,*[136] the HKCFA had to determine the applicable law on state immunity in Hong Kong, which hinged on an interpretation of Article 13[137] HKBL (Central People's Government's responsibility over foreign affairs) and Article 19[138] (acts of state) HKBL. In this Interpretation,[139] the NPCSC decided that Hong Kong's law on state immunity was "an act of state involving foreign affairs"[140] and Hong Kong must "give effect to the rules or policies on state immunity as determined by the Central People's Government."[141] This Interpretation basically required Hong Kong to apply an "absolute" doctrine of state immunity applicable across the entire PRC and overruled the city's

134 Article 53(2) of the HKBL reads:

> In the event that the office of Chief Executive becomes vacant, a new Chief Executive shall be selected within six months in accordance with the provisions of Article 45 of this Law. During the period of vacancy, his or her duties shall be assumed according to the provisions of the preceding paragraph.

135 Interpretation by the Standing Committee of the National People's Congress Regarding the Second Paragraph in Article 53 of the Basic Law of the Hong Kong Special Administrative Region of the People's Republic of China (Adopted at the 15th Meeting of the Standing Committee of the Tenth National People's Congress on 27 April 2005).

136 (2011) 14 HKCFAR 95.

137 Article 13 of the HKBL reads: 'The Central People's Government shall be responsible for the foreign affairs relating to the Hong Kong Special Administrative Region…'.

138 Article 19(3) of the HKBL reads: "The courts of the Hong Kong Special Administrative Region shall have no jurisdiction over acts of state such as defence and foreign affairs…".

139 Interpretation by the Standing Committee of the National People's Congress Regarding the First Paragraph of Article 13 and Article 19 of the Basic Law of the Hong Kong Special Administrative Region of the People's Republic of China (Adopted at the 22nd Meeting of the Standing Committee of the 11th National People's Congress on 26 August 2011).

140 Interpretation by the Standing Committee of the National People's Congress Regarding the First Paragraph of Article 13 and Article 19 of the Basic Law of the Hong Kong Special Administrative Region of the People's Republic of China (Adopted at the 22nd Meeting of the Standing Committee of the 11th National People's Congress on 26 August 2011), Para 3.

141 Interpretation by the Standing Committee of the National People's Congress Regarding the First Paragraph of Article 13 and Article 19 of the Basic Law of the Hong Kong Special Administrative Region of the People's Republic of China (Adopted at the 22nd Meeting of the Standing Committee of the 11th National People's Congress on 26 August 2011), Para 4.

longstanding practice since its colonial days of applying a "restrictive" doctrine of state immunity, which had hitherto carved out an exception to state immunity for commercial transactions States undertook.

In 2016, the NPCSC handed down its Fifth and most controversial Interpretation to date in Hong Kong. It was handed down *sub judice* to pre-empt a potential adverse judicial ruling. As elaborated upon more fully in Chapter 3, a slew of young incoming Hong Kong lawmakers had intentionally denigrated China when taking their inaugural oaths-of-office in 2016. Their oaths were rejected by the President of the Hong Kong Legislative Council and the HKSAR government went to court to seek a judicial declaration that these errant lawmakers – by virtue of their conduct – were ipso facto disqualified from office. Days after judicial proceedings began but before the court handed down a ruling, the NPCSC unilaterally issued an Interpretation of Article 104 of the HKBL,[142] unequivocally ruling that any oath taker assuming public office who "intentionally reads out words which do not accord with the wording of the oath prescribed by law, or takes the oath in a manner which is not sincere or not solemn, shall be treated as declining to take the oath".[143] Such errant political office holders are not only "disqualified forthwith from assuming the public office"[144], "no arrangement shall be made for retaking the oath".[145]

While the NPCSC's First Hong Kong Interpretation (1999) overruled the HKCFA upon the formal request of the local government, and the NPCSC's Fourth Hong Kong Interpretation (2011) responded to a judicial reference from the HKCFA, the NPCSC's Fifth Interpretation (2016) posed the greatest challenge yet to the autonomy conferred on Hong Kong courts as it was a blatant *unilateral* intervention in *ongoing* judicial proceedings to pre-determine the legal outcome, thereby underscoring the

142 Article 104 of the HKBL reads:

> When assuming office, the Chief Executive, principal officials, members of the Executive Council and of the Legislative Council, judges of the courts at all levels and other members of the judiciary in the Hong Kong Special Administrative Region must, in accordance with law, swear to uphold the Basic Law of the Hong Kong Special Administrative Region of the People's Republic of China and swear allegiance to the Hong Kong Special Administrative Region of the People's Republic of China.

143 Interpretation of Article 104 of the Basic Law of the Hong Kong Special Administrative Region of the People's Republic of China by the Standing Committee of the National People's Congress (Adopted by the Standing Committee of the 12th National People's Congress at its 24th Session on 7 November 2016), Para 2(3).

144 Interpretation of Article 104 of the Basic Law of the Hong Kong Special Administrative Region of the People's Republic of China by the Standing Committee of the National People's Congress (Adopted by the Standing Committee of the 12th National People's Congress at its 24th Session on 7 November 2016), Para 2(3).

145 Interpretation of Article 104 of the Basic Law of the Hong Kong Special Administrative Region of the People's Republic of China by the Standing Committee of the National People's Congress (Adopted by the Standing Committee of the 12th National People's Congress at its 24th Session on 7 November 2016), Para 2(4).

comprehensive/ overall jurisdiction that the Central Authorities now assert over the city.

NPCSC Decisions

The NPCSC also issued "Decisions" on matters relating to Macau and Hong Kong. Interestingly, unlike Interpretations,[146] both the Basic Laws of Macau and Hong Kong are silent on the legal status of these Decisions operating in their territories. While such Decisions are provided for under the PRC Constitution and Mainland Chinese law,[147] both Basic Laws make no mention of their applicability in the SARs at all.

In fact, the number of such SAR-related Decisions issued by the NPCSC post-handover (8 in Macau and 16 in Hong Kong) far exceeds the number of Interpretations (one in Macau and five in Hong Kong) issued by this same legislative body.

First, NPCSC Decisions have been used to add National Laws to Annex III of both the HKBL[148] and MABL.[149] For the addition of National Laws, Article 18 of the two Basic Laws provide textual justification for such Decisions: The NPCSC is empowered to add to or delete from the list of laws in Annex III after consulting the respective SAR governments and the National Laws listed in Annex III shall be "confined to those relating to defence and foreign affairs as well as other matters outside the limits of the autonomy of the Region".[150] As discussed in Chapter 4, the only problematic National Law inserted this way is the 2020 HKNSL as it is highly questionable whether this law falls outside the limits of the SAR's autonomy since

146 HKBL, Article 158; MABL, Article 143.

147 Articles 62 and 67 of the PRC Constitution; Article 68 of the PRC Legislation Law (全国人民代表大会及其常务委员会作出有关法律问题的决定，适用本法的有关规定).

148 NPCSC Decision on Adding to and Deleting from the List of the National Laws in Annex III to the Basic Law of the HKSAR of the PRC (Law of the PRC on the National Flag; Regulations of the PRC Concerning Consular Privileges and Immunities; Law of the PRC on the National Emblem; Law of the PRC on the Territorial Sea and the Contiguous Zone; Law of the PRC on Garrisoning the Hong Kong Special Administrative Region) (1 July 1997); NPCSC Decision on Adding a Law to the List of the National Laws in Annex III to the Basic Law of the HKSAR of the PRC (Law on the Exclusive Economic Zone and Continental Shelf of the PRC) (4 November 1998); NPCSC Decision on Adding a Law to the List of the National Laws in Annex III to the Basic Law of the HKSAR of the PRC (Law of the PRC on Judicial Immunity from Compulsory Measures Concerning the Property of Foreign Central Banks) (27 October 2005); NPCSC Decision on Adding a Law to the List of the National Laws in Annex III to the Basic Law of the HKSAR of the PRC (Law of the PRC on the National Anthem) (4 November 2017); NPCSC Decision on Adding a Law to the List of the National Laws in Annex III to the Basic Law of the HKSAR of the PRC (Law of the PRC on Safeguarding National Security in the HKSAR) (30 June 2020). See Appendices 1 and 3 of this chapter.

149 NPCSC Decision on Adding a Law to the List of the National Laws in Annex III to the Basic Law of the MASAR of the PRC (20 December 1999); NPCSC Decision on Adding a Law to the List of the National Laws in Annex III to the Basic Law of the MASAR of the PRC (27 October 2005); NPCSC Decision on Adding a Law to the List of the National Laws in Annex III to the Basic Law of the MASAR of the PRC (4 November 2017).

150 HKBL, Article 18; MABL, Article 18.

Article 23 HKBL explicitly states that national security legislation was for the local government to pass "on its own".[151]

Second, NPCSC Decisions have been used to empower the SAR to *relinquish* legal control over its own land or *extend* legal control over Mainland territory. The NPCSC authorised the HKSAR to exercise jurisdiction over the Shenzhen Bay Port area in 2006.[152] Similarly, the MASAR was authorised by the NPCSC to exercise legal jurisdiction over a new campus for the University of Macao on neighbouring Hengqin Island (Guangdong Province)[153] in 2009, and to exercise legal jurisdiction over Macau's Port Zone at Hengqin in 2019.[154] For the *extension* of SAR legal control over Mainland land, this is uncontroversial. Notably, Article 20 of both Basic Laws explicitly state that the SARs may "enjoy other powers granted to it" by the NPCSC. But the *relinquishment* of legal control over Hong Kong land to Mainland immigration authorities has been controversial. As discussed above, a public ruckus ensued when the HKSAR government decided to implement Mainland Chinese CIQ procedures at a high-speed train terminus in Hong Kong.[155] The objective of creating an MPA in the West Kowloon Station of Hong Kong was to allow Mainland immigration personnel to conduct CIQ procedures therein so that travellers can enjoy one-stop seamless travel into Mainland China. The NPCSC approved this Arrangement in 2017,[156] noting that this Arrangement is consistent with Article 7 of the HKBL, which empowers the HKSAR government to lease land to individuals, legal persons or organisations for use and development. In a subsequent challenge to the legality of this Co-location Arrangement, the Hong Kong Court of Appeal ruled that NPCSC Decisions must "carry a highly persuasive

151 HKBL, Article 23. See Chapter 4 of this book.

152 NPCSC Decision on Empowering the HKSAR to Exercise Jurisdiction over the Shenzhen Bay Port Hong Kong Port Area (31 October 2006).

153 NPCSC Decision on Empowering the MASAR to Exercise Jurisdiction over the New Campus of the University of Macao on Hengqin Island (27 June 2009).

154 NPCSC Decision on Authorising the MASAR to Exercise Jurisdiction over Macau's Port Zone at Hengqin Port and Related Extended Areas (26 October 2019).

155 See Hong Kong Bar Association, 'Statement of the Hong Kong Bar Association on the Decision of the NPCSC of 27 December 2017 on the Co-operation Agreement Between the Mainland and the HKSAR on the Establishment of the Port at the West Kowloon Station of the Guangzhou-Shenzhen-Hong Kong Express Rail Link for Implementing Co-location Arrangement' (28 December 2017) < chrome-extension://efaidnbmnnnibpcajpcglclefindmkaj/https://www.hkba.org/uploads/20171228%20-%20Bar%20Co-Location%20Arrangement%20Statement%20(English)%20FINAL_0.pdf > last accessed 1 January 2026; Albert Chen, 'A Legal Analysis of the NPCSC Decision on Co-location (Part I)' *Ming Pao* (8 January 2018) A18; Albert Chen, 'A Legal Analysis of the NPCSC Decision on Co-location (Part II)' *Ming Pao* (9 January 2018) A27; Joyce Huang, 'Critics: Hong Kong Sets Bad Precedent with Mainland Police in Rail Station' *VOA* (28 July 2017)<www.voanews.com/a/hong-kong-mainland-police-high-speed-rail/3962653.html> last accessed 1 January 2026.

156 NPCSC Decision on Approving the Co-operation Arrangement between the Mainland and the HKSAR on the Establishment of the Port at the West Kowloon Station of the Guangzhou-Shenzhen-Hong Kong Express Rail Link for Implementing Co-location Arrangement (27 December 2017).

weight in the courts' construction of the Basic Law"[157] and the courts must be "very circumspect in adopting a construction of the Basic Law that is inconsistent with the NPCSC Decision"[158] as the NPCSC can simply reinstate its original views via an Interpretation.

The final tranche of NPCSC Decisions pertains to the electoral systems in the SARs and the NPCSC used these Decisions to set the pace of the cities' political reform. In 2004, the NPCSC ruled out any move toward universal suffrage for the Hong Kong Chief Executive Election in 2007 or its Legislative Council in 2008.[159] In 2007, the NPCSC once again demurred on any universal suffrage for the Hong Kong Chief Executive and Legislative Council Elections that were upcoming in 2012.[160] But in 2010, the NPCSC endorsed constitutional amendments that expanded the size of the Chief Executive Election Committee to 1200 members (from 800 members) and expanded the Legislative Council to 70 members (from 60 members), with 35 members directly elected by universal suffrage in geographical constituencies and 35 members returned by functional constituencies.[161] These constitutional changes were timed to take effect in the 2012 Hong Kong Chief Executive and Legislative Council elections.

For Macau, the NPCSC also issued a Decision in February 2012 to authorise the MASAR to undertake limited electoral reforms to its Chief Executive and Legislative Assembly Elections, but on condition that the Chief Executive be selected by a "broadly representative" nominating committee and the Legislative Assembly be constituted by directly-elected members, indirectly-elected members, and appointed members.[162] Basically, universal suffrage was also ruled out in Macau. In the end, the Macau government chose to proceed with modifying the Chief Executive electoral model with a meagre expansion of the number of

157 *Kwok Cheuk Kin v Secretary for Justice* [2021] 3 HKLRD 140 at [69].

158 *Kwok Cheuk Kin v Secretary for Justice* [2021] 3 HKLRD 140 at [70].

159 Decision of the Standing Committee of the National People's Congress on Issues Relating to the Methods for Selecting the Chief Executive of the Hong Kong Special Administrative Region in the Year 2007 and for Forming the Legislative Council of the Hong Kong Special Administrative Region in the Year 2008 (Adopted at the Ninth Session of the Standing Committee of the Tenth National People's Congress on 26 April 2004).

160 Decision of the Standing Committee of the National People's Congress on Issues Relating to the Methods for Selecting the Chief Executive of the Hong Kong Special Administrative Region and for Forming the Legislative Council of the Hong Kong Special Administrative Region in the Year 2012 and on Issues Relating to Universal Suffrage (Adopted at the 31st Session of the Standing Committee of the Tenth National People's Congress on 29 December 2007).

161 Decision of the Standing Committee of the National People's Congress on Approving the Amendment to Annex I to the Basic Law of the Hong Kong Special Administrative Region of the People's Republic of China Concerning the Method for the Selection of the Chief Executive of the Hong Kong Special Administrative Region (Adopted at the 16th Session of the Standing Committee of the 11th National People's Congress on 28 August 2010). See Chapter 2 of this book.

162 Decision of the NPCSC on Issues Relating to the Methods for Forming the Legislative Assembly of the MASAR in the Year 2013 and for Selecting the Chief Executive of the MASAR in the Year 2014 (Adopted at the 25th Session of the 11th NPCSC on 29 February 2012).

Election Committee members from 300 to 400.[163] These constitutional proposals were endorsed by another NPCSC Decision in June 2012.[164] No other constitutional amendments have been made to the Macau electoral models since then.

In 2014, the NPCSC agreed that universal suffrage elections *may* be introduced for the Hong Kong Chief Executive Election starting from 2017, but it was for a nominating committee, which would be based on the pre-existing Chief Executive Election Committee, to short-list "two to three candidates" for the public to vote on.[165] In essence, the Decision allows for the Election Committee that picks the Chief Executive to transition into a nominating committee, and all registered Hong Kong voters would then vote on candidates who have been pre-screened by the pro-Beijing delegates on this nominating committee. The pro-democracy camp in the Hong Kong Legislative Council rejected this political compromise[166] and the status quo has remained since.

After the imposition of the National Security Law on Hong Kong in June 2020, the NPCSC passed a Decision to postpone the Hong Kong Legislative Council elections by one year.[167] In view of the ongoing COVID-19 pandemic and the city's relentless adherence to the country's draconian zero-COVID policy, the staging of large in-person events became untenable. As the local government lacked the constitutional authority to postpone such elections – the term-of-office of the Legislative Council was explicitly limited to four years[168] – the NPCSC stepped in. Without naming which specific provision of the PRC Constitution or the HKBL it was acting in pursuance of, the NPCSC authorised by fiat pre-existing legislators to stay on in office for one additional year.

Three months later, the NPCSC followed up with another Decision in November 2020 that disqualified any Hong Kong lawmaker from office if they did not "meet the legal requirements and conditions on upholding the Basic Law... and [bear] allegiance to the [HKSAR]"[169]. This Decision effectively barred four incumbent

163 See Table 2.1 in Chapter 2.

164 Decision of the NPCSC on Approving the Amendment to the Annex I to the Basic Law of the MASAR of the PRC concerning the Method for the Selection of the Chief Executive of the MASAR (Approved at the 27th Session of the 11th NPCSC on 30 June 2012), art 1.

165 Decision of the Standing Committee of the National People's Congress on Issues Relating to the Selection of the Chief Executive of the Hong Kong Special Administrative Region by Universal Suffrage and on the Method for Forming the Legislative Council of the Hong Kong Special Administrative Region in the Year 2016 (Adopted at the Tenth Session of the Standing Committee of the 12th National People's Congress on 31 August 2014).

166 Albert Chen and Po Jen Yap, *The Constitutional System of the Hong Kong SAR: A Contextual Analysis* (Hart 2023) 19–20.

167 Decision of the Standing Committee of the National People's Congress on the Continuing Discharge of Duties by the Sixth-Term Legislative Council of the Hong Kong Special Administrative Region (Adopted at the 21st Session of the Standing Committee of the 13th National People's Congress on 11 August 2020).

168 Article 69 of the HKBL.

169 Decision of the Standing Committee of the National People's Congress on Issues Relating to the Qualification of the Members of the Legislative Council of the Hong Kong Special Administrative

pro-democracy Hong Kong lawmakers from serving in the extended Legislative Council because they were previously disqualified by electoral returning officers from contesting the 2020 Hong Kong Legislative Council election prior to its postponement.[170] This time, the NPCSC buttressed the disqualification by referencing specific provisions of the PRC Constitution – Article 52 (Citizen's Obligation to Safeguard National Unity); Article 54 (Citizen's Obligation to Safeguard National Security); and even Article 67(1), which empowers the NPCSC to supervise the implementation of the PRC Constitution. As discussed previously, this marked the first instance when PRC constitutional provisions were invoked to legitimise the NPCSC's Decisions over political issues in Hong Kong. In a sign of solidarity with their ousted brethren, 15 additional pro-democracy lawmakers resigned *en masse*.[171]

Despite the sheer number of NPCSC Decisions that operate in the SARs, particularly vis-à-vis Hong Kong, it is surprising that neither Basic Law stipulates the circumstances under which these instruments can apply in the territories. While NPCSC Interpretations – in theory anyway – are tethered ostensibly to "uncovering" the meaning of specific Basic Law provisions, these NPCSC Decisions run the gamut as they make extra-textual constitutional determinations writ large. In essence, these Decisions allow Beijing to fill in the gap in the Basic Laws and their ubiquity and scope run the risk of undermining the autonomy granted to the two SARs.

Conclusion

From inception, the MASAR has been closely integrated with Mainland China. Affectionately termed the "apple of the country's eye",[172] the MASAR's economic growth has hitherto been driven by its casino industry that is heavily reliant on

Region (Adopted at the 23rd Session of the Standing Committee of the 13th National People's Congress on 11 November 2020).

170 The electoral returning officers had disqualified these four incumbent lawmakers from contesting the then-upcoming elections because the latter had allegedly called on the US government to impose sanctions on Hong Kong after the passage of the 2020 HKNSL. See Tony Cheung et al., 'Hong Kong Elections: Mass Disqualification of Opposition Hopefuls Sparks Political Storm' *SCMP* (30 July 2020) <www.scmp.com/news/hong-kong/politics/article/3095327/hong-kong-elections-12-opposition-candidates-disqualified> last accessed 1 January 2026.

171 'Hong Kong Opposition Lawmakers to Resign En Masse over Beijing Resolution Empowering Local Government to Bypass Courts and Unseat Politicians' *SCMP* (11 November 2020) <www.scmp.com/news/hong-kong/politics/article/3109330/top-beijing-body-makes-patriotism-mandatory-hong-kong> last accessed 1 January 2026.

172 Willa Wu, ' "Apple of Country's Eye": Top Official Tells Macau to Maximise Business Advantages, Economic Foundations and Cultural Inclusiveness' *SCMP* (19 May 2024) <www.scmp.com/news/hong-kong/politics/article/3263258/apple-countrys-eye-top-official-tells-macau-maximise-business-advantages-economic-foundations-and> last accessed 1 January 2026.

Chinese visitors,[173] and it has no real alternative but to be reliant on the Mainland and its good graces.

On the other hand, Hong Kong has the privilege of being an international financial centre that connects China's state-owned enterprises and private conglomerates to global capital. To preserve this "golden goose", Beijing exercised self-restraint and adopted a hands-off approach to the city in the early years. The Central Government's dilemma over Hong Kong can be summed up in this Chinese adage: "一管就死，一放就亂" (to control is death, to loosen is chaos).[174] Free-market constitutionalism prevailed in Hong Kong.[175] But with the demise of the local national security legislative bill in 2003, and the rise of localism in Hong Kong politics after 2012, Beijing decided it had to change tack.[176]

The Guangdong–Hong Kong–Macau Greater Bay Area ("GBA") initiative was birthed in 2015,[177] with the objective of establishing a long-term, institutionalised mechanism for expanding inter-regional coordination between nine cities in Guangdong Province and the SARs, and deepening Hong Kong's dependency on the Mainland. The GBA initiative is a state-initiated, top-down cluster-city development plan that not only encompasses regional economic interactions, but also seeks to enhance regional cooperation on technological innovation, accelerate regional transport connectivity, and promote legal and administrative coordination.[178] Nevertheless, progress on the GBA was stymied by the COVID-19 pandemic[179] and China's post-COVID economic

173 Jason Buhi, 'Corporate Social Responsibility, Casino Capitalism, and the Constitution of Macau' (2020) 37(1) *UCLA Pacific Basin Law Journal* 1, 7.

174 This well-known saying has been used to characterise the intricate balance between the central and local governments, as well as state-society relations in China since the 1970s. See Xueguang Zhou (周雪光), '論"一管就死，一放就亂" On "to Control is Death, to Loosen is Chaos"' in Xueguang Zhou (ed), *The State-Society Relationship in Contemporary China* (當代中國的國家與社會關係) (桂冠出版社 Laureate Press 1992) 149–163; Sonny Shiu-Hing Lo also traces the oscillation between control (shou) and loosening (fang) in Beijing's policy towards Hong Kong in *The New Politics of Beijing–Hong Kong Relations: Ideological Conflicts and Factionalism* (Hong Kong University Press 2025) 19–20.

175 Gonzalo Villalta Puig and Eric Ip, *The Freest Market in the World: The Constitutional Logic of Economic Liberty in China's Hong Kong* (Routledge 2023).

176 Peter Cheung, 'The Changing Relations between Hong Kong and the Mainland since 2003' in Wai-man Lam, Percy Luen-tim Lui, and Wilson Wong (eds), *Contemporary Hong Kong Government and Politics* (Hong Kong University Press 2012) 325, 339–341.

177 See 'Vision and Actions on Jointly Building Silk Road Economic Belt and 21st-Century Maritime Silk Road 推動共建絲綢之路經濟帶和21世紀海上絲綢之路的願景與行動' (jointly issued by the National Development and Reform Commission, Ministry of Foreign Affairs, and Ministry of Commerce on 28 March 2015) <http://2017.beltandroadforum.org/n100/2017/0407/c27-22.html> last accessed 1 January 2026.

178 See Hong Yu, 'The Guangdong-Hong Kong-Macau Greater Bay Area in the Making: Development Plan and Challenges' (2021) 34(4) *Cambridge Review of International Affairs* 481–509.

179 Lilian Cheng, 'Coronavirus Disrupted Plans for Greater Bay Area but Region Now Poised for Lift-Off, Says Newly Promoted Guangdong Party Chief Huang Kunming' *SCMP* (24 February

slowdown.[180] After the full resumption of cross-border travel between the Mainland, Hong Kong, and Macau in early 2023,[181] both the central and local authorities have actively revived the integration of the GBA. The Hengqin Cooperation Zone[182] – a Mainland area in southern Zhuhai and adjacent to Macau – became an autonomous customs territory in March 2024, with tax exemptions and streamlined customs procedures introduced to further facilitate the movement of people, goods, and capital between Macau and the Mainland.[183] In October 2024, the Central Government amended the Closer Economic Partnership Arrangements (CEPAs)[184] – bilateral trade pacts between Mainland and the two SARs – to facilitate greater market access for service providers from Hong Kong and Macau to enter the Mainland market.[185] Notably, the amendments allow registered Hong Kong and Macau companies, when doing business in the GBA, to apply SAR laws or choose the SARs as the arbitration forum.[186] Since 2020, the NPCSC has made Decisions

2023) <www.scmp.com/news/hong-kong/politics/article/3211486/coronavirus-disrupted-plans-greater-bay-area-region-now-poised-lift-says-newly-promoted-guangdong?module=perpetual_scroll_0&pgtype=article> last accessed 1 January 2026.

180 Alicia Garcia Herrero, 'China's Economic Woes: How They will Impact the Greater Bay Area and Hong Kong', *AmCham HK e-Magazine* <https://amchamhk.online/chinas-economic-slowdown-impacts-greater-bay-area-hong-kong/> last accessed 1 January 2026.

181 Farah Master and Twinnie Siu, 'China to Fully Resume Travel with Hong Kong, Macau on Feb 6' *Reuters* (4 February 2023) <www.reuters.com/world/asia-pacific/china-fully-resume-travel-with-hong-kong-macau-feb-6-2023-02-03/> last accessed 1 January 2026.

182 The full name for this area is 'Guangdong-Macao In-Depth Cooperation Zone in Hengqin', which was formally established in 2021. It is managed by a committee headed by the Governor of Guangdong Province and the Macau Chief Executive. It has been designated as a high-priority free-trade area, designed for fostering collaboration between Macau and Guangdong. See Long Zhou et al., *Urban and Regional Cooperation and Development: Challenges and Strategies for the Planning and Development of the Guangdong-Macao Intensive Cooperation Zone in Hengqin Island* (Springer 2023) 1–15.

183 'China's Hengqin Lifts Tariffs for Most Imports from Macau' *Xinhua* (1 March 2024) <https://english.news.cn/20240301/868066189dfe4420946bb3f11ee5c882/c.html> last accessed 1 January 2026.

184 The full names of the two CEPAs are 'Mainland and Hong Kong Closer Economic Partnership Arrangement' (內地與香港關於建立更緊密經貿關係的安排) and 'Mainland and Macau Closer Economic Partnership Arrangement' (內地與澳門關於建立更緊密經貿關係的安排). Both are bilateral trade agreements signed in 2003 to boost the economy in the two SARs by easing restrictions on cross-border travel and facilitating the movement of goods and services between the Mainland and the two SARs. See Peter Chiu, 'CEPA: A Milestone in the Economic Integration between Hong Kong and Mainland China' (2006) 15(47) *Journal of Contemporary China* 275–295.

185 'HKSAR Government and Ministry of Commerce sign Second Agreement Concerning Amendment to CEPA Agreement on Trade in Services' (9 October 2024) <www.info.gov.hk/gia/general/202410/09/P2024100900266.htm> last accessed 1 January 2026; 'Macau and Mainland Sign New Upgrade to CEPA Trade Agreement' *Macau Business* (11 October 2024) <www.bilaterals.org/?macau-and-mainland-sign-new> last accessed 1 January 2026.

186 Article 1 (ii) of the Second Agreement Concerning Amendment to the Agreement on Trade in Services of the Mainland and Hong Kong Closer Economic Partnership Arrangement (9 October

allowing legal practitioners from Hong Kong and Macau, after passing a bar examination, to practise in the GBA.[187]

On national security, the SARs' integration with the PRC apparatus is equally palpable. The Central Government is now authorised to dispatch its own national security team to operate in Hong Kong[188] and Macau,[189] and suspects from Hong Kong can even be transferred to the Mainland to face trial in "complex"[190] cases, though the latter has yet to occur. Both the 2023 MANSL and the 2024 HKNSL were also heavily influenced by the PRC version, as we discussed more fully in Chapter 4. After the debacle over the 2019 extradition bill, its revival is no longer on the cards in Hong Kong.[191] Vis-à-vis Macau, there are also no formal extradition arrangements between the city and Mainland China. In fact, back in 2008, the MACFA ruled that in the absence of specific legislation authorising rendition to the Mainland, the local government's attempts to transfer fugitives to Mainland China were illegal.[192] In that landmark decision, the MACFA – with unusual alacrity – openly criticised the Macau government for "undermining justice, shaking the rule of law, and tarnishing the reputation of the MASAR" ("這些行為違背公正，動搖法治，影響澳門特別行政區的威望")[193] by seeking to detain and transfer these fugitives. But even if formal rendition is unavailable, informal assistance and coordination now abound. In 2021, Alvin Chau Cheok-wa – the biggest junket

2024) <www.tid.gov.hk/en/our_work/cepa/legal_text/files/cepa19_main.pdf > last accessed 1 January 2026; Article 1(2) of the Second Agreement Concerning Amendment to the Agreement on Trade in Services of the Mainland and Macau Closer Economic Partnership Arrangement (10 October 2024) <www.dsedt.gov.mo/zh_MO/web/public/pg_cepa_cepa_aacs2> last accessed 1 January 2026.

187 Decision of the NPCSC to Authorise the State Council to Carry out the Pilot Program of Allowing Hong Kong Legal Practitioners and Macau Practising Lawyers to Obtain Mainland Practising Qualification and Practice Law in Nine Mainland Cities of the GBA 全国人民代表大会常务委员会关于授权国务院在粤港澳大湾区内地九市开展香港法律执业者和澳门执业律师取得内地执业资质和从事律师职业试点工作的决定 (11 August 2020). The 2020 NPCSC decision authorised the State Council to initiate this pilot program for a period of three years. In 2023, the NPCSC further authorised the State Council to extend the duration of the program for an additional three years, see Decision of the NPCSC to Extend the Period of the Pilot Program of Practice of Law in Nine Mainland Cities of the GBA by Hong Kong Legal Practitioners and Macao Practising Lawyers after Obtaining Mainland Practising Qualifications Conducted by the State Council as Authorised 全国人大常委会关于延长授权国务院在粤港澳大湾区内地九市開展港澳律師取得内地执业资质和从事律师职业试点工作期限的决定 (1 September 2023).

188 Articles 48–53 of the 2020 HKNSL.

189 See Official Reply of the State Council to Approve the Appointment of a National Security Affairs Advisor and National Security Technical Advisors to the Committee for Safeguarding National Security of the Macao SAR (30 November 2021).

190 Article 55 of the 2020 HKNSL.

191 'John Lee says He "Definitely" won't Promote Extradition Bill Again' *The Standard* (5 July 2023) <www.thestandard.com.hk/breaking-news/section/4/205633/John-Lee-says-he-'definitely'-won't-promote-extradition-bill-again> last accessed 1 January 2026.

192 Case 3/2008 (12 February 2008); See also Case 12/2007 (20 March 2007).

193 Case 3/2008 (12 February 2008).

operator in Macau – was arrested by Macau authorities within 12 hours after the Mainland police issued an arrest warrant for him on cross-border money laundering and illegal gambling charges,[194] thereby underscoring the formidable informal influence Mainland law enforcement wields in Macau. But notably, Alvin Chau was not extradited to Mainland China but was prosecuted and convicted locally for the said offences.[195]

Politically, both cities have been overhauled. For Hong Kong, Beijing directly intervened in 2021 and only allowed "patriots" to run for office.[196] Macau was left alone by the Central Authorities, but the local government genuflected to the prevailing national ethos and – of its own accord – barred all pro-democracy lawmakers from contesting the 2021 and 2025 Legislative Assembly elections.[197]

After the 2019 protests in Hong Kong, Beijing also revamped its chain of reporting and command over Hong Kong and Macau affairs. In February 2020, the pre-existing Central Coordination Group on Hong Kong and Macau Affairs (中央港澳工作協調小組) – the CCP's top body in charge of SAR affairs – was upgraded and became the Central Leading Group on Hong Kong and Macau Affairs (中央港澳工作領導小組),[198] a move intended to enhance direct Party control over SAR affairs.[199] This Central Leading Group is currently headed by Ding Xuexiang, a member of the CCP Politburo Standing Committee. In tandem with this change, the HKMAO[200] in March 2023 was transferred from an administrative agency within the PRC State Council to become the Secretariat Office of the Central Leading Group on Hong Kong and Macau Affairs. This

194 Ng Kang-chung and Jeffie Lam, 'Macau Police Arrest Casino Junket Boss Alvin Chau, 10 Other over Alleged Gambling Offences' *SCMP* (28 November 2021) <www.scmp.com/news/hong-kong/law-and-crime/article/3157657/macau-police-arrest-casino-junket-boss-alvin-chau-10> last accessed 1 January 2026.

195 Emily Hung, 'Macau "Junket King" Alvin Chau Jailed for 18 Years on 162 Charges of Fraud, Illegal Gambling and Criminal Association' *SCMP* (18 January 2023) <www.scmp.com/news/hong-kong/law-and-crime/article/3207267/macau-junket-king-alvin-chau-jailed-18-years-charges-fraud-illegal-gambling-and-criminal-association> last accessed 1 January 2026.

196 Decision of the National People's Congress On Improving the Electoral System of the Hong Kong Special Administrative Region (Adopted at the Fourth Session of the 13th National People's Congress on 11 March 2021).

197 See Chapter 2 of this book.

198 HaimingTu (屠海鳴), 'Deeper Implications of the Appearance of the New Team of the Central Hong Kong and Macau Office 中央港澳辦新班子亮相的深意' *Bauhinia Magazine* (紫荊) (12 July 2023) <https://bau.com.hk/article/2023-07/12/content_1128626977812389888.html> last accessed 1 January 2026.

199 HaimingTu (屠海鳴), 'Deeper Implications of the Appearance of the New Team of the Central Hong Kong and Macau Office (中央港澳辦新班子亮相的深意)' *Bauhinia Magazine* (紫荊) (12 July 2023) <https://bau.com.hk/article/2023-07/12/content_1128626977812389888.html> last accessed 1 January 2026.

200 Prior to the 2023 restructuring, the HKMAO was an administrative agency within the State Council. The Liaison Offices serve as the representatives of the Central People's Government in Hong Kong and Macau. Before 2023, the HKMAO functioned as the primary SAR policy-making and research institution in Beijing, while the Liaison Offices operated on the front-lines

move established a direct line of reporting from the SAR Liaison Offices to the CCP leadership, with the Directors of the two Liaison Offices now serving as Deputy Directors of the HKMAO.[201]

The two SARs were birthed when Britain and Portugal respectively relinquished control over their erstwhile colonies. A new constitutional order was forged in both cities as the 20th century drew to a close. But over two decades later, the so-called "autonomous" regions were constitutionally re-ordered again as they both succumbed to and integrated with the authoritarian impulses of their Motherland.

in the SARs, gathering information and liaising with various sectors of Hong Kong and Macau societies. The HKMAO and the Liaison Office were parallel institutions, both reporting to the then Central Coordination Group on Hong Kong and Macau Affairs, led by a senior Politburo Standing Committee member. The 2023 restructuring converted this parallel relationship into a vertical one, with the HKMAO being elevated to a CCP party organ and supervisor of the two Liaison Offices. See Chuchu Chen (陳楚楚),'Decoding "Two Offices" Governing Hong Kong: Who Will be the Future Governor of Hong Kong? 解密"兩辦"治港：誰才是香港未來的管治者？' *Initium Media* (端传媒) (19 May 2020) <https://theinitium.com/zh-hans/opinion/20200519-hongkong-the-liaison-office-new-boss> last accessed 1 January 2026.

201 The State Council Appoints and Removes National Staff《國務院任免國家工作人員》(11 July 2023) <https://paper.people.com.cn/rmrb/html/2023-07/12/nw.D110000renmrb_20230712_6-04.htm> last accessed 1 January 2026.

Appendix 1

National Laws Listed in Annex III of the Hong Kong and Macau Basic Laws (as of 1 March 2026)

Hong Kong		
1	1990	Resolution on the Capital, Calendar, National Anthem and National Flag of the PRC 《關於中華人民共和國國都、紀年、國歌、國旗的決議》
2		Resolution on the National Day of the PRC 《關於中華人民共和國國慶日的決議》
3		Declaration of the Government of the PRC on the Territorial Sea 《中華人民共和國政府關於領海的聲明》
4		Nationality Law of the PRC 《中華人民共和國國籍法》
5		Regulations of the PRC Concerning Diplomatic Privileges and Immunities 《中華人民共和國外交特權與豁免條例》
6	1997	Law of the PRC on the National Flag 《中華人民共和國國旗法》
7		Regulations of the PRC Concerning Consular Privileges and Immunities 《中華人民共和國領事特權與豁免條例》
8		Law of the PRC on the National Emblem 《中華人民共和國國徽法》
9		Law of the PRC on the Territorial Sea and the Contiguous Zone 《中華人民共和國領海及毗連區法》
10		Law of the PRC on Garrisoning the Hong Kong Special Administrative Region 《中華人民共和國香港特別行政區駐軍法》
11	1998	Law on the Exclusive Economic Zone and Continental Shelf of the PRC 《中華人民共和國專屬經濟區和大陸架法》
12	2005	Law of the PRC on Judicial Immunity from Compulsory Measures Concerning the Property of Foreign Central Banks 《中華人民共和國外國中央銀行財產司法強制措施豁免法》
13	2017	Law of the PRC on the National Anthem 《中華人民共和國國歌法》
14	2020	Law of the PRC on Safeguarding National Security in the HKSAR 《中華人民共和國香港特別行政區維護國家安全法》
Macau		
1	1993	Resolution on the Capital, Calendar, National Anthem and National Flag of the PRC 《關於中華人民共和國國都、紀年、國歌、國旗的決議》
2		Resolution on the National Day of the PRC 《關於中華人民共和國國慶日的決議》
3		Nationality Law of the PRC 《中華人民共和國國籍法》
4		Regulations of the PRC Concerning Diplomatic Privileges and Immunities 《中華人民共和國外交特權與豁免條例》
5		Regulations of the PRC Concerning Consular Privileges and Immunities 《中華人民共和國領事特權與豁免條例》
6		Law of the PRC on the National Flag 《中華人民共和國國旗法》

(*Continued*)

Macau		
7		Law of the PRC on the National Emblem《中華人民共和國國徽法》
8		Law of the PRC on the Territorial Sea and the Contiguous Zone《中華人民共和國領海及毗連區法》
9	1999	Law on the Exclusive Economic Zone and Continental Shelf of the PRC《中華人民共和國專屬經濟區和大陸架法》
10		Law of the PRC on Garrisoning the MASAR《中華人民共和國澳門特別行政區駐軍法》
11	2006	Law of the PRC on Judicial Immunity from Compulsory Measures Concerning the Property of Foreign Central Banks《中華人民共和國外國中央銀行財產司法強制措施豁免法》
12	2017	Law of the PRC on the National Anthem《中華人民共和國國歌法》

Appendix 2

Post-Handover NPCSC Interpretations on the Hong Kong and Macau Basic Laws (as of 1 March 2026)

Hong Kong		
26 June 1999	Interpretation by the NPCSC Regarding Paragraph 4 in Article 22 and Category (3) of Paragraph 2 in Article 24 of the Basic Law of the HKSAR《全國人民代表大會常務委員會關於〈中華人民共和國香港特別行政區基本法〉第二十二條第四款和第二十四條第二款第（三）項的解釋》	Constitutional right of abode of Mainland immigrants born to Hong Kong Permanent Residents
6 April 2004	Interpretation by the NPCSC Regarding Annex I (7) and Annex II (III) to the Basic Law of the HKSAR《全國人民代表大會常務委員會關於〈中華人民共和國香港特別行政區基本法〉附件一第七條和附件二第三條的解釋》	Method for amending Basic Law on political system
27 April 2005	Interpretation by the NPCSC Regarding the Second Paragraph in Article 53 of the Basic Law of the HKSAR《全國人民代表大會常務委員會關於〈中華人民共和國香港特別行政區基本法〉第五十三條第二款的解釋》	Length of term of Chief Executive filling mid-term vacancy
26 Aug 2011	Interpretation by the NPCSC Regarding the First Paragraph of Article 13 and Article 19 of the Basic Law of the HKSAR《全國人民代表大會常務委員會關於〈中華人民共和國香港特別行政區基本法〉第十三條第一款和第十九條的解釋》	Doctrine of state immunity applied in Hong Kong

Hong Kong		
7 Nov 2016	Interpretation of Article 104 of the Basic Law of the HKSAR by the NPCSC 《全國人民代表大會常務委員會關於〈中華人民共和國香港特別行政區基本法〉第一百零四條的解釋》	Oath-taking requirements and consequences of non-compliance for public office holders
Macau		
31 Dec 2011	Interpretation by the NPCSC Regarding Annex I (7) and Annex II (III) to the Basic Law of the MASAR 《全國人民代表大會常務委員會關於〈中華人民共和國澳門特別行政區基本法〉附件一第七條和附件二第三條的解釋》	Method for amending Basic Law on political system

Appendix 3

Post-Handover NPCSC Decisions on Hong Kong (as of 1 March 2026)

1	1 July 1997	NPCSC Decision on Adding to and Deleting from the List of the National Laws in Annex III to the Basic Law of the HKSAR of the PRC 《全國人民代表大會常務委員會關於〈中華人民共和國香港特別行政區基本法〉附件三所列全國性法律增減的決定》
2	3 July 1997	NPCSC Decision on Approval of the Suggestion on the Conclusion of the Work of the Preparatory Committee for the HKSAR of the NPC 《全國人民代表大會常務委員會關於批准全國人民代表大會香港特別行政區籌備委員會結束工作的建議的決定》
3	27 Oct 1998	NPCSC Decision on the By-election of Deputies of the HKSAR to the Ninth NPC 《全國人民代表大會常務委員會關於補選出缺的香港特別行政區第九屆全國人民代表大會代表的決定》
4	4 Nov 1998	NPCSC Decision on Adding a Law to the List of the National Laws in Annex III to the Basic Law of the HKSAR of the PRC 《全國人民代表大會常務委員會關於增加〈中華人民共和國香港特別行政區基本法〉附件三所列全國性法律的決定》
5	29 June 2002	NPCSC Decision on Continuous Performance of Duty by the Members of the First Basic Law Committee of the HKSAR Under the NPCSC 《全國人民代表大會常務委員會關於第一任全國人民代表大會常務委員會香港特別行政區基本法委員會成員繼續履行職責的決定》
6	26 Apr 2004	NPCSC Decision on Issues Relating to the Methods for Selecting the Chief Executive of the HKSAR in the Year 2007 and for Forming the Legislative Council of the HKSAR in the Year 2008 《全國人民代表大會常務委員會關於香港特別行政區2007年行政長官和2008年立法會產生辦法有關問題的決定》
7	27 Oct 2005	NPCSC Decision on Adding a Law to the List of the National Laws in Annex III to the Basic Law of the HKSAR of the PRC 《全國人民代表大會常務委員會關於增加〈中華人民共和國香港特別行政區基本法〉附件三所列全國性法律的決定》

(*Continued*)

8	31 Oct 2006	NPCSC Decision on Empowering the HKSAR to Exercise Jurisdiction over the Shenzhen Bay Port Hong Kong Port Area 《全國人民代表大會常務委員會關於授權香港特別行政區對深圳灣口岸港方口岸區實施管轄的決定》
9	29 Dec 2007	NPCSC Decision on Issues Relating to the Methods for Selecting the Chief Executive of the HKSAR and for Forming the Legislative Council of the HKSAR in the Year 2012 and on Issues Relating to Universal Suffrage 《全國人民代表大會常務委員會關於香港特別行政區2012年行政長官和立法會產生辦法及有關普選問題的決定》
10	28 Aug 2010	NPCSC Decision on Approving the Amendment to Annex I to the Basic Law of the HKSAR of the PRC Concerning the Method for the Selection of the Chief Executive of the HKSAR 《全國人民代表大會常務委員會關於批准〈中華人民共和國香港特別行政區基本法附件一香港特別行政區行政長官的產生辦法修正案〉的決定》
11	31 Aug 2014	NPCSC Decision on Issues Relating to the Selection of the Chief Executive of the HKSAR by Universal Suffrage and on the Method for Forming the Legislative Council of the HKSAR in the Year 2016 ("831 Decision") 《全國人民代表大會常務委員會關於香港特別行政區行政長官普選問題和2016年立法會產生辦法的決定》
12	4 Nov 2017	NPCSC Decision on Adding a Law to the List of the National Laws in Annex III to the Basic Law of the HKSAR of the PRC 《全國人民代表大會常務委員會關於增加<中華人民共和國香港特別行政區基本法>附件三所列全國性法律的決定》
13	27 Dec 2017	NPCSC Decision on Approving the Co-operation Arrangement between the Mainland and the HKSAR on the Establishment of the Port at the West Kowloon Station of the Guangzhou-Shenzhen-Hong Kong Express Rail Link for Implementing Co-location Arrangement 《全國人民代表大會常務委員會關於批准<內地與香港特別行政區關於在廣深港高鐵西九龍站設立口岸實施"一地兩檢"的合作安排>的決定》
14	30 June 2020	NPCSC Decision on Adding a Law to the List of the National Laws in Annex III to the Basic Law of the HKSAR of the PRC 《全國人民代表大會常務委員會關於增加〈中華人民共和國香港特別行政區基本法〉附件三所列全國性法律的決定》
15	11 Aug 2020	NPCSC Decision on the Continuing Discharge of Duties by the Sixth Term Legislative Council of the HKSAR 《全國人民代表大會常務委員會關於香港特別行政區第六屆立法會繼續履行職責的決定》
16	11 Nov 2020	NPCSC Decision on Issues Relating to the Qualification of the Members of the Legislative Council of the HKSAR 《全國人民代表大會常務委員會關於香港特別行政區立法會議員資格問題的決定》

Appendix 4

Post-Handover NPCSC Decisions on Macau (as of 1 March 2026)

1	20 Dec 1999	NPCSC Decision on Adding a Law to the List of the National Laws in Annex III to the Basic Law of the MASAR of the PRC 《全國人民代表大會常務委員會關於增加〈中華人民共和國澳門特別行政區基本法〉附件三所列全國性法律的決定》
2	25 Dec 1999	NPCSC Decision on Approving the Report on the Work of the NPC Preparatory Committee for the MASAR and the Suggestion on the Conclusion of the Work of the NPC Preparatory Committee for the MASAR 《全國人民代表大會常務委員會關於批准〈全國人民代表大會澳門特別行政區籌備委員會工作情況的報告〉和全國人民代表大會澳門特別行政區籌備委員會結束工作的建議的決定》
3	27 Oct 2005	NPCSC Decision on Adding a Law to the List of the National Laws in Annex III to the Basic Law of the MASAR of the PRC 《全國人民代表大會常務委員會關於增加〈中華人民共和國澳門特別行政區基本法〉附件三所列全國性法律的決定》
4	27 June 2009	NPCSC Decision on Empowering the MASAR to Exercise Jurisdiction over the New Campus of the University of Macao on Hengqin Island 《全國人民代表大會常務委員會關於授權澳門特別行政區對設在橫琴島的澳門大學新校區實施管轄的決定》
5	29 Feb 2012	NPCSC Decision on Issues Relating to the Methods for Forming the Legislative Assembly of the MASAR in the Year 2013 and for Selecting the Chief Executive of the MASAR in the Year 2014 《全國人民代表大會常務委員會關於澳門特別行政區2013年立法會產生辦法和2014年行政長官產生辦法有關問題的決定》
6	30 June 2012	NPCSC Decision on Approving the Amendment to Annex I of the Basic Law of the MASAR of the PRC Concerning the Method for the Selection of the Chief Executive of the MASAR 《全國人民代表大會常務委員會關於批准〈中華人民共和國澳門特別行政區基本法附件一澳門特別行政區行政長官的產生辦法修正案〉的決定》
7	4 Nov 2017	NPCSC Decision on Adding a Law to the List of the National Laws in Annex III to the Basic Law of the MASAR of the PRC 《全國人民代表大會常務委員會關於增加〈中華人民共和國澳門特別行政區基本法〉附件三所列全國性法律的決定》
8	26 Oct 2019	NPCSC Decision on Authorising the MASAR to Exercise Jurisdiction over Macau's Port Zone at Hengqin Port and Related Extended Areas 《全國人民代表大會常務委員會關於授權澳門特別行政區對橫琴口岸澳方口岸區及相關延伸區實施管轄的決定》

References

Buhi, Jason, 'Corporate Social Responsibility, Casino Capitalism, and the Constitution of Macau' (2020) 37(1) *UCLA Pacific Basin Law Journal* 1–23.

Cao, Xudong 曹旭东，'宪法在香港特别行政区的适用:理论回顾与实践反思 Application of the Constitution in the Hong Kong Special Administrative Region: Theoretical Review and Practical Reflection' (2018) 1 *政治与法律 Political Science and Law* 79–89.

Chan, Johannes, 'Hong Kong's Constitutional Journey, 1997–2011'in Albert Chen (ed), *Constitutionalism in Asia in the Early Twenty-First Century* (Cambridge, Cambridge University Press 2014) 169–193.

Chen, Albert and Po Jen Yap, *The Constitutional System of the Hong Kong SAR: A Contextual Analysis* (Oxford, Hart 2023).

Chen, Albert, 'Constitutional Controversies in the Aftermath of the Anti-Extradition Movement of 2019' (2020) 50 *Hong Kong Law Journal* 609–632.

Chen, Albert, '香港特別行政區政治體制中的行政與立法機關 The Executive and Legislative Organs in the Political System of the HKSAR' (2014) 1 *"一國兩制"研究 Journal of "One Country Two Systems" Studies* 6–14.

Chen, Albert, 'Executive-Led Government, Strong and Weak Governments and "Consensus Democracy"' in Johannes Chan and Lison Harris (eds), *Hong Kong's Constitutional Debates* (Hong Kong, Hong Kong Law Journal 2005) 9–14.

Cheng, Joseph Yu-shek, 'Beijing's Changing Hong Kong Policy: The Rise and Fall of Pragmatism' (2023) 53(4) *Journal of Contemporary Asia* 626–647.

Cheung, Peter, 'The Changing Relations between Hong Kong and the Mainland since 2003' in Lam Wai-man et al. (eds), *Contemporary Hong Kong Government and Politics* (Hong Kong, Hong Kong University Press 2012) 325–347.

Chiu, Peter, 'CEPA: A Milestone in the Economic Integration between Hong Kong and Mainland China' (2006) 15(47) *Journal of Contemporary China* 275–295.

Clift, Brendan, 'Mandating Symbolic Patriotism: China's Flag and Anthem in the Hong Kong Special Administrative Region' (2022) 9 *Asian Journal of Law and Society* 500–518.

Ding, Huanchun 丁焕春, '论我国宪法对香港特别行政区的法律效力 On the Legal Effect of the PRC Constitution on the Hong Kong Special Administrative Region' (1991) 3 *法学评论 Law Review* 8–13.

Fu, Hualing, 'Supremacy of a Different Kind: The Constitution, the NPC, and the Hong Kong SAR' in Johannes Chan et al. (eds), *Hong Kong's Constitutional Debate: Conflict Over Interpretation* (Hong Kong, Hong Kong University Press 2000) 97–111.

Ghai, Yash, *Hong Kong's New Constitutional Order: The Resumption of Chinese Sovereignty and the Basic Law* (Hong Kong, Hong Kong University Press 1999).

Han, Dayuan 韩大元, '论《宪法》在《香港特别行政区基本法》制定过程中的作用 On the Role of the Constitution in the Drafting Process of the Hong Kong Basic Law' (2017) 5 *现代法学 Modern Law Science* 3–10.

Ho, Bryan, 'Political Culture, Social Movements, and Governability in Macao' (2011) 38(2) *Asian Affairs: An American Review* 59–87.

Huang, Hai 黃海, *疏離的人心：香港社會思潮評析 Alienated Hearts: An Analysis of the Social Ethos in Hong Kong* (Hong Kong, 香港城市大學出版社 City University of Hong Kong Press 2019).

Hung, Steven Chung Fun, 'The Occupy Central Campaign in 2014 Hong Kong' (2016) 2(2) *Contemporary Chinese Political Economy and Strategic Relations* 669–734.

Lo, Sonny Shiu-Hing, *The New Politics of Beijing–Hong Kong Relations: Ideological Conflicts and Factionalism* (Hong Kong, Hong Kong University Press 2025).

Lo, Sonny Shiu-Hing, 'One Formula, Two Experiences: Political Divergence of Hong Kong and Macao since Retrocession' (2007) 16(52) *Journal of Contemporary China* 359–387.

Lo, Sonny Shiu-Hing, 'The Mainlandization and Recolonization of Hong Kong: A Triumph of Convergence over Divergence with Mainland China' in Joseph Cheng (ed), *The Hong Kong Special Administrative Region in its First Decade* (Hong Kong, City University of Hong Kong Press 2007) 179–231.

Petersen, Carole, 'The Disappearing Firewall: International Consequences of Beijing's Decision to Impose a National Security Law and Operate National Security Institutions in Hong Kong' (2020) 50 *Hong Kong Law Journal* 633–656.

Petersen, Carole, 'Hong Kong's Spring of Discontent: The Rise and Fall of the National Security Bill in 2003' in Fu Hualing, Carole Petersen and Simon Young (eds), *National Security and Fundamental Freedoms: Hong Kong's Article 23 under Scrutiny* (Hong Kong, Hong Kong University Press 2005) 13–62.

Puig, Gonzalo Villalta and Eric Ip, *The Freest Market in the World: The Constitutional Logic of Economic Liberty in China's Hong Kong* (Oxford, Routledge 2023).

Wang, Shuwen 王叔文 (ed),香港特别行政区基本法导论 *Introduction to the Hong Kong Special Administrative Region Basic Law* (Beijing, 中共中央党校出版社 Chinese Communist Party Central Party School Press 1997).

Wang, Shuwen 王叔文, '基本法是体现"一国两制"方针的全国性法律 The Basic Law Is a National Law that Embodies the "One Country, Two Systems" Policy' (1990) 2 *法学研究 Chinese Journal of Law* 1–10.

Xiao, Weiyun 肖蔚雲, *一國兩制與香港基本法制度 One Country Two Systems and the Hong Kong Basic Law System* (Beijing, 北京大学出版社 Beijing University Press 1990).

Xu, Chongde 许崇德, *港澳基本法教程 Hong Kong and Macau Basic Law Textbook* (Beijing, 中国人民大学出版社 China Renmin University Press 1994).

Yap, Po Jen, 'Judging Hong Kong's National Security Law' in Hualing Fu and Michael Hor (eds), *The National Security Law of Hong Kong: Restoration and Transformation* (Hong Kong, Hong Kong University Press 2022) 149–166.

Yap, Po Jen and Zixin Jiang, 'Co-location Is Constitutional' (2018) 48 *Hong Kong Law Journal* 37–50.

Yu, Hong, 'The Guangdong-Hong Kong-Macau Greater Bay Area in the Making: Development Plan and Challenges' (2021) 34(4) *Cambridge Review of International Affairs* 481–509.

Yuan, Qiushi 袁求實 (ed), *香港過渡時期重要文件彙編 Compilation of Important Documents During the Hong Kong Transition Period* (Hong Kong, 三聯出版社 Joint Publishing 1997).

Zhou, Long et al., *Urban and Regional Cooperation and Development: Challenges and Strategies for the Planning and Development of the Guangdong-Macao Intensive Cooperation Zone in Hengqin Island* (Singapore, Springer 2023).

Zhou, Xueguang 周雪光, '論"一管就死，一放就亂" On "to Control Is Death, to Loosen Is Chaos"' in Xueguang Zhou (ed), *當代中國的國家與社會關係 The State-Society Relationship in Contemporary China* (Taipei, 桂冠出版社 Laureate Press 1992) 149–163.

Zhu, Han, 'The Hong Kong National Security Law: The Shifted Grundnorm of Hong Kong's Legal Order and Its Implications' in Hualing Fu and Michael Hor (eds), *The National*

Security Law of Hong Kong: Restoration and Transformation (Hong Kong, Hong Kong University Press 2022) 49–71.

Zou, Pingxue 邹平学, '1982 年《宪法》第31条辩析——兼论现行《宪法》在特别行政区的适用 An Analysis of Article 31 of the 1982 Constitution and the Application of the Current Constitution in the SARs' (2013) 1 *当代港澳研究 Studies on Hong Kong and Macau* 78–96.

6
CONCLUSION

The punishing "zero-COVID" policy that locked Hong Kong down for three years has receded from the local consciousness, but the city is still scarred by the trauma that followed its "decade of protests".[1] The national security laws and constitutional overhauls to the political system now undergird Hong Kong's new political compact, albeit one foisted unilaterally by Beijing. Protest marches for universal suffrage are no more; Tiananmen public candlelight vigils have ended; pro-democracy lawmakers are driven out of office; and scores of dissidents languish in jail or live overseas in exile, fearing or fleeing arrest. The cityscape is now awash with exuberant exultations of the Motherland and patriotic odes to the country, just as Macau had been all along. Unbeknownst to most Hong Kong residents and international observers, Macau has been the harbinger of Hong Kong's future all along – the gradual purging of both Special Administrative Regions' (SARs) colonial past and the incremental alignment with the country's contemporary ethos.

Chapter 1 traces how Hong Kong reached this inflection point. In particular, two epochal social movements redefined the local political consciousness. "Occupy Central" – the occupation of the Central financial district in Hong Kong – was originally floated in 2013 as a pressure tactic by the pro-democracy movement to press the local and Mainland governments to take substantive genuine steps towards universal suffrage. The occupation eventually materialised on 28 September 2014 and the riot police responded by deploying tear-gas to disperse the crowd, forcing the peaceful protestors to shield themselves with umbrellas. Television images of Hong Kongers being teargassed – hitherto unseen since the 1960s – drew thousands

1 Tessa Wong et al., 'Silenced and Erased, Hong Kong's Decade of Protest is Now a Defiant Memory' *BBC* (30 November 2024) <www.bbc.com/news/articles/c888jnvq4x4o> last accessed 1 January 2026.

DOI: 10.4324/9781003683872-6

more into the streets. With the surge in protestors, the riot police were withdrawn, and road occupiers swiftly pitched tents along the main arteries of the financial district. The "Umbrella" movement was born as the ubiquitous umbrella became a symbol of resilience and defiance for the unlawful occupation. The road blockades lasted 79 days and were eventually cleared with minimal opposition and fanfare. But the street protestors returned in 2019 with a vengeance. In February 2019, the Hong Kong government attempted to pass a law that would have allowed Hong Kong residents to be extradited to Mainland China to face trial. Unsurprisingly, public opposition grew, and mass street protests returned, with regular violent altercations between the police and protestors. Notably, the social unrest did not abate, even after the bill was suspended, with close to 2 million people out in the streets at one point. Over the course of that sweltering summer in 2019, Hong Kong saw its legislature ransacked, public facilities vandalised, and university campuses became war zones. "Defying the Dragon"[2] with violence was always going to be a fool's errand. The rampage only hardened the Central Government's resolve to restore order and turbo-charge Hong Kong's integration with the Mainland. Unfortunately for Macau, it was a mere innocent bystander to Hong Kong's unravelling. And when the Central Government clamped down on Hong Kong, with the imposition of the National Security Law in 2020, and the overhaul of the electoral system in 2021, the obedient younger sibling felt it had to do more and, of its own accord, Macau genuflected to the national zeitgeist.

Chapter 2 analyses the political systems of the Hong Kong and Macau SARs. Both were similarly structured at conception. Each SAR is headed by a Chief Executive, drawn from *outside* a political party, who is chosen by the Central Government but formally "elected" by a small circle of pro-Beijing loyalists. As for the legislature, the public in both cities can only directly vote for a segment of the seats; these "universal suffrage" seats co-exist with allocations reserved for proxies of different business and professional sectors that are overwhelmingly pro-Beijing but all serve their own sectoral interests. In this way, a dominant political party never emerged in either SAR as political power is intentionally fragmented between different factions *within* the pro-Beijing political coalition, so that the Central Government can be the focal point to coordinate between all its allies and to determine core personnel and policy decisions. Unwittingly, this deliberate fragmentation of legislative power led to legislative gridlock in Hong Kong. Unlike Macau, Hong Kong used to have a strong civil society and a strong pro-democracy movement that elected enough like-minded lawmakers to occupy over a third of its legislature. The Macau legislature, on the other hand, never had more than three pro-democracy lawmakers in its ranks. Despite not having a numerical majority, the Hong Kong pro-democracy lawmakers had sufficient

2 Stephen Vines, *Defying the Dragon: Hong Kong and the World's Largest Dictatorship* (Hurst & Company 2021).

political leverage to decry, delay, and even derail its Chief Executive's legislative agenda. But everything changed after 2019. Political turmoil rocked Hong Kong for months over the extradition bill, which saw escalating violent confrontations between the police and protestors and rampant vandalism of public facilities. China was equally incensed by the relentless pro-democracy lawmakers who incessantly roused and rallied the crowd, disrupting legislative proceedings to reflect public sentiments. And, in 2021, the Central Government overhauled Hong Kong's electoral system so that it could terminate all anti-China mobilisation by the local lawmakers once and for all. The "universal suffrage" seats in the legislature were slashed and only "patriots" as certified by the Hong Kong SAR government can now run for any political office. Today, there are only pro-Beijing lawmakers left in Hong Kong and Macau. Both SARs have been politically tamed and their "arrested democratisation"[3] is now complete.

Even as both SARs are politically homogenised, their judiciaries remain starkly different, especially their top courts. Chapter 3 explains why and how. Since the creation of the Hong Kong Court of Final Appeal (HKCFA) in 1997, the Court has declared local laws unconstitutional on 27 occasions.[4] On the other hand, the Macau Court of Final Appeal has only declared laws unconstitutional three times, and none since 2011.[5] Even on these three occasions, the impugned Macau laws were only ruled inapplicable vis-à-vis the victorious applicants but remain operative otherwise. On the other hand, even after Beijing clamped down on Hong Kong after 2020, the HKCFA has continued to hand down landmark freedom-friendly rulings particularly on gay rights. In 2023, the HKCFA declared that the local government's failure to provide an alternative legal framework for protecting the core rights of same-sex partnerships was unconstitutional and gave the city authorities two years to pass the requisite legislation.[6] In November 2024, as the clock ticked down to the 2025 deadline, the HKCFA handed down a pair of gay-friendly decisions, granting same-sex couples equal access to public housing[7] and intestacy[8] rights. Macau, let alone Mainland China, never comes anywhere close on such same-sex protections. While both Basic Laws guarantee that the respective local judges would be chosen by an "independent commission"[9], in practice only Hong Kong's commission is so. Hong Kong's judicial commission has always been chaired by its non-partisan Chief Justice, and the commission is dominated by senior judges and lawyers. Conversely, Macau's judicial commission is chaired and dominated by local officials with explicit pro-Beijing political affiliations. Macau's

3 Ma Ngok, 'Party Underdevelopment in Hong Kong: Hybrid Constraints and Value Changes' (2018) 58 (3) *Asian Survey* 416.
4 See Chapter 3 of this monograph, Appendix 1.
5 See Chapter 3 of this monograph, Appendix 2.
6 *Sham Tsz Kit v Secretary for Justice*, (2023) 26 HKCFAR 385.
7 *Infinger, Nick v Hong Kong Housing Authority*, [2024] HKCFA 29.
8 *Ng Hon Lam Edgar v Secretary for Justice*, [2024] HKCFA 30.
9 Article 87 of the Macau Basic Law (MABL); Article 88 of the Hong Kong Basic Law (HKBL).

first and long-serving Chief Justice Sam Hou-Fai (1999–2024) was deemed so politically reliable that he was enlisted by the Central Government to become the city's current Chief Executive. This crucial difference in the judicial appointment system directly impacts the composition and background of the judges appointed to the respective cities' top courts, which correspondingly shapes the local constitutional jurisprudence. Furthermore, Hong Kong is an international financial hub – third in the world[10] – on which China relies for international capital. This is unlike Macau whose economy is conjoined with Mainland China in a one-way dependence. On the other hand, as of 2024, 68.1% of China's *inward* Foreign Direct Investment originates from Hong Kong.[11] So long as both the HKSAR and Central Governments need Hong Kong to attract foreign capital and overseas talent, the rule of law – particularly the *common law* – undergirded by an independent judiciary must remain a cornerstone of the city's governance. With the National People's Congress Standing Committee legally empowered to overrule every constitutional law ruling of the HKCFA,[12] the Court is significantly constricted on "core" issues pertaining to Hong Kong's political system and national security. But on matters less fundamental to the political hegemony or survival of the regime, such as gay rights and the application of common law rules, the HKCFA has retained its independence to chart a path distinct from the rest of Communist China.

National security has become the country's top preoccupation after President Xi Jinping's rise to power and it was our focus in Chapter 4. As Hong Kong careened into civil war in 2019, the Central Government was determined to prevent similar "uprisings" from ever occurring again. Under the pretext that Hong Kong had failed to discharge its constitutional duty to pass a national security law "on its own",[13] Beijing foisted a customised one for Hong Kong in 2020, criminalising secession, subversion, terrorism, and external collusion. But notably, this 2020 Hong Kong National Security Law (2020 HKNSL) sweeps wider than what Hong Kong was constitutionally obligated to enact under the Basic Law. Under the 2020 HKNSL, Beijing criminalised terrorism, subversion against the Hong Kong authority, and collusive links with foreign *individuals* and *non-political* bodies, but notably all these offences fall outside the scope of Article 23 HKBL.[14]

10 'The Global Financial Centres Index 38' (September 2025) <www.longfinance.net/media/documents/GFCI_38_Report_2025.09.25_v1.0.pdf> last accessed 3 January 2026.

11 National Bureau of Statistics of China, *2025 China Statistical Yearbook*, section 11–14 (Foreign Direct Investment by Country (Region)) <www.stats.gov.cn/sj/ndsj/2025/indexch.htm> last accessed 3 January 2026.

12 Article 158 of the HKBL.

13 Article 23 of the HKBL.

14 Article 23 of the HKBL reads: The Hong Kong Special Administrative Region shall enact laws on its own to prohibit any act of treason, secession, sedition, subversion against the Central People's Government, or theft of state secrets, to prohibit foreign political organisations or bodies from conducting political activities in the Region, and to prohibit political organisations or bodies of the Region from establishing ties with foreign political organisations or bodies.

With the constitutional overhauls firmly in place after 2021, the "patriots-only" Hong Kong passed its own local national security law in 2024 (2024 HKNSL) to complement the Beijing-annexed one, criminalising five additional offences that include treason; insurrection and sedition; offences relating to state secrets and espionage; sabotage; and external interference.[15] From the start of the public consultation to the passage of the law, the entire process of the 2024 HKNSL took less than 50 days – the fastest legislative bill passed in the history of the HKSAR.[16] Not to be outdone by its elder sibling, Macau toughened and revised its national security law in 2023 (2023 MANSL), even though a comprehensive one had already been in place since 2009. The greatest difference between the national security laws of the two cities lies in their implementation. Only one person has been charged with a national security offence in Macau. On the other hand, as of 1 March 2026, 148 people have been charged, with 130 convictions so far, under Hong Kong's national security laws. The PRC national security apparatus now legally operates in Hong Kong;[17] bail is typically denied to persons charged under either of Hong Kong's national security laws;[18] and all national security related proceedings are heard by "designated"[19] national security judges handpicked by the Chief Executive from the pre-existing bench of local judges. The largest crackdown under Hong Kong's revamped national security landscape has been the conviction of 45 pro-democracy activists and legislators for participating in an unofficial election primary in July 2020 to select pro-democracy candidates who could win a majority of seats in the Legislative Council, and subsequently use this legislative majority to veto budgetary bills and force the Chief Executive to resign.[20] With civil society crushed, rambunctious media outlets closed, political protests silenced, and patriotism exalted, Hong Kong's defiant streak has been tamed. The city is now as docile as Macau has been all along.

Chapter 5 examines the constitutional interface between Mainland China and its two SARs. In the early days, especially vis-à-vis Hong Kong, there was an unspoken understanding of mutual non-interference. But as the Hong Kong SAR tugged at its political leash in the second decade of its establishment, Beijing started

15 2024 HKNSL, Part 2 to Part 6.

16 Lilian Cheng, '"Historic Moment": Hong Kong Passes Domestic National Security Law after Marathon Session, Fast-Tracking Legislation Shelved for 2 Decades' *SCMP* (20 March 2024) <www.scmp.com/news/hong-kong/politics/article/3255999/historic-moment-hong-kong-passes-domestic-national-security-law-after-marathon-session-fast-tracking> last accessed 1 January 2026.

17 2020 HKNSL, Chapter V.

18 2020 HKNSL, Article 42.

19 2020 HKNSL, Article 44.

20 Chris Lau and Brian Wong, 'Hong Kong National Security Trial: Prosecutors Accuse 47 Opposition Figures of Plotting to Turn Legislature into "Lethal Constitutional Weapon" against Beijing' *SCMP* (6 February 2023) <www.scmp.com/news/hong-kong/politics/article/3209209/national-security-law-16-47-hong-kong-opposition-figures-contest-subversion-charge-major-trial> last accessed 1 January 2026.

asserting its "comprehensive jurisdiction"[21] over the city. The PRC Constitution, which used to exist in the constitutional shadows, began to emerge as a direct reference of legal power, and it is now front and centre of constitutional discourse in both Hong Kong and Macau. Furthermore, not only did Beijing foist the bespoke 2020 HKNSL on the city, PRC legal concepts on national security now permeate local laws of both SARs.[22] The Standing Committee of the National People's Congress (NPCSC) is legally empowered to interpret both Basic Laws, but it has intervened more often in Hong Kong to keep this "delinquent" child in line. In its first Interpretation concerning Hong Kong,[23] the NPCSC in 1999 limited, by overruling a pair of HKCFA decisions, the constitutional right of abode of Chinese nationals born to Hong Kong Permanent Residents. In 2016,[24] the NPCSC even handed down an Interpretation *sub judice* to pre-empt an adverse judicial ruling concerning the legal consequences that followed when local lawmakers declined to take their inaugural oaths in the prescribed form. For Macau, the NPCSC has only issued an Interpretation once in 2011, which imposed new hurdles for enacting constitutional amendments on the city's elections.[25] A similar Interpretation was previously issued in 2004 to impose the same hurdles in Hong Kong.[26] Equally, if not more, controversial are NPCSC Decisions, of which both Basic Laws make no mention, and they are more regularly applied to the SARs than the formally authorised Interpretations. These Decisions have been used to empower the SARs to relinquish legal control over their own land (in the case of Hong Kong) or extend legal control over Mainland territory (in the case of Macau). But crucially, these Decisions are used by Beijing to set the pace of electoral reforms in both cities, which included the infamous 2020 Decision[27] to delay Hong Kong legislative elections

21 The State Council, 'The Practice of the "One Country, Two Systems" Policy in the Hong Kong Special Administrative Region' (10 June 2014) <https://english.www.gov.cn/archive/white_paper/2014/08/23/content_281474982986578.htm> last accessed 1 January 2026.

22 Section 4 of the 2024 HKNSL and Article 2 of the 2023 MANSL.

23 The Interpretation by the Standing Committee of the National People's Congress Regarding Paragraph 4 in Article 22 and Category (3) of Paragraph 2 in Article 24 of the Basic Law of the Hong Kong Special Administrative Region of the People's Republic of China (Adopted at the Tenth Meeting of the Standing Committee of the Ninth National People's Congress on 26 June 1999).

24 Interpretation of Article 104 of the Basic Law of the Hong Kong Special Administrative Region of the People's Republic of China by the Standing Committee of the National People's Congress (Adopted by the Standing Committee of the 12th National People's Congress at its 24th Session on 7 November 2016).

25 The Interpretation by the Standing Committee of the National People's Congress Regarding Annex I (7) and Annex II (III) to the Basic Law of the Macau Special Administrative Region of the People's Republic of China (Adopted at the 24th Meeting of the Standing Committee of the 11th National People's Congress on 31 December 2011).

26 The Interpretation by the Standing Committee of the National People's Congress Regarding Annex I (7) and Annex II (III) to the Basic Law of the Hong Kong Special Administrative Region of the People's Republic of China (Adopted at the Eighth Meeting of the Standing Committee of the Tenth National People's Congress on 6 April 2004).

27 Decision of the Standing Committee of the National People's Congress on the Continuing Discharge of Duties by the Sixth-Term Legislative Council of the Hong Kong Special Administrative Region

by a year so that the Central Authorities could buy time and overhaul the electoral system altogether in 2021. Cleansed of political opposition, and constitutionally re-ordered, Hong Kong now joins its domesticated sibling in goose-stepping to the Party's drumbeat, ebulliently propagating national education, national security, and national integration.

In the face of "coercive assimilation",[28] critics lament the "freedom undone"[29]. What China views as Hong Kong's "new beginnings",[30] the West sees as Hong Kong's end game.[31] With Donald Trump back in the White House, threats of new sanctions and tariffs hang over this international financial hub; anxieties abound too as China's economy remains in the doldrums. In China's "age of counterreform",[32] strongman rule has returned, and Maoism is revived. The pursuit of President Xi Jinping's "Chinese Dream" requires the entire Chinese nation to march in lockstep, and Hong Kong and Macau are no longer spared from this draft. China is now erasing Hong Kong's past[33] so that it can define the city's future. Even for Macau, China is weaning the city off gambling[34] – a colonial legacy protected under its Basic Law.[35] "Borrowed Place, Borrowed Time"[36] was a maxim used to depict Britain's 99-year occupation of its erstwhile colony, but this slogan is equally apposite in characterising the temporary reprieve China granted its two SARs upon establishment to keep their "way of life… unchanged for 50 years".[37] Time is not officially up, yet much has already changed.

(Adopted at the 21st Session of the Standing Committee of the 13th National People's Congress on 11 August 2020).

28 Ho-fung Hung, *City on the Edge: Hong Kong under Chinese Rule* (CUP 2022) 122.

29 Michael Davis, *Freedom Undone: The Assault on Liberal Values and Institutions in Hong Kong* (Association for Asian Studies 2024).

30 'Hong Kong Restarts: A New Chapter from Stability to Prosperity 香港再出发：开启由治及兴新篇章' *Xinhua Net* (26 December 2022) <www.news.cn/gangao/2022-12/26/c_1129234224.htm> last accessed 1 January 2026.

31 Rosalind Mathieson, 'China's Playing Out Its End Game in Hong Kong' *Bloomberg* (30 June 2020) <www.bloomberg.com/news/newsletters/2020-06-30/china-s-playing-out-its-end-game-in-hong-kong> last accessed 1 January 2026.

32 Carl Minzner, 'China's Age of Counterreform' (2024) 35 *Journal of Democracy* 5.

33 Kenji Kawase, 'Hong Kong Lets 40th Anniversary of Sino-British Declaration Pass Quietly' *Nikkei Asia* (19 December 2024) <https://asia.nikkei.com/Spotlight/Hong-Kong-security-law/Hong-Kong-lets-40th-anniversary-of-Sino-British-declaration-pass-quietly> last accessed 1 January 2026.

34 Alexandra Stevenson and Zixu Wang, 'Macau Is the Casino Capital of the World. For China, That's Not Enough' *The New York Times* (19 December 2024) <www.nytimes.com/2024/12/19/business/macau-china-xi-jinping.html> last accessed 1 January 2026.

35 Article 118 of the MABL.

36 Richard Hughes, *Borrowed Place, Borrowed Time: Hong Kong and Its Many Faces* (Andre Deutsch 1968).

37 Article 5 of the HKBL; Article 5 of the MABL.

References

Davis, Michael, *Freedom Undone: The Assault on Liberal Values and Institutions in Hong Kong* (Ann Arbor, Association for Asian Studies 2024).

Hughes, Richard, *Borrowed Place, Borrowed Time: Hong Kong and Its Many Faces* (London, Andre Deutsch 1968).

Hung, Ho-fung, *City on the Edge: Hong Kong under Chinese Rule* (New York, Cambridge University Press 2022).

Ma, Ngok, 'Party Underdevelopment in Hong Kong: Hybrid Constraints and Value Changes' (2018) 58 (3) *Asian Survey* 416–438.

Minzner, Carl, 'China's Age of Counterreform' (2024) 35 *Journal of Democracy* 5–19.

Vines, Stephen, *Defying the Dragon: Hong Kong and the World's Largest Dictatorship* (London, Hurst & Company 2021).

INDEX

Note: Page numbers in **bold** refers to tables.

For Product Safety Concerns and Information please contact our EU representative GPSR@taylorandfrancis.com
Taylor & Francis Verlag GmbH, Kaufingerstraße 24, 80331 München, Germany

www.ingramcontent.com/pod-product-compliance
Ingram Content Group UK Ltd.
Pitfield, Milton Keynes, MK11 3LW, UK
UKHW020008200926
475702UK00015B/2541
9781041163145